Robert Southey, David Hannay

English Seamen

Howard, Clifford, Hawkins, Drake, Cavendish

Robert Southey, David Hannay

English Seamen
Howard, Clifford, Hawkins, Drake, Cavendish

ISBN/EAN: 9783337013707

Printed in Europe, USA, Canada, Australia, Japan

Cover: Foto ©ninafisch / pixelio.de

More available books at **www.hansebooks.com**

ENGLISH SEAMEN

HOWARD, CLIFFORD, HAWKINS, DRAKE

CAVENDISH

BY

ROBERT SOUTHEY

EDITED, WITH AN INTRODUCTION

BY

DAVID HANNAY

CHICAGO
STONE AND KIMBALL
1895
LONDON: METHUEN & COMPANY

CONTENTS

	PAGE
LORD HOWARD OF EFFINGHAM	1
THE EARL OF CUMBERLAND	101
HAWKINS AND DRAKE	170
THOMAS CAVENDISH	359

INTRODUCTION

WRITING to his friend Mrs. Hodson, on the 20th January, 1830, Southey tells her, "I have engaged to compose a volume of Naval History in biographical form for the *Cabinet Cyclopædia*, not for love but for lucre, though it will be done lovingly when in hand". The volume grew into volumes. In 1838 he had still to write that he was "getting through the admirals". Next year his strength broke down under the strain of incessant writing, and what was more fatal still, of reading continually through the walks which he was, with some difficulty, persuaded to take for the good of his health. The admirals remained a fragment. The whole work was to have included an introductory sketch of the Naval History of England down to the reign of Elizabeth. From that point, in the words of Southey's Preface, "it may be best continued in a biographical form; because there are then materials for such biography, whereby we are enabled to understand how much depended upon the character of individual commanders". The introduction filled the whole of one volume, and overflowed much the greater part of a second. The biographies had extended into a fifth volume when the failure of Southey's intellect stopped his share of the work, at the end of the life of Sir William Monson. A life of the first Earl of Sandwich was added by Mr. Robert Bell, and then in accordance with the evil fate which has ordained that all histories of the Navy above the rank of mere compilations shall be partial or fragmentary, there was an end of the effort of the *Cabinet Cyclopædia* to make good a discreditable defect in English literature.

Some portion of the blame for this want of completeness must, even by those who are least inclined to find fault with him, he allowed to rest on Southey. From a passage in a letter written to John May on the 20th January, 1836, he appears to have had an uneasy consciousness that he had not so executed his work as to leave him the possibility of rounding it fairly off in good proportions.

"The fourth volume," he writes, "will contain the lives of Essex, Raleigh, Sir William Monson, Blake, and Monk. Then, not to extend unreasonably a work which was not intended by the publisher at first for more than two volumes, I shall drop the biography and wind up in one volume more, with the Naval History from the Revolution in continuous narrative. A good pretext for this is, that the age of naval enterprise and adventure, and consequently of personal interest, was past; and the interest henceforth becomes political, events are regarded, not with reference to the principal actors, as in Drake's time, but to their bearings upon the national affairs."

The word pretext is used, as was indeed uniformly the case with Southey's English, in the most strictly accurate sense. The distinction which he draws here is quite arbitrary, and must be taken to be a species of confession on the part of the writer, that he had allowed his work to break far beyond all reasonable bounds, and must make an effort to reduce it. Even if he had kept to the limits which he set himself in this letter, his scheme would have been out of all proportion. A Naval History of England in which nearly two volumes were given to the period before Elizabeth, more than two volumes to the lives of the men of her reign, of whom several were little at sea, and others were mainly privateersmen and explorers, while one poor volume was left for all the great series of naval events between 1660 and 1815, would have been egregiously out of drawing. But Southey did not even keep to the scheme he sketched to Mr. May. His biographies ran beyond the fourth volume as far as the middle of the fifth. He would assuredly have been at the end of a seventh before he was done with Monk; and not five volumes, but five and twenty, if not five and fifty would have been required to complete the work on the scale on which it had been begun. No publisher of any cyclopædia has the purse or the patience for such colossal enterprise, not even "the Long-Man of the Row," who knew Southey of old and was his friend. So the "British Admirals" was doomed by the act of the author to be cut short. It was easy for Southey to talk of giving one volume to the history of the Navy after 1660. Such promises pass well in a letter, but it was not in his nature to tie himself down to these narrow limits.

This attempt at a history of the English Navy was deprived of all hope of ever being a complete work by the fact that the author had to the full the defect of his qualities. Whoever has gone over the authorities on whom Southey drew, must have noticed the unerring tact with which he quoted. It is commonly impossible to find anything which he passed over, and which is yet conspicuously worth quotation. But this fine quality of seeing, which in his case was accompanied by an extraordinary dexterity in extracting and weaving together, has also its shadow from which the possessor cannot jump. He who can see what is worth quoting is sorely tempted to quote every worthy thing he sees. When he is, as Southey was, a man of enormous circumambient reading (if the expression may pass); when he has not only read but remembers; when all his knowledge has always been noted, marked for reference, extracted into common-place books, docketed and indexed so that it lies ready to the "wet finger" when wanted, it is odds but he will find it hard to keep within bounds. The temptation to bring out all that bears on the case, or even only illustrates by comparison, is not all the writer has to fight against, though in this, legitimate as it is, there may be excess. He is very likely to be drawn into speaking of things only indirectly bearing on his subject, but none the less picturesque, or pathetic, or perhaps only quaint and forgotten, which he has met in his reading, and are brought to his memory by his writing. Southey certainly found it hard not to be prodigal of his learning. Old chronicles, old narrative poems of Spaniards and Portuguese, lives of the saints, stories of shipwreck, and of savage life which he had read, in sober truth, by the thousand, and reading had marked for reference, were habitually drawn upon by him. It is never mere compilation. It is always an extracting, arranging and fitting together of the pure ore of his matter into something which is emphatically Southey's own. What would be bookmaking in a mere compiler is in his case the making of literature. But at its best this pouring out of the stores of knowledge is hard to reconcile with brevity, and Southey could not be brief. He could tell a story in the minimum of words, but he could not limit himself in the number of stories he wished to tell. In his Preface, he gravely promised that "no more of our general history is included than was necessary for forming a connected narrative, and for tracing the causes and consequences of those events which are the proper subject of the work". In his text he observes his own excellent rule so laxly that he cannot refrain from giving pages to the adventures in love and war of the Conde Don Pero Niño, which he has to confess "are matters with which this history has no concern". But they were picturesque; they came from a romantic old Spanish chronicle; they supplied vivid little pictures of the life and the men of old; they were little known. Pero Niño plundered on our coast about 1405, and with that excuse to give him countenance Southey could do no other than decant the best of the chronicle written by the Alferez Gutierre Diez into his own pages.

This inability to turn from the picturesque, which was not immediately *germaine* to the matter, may have stopped "The Lives of the British Admirals" from becoming a history of the Navy, but it gives their charm and much of their merit to the biographies from which this selection is taken. One criticism which has been made on the naval portions of Southey's vast literary work, must be noticed for the purpose of estimating it at its real value. It is said that he was ignorant of sea affairs, and therefore incapable of either understanding them himself, or making them clear to others. Now Southey was perfectly well aware of his deficiencies in this respect. When he was engaged in extending his quarterly article on Clarke and McArthur's compilation into the immortal *Life of Nelson*, he wrote to his brother, Captain Thomas Southey of the Navy, who had fought at Copenhagen, a letter containing a string of questions, and this paragraph :—

"I am such a sad lubber that I feel half ashamed of myself for being persuaded ever even to review the *Life of Nelson*, much more to write one. Had I not been a thorough lubber, I should have remembered half a hundred things worthy of remembrance which have all been lost, because though I do indeed know the binnacle from the mainmast, I know little more; tackle and sheets, and tally and belay are alike to me; and if you ask me about the lee-clue garnets, I can only tell that they are not the same kind of garnets as are worn in necklaces and bracelets, and so fine facts have been lost because I did not know where to store them in the ship, or in my recollection-closet upstairs. There is something ridiculous, and something like quackery in writing thus about what I so little understand. I walk among sea terms as a cat does in a china pantry, in bodily fear of doing mischief and betraying myself; and yet there will come a good book of it I verily believe."

Southey knew wherein he was deficient, and knew also where to go for help to make his deficiencies good. He had many naval officers among his acquaintance, and applied to them, to his brother, and to his friend Admiral Burney, the author of the *Discoveries in the South Seas*, for help. Moreover he had what was better than this, namely, a literary honesty which kept him from writing about those technical things which he knew he did not understand, and a literary instinct which taught him to extract what is of universal interest from amid a mass of technicalities. Human character and the motives of human action in what is general to the race, were the matters possessing interest to him. No doubt his work would have been better still if he could have added his brother's professional knowledge to his own vast reading and artistic faculty. Then indeed we might have obtained a History of the English Navy such as we can hardly hope to have. But the combination is yet to seek. Only pedantry (and it is quite possible to be pedantic about the bobstay and the brailing of the lee yard-arm) will prefer the merely particular and technical to the universal and human. If any one wishes to see how little professional knowledge will avail of itself, let him turn from Southey's *Nelson*, or any of the lives given here, to Schomberg or Brenton. If he wishes to see how poor a guarantee it is for mere mechanical accuracy let him read Captain White's strictures on Admiral Ekins' account of the fighting in the Basse Terre of St. Kitts. He will find one experienced naval officer accusing another of grossly misunderstanding the meaning of a simple sea term.

Accuracy in technical matters is no doubt one of the virtues of the author of biographies, but at the risk of appearing to speak lightly of the expert, it may be affirmed to belong distinctly to the minor class. The first duty of the biographer is to give a living and credible picture of his man. To do this he must possess the general knowledge which gives him a fair understanding of the surroundings of that man's life, and the sanity of judgment which makes him a safe critic of character or conduct. The general knowledge brought by Southey to these studies of the Elizabethan seamen has never been equalled by any other English writer on the subject. He was minutely familiar with the history of the Spaniards and Portuguese. With the colonial and maritime sides he was perhaps better acquainted than with any other. He had therefore always at command a vast stock of instances with which to illustrate the actions of our own adventurers, and to complete the picture by showing against what manner of men it was they fought. When he has to tell of the capture of Portuguese carracks he draws on his learning for tales of their disasters in Eastern Seas, in the beginning of the voyage which ended with the attack of the English rovers. When his story takes him to the Straits of Magellan he seizes the first plausible excuse to recount the dreadful fate of Sarmiento de Gamboa's settlement. These digressions may be proofs of his tendency, of which he was himself fully conscious, to "allow his steed to expatiate on the fields of prolixity," but they fill up the picture, and complete its general truth.

The sanity of judgment which Southey brought to these studies of the Elizabethan heroes is hardly less rare, and is assuredly not less necessary, than his learning.

Writers on this, the most romantic period in the history of our adventures at sea, have commonly found it difficult to avoid one of two kinds of excess. Some have condemned the generation of Drake and Hawkins as mere slavers and pirates. These have been the smaller number, and in our time they have fallen silent. There is therefore no call to insist upon their error. Of late the tendency has been to go into the other extreme, and to maintain, by implication if not in so many words, that slave-hunting and piracy were intrinsically very noble occupations when they had as their consequence the doing of a damage to the Spaniards or Portuguese. They are excused, or even gloried in, as parts of the strife between the children of Light and the children of Darkness. In a sense perhaps they were; but it must be confessed that the methods of the children of Light, and their motives as they are to be gathered from their own words, were curiously like those of their enemies. Both indeed could appeal to religion as sanctifying their gold-hunting adventures. Cortes and Pizarro had the extension of the true faith much in their mouths, and in some measure in their hearts. Hawkins, sailing from the coast of Senegambia with a holdful of kidnapped negroes, on his way to a smuggling venture on the Spanish main, supported himself amid the miseries of a tropical calm, by remembering that the Lord will not suffer His elect to

INTRODUCTION xiii

perish. We need not think him a hypocrite, but we shall be very credulous if we see more in his religious faith than a proof of the happy facility with which men can persuade themselves that what is agreeable to their interests or passions is also acceptable to God. There is a sentence in Raleigh's *Discoverie of Guiana* which throws a most instructive light on the motives of the Elizabethan adventurer. Sir Walter had been descanting at length on the many advantages which El Dorado, the gilded king of Manoa, would derive from the protection to be afforded him by a garrison of English " younger brothers, and all chieftaines, and captains that want employment". He ends with the following significant sentence: " In which respects no doubt he will be brought to tribute with great gladnesse; if not, he hath neither shot nor yron weapon in all his empire and therefore may easily be conquered ". Let me protect you, for a consideration, or I will plunder you. It may be doubted whether the great " Inga " of Manoa would have found much to choose between Sir Walter Raleigh of the county of Devon, and Don Gonzalo de Pizarro of the kingdom of Estremadura.

Southey never forgot such revelations as this, and his picture of the Elizabethans is the better for it. He drew them the more like what they unquestionably were, namely, such men as the Spanish " conquistadores," with the advantage of belonging to a more many-sided and capable race; as lovers of adventure and lovers of gold, with a business and governing faculty, which the Spaniard had possessed in an eminent degree, but was losing rapidly as the sixteenth century drew to its close. The picture agrees better with the evidence than that figure of the Protestant hero or humane knight-errant which has been made to do duty for that slave-hunter and intrepid liar, Hawkins, or the self-seeking intriguer who was Raleigh. Yet Southey knew that a man may be a slave-hunter, may be greedy for gold, may intrigue, and still be brave, be patriotic, be loyal to his comrades, magnanimous at times, and ready to risk life and fortune for a cause. There are some who cannot be taught by any evidence that this combination of apparently incompatible qualities is not only possible but very human. It is too what supplies the humour of life.

Some few words may be said on the style of these lives. Southey himself denied that he had any style. " As for composition," he wrote to his son-in-law Warter, " it has no difficulties for one who will ' read, mark, learn and inwardly digest' the materials upon which he is to work. I do not mean to say that it is easy to write well, but of this I am sure, that most men would write better if they did not take half the pains they do. For myself, I consider it no compliment when any one praises the simplicity of my prose writings; they are written, indeed, without any other immediate object than that of expressing what is to be said in the readiest, and most perspicuous manner. But in the transcript (if I make one) and always in the proof sheet, every sentence is then weighed upon the ear, euphony becomes a second object, and ambiguities are removed. But of what is now called style not a thought enters my head at any time."

By what "is now called style," it is to be presumed that Mr. Warter was understood by his father-in-law to mean mannerism. Southey could with complete truth protest that no wish to write differently from the accepted standard of English had at any time entered his head. To write "English such as every one from Chaucer to Sir Thomas More, and from More to Cowper, could understand," to write it with perspicuity as a first " and with euphony as a second" object was his aim. But to succeed in doing so much was to attain to a style, and not only so, but it was to write in the only way which it is safe to take as a model. Those whose style is individual are some of them among the greatest of men of letters; but though they may be delightful to read, and great to inspire, it is fatal to follow them. Now when, as at some other times, what is called style is too often only a deliberate attempt to be peculiar, the prose of Southey cannot be too carefully read. It will show those who may be in danger of being misled by the popularity of certain models that it is possible to be perspicuous without being pedestrian, to consider euphony and yet not to be precious, to be manly and yet not violent. They may be sure, at least, that in following his path they will be in no danger of falling into absurdity.

The lives contained in this volume have been chosen for reasons which perhaps ought to be given. No excuse need be assigned for reprinting the "Hawkins and Drake". The life of Lord Howard of Effingham contains as full an account of the Armada as could be written on the evidence accessible to Southey. The Earl of Cumberland was an accomplished and adventurous noble, which would of itself entitle him to a place among the typical heroes of an aristocratic age, but his voyages to the isles also show the character of the naval warfare of the time exceptionally well. Of Cavendish we cannot say that he was one of the greatest in achievement, still less that he was one of the highest in character of the Elizabethans, yet he was the third captain of any race, the second among Englishmen, who circumnavigated the globe, and his life has this value, that it shows the cruel and greedy side of that aristocratic spirit of which Cumberland was the chivalrous representative.

A few notes are appended merely to point out what research has added to Southey's knowledge. It is but little, and no part modifies in any way the estimates of characters which are to be found in this selection from what I will venture to describe as on the whole the finest portrait gallery of the Elizabethan sea heroes in the English language.

DAVID HANNAY.

ENGLISH SEAMEN

LORD HOWARD OF EFFINGHAM

CHARLES, eldest son of Lord William Howard, and grandson of Thomas, second Duke of Norfolk, was born in 1536. Margaret, his mother, was daughter of Sir Thomas Gamage of Coity, in Glamorganshire. His father was one of the courtiers who accompanied King Henry to the Field of the Cloth of Gold, having (it is recorded) in his retinue eleven servants and two horsekeepers; he assisted as proxy for his brother, the duke and earl marshal, at the coronation of Anne Boleyn; and, after the conviction of his niece, Queen Catherine Howard, was found guilty, with his lady, of misprision of treason, for not having revealed what they knew of her misconduct, and condemned to perpetual imprisonment, with forfeiture of their goods, and of the profits of their lands during life. This sentence was soon remitted, in consideration of his services, "and it may be of his innocence". He attended on Henry at the siege of Boulogne; and, in the ensuing reign, was "one of the first favourers and furtherers, with his purse and countenance, of" what Fuller calls "the strange and wonderful discovery of Russia," being one of those who were incorporated as merchant-adventurers to Moscovy; and, "at their own cost and charges, provided those ships to discover territories unknown, northwards, north-eastwards, and north-westwards". The expedition is memorable both in naval and commercial history: for the commander,

Sir Hugh Willoughby, after discovering Greenland, was frozen to death, with all his ship's company, in a haven on the coast of Lapland; and the second in command, Richard Chancellor, who had fortunately parted company with him, entered the river of St. Nicholas, travelled to the court of the Czar Ivan Basilowitz, delivered the king's letters to that sovereign, and obtained for the English the privilege of a free trade in any part of his dominions, being their first entrance into Russia. On the accession of Queen Mary, he was created a peer of the realm, by the title of Lord Howard of Effingham, and appointed High Admiral of England and Wales, Ireland, Gascony, and Aquitaine; the queen, "in consideration of his fidelity, prudence, valour and industry," constituting him "her lieutenant-general and chief commander of her whole fleet and royal army going to sea for the defence of her friends". In the discharge of this office, he kept the seas about three months; and having met with Philip, then Prince of Asturius, escorted him to Southampton, and attended his marriage with the queen. At the commencement of the following reign, he was one of the persons empowered to conclude peace with France.

Under such a father Charles Howard was trained, serving under him by land and sea. He was about twenty-two years of age at the accession of Elizabeth; and his "most proper person" is said to have been one reason why that queen "(who, though she did not value a jewel *by*, valued it the more *for*, a fair case) reflected so much upon him ".* She sent him to France, after the death of Henry II., on an embassy of condolence and congratulation to the young king. He was elected one of the knights for his native county of Surrey, in the Parliament of 1562-3; and afterwards distinguished himself as general of the horse in quelling the rebellion of the Earls of Northumberland and Westmoreland. In the ensuing

* Fuller.

year, he commanded ten ships of Her Majesty's " navy royal"; which, when the Emperor Maximilian's daughter, Anne, sailed from Zeeland to marry her uncle, Philip II., were ordered to convoy her through the British seas, as a singular testimony of the queen's respect for the house of Austria; and on this occasion it is said that he enforced the Spanish fleet, " to stoop gallant, and to veil their bonnets to the Queen of England ". It was probably at this time that he received the honour of knighthood. Having a second time been elected for Surrey, he was installed Knight of the Garter in 1574, and made Lord Chamberlain of the Household,—an office which had been held by his father, who, dying in 1572-3, had bequeathed to him his collar of gold, and all his robes belonging to the order of the garter. Upon the death of the Earl of Lincoln, he was raised to the office of Lord High Admiral of England; in which capacity he was called upon to perform a more serious service with regard to the Spaniards than when he required from them in peace a recognition of the queen's sovereignty in the English seas.

Elizabeth, when she succeeded in happy hour to the English throne, was far from entertaining any sentiments of ill-will toward the King of Spain. "Whatsoever," saith Fox[*] the martyrologist, " can be recited touching the admirable working of God's present hand in defending and delivering any one person out of thraldom, never was there, since the memory of our fathers, any example to be showed, wherein the Lord's mighty power hath more admirably and blessedly showed itself, to the glory of His own name, to the comfort of all good hearts, and to the public felicity of this whole realm, than in the miraculous custody and out-scape of the then Lady Elizabeth, in the strict time of Queen Mary". To be near the throne was almost as perilous in the Plantagenet and Tudor families as in the Ottoman house; and in her case the danger

[*] Vol. iii., 792.

was fearfully enhanced by a clear apprehension, on the part of the Romish hierarchy, that the reformed religion, which they were labouring to extirpate by fire and sword, would be re-established if Elizabeth would succeed to her sister. Some of the laity, who in their station forwarded the persecution which has rendered Queen Mary's reign for ever infamous, entered fully into this fear; and if Elizabeth was not brought to the scaffold, or made away with in confinement, it was not for want of wicked counsellors, or fitting keepers. One who was in authority is said to have declared in his place that there would never be " any quiet commonwealth in England unless her head were stricken from the shoulders ";* and " it would make a pitiful story to recite what examinations and rackings of poor men there were to find out that knife which should cut her throat". To the honour of the Spaniards, in that persecuting age, it ought never to be forgotten in this country, that their good offices were effectually interposed in her behalf, and that Philip "showed himself in that matter a very friend ". Nor will it be regarded by an equitable mind as any impeachment of his motives, that the part which he took on this occasion was that of sound policy, if policy alone had influenced him. Let him have credit for justice in this instance, if not for humanity! He had some great qualities, and some good ones; and his worst actions must be imputed to a deluded conscience, acting under a mistaken sense of religious duty.

If Elizabeth had been at that time cut off, Mary Stuart,

---

* Fox, iii., 794, 797, 798. The queen's feelings towards her sister are truly stated by Ribadeneira, who had opportunity of knowing them well, and who may be believed when he had no motive for writing falsely: " Una muger," he says, speaking of Elizabeth, " que ella nunca tuvo por hermana, sino por bastarda y enemiga suya, y de la religion catolica; y que siempre temio que la avia de arruynar y destruyr, y a quien por estas causas desseó y procuró excluyr de la succession del reyno" (*Hist. Eccl. de Inglaterra*, l. ii., c. xix.).

then dauphiness, would have become presumptive heiress to the crown of England; and her succession, by uniting England, Scotland and Ireland to the crown of France, would have been, of all possible contingencies, the most injurious to the interests of Spain. That contingency became more probable upon Queen Mary's death; and it seemed as if the French Government, in pursuit of its ambitious hopes, was too impatient to wait for it, for Henry II. commanded that the dauphin and dauphiness should, in all public instruments, style themselves by the grace of God King and Queen of Scotland, England and Ireland.* The arms of England, quartered with those of Scotland, were set forth everywhere in their household stuff, and painted upon the walls, and wrought into the heralds' coats of arms; and by his agents at Rome, Henry ceased not to importune the Pope that he would pronounce Elizabeth a heretic and illegitimate, and Mary of Scotland to be the lawful Queen of England. But here both Philip and the emperor earnestly, though closely, interfered. The question of illegitimacy no longer touched the pride, or affected the interests, of their house; and that of heresy even Spain and Austria could be contented to postpone, rather than allow the power of France to be aggrandised. Philip, therefore, ceased not secretly to oppose the practices of the French at the papal court, even when he refused to renew the league made of old between the kings of England and

---

* Pollini, *Istoria Eccles. della Revol. d'Inghilterra*, p. 406. " In very deed from this title and arms, which through the persuasion of the Guises, Henry, King of France, had imposed upon the Queen of Scots, being now in her tender age, flowed as from a fountain all the calamities wherein she was afterwards wrapt. For hereupon Queen Elizabeth bare both enmity to the Guises, and secret grudge against her, which the subtle malice of men on both sides cherished, emulation growing betwixt them, and new occasions daily arising, in such sort that it could not be extinguished but by death. For a kingdom brooketh no companion; and majesty more heavily taketh injuries to heart " (Camden, 34).

his forefathers, and sent back his insignia of the garter, whereby he seemed quite to renounce amity with the English. Still there remained the bond of mutual interest between Philip and Elizabeth, and not, it may be believed, without some sense of grateful remembrance on one part, and of personal respect on both. That bond was broken by the decease of Francis II., a few months after his succeeding to the throne; and no kindly feelings, in a man of Philip's temperament, could long withstand that bigotry which was in him a principle and passion,—a principle, indeed, to which, under a dreadful persuasion of duty, he would have made any sacrifice. The first animosity that he felt was excited by a trifling circumstance. He requested, through his ambassador, that four persons, who had withdrawn themselves without licence into his dominions, for religion's sake, might be exempted from the existing laws, and permitted to remain there.* One of these persons was grandmother to the Condesa de Feria; another was an old lady who had been much in Queen Mary's confidence, and used to distribute her private alms to those of her own sex; the other two were men "most devoted to the popish religion, and most dear to the Spaniard". A distinction might well have been made between these persons, especially in the first instance, where there existed so valid a plea. Elizabeth, however, replied, it was without example that such a licence of perpetual absence from their own country should be granted to women; and though it seemed in itself a matter of no moment, yet she thought it a thing not to be granted, "seeing the private benefit to the

---

* " For by the ancient laws of England it was provided, under pain of confiscation of goods and lands, that none but the great noblemen of the land and merchants should without the king's special licence depart the realm, nor abide in foreign countries beyond a time prefixed, and this, either for the recovery of their health in a hotter climate, or for the more plentiful adorning of their wits in the universities, or else to learn the discipline of the wars " (Camden, 46).

individuals would not be so great as the hurt to the community, when others should take courage by their example ". The Conde de Feria * resented this refusal as a private injury, though made upon public grounds: he caused a servant of the English ambassador to be seized by the Inquisition, and " kindled the coals of the displeased king's mind, his wife in vain labouring to the contrary ".†

But though Philip became more and more estranged from Elizabeth, that wise queen avoided all occasion for a breach with Spain; and when her ambassador, Sir Thomas Chaloner, who when employed in Germany found nothing but courtesy there, requested to be recalled, because his coffers had been searched, she admonished him, that an ambassador must take all things in good part, so as his prince's honour were not directly violated. Early, however, in her reign, " finding the realm greatly unfurnished of armour, munitions, and powder," she began to provide against war, that she " might the more quietly enjoy peace ". Arms and weapons were purchased for her at Antwerp, but the Spaniards refused to allow the exportation, in policy, not with any hostile disposition at that time. They were procured, therefore, from Germany, at great cost, but so largely that the land was said never to have been

---

* No doubt he felt that he had rendered himself personally obnoxious to Elizabeth, for refusing, though residing in London as Philip's representative, to be present at her coronation; which refusal, Ribadeneira says, he made " como cavallero catolico y valeroso ". For he inquired: " Si se avian de guardar en la coronacion todas las ceremonias de los otros reyes Christianos conforme al uso de nuestra santa madre yglesia Romana, y como supiesse que avia de aver alguna alteracion, nunca se pudo acabar con el que assistiesse a la solennedad, ni estuviesse en la yglesia, ni en publico, ni encubierto, ni con los otros grandes del reyno, ni aparte en un tablado que le quisieron hazer, por no autorizar con su presencia aquel auto impio, y dar exemplo del recato y circunspecion que en semejantes cosas, por pequenas que parezcan, deven tener los catolicos para no contaminarse " (l. ii. c. xxii.).

† Camden, 46.

so amply stored at any former time with "all kinds of convenient armour and weapons". "Very many pieces of great ordnance of brass and iron she cast; and God," says Camden, "as if He favoured what she undertook, discovered a most rich vein of pure and native brass, which had been long time neglected, near Keswick,* in Cumberland, which abundantly sufficed for that use, and afforded brass to other countries also. The stone, also, called *lapis calaminaris,* which is most necessary for the brass works, was now, by God's favour, first found in England, and that in abundance. And she, also, was the first that procured gunpowder to be made in England, that she might not both pray and pay for it too to her neighbours. The noblemen, too, and common people, with no less cheerful diligence, provided them arms everywhere; so as in noblemen's houses most complete armouries were furnished. Musters and views of arms were often kept, and the youth trained to the science of war, and audacity of skirmishing. In those days, also, the queen restrained, by a strict proclamation, the covetousness of merchants, which supplied munition for war to the Emperor of Russia against the Polonians, and also to the enemies of Christendom." † For the better maintenance and increase of the navy, the free exportation of herrings and all other sea fish, in English bottoms, was allowed for four years, and so further during pleasure: a partial exemption from impressment was granted to all fishermen; and for their encouragement and "the repairing of port towns and navigation," Wednesdays, as well as Saturdays, were ordered to be

* In his *Britannia* Camden says that "this place was formerly noted for mines, as appears by a certain charter of Edward IV.". And Philemon Holland adds that the miners "have here their smelting-house by Derwent side, which with his forcible stream and their ingenious inventions serveth them in notable stead for easy bellows-works, hammer-works, forge-works, and saving of boards, not without admiration of those that behold it". These works, however, were on the side of the Greta, not the Derwent.

† Camden, 56. Holinshed, 202.

observed as fish-days, under penalty of a heavy fine; and this, it was stated, " was meant politicly, not for any superstition, to be maintained in the choice of meats ".* Her navy was, ere long, so well appointed, that she had no need (like her father and predecessors) to hire ships from Hamburgh, Lubeck, Dantzic, Genoa, and Venice. "Foreigners named her the restorer of the glory of shipping, and the queen of the North Sea." For the protection of the fleet she built Upnore Castle; and she increased the sailors' pay. " The wealthier inhabitants of the sea coast," says Camden, " in imitation of their princess, built ships of war, striving who should exceed; insomuch that the queen's navy, joined with her subjects' shipping, was, in short time, so puissant, that it was able to bring forth 20,000 fighting men for sea service." †

The world in those days offered occupation enough to restless spirits. At one time many of the young English gentry " who, according to their innate courage, thought themselves born to arms, not to idleness," repaired to Hungary, as volunteers against the Turks. A few years later they began to flock into the Low Countries, taking different sides, some for principle, others preferring that service in which best entertainment was to be found; the far greater number, however, engaged in the Protestant cause, the strong feeling that had been excited by the Marian persecution in their own country being roused by the cruelty of the Spanish Government under Alva,—a great but merciless man, who in his last illness accounted those actions which have entailed an everlasting reproach on his name among his good works! He had used his influence in Spain to restrain ‡ the violence with which the English in that country were persecuted on the score of their religion,—either because that persecution was urged by a rival statesman, or because he deemed it politic at that time to keep up a friendly understanding with England,

* *Eliz.*, c. v.   † Camden, 56.   ‡ *Ibid.*, 61.

certainly not from any toleration or feeling of compassion. But when Governor of the Netherlands he clearly saw that in England lay the strength of that Protestant cause, for the extirpation of which he was exerting all the energies of his strong head and obdurate heart. No direct or open offence had as yet been offered by either party, when some French privateers whom the Prince of Condé had equipped, but who infested the seas as pirates, fell in with five Spanish vessels which with difficulty escaped, some getting into Falmouth, the others into Plymouth and the Southampton River. The French also put into an English port, waiting to renew the pursuit, whenever the Spaniards should depart from their asylum.

The Spanish ambassador, being apprised of this, applied to the queen: he informed her that there was money on board, for the payment of the king's troops in the Low Countries, and requested that she would protect it in her harbours, and grant it a safe convoy to Antwerp; or, if advisable, let it be carried through the country to a port where it might be safely re-embarked. This the queen granted, and promised security both by sea and land. Even in harbour the freebooters would have mastered one of these ships, if they had not been beaten off by the English: and after this danger, the money was landed. No sooner had this been done than the Spanish resident began to fear that it was trusted to dangerous hands, and he imparted his suspicions to Alva. Meantime Cardinal Chastillon, who was then in England, assured the queen that the money was not in fact the King of Spain's, but belonged to certain Genoese, from whom Alva intended to take it as a loan, against their will. The matter was then laid before the council, and it was debated whether this money, which was to be employed for the destruction of the Protestants in the Low Countries, should not be borrowed by the queen, security being given; a practice then usual among princes, and to which Philip himself had sometimes resorted; and upon this the queen resolved, though most of her advisers were of a different opinion, and feared to exasperate a powerful king who was already sufficiently incensed against the English. This resolution was communicated to the Spanish ambassador, with a solemn engagement to restore the money, if it should prove to belong not to the merchants but to the King of Spain. Alva, on the very day that this communication was made to the resident, upon the first suspicion seized the goods of all the English in the Netherlands, and arrested the owners. He thought to intimidate a Government, the strength of which had not been tried, and the foundations of which he was then working to undermine. But the courageous queen immediately made reprisals upon the ships and property belonging to the Netherlanders.*

Ships were now sent out to cruise against the English, not only from the Netherlands, but from the ports of Spain, where the English merchants and mariners were arrested by the Inquisition, and condemned to the galleys, and their goods confiscated. When this was known in England, privateers were fitted out with the utmost activity; but they acted with such indiscriminating rapacity, that it became necessary to issue proclamations forbidding all men from purchasing any merchandise from sea rovers. Meantime Alva was prosecuting what he hoped would prove a far more effectual plan of operations against Elizabeth, and in her person against the Protestant religion, whereof she was the chief earthly support. The hostile disposition of Philip towards England was such, that he had reprimanded this minister not long before for having written as if he were well inclined towards what the king

---

* Camden, 120. Pieter Bor, *Oorsprongk.* etc., *der Netherlandsche Oorlogen,* i., 272.

The property embargoed here is said to have far exceeded in value what was seized in the Netherlands, though Pieter Bor states the yearly value of our exports to those countries at more than 12,000,000 crowns of gold (i., 69).

called that "lost and undone kingdom";* for the Inquisition had now obtained as much influence over the councils of that monarch, prudent as he was deemed, as over his conscience. The language of the Pope was, that for the diseases which then afflicted Christendom fiery cauteries were required; that corrupt members must be cut off; that nothing was more cruel than to show mercy to the heretics; that all who fell into the hands of the true servants of the Church ought immediately to be put to death, and that no king who suffered himself to be entreated in their favour could satisfy his Redeemer.† They acted themselves in the spirit of these exhortations. Pius V. laid a plot for restoring the Romish religion in England by taking off Elizabeth,‡ and raising the Queen of Scots to the throne. Her agents in this country conducted it with great dexterity, so as to engage in it some who were in Elizabeth's council, and in her favour as well as confidence, but who were now actuated by ambition, or by envy and hatred of their rivals, or by a dreadful persuasion of duty to the Papal Church; and all things seemed ripe when the dispute concerning the money which the English Government had retained afforded Pius a favourable opportunity § for engaging Philip in the conspiracy. Philip lent an obedient ear. Alva was ordered to hold 3000 harquebussiers in readiness for embarkation: the Marquis Vitelli was sent to London under the pretext of an embassy, but with the intent that he should take the command of those troops as soon as they should have landed near London, where an understanding

* Turner's *Elizabeth*, 454, n. 2.

† *Ibid.*, 461, 480, n. 45; 481, n. 56.

‡ " Unâ quidem ex parte ipsi Scotorum reginæ—opem ferre, eamque omnino liberare; ex alterâ vero lapsam in Angliâ religionem renovare cogitabat, simul et illam malorum omnium sentinam, seu, ut appellabat ipse, flagitiorum servam *de medio tollere*, si minus posset ad sanitatem revocari" (Gabutius, *Vita B. Pii. V. Acta SS.*, 2. Mar., t. i., p. 658).

§ " Oblatam occasionem haud contemnendam esseratus " (*Ibid.*).

had been established with the Tower, at the palace, and among the queen's guards.*

These arrangements having been made, the Pope fulminated that memorable bull, wherein, as one whom the Lord had made prince over all people and all kingdoms, to pluck up, destroy, scatter, consume, plant, and build, he passed sentence of excommunication against Elizabeth, as being a heretic, and a favourer of heretics; pronounced that she was cut off from the unity of the body of Christ, and deprived of her pretended title to the kingdom; absolved her subjects from the oath of allegiance, and all manner of duty towards her, and included all who should obey her in the same sentence of anathema. It was thought imprudent to let this bull appear in Spain or France before it had been published in England, lest it should provoke the queen † to take more active measures against the Spaniards, and to appear decidedly in support of the French Protestants. Its first appearance, therefore, was in London, where Felton nailed it upon the Bishop of London's palace gate. But an earlier insurrection in the north had broken the strength and abated the hopes of the more eager Papists; and secret information of the conspiracy was given to the English ministers by the French Government,‡ which, though possessed with the most deadly hatred against the Protestant cause, dreaded the union of England and Scotland under one sovereign, and the subjugation of this country to the influence,

---

* Turner, 505, 509.

† *Acta Sanctorum*, 658. Pollini, 458.

‡ Turner, 509. This most diligent historian, whose industry and integrity, and perfect fairness, entitle him always to be trusted, has shown that this information was given by Catherine de Medicis, upon the Cardinal of Lorraine's advice.

"... divino judicio permissum est (Gabutius says) ut de rerum seria totâ ad Elizabetham referretur à nonnullis, Galliæ regno politicè magis quam piè consulentibus, statusque jure (quod Pius diabolicum jus appellare solebat) atque vanâ suspicione implicitis, ne scilicet Angliâ recepâ, Galliarum regno potirentur Hispani" (*Acta SS.*, 658).

or possibly * to the power of Spain. Thus did France, at this critical time, interpose in favour of Elizabeth against the Spaniards, upon motives precisely similar to those by which Spain had before been led to interfere for her against the French ; and the conspiracy was frustrated,† though its extent was not discovered, nor the magnitude of the danger as yet fully understood.

But though the treason had failed, and the Duke of Norfolk, who was to have been the Catholic husband of a second Queen Mary, suffered death, the design was still pursued by the Spaniards and the Pope : the latter spared no money for this pious purpose, as it was deemed at the Vatican, and declared that, were it necessary, for such an object he would expend the whole revenues of the apostolic see, and sell the chalices and the crosses, and even the very vestments.‡ That the blow might more surely be struck, the semblance of peace, if not of amity, was still maintained ; not with sincerity, indeed, on

---

* "Verentes nimirum ne Anglia in Hispanorum caderet potestatem."

† Pollini imputes the delay to Alva's fear of bringing about a league between France and England in aid of the Protestants in the Netherlands; and afterwards to his desire that his son D. Fadrique should command the expedition instead of Vitelli. The first fear he ascribes to the suggestion of the devil, and insinuates (falsely beyond all doubt) that, owing to his resentment at being disappointed in his views for his son, Elizabeth was made acquainted with the plot; whereby "hebbe finalmente quello che desiderava il diavolo " (471, 472).

Philip is asserted to have said to the legate : " Nullam unquam hoc ipso vel preclarius vel sanctius compositum stratagema fuisse ; neque vero majorem unquam visam esse conjuratorum sive concordiam, sive constantiam ; siquidem per tot dies nihil unquam ab ipsis temere enuntiatum erat, magnaque res bene gerendæ atque opportuna sese offerebat occasio. Sed enim summus ille mundi Opifex, cujus nutu omnia gubernantur, seu mortalium peccatis id emerentibus, seu ut ex Angliâ vigente persecutione plures interim Christi martyres, uti deinceps factum est, in cœlum volarent, nos alioqui pios conatus irritos esse permissit " (*Acta SS.*, 659).

‡ *Ibid.*

Elizabeth's part; but on the part of Philip perfidiously. She did not restrain her subjects from those maritime adventures which nourished her naval strength; and he, in conformity to what was then the avowed doctrine of the Romish Church, acted upon the principle that all means were justifiable whereby the interests of that Church could be promoted. The Spanish ambassador complained that the rebellious Netherlanders were supplied with warlike stores from England, and harboured in the English ports; and, in consequence of his complaint, she ordered their ships of war to be detained, and those persons who were suspected of being implicated in the disturbances to leave the land. The most important events in public affairs, as well as in private life, often arise from circumstances which, when they occur, appear of little moment. The ships which the Prince of Orange had commissioned, though they were expressly enjoined not to injure any but their enemies, had brought a scandal upon his cause * by their piracies: insomuch that he had displaced the admiral and appointed the Lord of Lumey, William Graave van der Marck, in his stead. That officer, acting either from timely apprehension, or upon secret intimation, collected his ships, twenty-four in number, and sailed from England, entered the Maas, and by a sudden assault got possession of the Briel. This was the first town in Holland which was delivered from the Spaniards, and with this enterprise, the naval power of the United Provinces commenced. The Water-Geusen, as the Prince of Orange's sailors were called, had before this time deserved no better appellation; they were mere pirates; and by their ill name had done more injury to him, than by their ill deeds to his enemies. But after this adventure, which had been undertaken by the exhortation of a better man than Lumey,† one success followed

---

* Pieter Bor, 289, 323.

† He was a mere freebooter, and most of his company little better: "Animi ferox, idque illi unum pro virtute erat," says Grotius; "et comitum plerisque consilium, aut animus, non nisi in prædam" (*Ann.*, l. ii., p. 35).

another. They obtained ports, entered earnestly into the national cause, and acquired character as they gathered strength.* Within four months after the capture of the Briel, they were joined by so many adventurers, French and English, that a fleet of 150 sail † was collected at Flushing, and by this fleet the project of an intended invasion of England was defeated, ‡ at a time when no apprehension of any such danger was entertained there. For the Duque del Medina Celi, coming to succeed Alva in the Government, and bringing with him reinforcements and orders to put in execution the design of entering the Thames and surprising London, approached the coast of Flanders, supposing it to be still in possession of the Spaniards, and that they were masters as well of the sea as of the shores. But the Admiral of Zeeland, Boudewijn Ewoutzoon, having intelligence of his approach, met and attacked him, and captured the far greater part of his richly laden fleet, the duque himself hardly escaping in a small vessel into Sluys.§ Dispirited at the unexpected aspect of affairs on his arrival, he solicited and obtained his recall; and Alva seeing that the scheme of foreign invasion, as well as of domestic treason, had been frustrated, deemed it advisable to dissemble still further with England, and renewed the commercial intercourse which had then for four years been suspended. By mutual agreement it was opened for two years, and among the articles was a clause, that "if this mutual good understanding and close amity should happen for a time to be disturbed, yet should it in no wise be construed to be broken and dissolved. But if the matter could not be com-

---

* *Tegenwoordige Staat der Ver. Netherlanden*, vol. v., pp. 330-336. Pieter Bor, 365.

† Strada, Dec. i., l. vii., p. 393.

‡ Camden, 191.

§ Pieter Bor, 393. *T'Vervolgh der. Chron. van de Netherlanden*, p. 64.

pounded by commissioners, within the time prescribed, the intercourse was to cease at the end of the two years."*

The good faith and honour of the realm was upon this occasion well maintained. Elizabeth made a full agreement with the Genoese merchants, concerning the money which was the first declared cause of difference: she indemnified the English merchants for their losses in the Netherlands, out of the produce of the Netherlanders' goods which had been embargoed here; and the residue was restored to Alva, who made no such restitution to his subjects out of the English property that he had detained.† It had never been Elizabeth's wish that the Netherlands should throw off their allegiance to Philip. Not contemplating the possibility, which, at that time, was not contemplated by themselves, that they could ever maintain themselves as an independent State, she knew that, as it regarded England, it was better they should be annexed to Spain than to France; and there was no other apparent alternative. Nor, if their independence had seemed feasible, could she, a sovereign princess, have desired that what she could not but deem a dangerous precedent should be established. As a Protestant, she sympathised with their sufferings for religion's sake ; as the queen of a free people, whose rights and privileges she respected as she ought, she acknowledged that they complained justly of the breach of their fundamental laws. But, on the other hand, Elizabeth felt that the cause of the Reformation had been disgraced and injured by the excesses the Netherlanders had committed under its name, by spoliation and havoc, and by cruelties which afforded the persecutors a recriminating plea, and which were not to be excused for having been exercised in retaliation. Moreover, she was sensible that, in such commotions, the foundations of civil society are loosened and endangered. These equitable views were fairly stated, both

* Camden, 191. † *Ibid.*

to the Spanish Government and to the States. When Requesens sent an agent into England to obtain her permission for engaging ships and seamen there, to act against the Hollanders and Zeelanders, she refused, and prohibited English seamen from serving under foreign powers, and all men from setting out ships of war without her licence: "her ships and sailors," she said, "should not be hazarded in foreign quarrels". The agent then requested that she would not be displeased if those English whom he called exiles, but whom she termed rebels, served at sea against the Hollanders; but that she would allow them free access to any of her ports. Her answer was, "that she could in no wise allow them to serve under the Spaniards; and that to give the use of her ports to rebels and sworn enemies would be nothing short of madness". One other request the agent made, that the Low Country emigrants might be expelled from her dominions. To this she replied, "that her consenting to a like request, three years before, had proved most prejudicial to the Spanish affairs; for from thence that maritime power had arisen, against which the Spaniards now found it so difficult to contend". In proof that she had neither forgotten nor disregarded the ancient league with the house of Burgundy, she forbade the Netherlanders' ships of war, which were then in her havens, from leaving them; and would, by public proclamation, give orders that none who were in arms against the Spaniards should be admitted into them, specifying by name the Prince of Orange, and some fifty of the most conspicuous persons of his party; but she would not expel the fugitives who had taken shelter upon her shores, . . . "poor, simple people, who had forsaken their country and their inheritance for peace; and whom it were inhuman, and against the laws of hospitality, to deliver into the hands of their enemies".*

On the other hand, she endeavoured to dissuade the Prince

* Camden, 20.

of Orange from inviting France to protect the States; and when she was entreated by Holland and Zeeland to take them into her own possession, or at least under her protection, as the person to whom, in defeasance of the Spanish line, the right of inheritance reverted (that line deriving it from a sister of Philippa of Hainault, Edward III.'s queen), she answered, that she esteemed nothing more glorious than to act with faith and honour as beseemeth a prince: in this case, she could not be satisfied that she could, consistently with honour and conscience, take those provinces under her protection, much less into her possession; but that she would earnestly endeavour to procure for them a happy peace. When Requesens died, and there were movements which indicated a disposition in the other States to recover their ancient liberties, she exhorted them to bend their minds to peace, desiring nothing so much as the restoration of order in their provinces, and good government. This, indeed, her subjects had great reason to desire; for while many of those unquiet spirits, who followed war as a trade, engaged on either side, the English merchants, seeking their own gain by less exceptionable means, were plundered by both. They who were resident in Antwerp, when that city was sacked by the mutinous Spaniards, were not only spoiled of their goods, but compelled to pay a large ransom for their lives. And the Dutch and Zeeland ships of war, with the connivance, if not the sanction of the States, detained English ships upon the plea that they imported provisions to their enemies the Dunkirkers, and that the trade from Flanders to Spain was now carried on in English bottoms, and boarded them "smally to the profit of those to whom the ships and goods appertained," even when they were not boldly seized and carried away as prizes. A breach had nearly been made between the States and England, when the States blockaded the Scheldt, and prohibited the English from trading by that river with Antwerp: the merchants, finding themselves thus damnified, complained to their own Government, reprisals took place, and the dispute was not adjusted till after much mutual injury and ill-will. The arrangement was facilitated by sending four vessels under the comptroller of the queen's ships, William Holstocke, to scour the narrow seas from the North Foreland to Falmouth. In that course, he recaptured fifteen merchantmen of sundry nations, took twenty ships and barques, "English, French, and Flemings, but all pirates, and in fashion of war"; and brought home 200 men prisoners for piracy, some thirty of whom were condemned to death.*

Such was the desire of Elizabeth that the Low Countries should remain united to Spain, rather than be annexed to France, that when Don John of Austria arrived as governor, she offered him her assistance in case the States should call in the French. At the same time when, upon the importunate entreaties of the States, she assisted them with 20,000*l.*, it was upon condition that they should neither change their religion nor their prince, nor receive the French into the Netherlands, nor refuse a peace if Don John would condescend to reasonable conditions; and that, if such a peace were obtained, this money should go toward the payment of the Spanish soldiers, who were then in a state of mutiny because of their arrears.† But it was with no amicable intentions towards the Queen of England that Don John took upon himself the command in the Netherlands. He had been bred up in ignorance that Charles V. was his father, but in a manner which qualified him for any rank to which he might be advanced; and Philip, after acknowledging him as his brother, though illegitimate, had placed him in circumstances the most favourable to an ambitious mind, by appointing him to the command of that fleet with which he achieved at Lepanto a naval victory more important and more famous than any

---

* Holinshed, 321-323, 329-332. Camden, 214.
† Camden, 208, 210, 215.

preceding one in modern history. Having taken possession of Tunis, he conceived the hope of becoming the founder of a Christian kingdom, which might one day vie in power and prosperity with ancient Carthage :* and when Philip refused his consent to a project the difficulties of which were well understood by Spanish statesmen, Don John, with the approbation of the Pope, fixed upon England as the seat of the kingdom to which he imagined himself born. A marriage with the Queen of Scots was to provide him with a claim to it, and possession was to be taken by force of arms. The English emigrants encouraged him in this design ; and he represented to Philip that England might be conquered more easily than Zeeland, and urged him to grant him some port in the north of Spain from whence he might invade it with a fleet. Meantime he had privately communicated with the Guises ; and this part of his negotiation was discovered and made known to Elizabeth by the Prince of Orange, as also that the intention was to occupy the Isle of Man, and that the aid of Mary's partisans in the south of Scotland was counted on, assistance from Ireland, and an insurrection of the Papists in the northern counties and in North Wales. When the truth of this information had been ascertained, Elizabeth entered into a league with the States.†

That league she notified by an ambassador to the King of Spain, praying him and the governors of the Netherlands to call to mind how often and how earnestly, and in how friendly an intent, she had long forewarned them of the evils impending over those countries ; how carefully she had endeavoured to keep them within their duty to the king ; how she had refused to take possession of the rich provinces which had been offered to her, and refused also to protect them ; and how she had supplied them largely with money, when all

* *Memorial de Ant. Perez*, 298.
† Camden, 220.

things were in a most desperate and deplorable state, that they might not, for want thereof, be necessitated to call in another power, and break the design of peace which had lately been set on foot; whether these things were unbeseeming a Christian queen, who affected peace, and was most desirous to deserve well of her confederate the Spaniard, let the Spaniard himself and all Christian princes judge! And now that the wars might cease, and the Netherlanders again be at his devotion, she advised him to receive his afflicted people into former grace and favour, to restore their privileges, to observe the conditions of the last agreement, and to appoint them another governor of his own family : for no peace could be concluded or observed unless Don John of Austria were removed, whom the States distrusted and hated, and whom she certainly knew, by his secret practices with the Queen of Scots, to be her most mortal enemy, insomuch that she could expect nothing from the Netherlands but assured danger, so long as he was governor there. It was because she knew what great forces Don John had raised, and how many auxiliary companies of French were ready to join him, that she, to preserve the Netherlands and Spain, and avert the danger from England, had now engaged to assist the States, they having promised on their part that they would continue in the king's obedience, and alter nothing in religion. If, however, the king would not listen to these representations, but was resolved to abrogate their rights and privileges, and reduce those miserable provinces into slavery, as if he had obtained possession of them by right of war, she in that case would not neglect to defend her neighbours, and provide for her own security.*

This was no palatable language to Philip; but that deep dissembler, feeling its force, and conscious of its truth, brooked it, and with simulated good-will besought her to continue her

* Camden, 221.

endeavours for bringing about a peace, and not hastily to credit false reports, nor believe that he attempted anything unbecoming a prince in amity with her. How far he favoured the designs of Don John as conformable to his own Catholic views, or discouraged them as tending more to the advantage of France than Spain, is uncertain.* But after the death of

* Strada says that when the Pope proposed a marriage between Don John and the Queen of Scots, " Cum dotali Angliæ regno, ad cujus aggressionem honestior inde titulus armis Austriacis adderetur "; Philip did not refuse his consent: " Neque rex abnuebat, immó licet expeditionem magis quam ducem probaret," are his cautious words (l. viii., p. 445).

There is a mystery about the fate of Don John. " Nam super natalium sortem Tunetense quondam regnum, tunc et Angliam sperasse manifestus, et cum Lotharingis in Gallicâ aulâ præpotentibus, clam Philippum, sociasse consilia, facile et res Belgicas in se versurus timebatur. Unde nec veneni suspicio abfuit, incertum tamen unde dati, quippe inventis sacerdotibus Romanæ professionis, qui suam in hoc operam patriæ imputarent. Anglos alii suspectabant, non ita dudum supplicio affectis, qui inde immissi in ipsum percursores dicebantur" (Grotius, p. 61).

The Englishmen here spoken of were Egremont Ratcliffe, and one Grey, the former son to the Earl of Sussex by a second wife, a man of a turbulent spirit, and one of the chiefs of the northern rebellion. The English emigrants accused him of intending to assassinate Don John, in whose army he was serving, and he and Grey were executed upon this. "The Spaniards," says Camden, " give out that Ratcliffe at his death voluntarily confessed he had been released from the Tower purposely to commit this murder, and encouraged to it by Walsingham with great promises. The English that were there present deny that he made any such confession, though the emigrants did what they could to extort it from him " (p. 227). They were put to the torture after Don John's death, by the Prince of Parma, and executed upon the confession thus extorted (Strada, 557). If Don John were poisoned, the cause of their execution is evident enough.

This was an absurd charge, and could be believed only by that party spirit which will believe anything. Common as the employment of assassins was in that age for party motives, the English Government stands free from all reproach on that score; and if it had been less scrupulous, Don John was no object of its jealousy or of its fear. There is a strange tale of his intriguing for a marriage with Elizabeth; this is

that ambitious chief, whose story is more like a fiction of romance or tragedy than a tale of real life, the plots against Elizabeth were renewed. Pope Gregory XIII. and Philip, by whom the scheme was now concerted, had each their separate views; the latter saw that he could not reduce the Netherlands to subjection unless he were master of the sea, and that he could not be master of the sea till he should have subdued England. The Pope, in the plenitude of his authority, was willing to confer upon him an apostolical title to that kingdom, giving Ireland at the same time to his own bastard son, whom he had made Marchese de Vineola. The notorious adventurer Stukely undertook to conquer Ireland for this king-aspirant, and to burn the ships in the Thames. For this service, he asked only 3000 men, while a larger force of Spaniards and Portuguese were to land in England. To show on what grounds he proceeded, this arch-traitor presented an instrument to Philip, " subscribed with the names of most of the Irish nobility, and of divers in England of good quality, ready

said to have been seriously affirmed by letters from the Low Countries, and it has also been affirmed that Escovedo passed two months in England endeavouring to bring about a negotiation for this end; but nothing that in the slightest degree supports this, appears in all that has come to light concerning Escovedo's fate, nor in any English documents. It is only not impossible, because Don John seems to have loved danger and dissimulation for their own sakes. Instead of taking a safe course to the Netherlands, when he went to assume the government, he chose to pass through France in the disguise of a negro servant, "infuscato ore, vibrato capillo ac barbâ" (Strada, Dec. iv., l. ix., p. 460). The man who could choose such a disguise, would think no plot too extravagant in which he was to perform a conspicuous part.

Strada suspects that the story was devised by the Prince of Orange, for the purpose of exasperating Philip against his brother (p. 556). But the Prince of Orange was a good man, engaged in a good cause, . . . too good a man ever to have served it by wicked means. When he charged Philip in his declaration, with the death of Don Carlos, I am as confident that he believed the charge as I am convinced that the charge itself was an atrocious calumny.

to be at his devotion ". In order to diminish the queen's means of naval defence, foreign merchants were employed to hire for distant voyages the greater part of those merchant ships which were built and furnished for sea-service.*

It is said that Sebastian of Portugal was intended for the command of this expedition. Such an undertaking would have well accorded with his temper, and with the principles wherewith his pernicious education had thoroughly imbued him. The massacre of St. Bartholomew's had been concerted with his knowledge: an armament, which he had prepared ostensibly against the Turks, was to have sailed in aid of the French Government, if that massacre had failed; and when the news of its perpetration arrived, Lisbon was illuminated, and processions made, and a thanksgiving sermon preached by the most eloquent of the Spanish preachers, Frey Luiz de Granada; and an ambassador was sent to congratulate Charles IX. † upon a crime—for which, as it regards himself, it may be hoped that the horror and remorse which speedily brought him to an untimely death may have atoned. But though Sebastian had proffered to the Pope his utmost services against Mahommedans and heretics, early impressions and national feeling led him to tread in the steps of his heroic ancestors, and endeavour to recover that dominion in Africa which they had unwisely abandoned for the sake of more distant and less tenable conquests. Though the Pope offered him a consecrated banner as for a holy war, he was not to be diverted from his purpose; and Stukely, who arrived in the Tagus with 800 men, raised for the invasion of Ireland, was induced to postpone that purpose, and accompany Sebastian to Barbary. Stukely met his death there, . . . in better company than he deserved to die in; for braver or nobler-minded men never fell in battle than some of those Portu-

* Camden, 230. Turner, 574.
† Bayam, *Portugal Cuidadoso y Lastimoso*, 271, 272.

guese who perished on that disastrous day. Whether Sebastian perished with them, is one of those secrets over which the grave has closed. But as his wilfulness had been the means of averting the intended invasion of England, so by the consequences of his defeat and disappearance Portugal became the immediate object of Philip's designs: his chief care was devoted to obtaining the succession for himself; and the forces which had been levied against Elizabeth were employed in establishing his ill-founded claim against a pretender whose pretensions were weaker than his own, and who had nothing to support them but the favour of the populace.

A few years earlier, Cecil, the greatest of English statesmen, thought that if an enemy were at hand to assail the realm it were a fearful thing to consider, because of its growing weakness, what the resistance might be. The cause of that weakness he perceived "in the queen's celibacy, and the want of a suitable successor, and the lack of foreign alliances; in the feebleness which long peace had induced, the weakness of the frontier, the ignorance of martial knowledge in the subjects, the lack of meet captains and trained soldiers, the rebellion which had then recently broken out in Ireland, the over-much boldness which the mildness of the queen's government had encouraged, the want of treasure, the excess of the ordinary charges, the poverty of the nobility and gentlemen of service (the wealth being in the meaner sort), the lack of mariners and munition, and the decay of morals and religion"; but the greatest danger he considered to be that which arose from " the determination of the two monarchies, next neighbours to England, to subvert not only their own subjects, but also all others refusing the tyranny of Rome, and their earnest desire to have the Queen of Scots possess this throne of England". * One alone of these causes of danger had been remedied, the lack of mariners: a race of seamen such as no

---

* Memorial of the state of the realm, quoted by Turner, 513.

former times had equalled, and no after ones have surpassed, was then training in voyages of discovery and of mercantile adventure. For the predatory spirit by which the speculators at home, as well as the adventurers themselves, were influenced, some provocation had been given; and when Elizabeth, in answer to the demand made by the Spanish ambassador for restitution of the treasure which Drake had brought home from that voyage which has immortalised his name, told him that Drake should be forthcoming to answer according to law, if he were convicted by good evidence of having committed anything against law or right; and that the property was set apart in order that it might be restored to its just claimants; she reminded him that a greater sum than Drake had brought home she had been compelled to expend in putting down those rebellions which the Spaniards had raised and encouraged both in Ireland and England: and as to the complaint which he preferred against the English for sailing in the Indian Ocean, she answered, she could not persuade herself that the Bishop of Rome's donation had conferred upon the kings of Spain any just title to the Indies: she acknowledged no prerogative in that bishop to lay any restriction upon princes who owed him no obedience; nor could she allow that he had any authority to enfeoff, as it were, the Spaniard in that new world, and invest him with the possession thereof. Neither was their only other claim to be admitted, which was no more than that they had touched here and there upon the coast, built huts there, and given names to a river or a cape. This donation of that which was another's, and this imaginary propriety, did not preclude other princes from trading to those countries, nor from transporting colonies (without breach of the law of nations) into those parts which were not inhabited by Spaniards (for prescription without possession was little worth); nor from navigating that vast ocean, seeing that the sea and air are common to all. A title to the ocean belonged not to any people or private persons, forasmuch as neither nature nor public custom warranted any possession thereof. She observed, also, that the Spaniards, by their hard dealing with the English, whom they had, contrary to the law of nations, prohibited from commerce, had drawn upon themselves the mischiefs which they now complained of.*

The charge against the Spanish Government, of having instigated rebellion, was incontestable. Stukely's preparations had not been secret, and an English fleet had been stationed on the Irish coast to intercept him; and that fleet had not long returned to England, in the belief that all present danger was past, before a body of Spaniards were landed in Ireland, in aid of the first Irish rebellion into which the Romish religion entered as an exciting cause, . . . a cause from whence have arisen the greatest evils that have afflicted, and are afflicting, and will long continue to afflict, that unhappy island. The Spaniards fortified themselves in Kerry; and when the lord deputy, Arthur Lord Grey of Wilton, marched against them, and sent a trumpet "to demand who they were, what they had to do in Ireland, who sent them, and wherefore they had built a fort in Queen Elizabeth's dominions, and withal to command them to depart with speed," they answered, that they were sent "some from the most holy father, the Pope, and some from the King of Spain, to whom the Pope had given Ireland, Queen Elizabeth having, as a heretic, forfeited her title to it. They would, therefore, hold what they had gotten, and get more if they could." The confidence which seemed to themselves to justify this language soon failed them; they discovered too late the vanity of the promises which had been held out to them, the condition of the people with whom they were to act, and the dreadful character of the war which, in reliance upon their support, had been begun. They were besieged by land; the protect-

* Camden, 255.

ing squadron was remanded from England, and cut off their escape by sea: they were compelled to surrender at discretion, and were put to the sword; a measure which grieved Elizabeth, and which she disapproved, even when she admitted that the plea of stern necessity was strongly urged in its vindication.*

It was easy for Elizabeth to justify the views of her Government, and the peaceable course which it had hitherto pursued. Upon general principles, too, the right of her subjects to explore distant seas and countries might well be asserted and maintained, but she made no attempt to defend what was not strictly defensible, and a great part of the money which Drake had brought home was restored to the Spaniards; † and some of the chief persons belonging to the court refused to accept the money which he offered them, because they considered it to have been gained by piracy. This is said to have troubled him greatly, for he no doubt was of opinion that the conduct of the Spaniards in their American conquests warranted any hostile proceedings against them; and he had this to encourage him, that, while statesmen openly condemned his conduct, or only covertly protected him, "the common sort of people admired and extolled his actions, as deeming it no less honourable to have enlarged the bounds of the English name and glory, than of their empire". ‡ Indeed, however desirous Elizabeth's ministers were of avoiding a war, they saw what the people felt, that it must soon be forced upon them, and that overt acts on the part of Philip would

---

Camden, 243.

† It was paid to a certain Pedro Sebura, of whom Camden says, that he "pretended himself an agent for retrieving the gold and silver," though he had no letters of evidence or commission so to do; and that he "never repaid it to the right owners, but employed it against the queen, and converted it to the pay of the Spaniards in the Netherlands, as was at length when it was too late, understood" (p. 255).

Fuller's *Church History*, sixteenth century, 180-182.

soon follow the covert hostility which had long been carried on. The Jesuits, who were now the moving spirits in every conspiracy, were at that time (to use a word current in that age) completely *hispaniolised*, and this was not because the founder, and the architect, and the great thaumaturgic saint of their order were Spaniards, but because the chimerical hope was entertained of establishing a universal monarchy of which Spain was to be the temporal and Rome the spiritual head. The important step of rendering Spain in all spiritual affairs absolutely subservient to Rome had been effected; and they who laboured to extend the Spanish dominion perceived that the succession of the Scottish line to the throne of England must be unfavourable to the interests of Spain, because of Mary's connection with the Guises; that of her son would be detrimental to the Romish Church, because he had been carefully and well educated in the principles of the Protestant faith, and it was now evident that those principles were well rooted in his mind. They set up, therefore, a title of the King of Spain to the English crown, by which, preposterous as it was, not a few of the English Papists were deluded.* Some of the queen's counsellors proposed to her, as a counter-project, that she should foment the difference which then existed between Philip and the Pope concerning the kingdom of Naples, and assist Gregory not as Pope, but

* This title, Fuller says (180), was "as much admired by their own party, as slighted by the queen and her loyal subjects. Indeed it is easy for any indifferent herald so to devise a pedigree, as in some seeming probability to entitle any prince in Christendom to any principality in Christendom; but such will shrink on serious examination. Yea, I believe Queen Elizabeth might pretend a better title to the kingdoms of Leon and Castile in Spain, as descended, by the House of York, from Edmond Earl of Cambridge, and his lady, co-heir to King Pedro, than any claim that the King of Spain could make out to the kingdom of England. However, much mischief was done hereby, many Papists paying their good wishes where they were not due, and defrauding the queen (their true creditor) of the allegiance belonging unto her."

in his character of temporal prince, with ships; thus, they argued, she might bring about a diversion of the Spanish forces, and prevent an invasion of her own dominions. It might have been a sufficient objection to any such proposal that the Papal claim rested upon Papal grounds, and was not maintainable as a political question. But Elizabeth saw it at once in the right point of view as a question of honour and of conscience: she refused to "entertain compliance with the Pope in any capacity, or any conditions, as dishonourable to herself, and distasteful to the Protestant princes; nor would she," says our good Church historian, "touch pitch in jest, for fear of being defiled in earnest".*

Part of the system which the hispaniolised faction pursued was to blacken the character of Elizabeth by every imaginable calumny, knowing that no calumnies can be too absurd for itching ears, and hearts that are prepossessed with hatred for the person whom it is proposed to injure. Not contented with contending that she was of illegitimate birth, they affirmed that she was the offspring of an incestuous intercourse between Henry VIII. and his own daughter! They arraigned her of the vilest ingratitude towards Philip, to whose intercession, they asserted, she had been three times beholden for her life, when sentence of death had been passed against her for treason against her sister. They represented the punishment of convicted traitors, and the preventive measures against preparatory treason, which for self-preservation her Government was compelled to pursue, in a religious persecution, against which the advocates and agents of the Inquisition,— yea, the very men who had kindled the fires in Smithfield,— filled Europe with their complaints. Books were set forth, wherein it was not contended, but dogmatically taught, that princes, when excommunicated for heresy, were to be deprived of kingdom and life. This doctrine received the sanction of

---

* Fuller's *Church History*, sixteenth century, 180-182.

the censorial authorities in Romish countries; and, by a libel which was secretly printed in England, the ladies of Elizabeth's household were exhorted to deal with her as Judith had dealt with Holofernes.* Bernardino de Mendoza, the Spanish ambassador in England, was detected in a correspondence with those Papists whose object it was, by foreign aid, to depose the queen and re-establish the Romish religion. He was ordered to depart the land, though he had rendered himself liable to the utmost severity of the law; and the queen was still so desirous of continuing at peace with Spain, that she sent the clerk of her council into that country, to inform the King of Spain for what just cause his minister had been sent away, and withal to assure him, lest, by having thus dismissed Mendoza, she "might seem to renounce the ancient amity that had subsisted between both kingdoms," that all amicable offices should still be shown by her, if Philip would send any other minister who should be desirous of preserving friendship,—provided only that a like reception might be given to her ambassador. But this minister could not obtain a hearing.†

Meantime the Prince of Orange, who had recovered after being desperately wounded by one assassin, perished by the hand of another; and the war in the Netherlands was vigorously prosecuted by the Prince of Parma, a general whose martial genius had then never been equalled in modern warfare, and, perhaps, has never since been surpassed. Elizabeth, in her cautious policy, hesitated at entering into any direct alliance with the united States, till he had taken Antwerp, after one of the most memorable sieges in military history. She then hesitated no longer, lest the war should be brought home to her own doors; and concluded a treaty, whereby she contracted to aid the States with 5000 foot and 1000 horse during the war, the States engaging to repay the expense thus

* Camden, 295, 307. † *Ibid.*, 296.

incurred, in the course of five years after the conclusion of a peace. Flushing, Rammakens, and the Briel, were to be occupied by English troops as caution towns. The contracting parties were to enter into no league, but on common consent; and ships for their mutual defence were to be equipped in equal numbers by both parties, at their common charge, and to be commanded by the admiral of England. The Zeelanders, in honour of this alliance, coined money with the arms of that province on one side, a lion rising out of the waves, and the motto *Luctor et emergo;* and on the other the arms of the several cities, with the motto, *Authore Deo, favente Regina.**
A declaration was published in the queen's name, " of the causes which had moved her to give aid to the defence of the people afflicted and oppressed in the Low Countries"; for "although kings and princes sovereign, it was said, were not bound to render account of their actions to any but to God, their only sovereign Lord, we are, notwithstanding this our prerogative, at this time specially moved to publish, not only unto our own natural loving subjects, but also to all others our neighbours, what our intention is at this time, and upon what just and reasonable grounds we are moved to give aid unto our next neighbours, the natural people of the Low Countries being, by long wars and persecutions of strange nations there, lamentably afflicted, and in present danger to be brought into a perpetual servitude".

"First," said this declaration, "it is to be understood that there hath been, time out of mind, even by the natural situation of those Low Countries and our realm of England, one directly opposite to the other, and by reason of the ready crossing of the seas, and multitudes of large and commodious havens respectively on both sides, a continual traffic and commerce betwixt the people of England and the natural people of those countries, and so continued in all ancient times, when

* Camden, 324.

the several provinces thereof, as Flanders, Holland, and Zeeland, and other countries to them adjoining, were possessed by several lords; and not united together as of late years they have been by inter-marriages, and at length by concurrence of many and sundry titles, reduced to be under the government of those lords that succeeded to the Dukedom of Burgundy: whereby there had been many special confederations, not only betwixt the kings of England and the lords of the said countries, but also betwixt the very natural subjects of both, as the prelates, noblemen, citizens, burgesses and other commonalties of the great cities and port towns of either country reciprocally, by special obligations and stipulations under their seals interchangeably, for maintenance of commerce and intercourse of merchants, and also of special mutual amity to be observed; and very express provision for mutual favours, affections, and all other friendly offices to be used and prosecuted by the people of the one nation towards the other. By which mutual bonds there hath continued perpetual union of the people's hearts together; and so, by way of continual intercourse, from age to age, the same mutual love hath been inviolably kept and exercised, as it had been by the will of nature, and never utterly dissolved, nor yet for any long time discontinued, howsoever the kings and the lords of the countries sometimes (though very rarely) have been at difference, by sinister means of some other princes, their neighbours, envying the felicity of these two countries. And so had the same mutual and natural concourse and commerce been continued in many ages, far above the like example of any other countries in Christendom, to the honour and strength of the princes, and to the singular great benefit and enriching of their people, until of late years the King of Spain had been (as it is to be thought) counselled by his counsellors of Spain to appoint Spaniards, foreigners, and strangers of strange blood,—men more exercised in war than in peaceful government, and some of them notably delighted in blood, as had appeared by their actions,—to be the chiefest governors of all his said Low Countries, contrary to the ancient laws and customs thereof. The Spaniards, having no natural regard to the maintenance of those people in their ancient manner of peaceable living, but being exalted to absolute government by ambition, and for private lucre, have violently broken the ancient laws and liberties, and, in a tyrannous sort, have banished, killed, and destroyed, without order of law, many of the most ancient and principal persons of the natural nobility, that were most worthy of government. And howsoever, in the beginning of these cruel persecutions, the pretence thereof was for maintenance of Romish religion, yet they spared not to deprive very many Catholics and ecclesiastical persons of their franchises and privileges; and of the chiefest that were executed of the nobility, none was in the whole country more affected to that religion than was the noble and valiant Count of Egmond, the very glory of that country, who neither for his singular victories in the service of the King of Spain can be forgotten in true histories, nor yet for the cruelty used for his destruction be but for ever lamented in the hearts of the people of that country."

The declaration proceeded to show how the horrible calamities thus brought upon the Low Countries had moved to compassion even such of their neighbours as had been at frequent discord with them in former times, insomuch that the French king thought, very many years ago, to have taken them under his protection, had not (as the deputies of the States were answered) the "complots of the house of Guise, stirred and maintained by money out of Spain, disturbed the peace of France, and thereby urged the king to forbear from the resolution he had made, not to aid those oppressed people of the Low Countries against the Spaniards, but also to have accepted them as his own subjects. But, in very truth, however, they were comforted and kept in hope by the French king, who had oftentimes solicited us, as Queen of England, both by message and writing, to be careful of their defence; yet, in respect that they were more strictly knit in ancient friendship to this realm than to any other country, we are sure that they could be pitied of none with more cause of grief generally than of our subjects, being their most ancient allies and familiar neighbours; and that in such manner that this our realm of England and those countries have been of long time resembled and termed as man and wife. For these urgent causes, and many others, we have by many friendly messages and ambassadors, by many letters and writings, to the said King of Spain, our brother and ally, declared our compassion of this so evil and cruel usage of his natural and loyal people. And furthermore, as a good loving sister to him, and a natural good neighbour to his Low Countries, we have often and often again most friendly warned him, that if he did not by his wisdom and princely clemency, restrain the tyranny of his governors, and cruelty of his men of war, we feared that the people should be forced, for safety of their lives, and for continuance of their native country in the former state of their liberties, to seek the protection of some other foreign lord, or rather to yield themselves wholly to the sovereignty of some mighty prince; as by the ancient laws, and by special privileges granted by some of the lords and dukes to the people, they do pretend and affirm that in such cases of general injustice, and upon such violent breaking of their privileges, they are free from their former homage, and at liberty to make choice of any other prince to be their head. By some such alteration, as stories testify, Philip, the Duke of Burgundy, came to his title, from which the King of Spain's interest is derived. And now, to stay them from yielding themselves in any like sort to the sovereignty of any other strange prince, we yielded some years past to the importunate requests of some of the greatest persons of degree and most obedient subjects to the king, and granted them prests of money, only to continue them as his subjects, and to maintain themselves in their just defence against the violence of the Spaniards, their oppressors; and during the time of that our aid thus given, and their stay in their obedience to the King of Spain, we did freely acquaint the same king with our actions, and did still continue our friendly advices to him, to move him to command his governors and men of war not to use such insolent cruelties against his people as might make them to despair of his favour, and seek some other lord.

"For we did manifestly see if the nation of Spain should make a conquest of those countries, as was and yet is apparently intended, and plant themselves there as they have done in Naples and other countries, adding thereto the late examples of the hostile enterprise of a power of Spaniards, sent by the King of Spain and the Pope into our realm of Ireland, with an intent, confessed by the captains, that their number was sent to seize upon some strength there, and with other great forces to pursue a conquest thereof, we did manifestly see in what danger our ourself, country and people might shortly be, if in convenient time we did not speedily otherwise regard to prevent or stay the same." The queen then complained, that notwithstanding her often requests and advices, the king's governors in the Low Countries increased their cruelties toward his own afflicted people, and his officers in Spain offered daily greater injuries to the English resorting thither for traffic: yea, her express messengers with her letters were not permitted to come to the king's presence,— " a matter very strange, and against the law of nations". She contrasted the unworthy treatment of her ambassadors in Spain, with her conduct towards the Spanish ambassadors, and especially Bernardino de Mendoza, "one," said she, " whom we did accept and use with great favour a long time, as was seen in our court, and we think cannot be denied by himself: but yet of late years (we know not by what direction), we found him to be a secret great favourer to sundry our evil-disposed and seditious subjects, not only to such as lurked in our realm, but also to such as fled the same, being notoriously condemned as open rebels and traitors, with whom, by his letters, messages, and secret counsels, he did in the end devise how, with a power of men, partly to come out of Spain, partly out of the Low Countries (whereof he gave them great comfort in the king's name), an invasion might be made into our realm; setting down in writing the manner how the same should be done, with what number of men and ships, and upon what coasts, ports, and places of our realm, and who the persons should be, therein of no small account, that should favour this invasion, and take part with the invaders: facts which have been most clearly proved, and confessed by such as were in that confederacy with him; yet when he had been charged with these practices, and it had been made patent to him how and by whom, with many other circumstances, we knew it, he was caused, in very gentle sort, to depart out of our realm, the rather for his own safety, as one in very deed mortally hated of our people".

The declaration proceeded to state what the queen had done for delivering Scotland from the servitude into which the house of Guise meant to have brought it, and that by her means only it had been restored to its ancient freedom, and was so possessed by the present king, whereby Scotland had remained in better amity and peace with England than could be remembered for many hundred years before. It concluded by saying how, upon the continued and lamentable requests of the States of Holland, Zeeland, Gueldres, and other provinces with them united, the queen had, with good advice, and after long deliberation, determined to aid them, "only to defend them and their towns from sacking and desolation, and to procure them safety, to the honour of God, whom they desire to serve sincerely as Christian people, according to His holy word, and to enjoy their ancient liberties, for them and their posterity, and so, consequently, to preserve the lawful and ancient commerce betwixt those countries and ours. And so," said this magnanimous queen, "we hope our intentions herein, and our subsequent actions, will be, by God's favour, honourably interpreted of all persons (saving of the oppressors themselves and their partisans), in that we mean not hereby either for ambition or malice, the two roots of all injustice, to make any particular profit hereof to ourself or to our people; only desiring at this time to obtain, by God's favour, for these countries a deliverance of them from war by the Spaniards and foreigners, a restitution of their ancient liberties, and government by some Christian peace, and thereby a surety for ourselves and our realm to be free from invading neighbours, and our people to enjoy their lawful intercourse of friendship and merchandise, according to the ancient usage and treaties of intercourse made betwixt our progenitors and the lords and earls of those countries, and betwixt our people and theirs. And though our further intention also is, or may be, to take into our guard some few towns upon the sea-side, next opposite to our realm, which otherwise might be in danger to be taken by the strangers, enemies of the country; yet therein considering we have no meaning at this time to take and retain the same to our own proper use, we hope all persons will think it agreeable with good reason and princely policy that we should have the guard and use of some such places, for sure access and recess of our people and soldiers in safety, and for furniture of them with victuals and other things requisite and necessary, whilst it shall be needful for them to continue in those countries, for the aiding thereof in these their great calamities, miseries, and imminent danger, and until the countries may be delivered of such strange forces as do now oppress them, and recover their ancient lawful liberties and manner of government, to live in peace as they have heretofore done, and do now most earnestly in lamentable manner desire to do, which are the very only true ends of all our actions now intended."

At the conclusion, the queen alluded to the "cankered conceits," uttered by malicious tongues, and blasphemous reports, in such infamous libels, that in no age had the devil employed more spirits replenished with all wickedness to utter his rage. An appendix was added to this declaration, in consequence of an account of the siege of Antwerp, printed at Milan, in which said she: "We found ourselves most maliciously charged with two notable crimes, no less hateful to the world than most repugnant and contrary to our own natural inclination. The one with ingratitude towards the King of Spain, who, as the author saith, saved our life, being justly by sentence adjudged to death in our sister's time; the other, that there were persons corrupted with great promises, and that with our intelligence, to take away the Prince of Parma's life. Now, knowing how men are maliciously bent, in this declining age of the world, both to judge, speak, and write maliciously, falsely, and unreverently of princes, and holding nothing so dear unto us as the conservation of our reputation and honour to be blameless, we found it very expedient not to suffer two such horrible imputations to pass under silence. And for answer of the first point, touching our ingratitude towards the King of Spain, as we do most willingly acknowledge that we were beholden unto him in the time of our late sister, which we then did acknowledge very thankfully, and have sought many ways since in like sort to requite, so do we utterly deny as a most manifest untruth, that ever he was the cause of the saving of our life, as a person by course of justice sentenced unto death, who ever carried ourself towards our said sister in such dutiful sort, as our loyalty was never called in question, much less any sentence of death* pronounced against us: a

---

* This accusation was not made by pamphleteers and mere libellers only. Herrera, the royal chronicler, in his *Historia General del Mundo* for the first seventeen years of Philip's reign, asserts that Elizabeth was on three several occasions condemned to death for treason against her sister, and as often pardoned through the king's intercession: "Y el librarla los Españoles con tanto cuydado de la muerte, dezian los Fran-

matter such as in respect of the ordinary course of proceeding, as by process in law, by place of trial, by the judge that should pronounce such sentence, and other necessary circumstances in like cases usual, especially against one of our quality, as it could not but have been publicly known, if any such thing had been put in execution. This, then, being true, we leave to the world to judge how maliciously and injuriously the author of the said pamphlet dealeth with us in charging us with a vice that of all others we do most hate and abhor. And by the manifest untruth of this imputation, men, not transported with passion, may easily discern what untruth is contained in the second, by which we are charged with an intended attempt against the life of the Prince of Parma. He is one of whom we have ever had an honourable conceit, in respect of those singular rare parts we always have noted in him, which hath won unto him as great a reputation as any man this day living carrieth of his degree and quality; and so have we always delivered out by speech unto the world, when any occasion hath been offered to make mention of him. And touching the prosecution, committed unto him, of the wars in the Low Countries, as all men of judgment know, that the

---

ceses que se hazia porque no sucediesse en la corona de Inglaterra Maria reyna de Escocia, casada con Francisco delfin de Francia; y los Españoles dezian contra los Franceses que procuravan de engañar a Ysabel, metiendola en estos trabajos, para que muriendo por ellos, quedasse desembarazada la sucession a la reyna de Escocia " (Let. vi., c. xiii., p. 399). Herrera probably believed what he asserted, if what Strada affirms be true, that the statement was made by Philip himself! That king, the Jesuit says, was incensed against Elizabeth, "tanto quidem acriore sensu, quanto pro beneficiis, proque vitâ ipsâ, quam ei bis terque se dedisse rex affirmabat, dum conspirationum insimulatam, è carcere, capitalique judicio liberaverat; pro his aliisque promeritis alias super alias accepisse se indesinenter injurias agnoscebat" (p. 526). The chronicler adds that Calais was betrayed, with Elizabeth's consent, she hoping thereby to break her sister's heart, " para acabar con estos enojos tanto mas presto la vida de su hermana ".

taking away of his life carrieth no likelihood that the same shall work any end of the said prosecution, so is it manifestly known that no man hath dealt more honourably than the said prince, either in duly observing of his promise, or extending grace and mercy where merit and desert hath craved the same; and, therefore, no greater impiety by any could be wrought, nor nothing more prejudicial to ourself (so long as the king shall continue the prosecution of the cause in that forcible sort he now doth), than to be an instrument to take him away from thence by such violent means, that hath dealt in a more honourable and gracious sort in the charge committed unto him, than any other that hath ever gone before him, or is likely to succeed after him. Now, therefore, how unlikely it is that we should be either author, or any way assenting to so horrible a fact, we refer to the judgment of such as look into causes, not with the eyes of their affection, but do measure and weigh things according to honour and reason. The best course, therefore, that both we and all other princes can hold, in this unfortunate age, that overfloweth with malignant spirits, is, through the grace and goodness of Almighty God, to direct our course in such sort, as they may rather show their wills through malice, than with just cause by desert to say ill either by speech or writing; assuring ourselves, that besides the punishment that such wicked libellers shall receive at the hands of the Almighty for depraving of princes and lawful magistrates, who are God's ministers, they both are and always shall be thought by all good men unworthy to live upon the face of the earth."*

When Elizabeth thus openly allied herself with the united States, which were, in fact, declaring war against Spain, the other Christian princes "admired such manly fortitude in a woman; and the King of Sweden said, she had taken the crown from her head and adventured it upon the chance of

* Holinshed, 621-630.

war ". * But no new or additional danger was drawn upon her by this declaration. The plan of invasion which Sebastian's expedition to Africa had frustrated, and which had been suspended in consequence of the subsequent events in Portugal, had been resumed two years before this treaty with the States was concluded. The Prince of Parma had at that time been ordered to obtain accurate information respecting the English ports and their means of defence: the Milanese engineer, Battista Piatti, who constructed the bridge over the Scheldt during the siege of Antwerp, was one of the persons thus employed; he had drawn up a report accordingly, and proceeded to Spain to give what further information might be required.† A negotiation pending with the Queen of Scots, for her release, upon her engagement that her agents should attempt nothing to the injury of Elizabeth or of England, was broken off, partly, says Camden, because of certain fears cast in the way by those who knew how to increase suspicions between women already displeased with one another; but chiefly in consequence of certain papers, which a Scotch Jesuit, on his passage to Scotland, when captured by some Netherlanders, tore in pieces and cast overboard: the wind blew them back into the ship, and from these fragments the designs of the Pope, the Spaniard, and the Guises, for invading England, were discovered.‡ The detection of a nearer treason led to the death of the Queen of Scots, an act by which Elizabeth, if she lessened her own immediate danger and that of the nation (which may well be doubted), brought upon herself an ineffaceable stain,§ purchasing self-preservation

* Camden, 321.   † Strada, 526.   ‡ Camden, 299.

§ Parry in a letter to the queen, after his condemnation, says: "The Queen of Scots is your prisoner. Let her be honourably entreated, but yet surely guarded. She may do you good; she will do you no harm, if the fault be not English. It importeth you much; so long as it is well with her, it is safe with you. When she is in fear, you are not without peril. Cherish and love her. She is of your blood, and your undoubted heir in succession. It is so taken abroad, and will be found so at home" (Strype's *Annals*, App. No. 46).

at a greater price than it is worth. But it is not upon Elizabeth that the blackest stigma should be affixed. The English Parliament called upon her for blood. Not a voice in either House was raised against the popular cry. The Commons came to a resolution, " that no other way, device, or means whatsoever could possibly be found or imagined, that safety could in any wise be had as long as the Queen of Scots were living.* To spare her," they said, " were nothing else but to spill the people, who would take all impunity in this case very much to heart, and would not think themselves discharged of their oath of association, unless she were punished according to her deserts. And they called upon Elizabeth to remember the fearful examples of God's vengeance upon King Saul for sparing Agag, and upon King Ahab for sparing Benhadad." †
To such purposes can public feeling be directed, and Scripture perverted! Some of those great personages who had corresponded with the royal prisoner, and were implicated more or less in the treasonable practices which under her name and with her concurrence were continually carried on, began now to act as her deadly enemies, thereby the better to conceal their own guilt.‡ The Spanish party thrust her forward to her own danger, that by her destruction the way might be cleared for the pretended title of the King of Spain.§ They had persuaded themselves that nothing but an absolute conquest of the island, like that by William of Normandy, could establish a Catholic prince here, and reinstate the Romish religion in its full powers. And when the French king, Henry III.,‖ sent a special ambassador publicly to speak in the

---

* *Parliamentary History*, 844.   † Camden, 363.
‡ *Ibid.*, 344.   § *Ibid.*, 331.
‖ Parry says of him, in the remarkable letter above quoted, in which he speaks with the freedom as well as the sincerity of a dying man: " The French king is *French;* you know that well enough. You will find him occupied when he should do you good. He will not lose a pilgrimage to save your crown."

Queen of Scots behalf, that ambassador was charged with secret instructions to press upon Elizabeth the necessity of putting her to death as an enemy, who, if she succeeded to the English throne, would, through her connection with the Guises, be as dangerous to him as she now was to the Queen of England!*

The death of Mary may have preserved England from the religious struggle which would have ensued upon her succession to the throne, but it delivered Elizabeth from only one, and that the weakest, of her enemies; and it exposed her to a charge of injustice and cruelty, which, being itself well founded, obtained belief for any other accusation, however extravagantly false. It was not Philip alone who prepared for making war upon her with a feeling of personal hatred: throughout Romish Christendom she was represented as a monster of iniquity; that representation was assiduously set forth, not only in ephemeral libels, but in histories, in dramas, in poems and in hawkers' pamphlets;† and when the King of Spain equipped an armament for the invasion of England, volunteers entered it with a passionate persuasion that they were about to bear a part in a holy war against the wickedest and most inhuman of tyrants. The Pope exhorted Philip to engage in this great enterprise for the sake of the Roman Catholic and Apostolic Church, which could not be more effectually nor more meritoriously extended than by the conquest of England; so should he avenge his own private and public wrongs; so should he indeed prove himself most worthy of the glorious title of Most Catholic King. And he promised, as soon as his troops should have set foot in that island, to supply him with a million of crowns of gold ‡ towards the expenses

---

* Turner, 643. Bayle's critique on Maimbourg's *Hist. of Calvinism* there quoted.

† They are circulated to this day in Spain and Portugal.

‡ The money, however, was not forthcoming. Strada, when he relates the offer, adds: "Quod magis Xysti magnanimitatem ostendit, quam belli

of the expedition. Opportunity could never be more favourable: he had concluded a truce with the Turk; the French were embroiled in civil war, and could offer to him no opposition. England was without forts or defences: long peace had left it unprovided of commanders or soldiers; and it was full of Catholics, who would joyfully flock to his standard. The conquest of Portugal had not been easier than that of England would be found; and when England was once conquered, the Low Countries would presently be reduced to obedience.

Such exhortations accorded with the ambition, the passions, and the rooted principles of the King of Spain. The undertaking was resolved on; and while preparations were making upon the most formidable scale, it was deliberated on what plan to proceed. Sir William Stanley, the most noted of those persons who for conscience' sake betrayed their trust, deserted to the enemy, and bore arms against this country, advised that Ireland should be the first point of attack. He knew that country well, having served in it fifteen years; and if Waterford, he said, were once taken and fortified, the Spaniards might from thence reduce the one island and invade the other. Piatti was of opinion that it were better to begin with Scotland, where he was led to believe the king might be induced to join with them for the sake of revenging his mother's death. Having established a footing there, he thought the Isle of Wight should next be occupied. A noble inhabitant of that island had promised the Prince of Parma to show him a place known only to himself, by which ships could approach, and in four and twenty hours obtain possession of it; and he laid before Philip a plan of the island, and a memoir concerning it, which had been drawn up at the Prince

subsidium fuit: quippe, ut partem hujus summæ aliquam pontifex elargiretur ante præfinitum hoc tempus, nullis adduci potuit aut Hispani legati, aut Cæsii comitis à Parmensi duce propterea Romam missi, persuasionibus " (p. 527).

of Parma's desire. The Marquis of Santa Cruz, who was to be commander-in-chief, objected to neither of these plans, but he urged the necessity of perpending all things well before an expedition should be sent out, in which Spain put forth all her strength: and he advised that a port should previously be secured, either in Ireland, or, which he thought more desirable, in Holland or Zeeland. The enterprise might safely be undertaken, if the fleet were thus rendered secure on that side. This was the opinion which the Prince of Parma supported in his letters. He represented the danger of venturing such a fleet in the British seas without providing a harbour into which it might retreat; and Flushing, he said, was the only one in the Low Countries capacious enough for so great a force. Now that he had taken Sluys, Flushing might more easily be captured; and he strongly advised that the capture of this place should be effected before the Armada ventured into those seas. It was a conquest which, with God's help, he undertook to make. But, in thus advising, the prince had a further object; he was not willing that Spain should divert its attention from the Low Countries, which he had no doubt of subjugating, if only a part of the force designed for England were employed for that purpose. Those countries once subdued, England would be open to invasion; and of this, which he saw clearly himself, he hoped to convince the king, if he could first persuade him to let the siege of Flushing be undertaken.*

But Philip would hear of no delay. The troubles in France and the treaty with the Turks allowed him at this time to direct his whole attention towards England: it was even less costly to punish that country by an invasion than to defend the coasts of his own empire against her piratical enterprises; and he felt himself bound to exact vengeance for the death of the Queen of Scots, in which cause all sovereign princes were

* Strada, 528-531.

concerned. Objecting, therefore, to any attempt upon Ireland, which would be opening a new theatre of war, or to any delay, which would allow the enemy time to prepare for defence, he directed the prince to take what measures he thought best for exciting the Scotch to arms; but meantime to make ready with all speed for co-operating with the expedition, which would set sail as soon as he should be in readiness.* Upon another point, also, there had been a difference of opinion among Philip's advisers: some of whom thought that war should be proclaimed against England, both to remove suspicion from other powers, and to alarm Elizabeth, who might then be induced to levy foreign troops for her defence; which, if she did, it was to be expected that those troops, according to the usual insolence of mercenaries, would so demean themselves, as to excite discontent among the English people, and consequent confusion.† The formality of declaring war was however disregarded as a mere form on both sides; and on the part of the Spaniards it was deemed more politic to disturb the English with apprehensions of some great but indefinite danger, and at the same time divert them from making any effectual preparation for defence, by carrying on negotiations in the Low Countries, without the slightest intention of assenting to any terms of reconciliation that could be proposed.

The Prince of Parma, therefore, while he prepared for the invasion with his characteristic diligence, which left nothing undone, opened a negotiation with England, to which Elizabeth, notwithstanding the urgent remonstrances of the States, gave ear, yet with a just suspicion that the proposal was insincerely made. Leicester, who had unwisely been entrusted with the command of the English auxiliaries, had conducted himself neither to the satisfaction of the States nor of his own Government: the English and Dutch had not been

* Strada, 582. † Camden, 404.

found to agree when they came to act together, under circumstances that brought their national qualities into close and unamiable contrast :* the Dutch, too, were divided among themselves ; so that there seemed little hope that England could afford them any such assistance as might enable them to obtain the objects for which they had taken up arms, and still less of any such happy termination, if they were left to themselves. With regard to England, it was the opinion of her greatest statesman, Cecil, that a peace was not only desirable, but most necessary ; but it must be such a peace as should be clear and assured, leaving no such occasion of quarrel as had hitherto existed ; the queen's subjects must be free from the Inquisition ; and the people of the Low Countries not impeached for anything which had passed ; but allowed to enjoy their liberties and franchises, and to have the use of their religion, now openly professed in their churches, for which they had so long stood to their defence.† The Dutch were well convinced that all negotiation was useless, and therefore refused to take any part : the English commissioners, however, met those of the King of Spain at Ostend : they first proposed a suspension of arms, " thereby to stay the coming of the Spanish fleet " ; and to this the Spanish commissioners seemed to incline, craftily thereby seeking to persuade them that it was not intended against England. They asked for the renewal of old treaties and intercourse ; the repayment of such sums as the queen had advanced to the States, not requiring this from the king, but that he should authorise the States to collect money for this purpose : further, they required that foreign governors and

* " Plurimum autem differunt harum nationum ingenia et mores ; nam Angli, ut addicte serviunt, ita evecti ad dignitates priorem humilitatem insolentia rependunt ; Belgarum est parere et imperare cum modo, nec gens ulla fidelius amat eminentes, aut iisdem, si contemtus adsit, implacabilius irascitur " (Grotius, 95).

† Strype's *Annals*, vol. iii., part ii., p. 5.

foreign troops should, for the queen's safety, be withdrawn from the Low Countries; that the people might enjoy their ancient liberties and privileges, and be governed by their countrymen, not by strangers; and that there might be a toleration for two years at least, during which time the matter of religion should be ordered and established by the States. If these terms were concluded, the queen would agree to any reasonable conditions concerning the cautionary towns, that all the world might know she had taken possession of them not to aggrandise herself, but for her own necessary assurance and defence.*

To the more important of these proposals it was replied, that the king could not withdraw his troops till the States had submitted themselves, nor while the French were in arms: that the Queen of England had nothing to do with the privileges of the Low Countries; nor was she to prescribe a law to him how he should govern his subjects; and that he would not hear of the free exercise of religion, but would grant a toleration, such as had been allowed to the towns that had yielded themselves to his obedience. The English commissioners made answer, that neither the queen nor the Netherlanders could be assured of any peace while foreign troops were maintained in that country: that in the privileges of these countries she had a special interest; first, in regard of neighbourhood; secondly, as being specially named in several pacifications; and thirdly, because it was not possible for her subjects to enjoy their privileges there, unless the provinces themselves were allowed them. And for the point of religion, if the king would not hear of any toleration of the exercise thereof, then must the Protestants be forced either to forsake the religion in which they had been born and bred, or go into perpetual exile. Not with any reason could the king refuse his subjects what in times past had been by his

* Grimestone, 986.

father, the Emperor Charles, accorded to the Germans, and by other princes, and namely by himself, in his perpetual edict. None but dilatory replies were made to this replication, the object of either party being to gain time; for Philip would have consented to no other terms than such as an absolute conquest of the revolted States might have enabled him to impose; and Elizabeth, though she sincerely wished for peace, knew that it could not possibly be obtained. At this time the Pope issued his bull, declaring that the Catholic king was about to direct his power against England, and enjoining the queen's subjects, by their obedience to the Church, to hold themselves in readiness for assisting the army which, under the Prince of Parma, was preparing for their deliverance. Allen, also, who had now been made a cardinal, published a book at Antwerp, which, for the audacity of its unhesitating falsehood, its vituperation, and its treason, may vie with any libel that ever issued from the press.* He called Elizabeth heretic, rebel, and usurper; an incestuous bastard, the bane of Christendom, and firebrand of all mischief; one who deserved not deposition alone, but all vengeance both of God and man; and he reproached the English Papists for their effeminate dastardy in suffering such a creature to reign almost thirty years, both over their bodies and their souls.† Nor was sophistry wanting in a composition thus highly seasoned with insolence and slander. He argued, that if there were no power by which apostate princes might be deposed, God would not have sufficiently provided for our salvation, and the preservation of His Church and holy laws. Our obligation to the Church far exceedeth all other that we owe to any human creature. The wife may depart from her husband, if he be an infidel or a heretic; the bond-slave, if his master become a heretic, may refuse to serve him; yea, *ipso facto*, he is made free; parents, if they become heretic, lose their

* Turner, 671. † Strype, iii., p. 2, App. No. 54.

natural authority over their children. "Therefore," said the cardinal, "let no man marvel that, in case of heresy, the sovereign loseth the superiority over his people and kingdom. The Pope," he added, "acting on a special canon of the great Council of Lateran, touching the chastisement of princes that will not purge their dominions of heresy and heretics, hath specially entreated the King of Spain to take upon him this sacred and glorious enterprise; who, by this his Holiness's authority and exhortation, moved also not a little by my humble and continual suit, hath consented and commanded sufficient royal forces to be gathered and conducted into our country."* The publication of this book at Antwerp was an

---

* Yet this very man had but a few years before protested, "that neither the reverend fathers of the Society of the Holy Name of Jesus, whom the people called Jesuits (an express clause being in the instructions of their mission into England, that they deal not in matters of State, which is to be showed, signed with their late general's hand, of worthy memory), neither the priests, either of the seminaries, or others, have any commission, direction, instruction, or insinuation, from his Holiness or any other their superior, either in religion, or of the colleges, to move sedition, or to deal against the State or temporal Government; but only by their priesthood and the functions thereof, to do such duties as be requisite for Christian men's souls, which consist in preaching, teaching, catechising, ministering the Sacraments, and the like" (*Apology of the English Seminaries*, p. 71).

In the same apology, alluding to a publication, very similar both in matter and spirit to that which he now fulminated in his capacity of cardinal, Allen says: "Touching some of our late repairing to the city of Rome, wherewith we are charged, the principal of that voyage (meaning himself) doth protest that he neither joined with rebel nor traitor, nor any one or other against the queen or realm; or traitorously sought or practised any prince or potentate to hostility against the same: further invocating upon his soul, that he never knew, saw, nor heard, during his abode in the court there, of any such writings as are mentioned in the proclamation of July, containing certain articles of confederation of the Pope, King of Spain, and other princes for the invasion of the realm; nor ever afterward gave counsel to publish any such thing, though he were at Rome at the day of the date, that some of those copies which

overt act of hostility; that of the bull amounted to nothing less than a declaration of war on the part of Spain.* The queen, therefore, directed Dr. Valentine Dale, who was one of her commissioners, to speak with the prince in person, charge him in good sort with the things contained in this publication, and require from him a direct answer, whether he were not appointed general of the army which was then preparing in Spain, and, as there publicly stated, for the invasion of England.†

The prince made answer, that he knew nothing either of the book or bull; nor had he undertaken anything in obedience to the Pope, nor attempted anything of himself but honourably, in the service of the king his master, whom, as his own sovereign, he must obey. And for the Queen of England, he had so high an esteem for her, for her royal virtues, that, next his own king, he honoured her above all persons, and desired to do her service. With that desire, he had persuaded the king to enter upon this treaty, which would be more afterwards he saw when they were common to all the world, do bear. Being also most assured that no other English Catholic would or could be the author thereof, nor (as it may be thought), any other of those princes or their ministers, that are pretended to be of the foresaid league; being neither wisdom nor policy, if any such thing were intended (as we verily think there was not), much less if it were never meant, to publish any such libels to give the realm warning to provide for it; specially all the world knowing that the pinching of the poor Catholics at home (a lamentable case) is their fence to repay for all adverse accidents abroad. And it may verily be thought (and so it is certain that some of the principal ministers of the forenamed princes have answered, being reminded thereof), that the Protestants, having exercised skill and audacity in such practices and counter-practices (of which France, Flanders, Scotland, and other countries have had so lamentable experience), did contrive them, to alter her Majesty's accustomed benignity and mercy towards the Catholics, into such rigour of justice as in the said edict is threatened" (pp. 15-16).

* Turner, 672.

† Bor, 320. Grimestone, 996. Camden, 409.

advantageous for the English than the Spaniards. "For if the Spaniards be overcome," said he, "they will soon repair their loss; but if you are once vanquished, your kingdom is lost." Dale made answer: "Our queen is provided of strength sufficient to defend her kingdom: and you yourself, in your wisdom, may judge that a kingdom cannot easily be won by the fortune of one battle, seeing that in so many years of war the King of Spain has not yet been able to recover his ancient inheritance of the Netherlands". "Be it so," replied the prince: "these things are in the disposal of the Almighty."*
This consummate general practised a duplicity more conformable to his religion than his own better nature, when he denied all knowledge of a bull then circulating throughout the States which he governed, and a book which had been printed at Antwerp, with the knowledge and approbation of the authorities that he had himself established there. In forwarding with the utmost activity the preparations for invasion during the negotiations, he did no more than circumstances fairly warranted, and his plain sense of duty required: in this point, neither party was duped into any loss of irretrievable time. Most happily for England, the provinces which the Prince of Parma had reduced were not the maritime ones; Flanders alone excepted. He had to seek, therefore, for shipwrights and for seamen: the former were brought from Italy, which still retained its reputation in this branch: the latter from Hamburgh, Bremen, and Embden. He thought also to obtain both ships and sailors from Denmark. The Danish king had endeavoured to act as mediator for bringing about, if that were possible, an accommodation between Philip and the States: but his ambassador, proceeding in company with some of the prince's soldiers, had been made prisoner by the Dutch in a skirmish; and as they either disbelieved or disregarded his pretensions to the character which he assumed,

* Camden, 409.

his papers had been opened. This so incensed the king, that he immediately detained 700 vessels which were bringing grain from the Baltic; for even if former experience had taught the Dutch to provide against such a danger, in the present circumstances of their country means and leisure for such provision were alike wanting, and they must have been reduced to immediate distress for food, if they had not, as necessity compelled, brought into their ports the French and English vessels * coming from the same sea. Spain, therefore, had less difficulty in contracting with the Danes for ships, mariners, and "soldiers upon the seas"; but the English resident at Copenhagen, having intelligence of this, represented to the governors of the king (for he was a minor), that this was contrary to the league between the two crowns, and nothing conformable to the sincere friendship which had subsisted between Queen Elizabeth and the king their master. This remonstrance prevailed; and though the parties pleaded their privileges, severe order was taken that no subjects of Denmark or Norway, or other parts appertaining to the king's dominions, should either then or thereafter serve against the queen.†

But in what was to be effected by human exertions under his own superintendence, the prince was in no danger of being disappointed. Two and thirty war ships he made ready at Dunkirk, hired for the same purpose five foreign vessels in that harbour, and engaged five more from Hamburgh to rendezvous there. Seventy flat-bottomed boats were fitted out in the little river Watene, each to carry thirty horses, with bridges for embarking and landing them; and at Nieuport about 200 similar vessels, but of smaller size. Here, too,

---

* "Ita vitatum discrimen sola pecuniæ a Danis expressæ jactura; quod ipsum tamen et quia rex missos ad se legatos audire dedignabatur, hæsit altius multorum animis judicantium minora regna majorum opibus obnoxia teneri" (Grotius, 105).

† Strype, 25.

he collected store of fascines, and all other materials for throwing up entrenchments and constructing sconces. At Gravelines many thousand casks were got together, with cordage or chain-work to connect them, for forming bridges or blocking havens. Stakes for palisades also were provided, horse furniture of every kind, and horses for draught, "with ordnance and all other necessary provision for the war". With such neighbours as the Zeelanders and the English at Flushing, even Antwerp did not give him the command of the Scheldt; and he was fain, therefore, to deepen and widen some of those channels by which Flanders is intersected, that ships might be brought from Antwerp by way of Ghent to Bruges, and so to Sluys; or by the Yperlee, which had also been deepened, to the other Flemish ports. At Nieuport he had thirty companies of Italian troops, two of Walloon, and eight of Burgundian. At Dixmude, eighty of Netherlanders, sixty Spanish, sixty German, and seven of English deserters, under Sir William Stanley, the traitor: each company consisted of 100 men, and better troops were never brought into the field than those who served under the Prince of Parma: 4000 horse were quartered at Courtray, 900 at Watene. "To this great enterprise and imaginary conquest divers princes and noblemen came from divers countries; out of Spain came the Duke of Pestrana, who was said to be the son of Ruy Gomez de Silva, but was held to be the king's bastard; the Marquis of Bourgou, one of the Archduke Ferdinand's sons by Philippina Welserine; Don Vespasian Gonzagua, of the house of Mantua, a great soldier, who had been viceroy in Spain; Giovanni de Medici, bastard of Florence; Amedeo, bastard of Savoy, with many such like, besides others of meaner quality." *

These preparations held the States in alarm, the more so because the prince endeavoured to make them apprehend that

* Grimestone, 999, 1000. Bor, 317.

his intention was to attack Goes, or Walcheren, or Tholen; on all these points they prepared for defence, and some were for cutting dykes, and drowning one part of the country for the sake of preserving the other. But the wiser opinion prevailed, not to incur this certain evil, till its necessity became evident; and the Dutch statesmen inferred that no movement would be made here till the great Spanish Armada, news of which was now bruited abroad, should arrive in the narrow seas; then they judged it would be joined by the Prince of Parma's forces, whether the expedition was intended against them, or against England first; whichever were attacked, they knew that the subjugation of both was in view. For themselves, they stood in little fear of the Spanish fleet, from which the nature of their coast, in great measure, would protect them; but they were in much greater danger from the prince's flotilla, against which their shoals and difficult harbours could afford them no security. Straitened as they were for means, and with the disadvantage of an unsettled Government, they exerted themselves manfully and wisely. All the vessels that they could muster were equipped; and after due consultation it was resolved that the larger vessels should be stationed between England at the coast of Flanders, outside the shoals, the smaller within the shoals, and the flotilla of smacks off Kleeyenburg, or between Rammekens and Flushing, according to circumstances. Their feelings toward England, notwithstanding the ill blood that had been stirred during Leicester's administration, was shown by a medal which they struck at this time. On the one side were the arms of England and of the united States, and two oxen ploughing, the motto *Trahite æquo jugo*—draw evenly; on the reverse two earthen pots floating upon the waves, the motto *Frangimur si collidimur*—if we strike we break.*

Meantime, though the negotiations at Ostend were still

---

* Grimestone, 994. Bor, 318,

carried on in policy by the Spanish commissioners, there was on the part of the Spanish Government a disdainful disregard of secrecy as to its intentions, or rather a proud manifestation of them, which, if they had been successful, might have been called magnanimous. The great king had determined upon putting forth his strength, and so confident were his subjects of success, that in the accounts which were ostentatiously published of its force, they termed it "The most fortunate and invincible Armada". The fleet, according to the official statement, consisted of 130 ships, having on board 19,295 soldiers, 8450 mariners, 2088 galley-slaves, and 2630 great pieces of brass; there were, moreover, twenty caravels for the service of the fleet, and ten six-oared *faluas*. The names of the most popular Romish saints and invocations appeared in the nomenclature of the ships; and holier appellations, which ought never to be thus applied, were strangely associated with the Great Griffin and the Sea Dog, the Cat and the White Falcon. There were in the fleet 124 volunteers of noble family, having among them 456 armed servants. There was no noble house in Spain but had a son, a brother, or a nephew in the voyage, embarked either at their own cost or in the king's pay. The religioners who embarked for the service of the fleet, and for after operations, were 180, consisting of Augustinians, Franciscans, Dominicans, and Jesuits. Don Martin Alarcon embarked, for the good of the heretics, as vicar-general of the holy Inquisition; and implements of conversion of a more cogent kind than argument or persuasion are said to have been embarked in sufficient quantity. The business of reconciling England to the Romish see was committed to Cardinal Allen, as it had formerly been to Cardinal Pole, and an English translation of the Pope's bull was ready for circulation as soon as a landing should be effected. The galleons, being above sixty in number, were "exceeding great, fair, and strong, and built high above the water, like castles, easy, says a contemporary writer, to be fought withal, but not so easy to board as the English and the Netherland ships; their upper decks were musket-proof, and beneath they were four or five feet thick, so as no bullet could pass them. Their masts were bound about with oakum, or pieces of fazeled ropes, and armed against all shot. The galleasses were goodly great vessels, furnished with chambers, chapels, towers, pulpits, and such like: they rowed like galleys, with exceeding great oars, each having 300 slaves, and were able to do much harm with their great ordnance." In place of the Marquez de Santa Cruz, who was dead, the Duque del Medina Sidonia was general of this great armament; Don Juan Martinez de Ricalde, admiral.[*]

In whatever spirit of vengeance this expedition was undertaken, and with whatever ambitious views on the part of Philip, it cannot be doubted but that he believed himself to be engaged in a religious war, and that a great proportion of the army embarked with as full a persuasion that they were engaging in God's service, as the first crusaders felt when they set forth for the Holy Land. The Duque of Medina Sidonia, in the general orders issued before his embarkation, said: "First, and before all things, it is to be understood by all in this army, from the highest to the lowest, that the principal cause which hath moved the king his Majesty to undertake this voyage, hath been and is to serve God, and to bring back unto His Church a great many contrite souls, now oppressed by the heretics, enemies to our holy Catholic faith. And for that every one may fix his eyes upon this mark, as we are bound, I do command, and much desire every one to enjoin those who are under his charge, that before they embark, they be shriven and receive the sacrament, with due contrition for their sins; which, if it be done, and we are zealous to do unto Him such great service, God will be with us, and conduct us to His great glory, which is what particularly

---

[*] Grimestone, 998.

and principally is intended." Strict command was given that no one should blaspheme or rage against God, or Our Lady, or any of the saints, on pain of condign punishment; " oaths of less quality " were to be punished by deprivation of wine, or otherwise, as might seem fitting. Gaming was forbidden, as a provocation to this and other sins; and all quarrels between any persons of what quality soever, were to be suppressed and suspended, as well by sea as by land, even though they were old quarrels, so long as the expedition lasted. Any breach of this truce and forbearance of arms was to be accounted as high treason, and punished with death. For further security, it was declared that on board the ships nothing should be offered to the disgrace of any man, and that whatever happened on board, no disgrace nor reproach should be imputed to any one on that account; moreover, no one might wear a dagger, nor thwart any one, nor give any provocation. " And for that it was known that great inconvenience and offence unto God arose from consenting that common women, and such like, went in such armies," none were to be embarked; if any person sought to carry them, the captains and masters of the ships were ordered not to consent thereto: whosoever did thus, or dissembled therewith, was to be grievously punished. Every ship's company was to give the good-morrow at day-break, by the main-mast, according to custom; and at evening, the *Ave Maria*, and some days the *Salve Regina*, or, at least on Saturdays, with a litany. A litany had been composed for the occasion, in which all archangels, angels, and saints were invoked to assist with their prayers against the English heretics and enemies of the faith. Should it happen because of the wind, that the word could not be given by the admiral, in such case the following words were appointed for the days of the week in order,—Jesus, the Holy Ghost, the Holy Trinity, Santiago, the Angels, All Saints, Our Lady. No men ever set forth upon a bad cause with better will, nor under a stronger delusion of perverted faith.

As needful preparations for action, the gunners were instructed to have half-butts, filled with water and vinegar* as usual, "with bonnets, old sails, and wet mantles, to defend fire"; and to have shot made in good quantity, and powder and match "ready, by weight, measure, and length"; and all soldiers to have "their room clean and unpestered of chests"; "and for that the mariners must resort unto their work, tackle, and navigation," their lodgings were to be on the upper works of the poop and forecastle, otherwise the soldiers would trouble them on the voyage. "The artillery," said the instructions, "must stand in very good order, and reparted among the gunners, being all charged with their balls; and nigh unto every piece his locker, wherein to put his shot and necessaries; and to have great care to the cartridges of every piece, for not changing, and not taking fire; and that the ladles and sponges be ready at hand. Every ship shall carry two boats-lading of stones, to throw to profit, in the time of fight, on the deck, forecastle, or tops, according to his burden; and shall carry two half-pipes, to fill them with water in the day of battle, and repart them among the ordnance, or other places as shall be thought necessary, and nigh unto them old clothes and coverings, which, with wetting, may destroy any kind of fire." The wildfire was to be entrusted only to those who understood well how to use it, "otherwise it might happen to great danger". That there might be no excuse for neglecting these orders on pretence of ignorance concerning them, they were to be publicly read, thrice a week, in every ship, by the purser.

Meantime Elizabeth and her wakeful ministers were well aware of the danger, and seeing it in its whole extent, they prepared to meet it with right English spirit. The lord lieu-

---

* Had then the wildfire, which was still in use, been derived from that of the Greeks, that vinegar was thought necessary for quenching it?

tenants of the several counties were required, by circular letters from the queen, to "call together the best sort of gentlemen under their lieutenancy, and to declare unto them these great preparations and arrogant threatenings, now burst forth in action upon the seas, wherein every man's particular state, in the highest degree, could be touched in respect of country, liberty, wives, children, lands, lives, and (which was specially to be regarded) the profession of the true and sincere religion of Christ. And to lay before them the infinite and unspeakable miseries that would fall out upon any such change, which miseries were evidently seen by the fruits of that hard and cruel government holden in countries not far distant. We do look," said the queen, "that the most part of them should have, upon this instant extraordinary occasion, a larger proportion of furniture, both for horsemen and footmen, but especially horsemen, than hath been certified; thereby to be in their best strength against any attempt, or to be employed about our own person, or otherwise. Hereunto as we doubt not but by your good endeavours they will be the rather conformable, so also we assure ourselves, that Almighty God will so bless these their loyal hearts borne towards us, their loving sovereign, and their natural country, that all the attempts of any enemy whatsoever shall be made void and frustrate, to their confusion, your comfort, and to God's high glory." * Letters also were addressed by the council to the nobility, because, in the directions given of late years for mustering, arming, and training all persons, there had been no special ones to the nobles, her Majesty having "certainly supposed that it was the natural disposition of the nobility, without direction, to be armed, both for themselves and for furniture of horsemen and footmen, according to their ability. The council, therefore, having a more certain knowledge than by common report, of what preparations were made beyond the

* Strype, App. L.

seas, very likely for the offence of this realm, required each lord, to whom this communication was addressed, to receive it as one whom her Majesty trusted, and as an argument of special love. And in regard thereof," the letter proceeds, "we do not doubt but that your lordship, with all the speed you can possible, will be furnished with armour and weapon meet for your calling; and of your servants and able tenants that are not already enrolled in the general musters of the country as special trained persons, to make as many horsemen as you can, both for lances and light horsemen. And for the more increase of horsemen, for want of sufficient number of great horse or geldings, we think your lordship may do well to increase your number, if you shall provide able men with petronels upon horses of smaller stature." *

A contemporary relates, that "all the noblemen in the realm, from east to west, from north to south, excepting such only as could not be absent from their charge in the country, and some few that were not able to make forces according to their desire, came to the queen, bringing with them, according to their degrees, and to the uttermost of their power, goodly bands of horsemen, both lances, light horsemen, and such other as are termed carbines or argelatiers, lodging their bands round about London, and maintaining them in pay at their own charges. And of these noblemen, many showed the bands of their horsemen before the queen, in the fields afore her own gate, to the great marvel of men; for that the number of them was so great, and so well armed and horsed, that, knowing they were no parcel of the horsemen limited in every country, it was thought there had not been so many spare horses of such valour in the whole realm, except the north part towards Scotland, whose forces consist chiefly of horse." The first who presented himself and his retainers to the queen was a Roman Catholic peer, the Viscount Moun-

* Strype, iii., part ii., pp. 13, 14.

tague, who at this time professed his resolution, " though he was very sickly, and in age, to live and die in defence of the queen and of his country, against all invaders, whether it were pope, king, or potentate whatsoever; and in that quarrel to hazard his life, his children, his lands, and goods. And to show his mind agreeably thereto, he came personally himself before the queen with his band of horsemen, being almost 200, the same being led by his own sons; and with them a young child, very comely, seated on horseback, being the heir of his house, that is, the eldest son to his son and heir: a matter much noted of many, to see a grandfather, father and son at one time on horseback, afore a queen, for her service." *

The clergy also were called upon by the primate, Archbishop Whitgift. " Being members," he said, " of one and the self-same commonweal, and embarked in the like common danger with others, if not more, in respect of our calling and public profession of religion, whereby we are also bound to go before others, as well in word as good example; we are, therefore, to remember, and advisedly to weigh with ourselves what dutiful forwardness against these extraordinary imminent dangers, of very congruence, is expected at our hands for the defence of our gracious sovereign, ourselves, our families, and country. And, beside the very good expectation of the best, the stirring up of those which otherwise are but slow to further such service, and the discouraging of the common enemy, our willing readiness herein will be a good means also to stop the mouths of such as do think those temporal blessings, which God hath in mercy bestowed upon us, to be too much; and, therefore, spare not in grudging manner to say that themselves are forced, to their great charges, to fight for us, while we live quietly at home, without providing any munition in these public perils." He required the bishops, therefore, as the letter of the council required

* Copy of a letter, etc. (Harl. Muse., 8vo ed., ii., p. 76).

him, "effectually to deal with those of their cathedral churches, and other beneficed men in their dioceses, but especially such as were of better ability, for the furnishing of themselves with lances, light horses, petronels on horseback, muskets, calivers, pikes, halberds, bills, or bows and arrows, as in regard of their several abilities might be thought most convenient: and he desired them, by all good persuasions, to move such ecclesiastical persons to be ready with all free and voluntary provision of man, horse, and furniture. This present necessary service," he said, "being no great charge, and so expedient for every one to have in readiness, for the defence of his own person, house, and family, upon any sudden occasion." *

The appeal from such a queen to such a nation was answered with just and enthusiastic loyalty. The city of London set an example worthy of London, such as the metropolis then was. When its aid was asked, the Lord Mayor requested that the council would state what would be deemed requisite. Accordingly, 5000 men and fifteen ships were required. The Lord Mayor asked two days for deliberation, and then, in the name of the city, prayed that the queen would accept of twice those numbers. Six thousand were immediately trained and regimented, being armed with muskets, pikes, calivers, and bills: the other 4000 were armed and put in readiness, and 10,000 more were reported as able men. The artillery company, which had originated about three years before, proved singularly useful now. At that time, "certain gallant, active, and forward citizens," says the old historian of London, "having had experience, both abroad and at home, voluntarily exercised themselves and trained others, for the ready use of war; so that there were almost 300 merchants, and others of the like quality, very sufficient and skilful to train and teach common soldiers the managing of their pieces, pikes, and halberds, and to march, countermarch, and ring. These

* Strype's *Whitgift*, book iii., App. No. 38.

merchants met every Tuesday to practise all points of war. Every man by turn bore orderly office, from the corporal to the captain. Some of them had now charge of men in the great camp, and were generally called captains of the artillery garden." Most erroneously had Cardinal Allen, and the King of Spain, and the Pope judged, when they thought that Elizabeth and the English nation were to be intimidated by a display of overpowering force, and denunciations "that the realm should be invaded and conquered, that the queen should be destroyed, and all the nobility and men of reputation, of honour, and wealth, who should obey her, and defend her, and would withstand the invasion, should, with all their families, be rooted out, and their places, their honours, their houses, and their lands bestowed upon the conquerors!" For "these things were universally so odiously taken, that the hearts of all sorts of people were inflamed,—some with ire, some with fear; but all sorts, almost without exception, resolved to venture their lives for the withstanding of all manner of conquest". The people, firmly devoted as they were to their magnanimous and excellent queen, were, by such insolent threats, "thoroughly irritated," says a contemporary, "to stir up their whole forces for their defence against such prognosticated conquests: so that, in a very short time, all her whole realm, and every corner, were furnished with armed men, on horseback and on foot; and those continually trained, exercised, and put into bands, in warlike manner, as in no age ever was before in this realm. There was no sparing of money to provide horse, armour, weapons, powder, and all necessaries; no, nor want of provision of pioneers, carriages, and victuals, in every county of the realm, without exception, to attend upon the armies. And to this general furniture every man voluntarily offered, very many their services personally without wages, others money for armour and weapons, and to wage soldiers: a matter strange, and never the like heard of in this realm or elsewhere. And this general reason moved all men to large contributions, that when a conquest was to be withstood wherein all should be lost, it was no time to spare a portion." *

There were some who advised the queen to place no reliance upon any means of maritime defence, but to expect the enemy's coming, and "welcome him with a land battle," as her father had resolved to do when he was threatened with invasion by a superior fleet; and as was intended in the time of the French Armada, in Richard II.'s reign. But Elizabeth, though her reliance was not upon any human strength, knew the worth of her seamen, and omitted none of those means of defence with which God and nature had provided her. The command of the whole fleet she gave to Charles, Lord Howard of Effingham, who had been appointed lord high admiral three years before, on the death of the Earl of Lincoln, Edward Clinton.† That office "seemed to have become almost hereditary in the Howard family. The queen had a great persuasion of his fortunate conduct, and knew him to be of a moderate and noble courage, skilful in sea matters, wary and provident, valiant and courageous, industrious and active, and of great authority and esteem among the sailors." Him she sent early in the year to the western coast with the main body of the fleet; Drake, who was her vice-admiral, joined him here, and Hawkins and Frobisher (great names in naval history) were in this division. Lord Henry Seymour, second

---

* Copy of a letter sent out of England (Harl. Muse., 8vo ed., vol. ii., 63, 64). The editor of this collection must have cast a careless eye over this letter, or he would not have supposed that it had really been written by a Papist in the Spanish interest.

"One strange speech," says the writer, "that I heard spoken, may be marvelled at, but it was avowed to me for a truth, that one gentleman in Kent had a band of 150 footmen which were worth in goods above 150,000*l.* sterling, besides their lands. Such men would fight stoutly before they would lose their goods" (p. 65).

† Camden, 325.

son of the Duke of Somerset, was ordered to lie off the coast of Flanders with forty ships, Dutch and English; blockade the enemy's ports there; and prevent the Prince of Parma from forming a junction with the Armada from Spain. Ten years before this time the royal navy consisted of no more than twenty-four ships of all sizes, the largest being of 1000 tons, the smallest under 60; all the ships throughout England of 100 tons and upwards were but 135, and all under 100 and above 40 tons were 656.* But if the ten years which had elapsed had done little toward the augmentation of the royal navy, it had added more than any preceding century to the maritime strength of the country in that race of sailors which had been trained up in adventurous expeditions to the new world. The whole number of ships collected for the defence of the country on this great occasion was 191, the number of seamen 17,472, the amount of tonnage 31,985. Eighteen of these ships were volunteers. There was one ship in the fleet (the *Triumph*) of 1100 tons, one of 1000, one of 900, two of 800 each, three of 600, and five of 500, five of 400, six of 300, six of 250, twenty of 200: all the rest were smaller. But, in the Armada, though there were only three ships that exceeded in size the *Triumph*, there were no fewer than 45 between 600 and 1000 tons burden; and though the English fleet outnumbered the Armada nearly by sixty sail, its tonnage amounted not to one-half of that of the enemy.†

For the land defence, somewhat more that 100,000 men were called out, regimented and armed, but only half of them were trained. Of these the cavalry, with the pioneers, amounted to 14,000. This was exclusive of the force upon the borders, and of the Yorkshire force, which was reserved for service northward. Twenty thousand men were disposed along the southern coast; an army of 45,000 was collected

---

* Campbell, i., 334.
† Charnock, vol. ii., 15, 17. Turner, 667.

under the Earl of Hunsdon to guard the queen's person, who, in case of the invaders' success, if she escaped from that malignant treason which had so often threatened her life, was to have been placed at the Pope's disposal. The band of pensioners was attached to this army. Another was formed at Tilbury under Leicester: it consisted of 1000 horse, and 22,000 foot; and 2000 troops were requested and obtained from Holland to act with this force, which was specially intended to engage the Prince of Parma, it being understood that London was the point for which he would immediately aim. "The Hollanders," says Stowe, "came roundly in, with threescore sail, brave ships of war, fierce and full of spleen, not so much for England's aid, as in just occasion for their own defence; these men foreseeing the greatness of the danger that might ensue, if the Spaniards should chance to win the day, and get the mastery over them; in due regard whereof their manly courage was inferior to none." Both sides of the river were fortified under the direction of Federico Giambelli, an Italian deserter from the Spanish service, who invented the famous fire-ships, or rather floating mines, employed against the Prince of Parma over the Scheldt at the siege of Antwerp. Gravesend was fortified, and western barges brought thither with the twofold intent of constructing a bridge like that of Antwerp, for blocking the river, and affording a passage for horse and foot between Kent and Essex, as occasion might require. Arthur, Lord Grey of Wilton, Sir Francis Knolles, Sir John Norris, Sir Richard Bingham, and Sir Roger Williams were appointed, as experienced soldiers, to consult upon the best means of defence. They advised that the most convenient landing-places for the enemy, whether coming from Spain, or from the Low Countries, should be well manned and fortified, "namely, Milford Haven, Falmouth, Plymouth, Portland, the Isle of Wight, Portsmouth, that open coast of Kent which we call the Downs, the Thames mouth, Harwich, Yarmouth, Hull. And that the trained bands all along the maritime counties should meet in arms upon a signal given, to defend the said parts, and do their best to prohibit the enemy's landing. And if the enemy did land, to lay all the country waste round about, and spoil all things that might be of any use to them; that so they might find no food but what they brought with them on their shoulders; and to busy the enemy night and day with continual alarms, so as to give them no rest; but not to put it to the hazard of a battle, till more commanders with their companies were come to them—one commander being nominated in every shire." *

The bull, Cardinal Allen's treasonable appeal to the English Romanists, and the opinion confidently expressed in Spain, that they would, as soon as Spanish aid afforded them opportunity, cast off the queen's yoke, and attempt something memorable for her destruction,† had rendered them objects of suspicion; and there were evil counsellors who argued that the Spaniards abroad were not so much to be feared as the Papists at home; that no invasion would be attempted were it not in reliance upon their co-operation; and, therefore, that for the sake of public safety, the heads of this dangerous party ought to be taken off; alleging, as an example, that in Henry VIII.'s time, when, at the Pope's instigation, the emperor and the King of France were about to invade England, their intention was abandoned as soon as he had put to death the persons whom he suspected of favouring it. This Elizabeth justly condemned as wicked counsel: on account, however, of the general murmurs, she thought it prudent not only to secure the priests and seminarists, but to commit some of the principal laity to custody, part in Wisbeach Castle, others in the bishop's palace at Ely.‡ This was not an indiscriminate

---

* Camden, 406. † Strype, vol. iii., p. 33.

‡ Camden, 406. Copy of a letter, etc., 66. Strype's *Whitgift*, i., 528-530.

LORD HOWARD OF EFFINGHAM

measure, nor can it be judged from the event to have been a needless one; for, after the failure of the Armada, when they might have been enlarged upon signing a bond, they took exception at a clause in it, engaging "for their good behaviour to the queen and the state," because, they said, it seemed to touch them in credit; they offered a form of their own, which was properly suspected of some mental reservation; and, in fact, three of the persons who were thus committed were afterwards engaged in the Gunpowder Plot.

While all human means for defence were provided by the queen and her wise ministers, they did not neglect to implore that aid without which all human means would have been unavailing. A form of prayer, "necessary for the present time and state," was set forth, and enjoined to be used on Wednesdays and Fridays every week, in all parish churches. "One of these prayers deserves," says Strype, "to be recorded, in eternal memory of this imminent national danger:" it ran thus: "O Lord God of Hosts, most loving and merciful Father, we, Thy humble servants, prostrate ourselves before Thy Divine Majesty, most heartily beseeching Thee to grant unto us true repentance for our sins past; namely, for our unthankfulness, contempt of Thy word, lack of compassion toward the afflicted, envy, malice, strife and contention among ourselves, and for all other our iniquities. Lord, deal not with us as we have deserved: but of Thy great goodness and mercy do away our offences; and give us grace to confess and acknowledge, O Lord, with all humble and hearty thanks, Thy wonderful and great benefits which Thou hast bestowed upon this Thy Church and people of England, in giving unto us, without all desert on our part, not only peace and quietness, but also in preserving our most gracious queen, Thine handmaid, so miraculously from so many conspiracies, perils, and dangers. We do instantly beseech Thee, of Thy gracious goodness, to be merciful to Thy Church militant here upon earth; and, as at this time, compassed about with most strong and subtle adversaries. And, especially, O Lord, let Thine enemies know, and make them confess, that Thou hast received England (which they, most of all for Thy Gospel's sake, do malign) into Thine own protection. Set, we pray Thee, O Lord, a wall about it, and evermore mightily defend it. Let it be a comfort to the afflicted, a help to the oppressed, a defence to Thy Church and people persecuted abroad. And, forasmuch as Thy cause is now in hand, we beseech Thee to direct and go before our armies, both by sea and land. Bless and prosper them, and grant unto them, O Lord, Thy good and honourable success and victory, as Thou didst to Abraham and his company against the four mighty kings; to Joshua, against the five kings, and against Amalek; and to David, against the strong and mighty-armed Goliath; and as Thou usest to do to Thy children when they please Thee. We acknowledge all power, strength, and victory to come from Thee. Some put their trust in chariots, and some in horses; but we will remember Thy name, O Lord our God! Thou bringest the counsel of the heathen to nought, and makest the devices of the people to be of none effect. There is no king that can be saved by the multitude of an host; neither is any mighty man delivered by much strength. Therefore we pray unto Thee, O Lord! Thou art our help and our shield!"* "This," says Strype, "we may call a prayer of faith, in regard of the strong hopes of success to be granted to this kingdom professing the Gospel." And such is the emphatic and scriptural language in which the prayers of the Church of England have always been composed; such the sober and earnest devotion which they breathe; such the spirit of Christian humility in which they are conceived.

History never impresses itself so strongly on the imagination as when, in great emergencies, it presents us with the hopes and feelings of the people in their own words. Never, indeed,

* Strype, vol. iii., p. ii., 15-17.

had England been threatened with an equal danger since the Norman conquest ; that was a danger of which there was no general apprehension throughout the nation ; nor was it in itself so formidable; and even the evils which it brought upon the Anglo-Saxon people were light in comparison with the horrors of a Romish persecution, and a war such as that which was then raging in the Netherlands, when there were no such defensive advantages as the Netherlanders possessed in their strong places and the nature of their country. If ever national prayers proceeded from the heart of a nation, it was at this momentous crisis. One of the most passionate was framed in these words: " For Preservation and Success against the Spanish Navy and Forces. O Lord God, Heavenly Father, without whose providence nothing proceedeth, and without whose mercy nothing is saved ; in whose power lie the hearts of princes, and the end of all their actions ; have mercy upon Thine afflicted Church, and especially regard Elizabeth, our most excellent queen, to whom Thy dispersed flock do fly, in the anguish of their souls, and in the zeal of Thy truth. Behold how the princes of the nations do band themselves against her, because she laboureth to purge Thy sanctuary, and that Thy holy Church may live in security. Consider, O Lord, how long Thy servant hath laboured to them for peace, but how proudly they prepare themselves unto battle. Arise, therefore, maintain Thine own cause, and judge Thou between her and her enemies. She seeketh not her own honour, but Thine ; nor the dominions of others, but a just defence of herself ; not the shedding of Christian blood, but the saving of poor afflicted souls. Come down, therefore, come down, and deliver Thy people by her. To vanquish is all one with Thee, by few or by many, by want or by wealth, by weakness or by strength. Oh ! possess the hearts of our enemies with a fear of Thy servants. The cause is Thine, the enemies Thine, the afflicted Thine : the honour, victory, and triumph shall be Thine. Consider, Lord, the end of our enterprises. Be present with us in our armies, and make a joyful peace for Thy Christians. And now, since in this extreme necessity Thou hast put into the heart of Thy servant Deborah, to provide strength to withstand the pride of Sisera and his adherents, bless Thou all her forces by sea and land. Grant all her people one heart, one mind, and one strength, to defend her person, her kingdom, and Thy true religion. Give unto all her council and captains wisdom, wariness and courage, that they may speedily prevent the devices, and valiantly withstand the forces of all our enemies; that the fame of Thy Gospel may be spread unto the ends of the world. We crave this in Thy mercy, O Heavenly Father, for the precious death of Thy dear Son, Jesus Christ. Amen." *

In this faith, with these preparations, and with a national spirit thus roused, the queen and the English people awaited the coming of the enemy. It was towards the latter end of May † that the then called Invincible Armada sailed from the Tagus for Corunna, there to take on board the remainder of the land forces and stores. Cardinal Albert of Austria, then Viceroy of Portugal, gave it his solemn blessing before it departed, and it set forth with all the confidence ‡ that could be derived from military and naval strength, and an entire belief that all the saints in the Romish Litany would befriend it. On the 30th, the lord admiral and Sir Francis Drake sailed from Plymouth: their fleet "amounted to 100 sail, whereof fifteen were victuallers, and nine voluntaries of Devonshire gentlemen, many a serviceable man returning back for

---

* Strype, book ii., App. No. 54.

† Most of the old accounts say the 19th. One which Mr. Turner follows makes it the 25th. The Dutch writers say the 29th or 30th, and with this Camden agrees; but the earliest date accords with the account given to Drake by the hulk from S. Lucar.

‡ "With the greatest pride and glory," says Sir W. Monsey, "and least doubt of victory that ever any nation did" (p. 156).

lack of employment or place". The easterly wind with which they set forth "continued but a short time; yet, nevertheless," says Drake, "all men were so willing of service, and none more than my lord admiral himself, that we endured a great storm (considering the time of the year), with the wind southerly and at south-west, for seven days; and longer we had, had not the wind come westwardly, and that so much, as in keeping sea, we should have been put to leeward off Plymouth, either for Portland or Wight, which places had not been so meet, either for the meeting of the enemy, or relieving ourselves of those wants which daily will be in so great an army of ships". He had met with intelligence that the enemy were at sea, and he inferred that either they would very shortly be heard of, or else go to Corunna, and there "make their full rendezvous". "I assure your good lordship," said he in his letter to Burleigh, "and protest it before God, that I find my lord admiral so well affected for all honourable services in this action, as it doth assure all his followers of good success and hope of victory. Thus humbly taking my leave of your good lordship, I daily pray to God to bless her Majesty, and to give us grace to fear Him. So shall we not need to doubt the enemy, although they be many. From aboard her Majesty's good ship the *Revenge*, riding in Plymouth Sound, this 6th of June, 1588. Your good lordship's very ready to be commanded, Francis Drake." This was the first despatch relating to the operations of this great campaign.

The storm which the English encountered dismasted some of the enemy's ships, dispersed others, and occasioned the loss of four Portuguese galleys. One sunk; a Welshman, David Gwynne * by name, who had been a galley-slave among these merciless people eleven years, took the opportunity of regain-

---

* Hakluyt, 596. Speed, 859. Bor, 321, 322. In the latter author the details are given.

ing his liberty, and made himself master of another, captured one galley with it, was joined by a third, in which the slaves were encouraged to rise by his example, and carried the three into a French port. The Armada, after this ominous commencement of the voyage, put back to Corunna; the lord admiral having received intelligence that it was broken in the storm, concluded rightly that its "storm-shaken" ships would return thither, and he set sail with the first fair wind, hoping to attack them in the harbour. But when he was not far from the coast of Spain, the wind came suddenly about into the south; and he, lest they should effect their passage with that wind, unperceived, returned to the entrance of the channel. "I myself," he wrote, "do lie in the midst of the channel, with the greatest force; Sir Francis Drake hath twenty ships, and four or five pinnaces, which lie towards Ushant; and Mr. Hawkins, with as many more, lieth towards Scilly. Thus we are fain to do, or else with this wind they might pass us by, and we never the wiser. The *Sleeve* is another manner of thing than it was taken for: we find it by experience and daily observation to be 100 miles over: a large room for me to look unto!"* Yet the delay of the enemy, and the report of what they had suffered, not from the storm alone, but also from sickness, deceived both the admiral and the Government; the ships withdrew, some to the coast of Ireland, the admiral, with the greater part of the fleet, to Plymouth, where the men were allowed to come ashore. Many of them were discharged,† and the officers amused themselves with revels, dancing, bowling, and making merry. The queen was verily persuaded that the invasion was not to be looked for this year; and in that rash confidence the secretary Walsingham wrote to the admiral to send back four of the tallest ships royal, as if the war for that season were surely at an end. Happily for England, and

---

* Turner, 675, n. † Monson, 157.

most honourably for himself, the Lord Effingham, though he had relaxed his vigilance, saw how perilous it was to act as if all were safe. He humbly entreated that nothing might be lightly credited in so weighty a matter, and that he might retain these ships, though it should be at his own cost. This was no empty show of disinterested zeal; for if the service of those ships had not been called for, there can be little doubt, that in the rigid parsimony of Elizabeth's Government, he would have been called upon to pay the costs.*

Meantime the Armada, having completely refitted, sailed from Corunna on the 12th of July. The Duque de Medina Sidonia † had been ordered to keep along the coasts of Bretagne and Normandy; and if he met with the English fleet, to keep on the defensive, and avoid an action; and to repair to the road of Calais, there to wait for the Prince of Parma: when their junction should have been affected, he was then to open the sealed instructions, which were directed to both. But as the news of the damage which he had sustained misled the English Government, so did the information which he received that the English were off their guard induce him to depart from his orders; "yet this was not done without some difficulty, for the council was divided in opinion; some held it best to observe the king's commands, others not to lose the opportunity of surprising our fleet in harbour, and burning and destroying it". This course was strongly advised by Diego Flores de Valdez, on whom the duke most relied, because of his experience; and with that determination they steered their course for England. The first land with which they fell in was the Lizard: they mistook it for the Ram's-head; and "night being at hand, they tacked off to sea, making

---

* " A man employed rather for his birth than experience; for so many dukes, marquises, and earls voluntarily going, would have repined to have been commanded by a man of less quality than themselves " (Monson).

† Camden, 410.

account in the morning to attempt the ships in Plymouth".*
One Thomas Fleming, a lucky pirate, had got sight of them
off the Lizard, and hastened to Plymouth with the intelligence;
—it was of such importance, that he obtained his pardon for
it, and a pension during life. It had been little looked for,—
and the wind at that time "blew stiffly into the harbour".
All hands were got on board with all speed; the ships were
warped out with great difficulty, "but indeed with singular
diligence and industry, and with admirable alacrity of the
seamen, whom the lord admiral encouraged at their halser-
work, towing at a cable with his own hands. "I dare boldly
say," says Fuller, "that he drew more, though not by his
person, by his presence and example, than any ten in the
place." He got out himself that night, with only six ships;
some four and twenty came out on the morrow, and with these,
though they were some of the smallest of the fleet, he stood
out to meet the enemy, resolving to impede their progress at
all hazards.

The next day the Armada was seen, "with lofty turrets
like castles, in front like a half-moon; the wings thereof
spreading out about the length of seven miles, sailing very
slowly, though with full sails, the winds," says Camden,
"being as it were weary with wafting them, and the ocean
groaning under their weight". The intent of surprising the
fleet in harbour being frustrated, they passed Plymouth, the
English willingly suffering them to pass, that they might chase

* Monson. In a discourse of Sir Robert Slingsby's it is said: "Had it
not been for the English privateer Fleming, Valdez's counsel to burn
our fleet as they lay in harbour without men had taken effect. The
Spaniards' ignorance in sea affairs taking the Lizard for the Ram's-head,
and tacking off that night, lost their opportunity of destroying our fleet
in Plymouth Sound. And although King Philip's counsel for his fleet to
sail along the coast of France was great and good, yet being to be put in
practice by gentlemen ignorant in sea affairs, and preferred only for their
birth, it lost the effect it might have had, and totally overthrew all their
design" (Charnock, Preface, lxxvi.).

them in the rear, with a foreright wind. And on the morrow, the lord admiral sending the *Defiance* pinnace forward, denounced war * by discharging her ordnance, and presently his own ship, the *Ark Royal*, thundered thick and furiously upon what he supposed to be the general's ship, but it proved to be the vice-admiral's, Alonso de Leyva's. Soon after, Drake, Hawkins, and Frobisher played stoutly with their ordnance upon the rear of the enemy, where Ricalde, the admiral, commanded; that officer endeavoured to prevent his ships from flying to the main fleet, till his own ship was rendered nearly unserviceable, and he was then fain, "with much ado," to hasten thither himself. "The duque then gathered together his fleet, which was scattered this way and that way, and hoisting more sail, held on his course with what speed he could. Neither could he do any other, seeing both the wind favoured the English, and their ships would turn about with incredible celerity which way soever they pleased to charge, wind, and tack about again." The Spaniards then felt a cause of weakness in their excess of strength, "their great ships being powerful to defend but not to offend, to stand but not to move, and therefore far unfit for fight in those narrow seas; their enemies nimble, and ready at all sides to annoy them, and as apt to escape harm themselves, by being low built, and easily shot over. Therefore they gathered themselves close in form of a half-moon, and slackened sail, that their whole fleet might keep together. After a smart fight, in which he had injured the enemy much, and suffered little or no hurt himself, Lord Effingham gave over the action, because forty of his ships were not yet come up, having scarcely indeed got out of the haven." †

During the night, the *St. Catalina*, which had suffered

* "Fire, smoke, and echoing cannons," says Speed, "began the parley; and bullets, most freely interchanged between them, were messengers of each other's mind."

† Hakluyt, 595. Speed, 860. Camden, 411.

greatly, was taken into the midst of the fleet to be repaired; and Oquendo's ship (of 800 tons) was set on fire (it is said) by a Flemish gunner, whose wife had been abused and himself outraged by the commanding officer of the troops on board. It was part of their general orders, that if any ship took fire, those that were near were to make from her, sending, however, their boats to succour her; this was so well observed that no other ship was injured, and the fire was quenched, though not before the upper works were consumed; but more diligence than humanity was shown in this, for after taking out whatever was of value that could be saved, when they abandoned the hulk they left in it some fifty of their countrymen, "miserably hurt". That night, also, in the confusion which this fire occasioned, Valdez's galleon ran foul of another ship, broke her foremast, and was left behind, and none coming to her assistance, "the sea being tempestuous and the night dark," the lord admiral supposed that the men had been taken out, and without tarrying to take possession of the prize, passed on with the *Bear* and the *Mary Wolf*, that he might not lose sight of the enemy in the darkness. He thought that he was following Drake's ship, which ought to have carried the lantern that night; it proved to be a Spanish light, and in the morning he found himself in the midst of the enemy's fleet, "but when he perceived it, he cleanly conveyed himself out of that great danger". In the eagerness of hope Drake had forgotten or disregarded his orders, and engaged in close pursuit of five great ships, which he supposed to be enemies, but which, when he came up with them, proved to be Easterlings, holding their course by these contending fleets, and protected by them from all danger of pirates. But the whole of the English ships, except the two which followed the admiral into so perilous a situation, lay to during the night, because the lantern was not to be seen, nor did they recover sight of the admiral till the following evening. Drake himself had the good fortune to fall in with

Valdez, who, after some parley, surrendered, seeing that resistance must have been vain. The prize was sent into Plymouth; and Drake's men paid themselves well with the spoil of the ship, wherein were 55,000 ducats in gold, which they shared merrily among them. The hulk of the galleon was also carried into Weymouth, to the great joy of the beholders; though the upper works had been consumed, and most of the crew burned. The gunpowder in the hold had not taken fire, "to the great admiration of all men".*

On Tuesday, the 23rd, the Spaniards were off Portland, and the wind came about into the north, so that they "had a fortunate and fit gale for invading the English". But the English, "agile and foreseeing all harms, recovered the vantage of the wind". After they had for some time manœuvred for this object, they prepared on both sides for action, the Spaniards "seeming more incensed to fight than before. And fight they did, confusedly, and with variable fortune; for on the one side the English manfully rescued some London ships that were hemmed in by the Spaniards, and on the other the Spaniards as stoutly rescued their admiral, Ricalde, when he was in danger." "On this day was the sorest fight, yet with no memorable loss on either side." A great Venetian ship and some smaller ones were surprised and taken by the English. On their part Captain Cock died with honour in the midst of the enemies, in a small ship of his own. Though this was the most furious and bloody skirmish of all, the loss was little, because the English, having given their broadsides, presently stood off, never exposing themselves in close action, but satisfied with levelling their guns with sure aim against those great ships, "which were heavy and altogether unwieldy. Neither did the lord admiral think good to adventure grappling with them, as some unadvisedly persuaded him. For the enemy had a strong army in

---

* Hakluyt, 597, 598. Speed, 860. Camden, 412.

his fleet, but he had none: their ships were of bigger burden, stronger and higher built, so as their men fighting from those lofty hatches must inevitably destroy those who should charge them from beneath. And he knew that an overthrow would endamage him much more than a victory would advantage him. For if he were vanquished he should very much endanger all England; and if he conquered he should only gain a little honour for beating the enemy." On the other hand the Spaniards were not less wary: they "gathered themselves close into a roundel, their best and greatest ships without, securing the smaller and those which had suffered most"; so that it was apparent that they meant as much as possible to avoid fighting, and hold on to the place appointed for their junction with the Prince of Parma.*

There was no wind stirring on the morrow, and only the four great galleasses were engaged, these having much advantage, by reason of their oars, while the English were becalmed; the English, however, galled the enemy with chain-shot, therewith cutting asunder their tacklings and cordage. But they were now constrained to send ashore for gunpowder, the want of which ministered displeasure, it is said, if not suspicion to many, that a scarcity should thus be felt on our own coast. Those persons did not reflect how freely it had been expended during the three preceding days. The same day a council of war was held, and it was resolved that the fleet should be divided into four squadrons under the command of the four "most skilful navigators, whereof the lord admiral in the *Ark Royal* was chief, Drake in the *Revenge* led the second, Hawkins the third, and Frobisher the fourth. Out of every squadron, also, small vessels were appointed to give the onset and attack the enemy on all sides simultaneously in the dead of the night." This design took no effect for want of wind. The Spaniards, meantime, "observed

* Hakluyt, 598. Speed, 860. Camden, 412.

very diligent and good order, sailing three and four, and sometimes more, in a rank, and following close up one after another, and the stronger and greater ships protecting the lesser ". The morrow was Santiago's day, and the Spaniards not improbably were animated by the hope that their patron saint might exert himself as visibly that day on their behalf as they had been taught to believe he had so often done against the Moors. The *St. Anna* not being able to keep up with the rest was set upon by some small ships: three galleasses came to her rescue; against these the lord admiral himself advanced, and Lord Thomas Howard in the *Golden Lion:* their ships being towed, because of the calm, they plied their guns with such effect that the galleon was not brought off without much difficulty, and from that time no galleasses would venture to engage. By this time they were off the Isle of Wight; and according to the Spaniards, the English, encouraged as it seems by success in the last encounter, battered the Spanish admiral (then in the rear of his fleet) with their great ordnance, approached closer than they had before done, and shot away his mainmast; but other ships came to his assistance, beat them off, and set upon the English admiral, who escaped only by favour of the wind which sprung up when he most needed it.* The English relate that they shot away the lantern from one of the enemy's ships, and the beak-head from a second, and did much hurt to a third, and that Frobisher extricated himself with great ability from a situation of great danger. The lord admiral knighted the Lord Thomas Howard, Lord Sheffield, Roger Townsend, Hawkins and Frobisher for their behaviour on that day. Both parties appear to have demeaned themselves gallantly, and both to have been rendered more cautious. The Spaniards say that from that time they gave over what they call the pursuit of their enemy; and they despatched a fresh messenger

* Camden, 413. Turner, 679.

to the Prince of Parma, urging him to effect his junction with them as soon as possible, and withal to send them some great shot, for they had expended theirs with more prodigality than effect. Without knowing of this intention on their part, the English also came to a resolution that they would make no further attack upon the Spaniards, till they should arrive in the Straits of Calais, where they should be joined by Lord Henry Seymour and Sir William Winter, with their squadrons.*

That same day the lord admiral received welcome assurances from Havre that no attempt in aid of the enemy would be made by the Guises, which there had been reason to apprehend. His own force now was continually increased by ships and men, resorting to him "out of all havens of the realm; for the gentlemen of England hired ships from all parts at their own charge, and with one accord came flocking thither as to a set field, where glory was to be attained and faithful service performed unto their prince and their country". Among the volunteers who thus came out were the Earls of Oxford, Northumberland, and Cumberland, with many others, whose names are conspicuous in Elizabeth's famous reign, the most illustrious of them being Walter Raleigh. So with a clear sky and a fair south-west wind the Armada held on its course, closely followed by the English fleet. On the evening of the 27th the Spaniards came to anchor before Calais just at sunset: their intention had been to hold on for Dunkirk in expectation of being joined there by the prince; but they were told by the pilots that if they proceeded any further they would be in danger of being carried by force of the tide into the northern sea. The English, also, anchored here, and within cannon shot. Seymour and Winter had joined with their squadrons. "And now were there in the English fleet 140 sail, all of them ships fit for fight, good sailors, nimble and

* Camden, 144. Hakluyt, 599.

tight for tacking about which way they would." Hitherto the whole brunt had been borne by not more than fifteen of them.

The conferences at Ostend had continued up to this time; but when the firing was heard at sea " all dissembling was laid aside ". The Prince of Parma has been accused of more dissimulation than was consistent with his honourable character, for having solemnly assured the English commissioners that the Armada was not intended against England, if the terms for which they were treating should be agreed on. There seems to have been no duplicity in this, because in that case it would immediately have been directed against the united provinces. Honourable dealing, however, was so little practised, or so little understood, in those times, that these commissioners thought themselves in danger, because no hostages had been taken for their safety; and when they obtained a passport and a convoy to the frontiers, " they gave great thanks to the Spanish commissioners, and much commended the prince's honourable disposition in that he had so justly kept his word with them ".* That prince, as soon as he was assured that the Armada was on its way, had made over his command in the Netherlands to the old Lord of Mansfelt; and in that same spirit of Romish devotion, in which the expedition was set forth, went in pilgrimage to our Lady of Halle, the most noted idol in those countries, that he might obtain her patronage and protection in this great attempt at the conquest of England. Returning from thence he repaired to Dunkirk, where he was to embark: there he heard the firing on the coast, found that Stanley's regiment of deserters was the only one which had embarked, and that the other troops were as little willing to go on board the ships as the ships themselves were likely to get out of the harbour.†

* Grimestone, 996.   † *Ibid.*, 1003.

It had been concerted with the States, that a squadron of about thirty ships, under Cornelius Lonke van Rosendael, should unite with Seymour's squadron, and take its station between Dover and Calais. It had sailed with this intention, but a storm had compelled it to put back to Zeeland; and some of the English, too prone to put a sinister interpretation upon all the actions of their allies, complained of this, as if there had been an intentional breach of faith. But the squadron performed better service than if the original plan had been carried into effect; for, when the weather allowed of its again coming forth, it joined the Admiral of Zeeland, Justinus van Nassau, and the Vice-Admiral of Holland, Jonker Pieter van der Does, who had with them about five and thirty sail of from 80 to 250 tons: 1200 soldiers were on board, selected from all the regiments in the service of the States, as good soldiers, accustomed to sea-service; and with part of this fleet they watched every creek and haven in Flanders, and with the remainder blockaded Dunkirk.* In vain did the Duke of Medina Sidonia despatch messenger after messenger to the prince, urging him to send forty light vessels for the immediate protection of the Armada, cumbered as it was by the unwieldy strength of its own ships, and entreating him to put to sea with his army, that they might proceed together to the Thames. His flat-bottomed boats were leaky; his provisions were not ready; his men were not willing: the sailors had been brought together by compulsion, and were deserting as fast as they could from what they knew to be a desperate service: the galleys which might have cleared the way for him (if it could have been cleared) had been lost on the voyage; and the great general of his age knew that if he attempted to sail from Dunkirk in the face of the Dutch fleet it would be wilfully exposing himself and his army to imminent and certain destruction.† Yet, unless some effort were made,

* Bor, 321, 323. † *Ibid.*

all these mighty preparations would be frustrated, and Spain would suffer a loss of reputation not to be repaired; and he promised, if wind and tide permitted, to join them within three days.*

Fair as the hopes of the English were at this time, and admirable as their conduct had been from the hour that the Armada came in sight, it has been justly observed † that the Spanish duke had thus far conducted his great expedition with as little evil and annoyance as could have been reasonably expected. The danger to England was still undiminished. The Armada had arrived unbroken at the point intended for its junction with the force from Flanders: it still appeared invincible to all except the English and the Dutch, and except those also who, in the confidence of its invincibility, had embarked in it. While it lay off Calais, in this anxious interval of expectation, " Flemings, Walloons, and French came thick and threefold to behold it, admiring the exceeding greatness of the ships and their warlike order. The greatest kept the outside next the enemy, like strong castles, fearing no assault; the lesser placed in the middle ward."‡ At this time the English might regret the loss of Calais; but never were the councils of England more wisely directed. The Spanish ships, " as castles pitched in the sea, had their bulks so planked with great beams, that bullets might strike and stick, but never pass through, so that little availed the English cannon, except only in playing on their masts and tackling". In this respect they seemed as invulnerable as the floating batteries employed against Gibraltar. And their height was such, that our bravest seamen were against any attempt at boarding them.

* Camden, 414. Grimestone, 1003. Turner, 680.

† Turner, 679.

‡ Stowe, 748. " Fresh victuals were straight brought abroad. Captains and cavaliers might have what they would for their money, and gave the French so liberally, that within twelve hours an egg was worth sixpence, besides thanks."

These things had been well prepended by Elizabeth's ministers, and the lord admiral was instructed to convert eight of his worst vessels into fire-ships. The orders arrived in such good time, and were obeyed with such alacrity, that within thirty hours after the enemy had cast anchor off Calais these ships were disburdened of all that was worth saving, filled with combustibles, and all their ordnance charged; and their sides being smeared with pitch, rosin, and wildfire, they were sent, in the dead of the night, with wind and tide, against the Spanish fleet; "which when the Spaniards saw the whole sea glittering and shining with the flames thereof, they remembered those terrible fire-ships which had been used in the Scheldt, and the fearful cry of 'The fire of Antwerp!'" ran through the fleet. They apprehended not the danger of fire alone, but all the evils that "deadly engines and murderous inventions" could inflict: some cut their cables; others let their hawsers slip, and in haste, fear, and confusion, put to sea, "happiest they who could first be gone, though few or none could tell which course to take".*

In this confusion, the largest of the galleasses, commanded by D. Hugo de Moncada, ran foul of another ship, lost her rudder, floated about at the mercy of the tide, and making the next morning for Calais, as well as she could, ran upon the sands. There she was presently assailed by the English small craft, who lay battering her with their guns, but dared not attempt to board, till the admiral sent a hundred men in his boats, under Sir Amias Preston. The Spaniards made a brave resistance, hoping presently to be succoured by the Prince of Parma, and the action was for a long time doubtful. At length Moncada was shot through the head, the galleass was carried by boarding, and most of the Spaniards, leaping into the sea, were drowned. The Veedor of the fleet, D.

* Hakluyt, 601. Strype, 861. Camden, 415. Grimestone, 1003. Bor, 324.

Antonio de Manrique, was one of those who reached the shore; and he was the first person that carried certain news to Spain of their "now vincible navy". This huge bottom, manned with 400 soldiers and 300 galley-slaves, had also 50,000 ducats on board; "a booty," says Speed, "well fitting the English soldiers' affections". Having ransacked all, and freed the slaves from their miserable fetters, they were about to set that vessel of emptiness on fire; but the Governor of Calais would not permit this, fearing, it is said, the damage that might thereupon ensue to the town and haven. He fired therefore, upon the captors, and the ship and ordnance became his prize.*

The duke, when the fire-ships were first perceived, had ordered the whole fleet to weigh anchor and stand off to sea, and when the danger was over, return every ship to its former station. The latter part of this order they were too much alarmed to wait for or to heed; and when he returned himself, and fired a signal for others to follow his example, the gun was heard by few, "because they were scattered all about, and driven by fear, some of them into the wide sea, and some among the shoals of Flanders". Little broken yet in strength, though now losing fast the hope and the confidence with which they had set forth, they ranged themselves again in order off Gravelines; and there they were bravely attacked. Drake and Fenner were the first who assailed them: Fenton, Southwell, Beeston, Cross and Reyman followed; and then the lord admiral came up, with Lord Thomas Howard and Lord Sheffield. They got the wind of the enemy, who were now cut off from Calais Roads, and preferred any inconvenience rather than change their array or separate their force, standing only upon their defence. "And albeit there were many excellent and warlike ships in the English fleet, yet scarce were there two or three and twenty

* Hakluyt, Strype, Camden, *ut supra*.

among them all which matched ninety of the Spanish ships in bigness, or could conveniently assault them. Wherefore, using their prerogative of nimble steerage, whereby they could turn and wield themselves with the wind which way they listed, they came oftentimes very near upon the Spaniards, and charged them so sore, that now and then they were but a pike's length asunder; and so continually giving them one broadside after another, they discharged all their shot, both great and small, upon them, spending a whole day, from morning till night, in that violent kind of conflict."* "We had such advantage," says Lord Monmouth, "both of wind and tide, that we had a glorious day of them, continuing fight from four o'clock in the morning till five or six at night." During this action the Spaniards, "lying close under their fighting sails," passed Dunkirk with a south-west wind, close followed by their enemies. Their great ships were found vulnerable in the close action of that day; many of them were pierced through and through between wind and water: one was sunk by Captain Cross, in the *Hope:* from the few of her people who were saved, it was learnt that one of her officers, having proposed to strike, was put to death by another; the brother of the slain instantly avenged his death, and then the ship went down. Two others are believed to have sunk. The *St. Philip* and the *St. Matthew*, both Portuguese galleons, were much shattered. D. Diego de Pimentel, in the latter, endeavoured to assist the former, but in vain; for being "sore battered with many great shot by Seymour and Winter," and the mast shot away, the *St. Philip* was driven near Ostend: as a last chance, the officers endeavoured to make for a Flemish port; but finding it impossible to bring the ship into any friendly harbour, they got to Ostend in the boats, and the galleon was taken possession of from Flushing. The *St. Matthew* suffered so much, and leaked so fast, that the

* Hakluyt, 602.

duke sent a boat to bring Pimentel and some of the chief persons on board his own ship. A sense of honour withheld them from abandoning their men, and looking solely to the preservation of their own lives. The duke then charged them to keep company with him; but this was impossible: in that danger the one vessel could not slacken its course, and the other could make little way; for the water came in so fast that fifty men were employed at the pumps. Seeing himself thus necessarily forsaken, Pimentel resolved to run aground on the Flemish coast; but here he was discovered by some of the Dutch ships, which had their station upon that coast; and, after losing some forty of his men in vain resistance, struck to Pieter van der Does. The ship sunk in one of the Zeeland ports; and its flag was suspended as a trophy in St. Peter's Church at Leyden; a city which had been in no light degree beholden for its own glorious deliverance to the illustrious family of Dousa.*

Still the duke did not despair of eventual success: an unexpected respite was afforded him; for the English had expended their ammunition, and were forced to send for a supply; and taking advantage of a strong west-north-wester, the Armada made an effort to regain his position in the straits, that the prince might join them. The spirit in which this resolution was taken was better than the seamanship: that wind carried them towards the shallows and sands on the Zeeland coast; and glad were they when it came to the south and enabled them to avoid the dangers by which they must otherwise soon have found themselves surrounded. That day Drake wrote to Walsingham: "We have the army of Spain before us, and mind to wrestle a pull with him. There was never anything pleased better than seeing the enemy flying with a southerly wind to the northward. I doubt not, but ere it be long, so to handle the matter with the Duke of

---

* Bor, 325. Hakluyt, 602, 603. Camden, 415. Grimestone, 1004.

Sidonia, that he shall wish himself at St. Mary's Port, among his vine trees. God give us grace to depend upon Him; so shall we not doubt victory, for our cause is good." But the hopes which Drake entertained of a brilliant victory * were not to be fulfilled. Enough had been achieved by the councils and the hand of man. That providence which had confounded the devices of the enemy effected by the agency of the elements the rest. The duke advised with his officers in the evening what course, after these unexpected disasters, should be pursued. They were now experimentally convinced that the English excelled them in naval strength. Several of their largest ships had been lost, others were greatly damaged: there was no port to which they could repair; and to force their way through the victorious English fleet, then in sight and amounting to 140 sail, was plainly and confessedly impossible. They resolved, therefore, upon returning to Spain

* "And here," says Sir William Monson, "was opportunity offered us to have followed the victory upon them; for if we had once more offered them fight, the general, it was thought, by persuasion of his confessor, was determined to yield; whose example, 'tis very likely, would have made the rest to have done the like. But this opportunity was lost; not through the negligence or backwardness of the lord admiral, but merely through the want of providence in those that had the charge of furnishing and providing for the fleet. For at that time of so great advantage, when they came to examine their provisions, they found a general scarcity of powder and shot, for want whereof they were forced to return home. Another opportunity was lost, not much inferior to the other, by not sending part of our fleet to the west of Ireland, where the Spaniards, of necessity, were to pass, after so many dangers and disasters as they had endured. If we had been so happy as to have followed their course, as it was both thought and discoursed of, we had been absolutely victorious over this great and formidable navy, for they were brought to that necessity, that they would willingly have yielded, as divers of them confessed that were shipwrecked in Ireland. By this we may see how weak and feeble the designs of man are in respect of the Creator; and how indifferently He dealt betwixt the two nations, sometimes giving one, sometimes the other, the advantage, yet so that He only ordered the battle" (*Churchill's Collection*, iii., 159).

by a northern course; and in that determination, "having gotten more sea room for their huge-bodied bulks, spread their mainsails, and made away as fast as wind and water would give them leave. But surely," says Speed, "if they had known the want of powder that our fleet sustained (a fault inexcusable upon our own coasts), they no doubt would have stood longer to their tacklings. But God, in this, as in the rest, would have us to acknowledge, that we were only delivered by His own gracious providence and arm, and not by any policy or power of our own." The lord admiral left Seymour to blockade the Prince of Parma's force, and followed what our chroniclers now call the Vincible Armada, not without some apprehension that they might put into Scotland; but leaving Scotland on the west, they bent towards Norway, "ill-advised, but that necessity urged, and God had infatuated their councils, to put their shaken and battered bottoms into those black and dangerous seas". And the English having, in Drake's words, "cast them so far to the northward, that they could neither recover England nor Scotland, thought it best to leave them to those boisterous and uncouth northern seas".*

But while the loss which they had hitherto sustained was as yet uncertain, and the opinion on shore was that they would return to the straits, it was still thought probable that the Prince of Parma might effect a landing. Elizabeth, who had not easily been dissuaded from her intention of being present in the battle wherever it should be fought, went to the camp at Tilbury. From the time that camp was formed, a true English spirit had been shown there. "It was a pleasant sight," says the good London chronicler,† who himself had seen it, "to behold the soldiers as they marched towards Tilbury, their cheerful countenances, courageous

* Hakluyt, 603. Speed, 862. Turner, 681.
† Stowe, 744.

words and gestures, dancing and leaping wheresoever they came. In the camp their most felicity was the hope of fighting with the enemy, where, ofttimes, divers rumours ran of their foes' approach, and that present battle would be given them; then were they as joyful at such news as if lusty giants were to run a race." When the queen came among them, "full of princely resolution, and more than feminine courage," she rode through the ranks with a general's truncheon in her hand, and sometimes with a martial pace, another while gently, like a woman: "Incredible it is," says Camden, "how much she encouraged the hearts of her captains and soldiers by her presence and her words". "I think," says Leicester, "the weakest person among them is able to match the proudest Spaniards that dare land in England!" Her speech at this memorable time has been preserved,* and well might it animate them. "My loving people," she said, "we have been persuaded by some that are careful of our safety to take heed how we commit ourselves to armed multitudes, for fear of treachery; but I assure you I do not desire to live to distrust my faithful and loving people. Let tyrants fear! I have always so behaved myself, that, under God, I have placed my chiefest strength and safeguard in the loyal hearts and good-will of my subjects; and, therefore, I am come amongst you, as you see, at this time, not for my recreation and disport, but being resolved in the midst and heat of the battle, to live or die amongst you all, to lay down, for my God, for my kingdom, and for my people, my honour and my blood even in the dust. I know I have the body but of a weak and feeble woman, but I have the heart and stomach of a king, and of a king of England too; and think it foul scorn that Parma, or Spain, or any prince of Europe, should dare to invade the borders of my realm; to which rather than any dishonour should grow by me, I

---

* Somer's *Tracts* (Scott's edition), i., 429.

myself will take up arms, I myself will be your general, judge, and rewarder of every one of your virtues in the field. I know already for your forwardness you have deserved rewards and crowns ; and we do assure you, on the word of a prince, they shall be duly paid you. In the meantime my lieutenant-general shall be in my stead, than whom never prince commanded a more noble or worthy subject, not doubting but by your obedience to my general, by your concord in the camp, and your valour in the field, we shall shortly have a famous victory over those enemies of my God, of my kingdom, and of my people."

While she was at dinner that day in the general's tent, there came a post with tidings that the Prince of Parma and all his forces had embarked for England, and that his arrival with all possible speed was to be looked for. The news was immediately published through the camp;* and assuredly, if the enemy had set foot upon our shores, they would have sped no better than they had done at sea, such was the spirit of the nation. This intelligence was soon disproved; but after it was certain that by God's mercy the danger had been averted, some time elapsed before the fate of the Armada was ascertained. Statements of its success were confidently circulated upon the continent, and credited according to the wishes of the hearer. It was affirmed that great part of the English fleet had been taken, great part sunk, and the poor remainder driven into the Thames " all rent and torn " ; that they were utterly discomfited, and that Drake was made prisoner.† Poems were composed in honour of the victory, as poems had been composed to predict it. It was

* Turner, 682, note.

† "And that there was found in his ship a piece of twenty-five spans, or one quintal of munition, made on purpose, of one only shot, to sink the Admiral of Spain ; but it pleased God, though she was hurt therewith, yet she was repaired again, and overcame the English fleet " (Strype, App. B, ii., No. 55).

believed at Rome that Elizabeth was taken, and England conquered; and Cardinal Allen is said to have made a feast in honour of the event, and invited to it the Scotch, Irish, and English who were in that city! But in vain, meantime, was the ship looked for in the Spanish ports that should bring good tidings home! The unhappy fleet, after the English had given over the pursuit, threw their mules and horses overboard lest their water should fail. They knew that they had no relief to expect in Scotland, and that Norway could not supply their wants; so taking some captured fishermen for pilots, they sailed between the Orkney and the Feroe Islands; and when they had reached the latitude of sixty-two, and were some 200 miles from any land, the duke ordered them each to take the best course they could for Spain. He, himself, with some five and twenty of the ships that were best provided, steered a straight course, and arrived in safety. The others, about forty in number, made for Cape Clear, hoping to water there; but a storm from the south-west overtook and wrecked many of them upon the Irish coast. Their treatment there is the only circumstance in the whole history of this enterprise which is disgraceful to an English name. For the lord deputy, Sir William Fitzwilliam, fearing they should join the rebels, and seeing that Bingham, the Governor of Connaught, refused to obey his merciless orders concerning them, sent his deputy marshal, "who drove them out of their hiding-places, and beheaded about 200 of them". The queen condemned this cruelty from her heart, though no such punishment as he deserved was inflicted upon Fitzwilliam. Terrified at this, the other Spaniards, "sick and starved as they were, committed themselves to the sea in their shattered vessels, and very many of them were swallowed up by the waves".* But with some of the officers who escaped this

* Camden, 417.

butchery Tyrone concerted his rebellion.* It is supposed that more than thirty of their ships perished off the coast of Ireland, with the greater part of their crews. Two vessels were cast away on the coast of Norway. Some few, having a westerly wind, got again into the English seas; of these, two were taken by the cruisers off Rochelle, and one (a great galleass) put into Havre. About 700 men who were cast ashore in Scotland were there humanely treated; and, with Elizabeth's consent, were, at the Prince of Parma's request, sent over to the Netherlands. Relics of this great destruction are still sometimes brought to light. It is not long since the remains of an anchor, which appeared to have belonged to the Armada, was picked up in a fisherman's trawl off Dover; and in 1832 one of their cannon † was found on the coast of Mayo. Of the whole Armada, only fifty-three vessels returned to Spain; eighty-one were lost; and of 30,000 soldiers who were embarked, nearly 14,000 were missing, the prisoners being about 2000.

Philip's behaviour when the whole of this great calamity was known should always be recorded to his honour. He received it as a dispensation of Providence; and gave, and commanded to be given, throughout Spain, thanks to God and the saints that it was no greater.

England having thus been "delivered by the hand of the Omnipotent, and the boar put back that sought to lay her vineyard waste," Elizabeth ordered a solemn thanksgiving to be celebrated at St. Paul's, where eleven of the Spanish ensigns were hung upon the lower battlements, "as palms of praise," says Speed, "for England's deliverance, a show, no doubt, more acceptable to God than when their spread colours did set out the pride of their ships, threatening the blood of

---

* Fiennes Moryson, 8. Carte's *Ormond*, i., 58.
† It is now in Lord Sligo's possession.

so many innocent and faithful Christians". On the following day, which was Southwark fair, the same flags were displayed upon London bridge. They were finally suspended in St. Paul's. Less perishable trophies were deposited in the Tower, where many of the arms taken in the captured ships are still preserved; and not a few instruments of torture, wickedly devised, but more probably intended for the punishment of offences on board, than for the use of their inquisitors, who, if the conquest had been effected, might have found racks in England, and would have had fire and faggot at command. Another great thanksgiving day was celebrated on the anniversary of the queen's succession, which was long and most fitly observed as a holiday in these kingdoms: one of greater solemnity, two days after, throughout the realm; and, on the Sunday following, the queen repaired as in public, but Christian triumph, to St. Paul's. Her privy council, her nobility, the French ambassador, the judges, and the heralds, attended her. The streets were hung with blue cloth, "the several companies, in their liveries, being drawn up on both sides the way, with their banners in becoming and gallant order". Her chariot* was made in the form of a throne with four pillars, and drawn by four white horses; alighting from it at the west door of St. Paul's, she there knelt, and, with great devotion, audibly praised God, acknowledging Him her only defender, who had thus delivered the land from the rage of the enemy. Pierce, Bishop of Salisbury, who was her lord almoner, preached a sermon, "wherein none other argument was handled, but only of praise and glory to be rendered unto God. And, when he had concluded, the queen herself (like unto another Joshua, David and Josias), with most princely and Christian speeches, exhorted the people to the due performance of those religious services of thankfulness

---

* "Coaches," says Camden, "were not then so much in use among princes as now they are amongst private men."

unto God." * It was manifest, indeed, that over-ruling Providence had preserved them. Well and properly has it been observed by the ablest of our naval biographers,† that, great as were the exploits of the English fleet, they were as nothing compared with what the elements wrought for England; and that this our ancestors proclaimed with one accord, "breathing the pure spirit of that blessed Reformation which had been so recently achieved for them". The people of England have never, since the Norman conquest, been chastised by the hand of a foreign enemy: when their own folly and their own sins have brought upon them God's judgments, the instructive punishment has been administered by their own hands.

Lord Effingham was rewarded with a pension. The queen many times commended him and the captains of her ships, as men born for the preservation of their country. A greater service it has never fallen to the lot of any Englishman to perform. "True it is," says Fuller, "he was no deep seaman (not to be expected from one of his extraction); but he had skill enough to know those who had more skill than himself, and to follow their instructions, and would not starve the queen's service by feeding his own sturdy wilfulness, but was ruled by the experienced in sea matters; the queen having a navy of oak, and an admiral of osier." He did good service afterwards at Cadiz, being joint commander with the Earl of Essex in that famous expedition, and, for that service, was advanced to the title of Earl of Nottingham, as descended from the Mowbrays, some of whom had been

* *Memoirs of Celebrated Naval Commanders*, illustrated by engravings from original pictures in the Naval Gallery of Greenwich Hospital, by Edward Hawke Locker, Esq. I cannot refer to this work without regretting that Mr. Locker should have been compelled by ill health to limit to a single volume a work for which he was in every respect so eminently qualified.

† Speed, 862. Camden, 418. Strype, 27.

earls of that county. On the apprehension of another invasion, at a time when it was known that Essex entertained rash and dangerous designs, Lord Nottingham was entrusted with the command of both fleet and army, "with the high and very unusual title of Lord Lieutenant-General of all England; an office scarcely known to former, never owned of succeeding times, and which he held with almost regal authority for the space of six weeks, being sometimes with the fleet in the Downs, and sometimes on shore with the forces".* It was to him, who, the queen said, was "born to serve and save his country," that Essex, after his insane insurrection, yielded himself a prisoner; and to him that the queen, upon her death, made that wise and constitutional declaration concerning her successor: "My throne has been held by princes in the way of succession, and ought not to go to any but my next and immediate heir".

James continued him in his post of lord admiral, appointed him lord high steward at his coronation, sent him ambassador to Spain, and chose him for one of the commissioners to treat of a union between England and Scotland. The last honour which fell to his lot was that of conveying the elector palatine and his bride, the Princess Elizabeth, to Flushing. At the age of eighty-three he resigned his post, retaining, by special patent, the precedence which it had given him; and, in his eighty-seventh year, dying in peace at Haling House, in Surrey, was buried in the family vault under the chancel of Ryegate Church. His office had been "of great profit, prizes being so frequent in that age; but great," says Fuller, "his necessary, and vast his voluntary, expenses; keeping seven standing houses at the same time: so that the wonder is not great if he died not very wealthy".

*Campbell, i., 377.

THE EARL OF CUMBERLAND

AMONG the naval adventurers who distinguished themselves during Queen Elizabeth's reign, there was no one who took to the seas so much in the spirit of a northern sea king as the Earl of Cumberland. Some of his most noted contemporaries were sailors by their vocation, some became so incidentally when called upon in the queen's service, and others pursued that course with the hope of repairing a broken fortune, or of raising one; but it was this nobleman's mere choice, which he followed to the great injury of his own ample estates, and to the neglect of all his private and domestic duties.

George Clifford, in the male line of his family, fourteenth Baron Clifford of Westmoreland, and sheriff of that county by inheritance, and in the same descent thirteenth Lord of the Honour of Skipton in Craven, and also Lord Vipont and Baron Vesey, was born in his father's castle at Brougham, on the 8th of August, 1558. Few names are more conspicuous than that of Clifford in the York and Lancaster wars, none more distinguished for fidelity to the cause it had espoused; and Shakespeare has given it a wider renown than could have been conferred by genealogists and chroniclers. To this family, also, Fair Rosamond belongs; and the Shepherd Lord, whose memory is embalmed in everlasting verse. Lord Clifford was yet a boy when his father began to treat concerning his marriage with a daughter of Francis, second Earl of Bedford; and he was in the twelfth year of his age when his father died. Upon the first intelligence that such an event was likely, Bedford, upon the alleged ground of this marriage-treaty, made suit to the queen for the wardship, and it was granted him. The boy was at Battle Abbey when the earl died at Brougham: no doubt he had been placed there to receive the first part of his education in the family by whom that venerable edifice was then possessed. It seems not to have been unusual in those days for youths of rank to connect themselves with both universities; thus this earl is said to have been educated at Peter House, Cambridge, and also to have studied at Oxford, under the tuition of Whitgift, afterwards archbishop; "and here he obtained some knowledge in the arts, and especially in the mathematics, which did not only incline him thereto, but rendered him more fit for maritime employment". Before he was nineteen he was married in St. Mary Overy's Church, Southwark, to his long-engaged spouse, the Lady Margaret Russell, who was some two years younger.

The earl is said to have excelled all the nobles of his time in tilting, so that in such exhibitions he was always the queen's champion; and in this and other costly recreations he consumed much of his ample patrimony. Elizabeth made him Knight of the Garter, and appointed him to be one of the forty peers by whom the Queen of Scots was tried, and one of the four earls who were present at the catastrophe of that tragedy. His first maritime adventure was designed for the South Seas: he did not embark in it himself, but fitted out at his own cost the *Red Dragon* of 260 tons, and the barque *Clifford* of 130: a pinnace of Raleigh's and another ship completed the force, and Master Robert Withrington was the commander. Instead of passing the Straits of Magellan, Withrington thought he might make a more profitable venture by plundering Bahia; but the Jesuits, with their Indian archers, preserved that city; and the expedition having committed much havoc upon the coast of Brazil, with little gain, he resolved upon returning home,—a resolution which was "taken heavily of all the company," and heard by them in silence, "for very grief to see my lord's hopes thus deceived, and his great expenses cast away ".*

In the ensuing year he sailed for Sluys, hoping to assist Sir Roger Williams in the defence of that town against the Duke of Parma; but it had surrendered before his arrival. He bore his part in the defeat of the Armada, on board the *Bonadventure*, Captain George Raymond, when, says Purchas, "they won that honour that no sea can drown, no age wear out ". The queen was so satisfied with his behaviour, that she gave him a commission to go the same year to the Spanish coast as general; and for his greater honour and ability, was pleased to lend him the *Golden Lion*, one of the ships royal, to be the admiral; but he victualled and furnished it at his own cost. After some fight he took a merchant ship in the narrow seas; but it was now late in the autumn: contrary winds baffled his course: he was compelled to cut away his mainmast in a storm, and returned when it was impossible for him to prosecute what Purchas calls his true designs.†

"His spirit remaining, nevertheless, higher than the winds, and more resolutely by storms compact and united in itself," he obtained of the queen one of the royal navy called the *Victory;* with which, two small ships, the *Meg* or *Margaret* and a caravel, set forth at his charges, and with 400 men on board, he sailed from Plymouth in June, 1589. The *Margaret*, being not able to endure the sea, was sent home in a few days, with two French ships, which, belonging to the party of the League, were deemed fair prizes. The earl was not very scrupulous on such occasions. He fell in with eleven ships from Hamburgh and the Baltic: after a few shot, they sent

---

* Sarracoll, 100. Hakluyt, iii., 769-778. *History of Brazil*, i., 377, 378.

† Purchas, part iv., 1142.

their masters on board, showing their passports; these were respected for themselves, but not for some property belonging to a Jew of Lisbon, which they confessed was on board, and which was valued at 4500*l*. He then made for the Azores, hoisted Spanish colours when he came in sight of St. Michael's, and in a night expedition succeeded in cutting four ships out of the road; one of them, however, proved to be a Londoner, trading there under the Scotch flag, and with a Scotch pilot. His great object was to intercept the carracks, and so reimburse himself for all his costs. At Flores he manned his boats, and obtained refreshments as being a friend to the prior, Don Antonio, whose pretended title to the Portuguese crown was acknowledged by England. "From thence rowing a ship-board, the boat was pursued two miles by a monstrous fish, whose fins many times appeared about the gills above water four or five yards asunder, and his jaws gaping a yard and a half wide, not without great danger of overturning the pinnace, and devouring some of the company." But from this, which was as formidable to the earl's boat as his ship was to a harmless trader, they at last escaped. Here he met and "accepted into consort" Captain Davies, with his ship and pinnace, Captain Markesbury, in a ship of Raleigh's, and the barque *Lime*.

The earl knew not at this time how narrowly the homeward-bound fleet from the East Indies had escaped him. Seven of its huge and richly laden vessels had sailed for Europe early in the year, separately, as they were ready, but with orders to rendezvous at St. Helena, and from thence to proceed in company, no danger being apprehended from cruisers on the first part of the voyage, but much afterwards. The richest of these vessels suffered, on the coast of Natal, one of the most lamentable shipwrecks of which the details have been recorded; the others reached the Azores in the middle of July; and some of the smaller cruisers fell in with them when they were ill able to defend themselves. What with the length of the voyage (for they had been six months on the way), the scarcity of water and of provisions, and the bad quality of the stores that were left (for every kind of knavery was practised in the equipment of the Portuguese ships), the scurvy was making great ravages on board; and every day men who had been some days dead were discovered in the places whither they had crept that they might lie down and die in peace.* If the light vessels which played about them and harassed them, in the hope, as it seemed, of delaying them till others should come up, had been aware of their condition, they might have carried some of them almost without resistance; for there was the utmost confusion as well as misery on board. Those who were in the best plight showed no disposition to assist their weaker comrades, all seeking to secure themselves with all speed under some of their own fortresses; while the English insulted them with reproaches for their cowardice, and annoyed them with musketry, and with such small pieces as vessels of thirty tons could carry. The Portuguese, however, made their way good to Tercera, and anchored in the road before the city of Angra: there, to their dismay, they found that the island was in arms, expecting to be attacked by Drake, and that instructions had arrived from Portugal, ordering them to remain there till they should receive further directions. The alarm occasioned by the destruction of the Armada, the attempt upon Lisbon, and the activity of the English privateers, was such, that it was thought better to expose these rich ships to the danger of an unsheltered road in the worst season of the year than let them run for the Tagus. Luckily for the Portuguese officers they were not expected to render more obedience to the Government than they could exact from their men; after a gale from the south had driven one of the ships on shore, the

* Linschoten, c. xcvi,

other captains ventured to act upon their own judgment, and sail for Lisbon, where they happily arrived.*

Some English prisoners who stole from Tercera in a small boat, having no other yard for their mainsail than two pipe staves, fell in with the earl, and gave him the unwelcome tidings that these carracks had sailed from that island a week before. This induced him to return to Fayal (where he had just taken some small Guinea ships and sent them to England): he now landed there, and took possession of the town, consisting of about 500 well-built houses. It was abandoned at his approach. He set a guard to preserve the churches and monasteries, and stayed there four days, till a ransom of 2000 ducats was brought him, mostly in church plate. He shipped from the platform fifty-eight pieces of iron ordnance; and the Governor of Graciosa, as if to deprecate such a visit, sent him sixty butts of wine. Here a Weymouth privateer, which arrived with a Spanish prize worth 16,000*l.*, brought news that the West India fleet was expected; and after plying three or four days to and fro in rough weather, he saw it, fifteen sail in number, enter Angra Roads; but he being "too far to leeward, and they being strong and fortified with castle and fort," he could make no attempt upon them; and the pinnace which he left to observe them returned with information that they had "taken off their sails and down their topmasts, with the intention of longer stay". The earl then made for St. Michael's, and was there repelled from watering; next he went to St. Mary's, where he found two Brazilian ships laden with sugar. The islanders endeavoured to bring them ashore; but Lister, the earl's captain, "hastening the attempt in the face of the enemy, and in danger of continual shoreshot, boarded the one, cut her cables

---

* Linschoten, *Schip vaert naer Oost, ofte Portugaels Indien*, c. xcvi. Linschoten was in the fleet, and he congratulates himself on having escaped *millort Commerlandt*, p. 146.

and hawser, and rowed her away". Captain Davies entered the other, which was aground, and had been abandoned; but he was forced to forsake her by a fire from the shore, with the loss of two slain and sixteen wounded. In bringing out their prize the bar detained them in a position exposed to an enemy whose force had been rashly undervalued: eighty men were killed; the earl received three shot upon his target, a fourth wounded him slightly in the side, "his head, also, was broken with stones, so that the blood covered his face," and both his face and legs were burnt with fire-balls. The prize, however, was brought off, and "the *Meg* being leaky" was sent with it to England.

The earl himself held his course for Spain. On the way he fell in with a Portuguese ship laden with sugar, from Brazil, and afterwards with one of the fleet which had taken shelter from him in Angra Roads. It proved to be a ship of 400 tons, from St. Juan de Ulloa, laden with hides, cochineal, sugar and silver, and the captain had with him a venture to the amount of 25,000 ducats. Full of joy at their good speed, they now resolved upon returning home. "But sea-fortunes," says Purchas, "are variable, having two inconstant parents, air and water"; and, in the words of one of the adventurers,[*] "these summer services and ships of sugar proved not so sweet and pleasant as the winter was afterwards sharp and painful". Captain Lister was sent in the Mexican prize for Portsmouth. She was wrecked at Helcliff, in Cornwall: everything was lost in her, and five or six only of the people were saved. Contrary weather delayed the earl so long upon his homeward passage that drink began to fail, and he endeavoured to make some Irish harbour, but there, too, was beaten off by the wind; and, the beer and water being by that time all spent, three spoonfuls of vinegar were allowed to each man at a meal, with some small relief, squeezed out of the lees of their

---

[*] Sir William Monson, *Churchill's Coll.*, iii., 161.

wine vessels. During fourteen days they had no other drink than this, except what they could collect in rain and hail storms in their sheets and napkins. "Some drank up the soiled running water at the scupper holes; others saved, by device, the running down the masts and tarred ropes; and many licked the moist boards, rails and masts with their tongues, like dogs. Yet was that rain so intermingled with the spray of the foaming sea, in that extreme storm, that it could not be healthful; yea, some in their extremity of thirst, drank themselves to death, with their cans of salt water in their hands." "By this time, the lamentable cries of the sick and hurt men for drink were heard in every corner of the ship." Many perished for want of it—"ten or twelve every night"; and in this manner more were lost "than otherwise had miscarried in the whole voyage". The mortality, indeed, was so great "that the like befell not any other fleet during the war.* The storm continuing added to their misery, tearing the ship in such sort that his lordship's cabin, the dining-room, and the half-deck became all one, and he was forced to seek a new lodging in the hold." Such circumstances call forth, in such men, the qualities by which alone, with God's blessing, they can be overcome; the earl, upon all occasions, encouraged his men by his promptitude, his presence of mind, and his example; and the small store of provisions was distributed equally to the prisoners and to his

* Sir William Monson, *Churchill's Coll.*, iii., 162. "All these disasters," Monson says, "must be imputed to Capt. Lister's rashness, upon whom my Lord of Cumberland chiefly relied, wanting experience himself. He was the man that advised the sending the ships of wine for England; otherwise we had not known the want of drink. He was as earnest in persuading our landing in the face of the fortifications of St. Mary's, against all reason and sense. As he was rash, so was he valiant: but paid dearly for his unadvised counsel; for he was the first man hurt, and that cruelly, in the attempt of St. Mary's, and afterwards drowned in the rich ship cast away at Mount's Bay." He values that ship at 100,000*l*.

own people. On the last of November they spoke a vessel, which promised them some barrels of wine the next morning; but their hopes were disappointed, for the vessel went on shore during the night. The next day, however, he fell in with another, which helped him with some beer, but not enough for him to venture upon making for England: so as the wind served, he put into Ventre haven, on the west coast of Ireland. There their sufferings ended, and on the 20th of December he sailed for England. On arriving in London, he learned the recent death of his eldest son; but was comforted a few weeks after by the birth of a daughter, the Lady Anne Clifford, afterwards the famous Countess of Pembroke.

In this voyage he had taken thirteen prizes; and although the one which was lost was worth more than all the rest, yet the profit doubled the outlay of his adventure. Encouraged by this success, as well as inflamed by former disappointments, and being thoroughly possessed by the spirit of the age, he obtained a ship of 600 tons from the queen, with which, and with four other vessels, he set forth in 1591, at his own charge, for the coast of Spain. On the way he met with several Dutch ships, coming from Lisbon, and with spices on board, which were Portuguese property: "So greatly," says Monson, "were we abused by that nation of Holland, who, though they were the first that engaged us in the war with Spain, yet still maintained their own trade into those ports, and supplied the Spaniards with ammunition, victuals, shipping, and intelligence against us". They who regarded the conduct of the Dutch merchants in this point of view, and made it a ground for reproaching the nation, did not bear in mind that the struggle in which the Low Countries were engaged with Spain was, in its origin, purely a religious war, and that many of these merchants might be of the Romish religion, consequently Spanish at heart, and acting as much in conformity with their own sense of duty, as Roman Catholic Christians and loyal subjects, as with their own immediate interest.

Still less were Englishmen likely to consider, what certainly was the case, that some of the Dutch, who thus endeavoured to save Portuguese property from the privateers, were Jews of Portuguese birth or blood, trading with their brethren who secretly held the same faith, and many of whom were desirous of removing themselves, as well as their property, from a land where they were in perpetual danger of the Inquisition. Least of all did our licensed sea rovers make allowance for the views of commercial men, who, in continuing a long-established trade with their old connections, had fair intentions, though they were compelled to use false colours, and knew that the commerce which they carried on was beneficial to their own Government, and, in fact, received from that Government all the secret encouragement that it could give.*

* Charnock, who hated the Dutch, says the rapid progress of their naval power "was effected by a steady and uniform perseverance in one system, from which they never suffered themselves to be diverted for a single moment by any supposed and imaginary evil attendant on the prosecution of it. This fundamental principle (for so it might truly be deemed, being the point or centre stone from whence all their maxims of government sprang, and on which alone, according to the mode in which the fabric was constructed, they depended for support) consisted in an unalterable resolution, that public hostilities should never be permitted, even for a single moment, to interrupt private commerce. So completely bigoted were the people and the Government to this opinion, that in the very height of the war the Dutch vessels entered the Spanish ports with their commodities (the want of which would have distressed their enemies extremely) with as much cordiality and unconcern as though they had been in perfect amity with them. They are even reported to have carried this idea, which by all other nations has been deemed extravagant and improper, to such an extent, as to have supplied their antagonists with ammunition and stores of different kinds, which, had they not obtained from some quarter or other, it would not have been possible for them to have carried on the war" (*Hist. of Marine Arch.*, ii., 168).

Charnock did not perceive how much might be alleged in defence of the system which he thus condemns; and he has altogether overlooked the other motives noticed in the text, powerfully as they must have influenced the Dutch at that time.

Proceeding to the coast of Spain, the earl "took good purchase," but to little profit. One prize, laden with sugar from St. Thomas's, he was forced to cast off because of an irremediable leak: another, which he sent for England, was, after long contrary winds, compelled to put into Corunna for want of victuals, and his men to render themselves to the enemy's mercy. He was not more fortunate with the spices which had been taken from the Hollanders. These were put on board a ship for England, the squadron convoyed her to the Berlings, from whence Captain Monson, who was on board, was to see her safely despatched. But the other ships did not observe the directions given them: the night fell calm; and in the morning six galleys from Peniche, seeing that this vessel was at a distance from her companions, and that, by reason of the calm, they could not come up to her assistance, attacked her. A brave resistance was made: but Captain Bayly and the principal men being slain, both ship and spices were taken; and Monson, with all the others who survived, made prisoners. Luckily for himself, Monson, but a little before, having surprised two vessels, merely for the sake of obtaining information, had let them go again without offering any injury to the people on board. His reason for dismissing the ships was, that they were not worth taking; but the men, thankful for their deliverance, made a favourable report of the usage which they had received at his hand,* and he now found the benefit of this good character. "Whether it was," he says, "the respect they had to the queen's ship, which was admiral of that fleet, or honour to my lord that commanded it, or hope by good usage of our men to receive the like again, I know not; but true it is, that the ordinary men were treated with more courtesy than they had been from the beginning of the war."† Some effect may also have been produced by a letter which the earl sent to

* Monson, 460. † *Ibid.*, 164.

the Archduke Albert, at that time Governor of Portugal, requesting that the prisoners might be well used; and intimating that upon their treatment would depend that of the Spaniards and Portuguese, "of whom, he presumed, he should take store ".* This led to an agreement, by which the other prisoners were released upon terms, for the performance of which Monson was detained as hostage.

The intelligence which the earl had obtained was of some importance. The Spaniards had, with great exertions, fitted out a formidable fleet.† As soon as he learnt this, he despatched one of his ships with the advice to Lord Thomas Howard, who was then off the Western Islands, waiting to intercept the West Indian fleet; and it arrived just in time to put him upon his guard, and enable him to avoid the danger.‡ But having sent off this vessel, and being weakened by the loss of another with its crew, and especially finding the queen's ship "but ill of sail, it being the first voyage she had had to sea, he durst not abide the coast of Spain, but thought it more discretion to return to England. Thus ended the third of his maritime adventures, and nothing whatever was taken in it toward defraying the great charges of its outfit."

The naval history of England is so much beholden to Sir William Monson that it would be treating him with ingratitude, as well as disrespect, if the story of his captivity were pretermitted. For some months he was kept on board the galleys at Cascaes and Lisbon, which "was most grievous to him"; and while lying in the Tagus, he planned means of escaping, by aid of a good-natured Dutchman, the master of a Dutch vessel, which had come from Brazil; "for at that time the Portuguese freighted Holland ships in most of their long voyages, though they pretended to be in war one with another". The war,

* Purchas, iv., 1144.
† "Little inferior," Monson says, "to that of 1588."
‡ Monson, 163, 164. Purchas, 1144.

however, was more than a pretence, as both nations found to their cost, and nowhere more dearly than in Brazil itself. But the day before this scheme was to have been put in execution, the galleys were ordered to sea. In September, when the galleys were commonly laid up for the winter, he and eight other Englishmen were sent to the castle at Lisbon, " there to be imprisoned till a course was taken for their redemption ". Each man had for his maintenance a daily allowance of $7\tfrac{1}{2}d.$,— " A proportion," he says, "that did not equal three-pence according to the rate of things in England". The humanities of war will always be in proportion to the established standard of military honour, one as it were regulating the other; and in wars which are exasperated by religious hatred both are disregarded. Monson and his comrades in captivity were closely confined all the time of their imprisonment; only in the morning they resorted to the castle walls, with a guard of soldiers,—even decent privacy being refused them. "It happened," says this officer, "on St. Andrew's Day, being upon the walls at our usual hour, we beheld a great galleon of the king's turning up the river in her fighting sails, being sumptuously decked with ancients, streamers, and pendants, with all other ornaments, to show her bravery. She let fly all her ordnance in a triumphant manner for the taking Sir Richard Grenville in the *Revenge*, at the Island of Flores, she being one of that fleet, and the first voyage she ever made. I confess it was one of the greatest and sorrowfullest sights that ever my eyes beheld, to see the cause the Spaniards had to boast, and no remedy in me to revenge it but in my tongue." He expressed, however, to his countrymen a hope of such future comfort, and offered to give them one on condition of receiving ten, should he live to be at the taking of that triumphal galleon: its name was not likely to escape his memory, for it was *St. Andrew*,—and some of the gala bravery which he attributed to the joy of this victory was no doubt intended in honour of its patron saint upon his festival. This passed only as an idle desire to see his word come to effect: to effect, however, it came, five years afterwards, in the Cadiz expedition; for the *St. Andrew* was one of the five galleons which were run ashore, and one of the two that were brought off by the conquerors, and Monson commanded in the boat that saved and took possession of her.*

A Portuguese, by name Manoel Fernandes, was at this time a prisoner in the castle. He had been in the service of the prior, Don Antonio, and having emigrated with him, had returned, as his emissary, to encourage the hopes of his party, and prepare them for taking up arms in his favour when opportunity might offer: in this he was discovered, and must have suffered death, if influence and money, which have always been all but all-powerful in Portugal, had not been employed with such effect in his behalf that, after seven years' imprisonment, he was now on the point of being enlarged. Among the persons who visited him in prison was a pilot, who was usually employed to meet the Indian fleets, with letters directing them what course they should hold, according as information had been obtained concerning the English cruisers. It occurred to Monson that, by means of Fernandes, it might be possible to corrupt this man, and give such intelligence to the queen's ships, as should enable them to fall in with the treasure fleet. He made no scruple of proposing this design to Fernandes, whose political feelings were in no degree mitigated either by time or the mercy that had been shown him; and the pilot, who, if he were an Antonian at heart, would be hardly the less villain for betraying his trust, entered into the scheme. Monson then wrote letters to Lord Burleigh, and to the lord admiral, informing them of the train which he had thus laid. As he had a page who was allowed to wait on him in his confinement this boy was to convey the letters, and they were secreted in the soles of

* Monson, 466.

his shoes. Unfortunately for all parties, Monson had been obliged to use an Englishman as an interpreter. No Englishman could then reside in Portugal unless he professed the Portuguese religion; and this person thought that he consulted best for his conscience and safety, and interest at the same time, by disclosing the plot. The boy was seized, and marched to Belem Castle, through one of those violent rains, which can hardly be imagined by those who have never witnessed them: to that rain both he and his master were indebted for their lives; for it was not till they had lodged their prisoner at Belem that they ripped the soles of his shoes, and the letters had by that time been so thoroughly soaked that they were quite illegible, so that no proof whatever could be drawn from them.

The Government, however, had such good reason for believing the informer's story, that they proceeded against Fernandes for his old treason, and a day was appointed for executing his sentence of death. He consulted with Monson, and was provided with a cudgel and a rope: by fixing the cudgel across two of the battlements of the wall, he might let himself down by the rope, and thus, it was hoped, take sanctuary in a church hard by: but upon closer inquiry it was found that this could not be done in the day-time. They then called to mind, that over the room in which he lay was a chamber wherein soldiers had been lodged, but which had been just left unoccupied. They cut a trap door through the ceiling of the one room, which was the floor of the other; and when night came, Fernandes, who had procured a scabbard and a wooden sword, ventured from the upper apartment, passed through the guards, who seeing the sword by his side took him for a soldier, to the wall, let himself down, and reached a place of concealment. Ere long the watch, or round as it is called, passing about the castle, espied the rope by which he had descended; the alarm was given; the prisoners were questioned; all agreed that Monson was the likeliest person to have been privy to the escape, and Monson accordingly was brought before a judge to be examined on the following morning. Every artifice was used that could either intimidate or tempt him to confess his part of the transaction; but he denied all knowledge of it; pretended that it was impossible for him to plot with a man with whom he could carry on no conversation, because each was ignorant of the other's language; and argued, that if he had done what he was accused of it could not be deemed an offence, for not having come into that land by his own will to carry on any designs against the state, but having been brought there as a prisoner of war, it was lawful for him to seek his own liberty, and to neglect no occasion wherein he might do service to his own prince and country. They could prove nothing against him that deserved punishment by the universal law of honour and arms; and he bade them be wary what violence they offered him, for he had friends in England, and was of a nation that both could and would revenge any cruelty that might be used towards him. The boldest defence was the best, and Monson took the right ground when he spoke of the strength and spirit of the English people; though the plea would have availed little if Fernandes had been taken, for he had provided him with a letter addressed to all English captains at sea; the design being that the fugitive should put himself into a fishing-boat and look out for a man-of-war to transport him to England. When the judge found that nothing could be drawn from him, he was remanded to the castle, with orders to be more strictly watched: no violence was used towards him, but no art left unattempted by which he might be entrapped.

Fernandes had faithful friends: among them he was concealed till the eagerness of the search for him had abated, and means could be taken for engaging a fishing-boat. At length he embarked, but with such ill fortune, that, having been a fortnight at sea without meeting an English ship, and wearied with sea-sickness, he was forced to return to shore, where he "lived some time among poor shepherds and herdsmen," till he thought that, disfigured as he was by fatigue, and sufferings, and exposure, and disguised also, he might venture to show himself, and ask alms. It so happened, however, that he begged at the house of one who had been fellow-prisoner with him. This person recognised him, and immediately called a servant; and Fernandes, not waiting to ascertain with what intention his old comrade had done this, ran into the church thereby, and took sanctuary, thus betraying himself by his own fears. Information was immediately despatched to the cardinal prince, and he, paying no regard to the sanctuary, ordered him to be reconveyed to his old lodging in the castle; the law then proceeded against him, and he was condemned to death, not without grief to many of the beholders; for Monson says: "He was a man of much goodness and great charity". The day of execution arrived, the last acts of religion were performed, and he was brought out of prison "with a winding-sheet lapped bandelier fashion about him". Many gathered around to give him their last adieu; and on taking leave of the soldiers he requested that in return for all his former kindness to them, one of them would with all speed hasten to the Misericordia, and inform the brethren of that institution of the injury done to God, themselves, and the Holy Church, by taking perforce a penitent sinner out of sanctuary. Fernandes had made himself so well liked during his long imprisonment, that happy was he who could make most speed upon this errand; and some of the brethren making no delay hastened on horseback to the place of execution, "where they found poor Senhor Fernandes ready to commend his spirit to God, and the hangman as ready to perform his office". Their interference was effectual, under a Government which implicitly conformed to whatever was required of it in the name of the Church; and thus his life was saved. Before this occurred Monson had been released; the conditions, for the performance of which he was detained in pledge, having been performed.*

The queen had given command "not to lay any Spanish vessel aboard with her ships, lest both might together be destroyed by fire"; and in this injunction the earl found so much inconvenience, that he chose rather "to seek out amongst the merchants than to make further use of the ships royal". So he hired the *Tiger* of 600 tons, for 300*l*. a month wages, in which, and with his own ship the *Samson*, the *Golden Noble*, and two small vessels, he set forth. The winds proved so adverse, that three months' victuals were spent in harbours before they could get to the westward of Plymouth. This frustrated his chief design, which was to intercept the outward-bound carracks, and it consumed also the stores that had been provided for a West India voyage: the earl therefore transferred the command to Captain Norton, with orders to go for the Azores, and returned to London. The voyage proved a most eventful one. They called at Flores, where the English cruisers used to take in water and refreshments at will, because the islanders had no means of resisting them; learning there that the homeward-bound East India ships must be near, they spread themselves in quest, and ere long came in sight of the *Santa Cruz*, which was some days' sail a-head of her comrades. The Portuguese made all sail for Angra; and the pursuers, when within half a league of her, discovered an English ship standing to cross her way, so that she was fain to luff up, the wind being westerly, and make for the road of Lagens on the south of the Isle of Flores. The English vessel proved to be the *Roebuck* of 200 tons, Sir John Burroughs, commander, the admiral of a squadron which Raleigh had fitted out. The wind soon fell, so as not to yield breath for spreading a sail; and, as no way could then be made on either side, Burroughs took his boat

* Monson, 461, 462.

and rowed near enough the enemy to ascertain what she was, of what burden, force, and countenance; having "made her exactly," he consulted with Norton, and they agreed to board her in the morning. A storm in the night forced them all to weigh anchor. "Yet their care was such in wrestling with the weather, not to lose the carrack, that in the morning, the tempest being qualified," they recovered the road and saw the carrack warped as near the shore as she could be brought, with all her sails up and flags flying. The Portuguese had carried all they could on shore, and then, at sight of the English, set fire to her, "that neither glory of victory nor benefit of ship might remain to their enemies". The guns went off as the fire reached them; and lest the English should endeavour to extinguish the fire, some of the Portuguese entrenched themselves near enough for defending the approach. Burroughs ordered 100 men to disperse them: the surge was so high that, for fear of losing their boats, the men were up to the neck in water, and some over head and ears, before they could reach the shore; and then they were forced to climb on hands and knees up a steep hill, from the top of which the islanders rolled great stones upon them; but all difficulties were overcome by resolution and hope: they entered the town without further opposition, and then possessed themselves of what little had been landed, or was drifted on shore from the wreck.

What was of more consequence, they obtained from some prisoners, by threats of torture, information that three larger carracks, at little distance, were holding the same course. By this time more of Raleigh's vessels had come up, with Sir Robert Cross in the *Foresight*, a queen's ship; their united numbers were now sufficient, by spreading from north to south, yet keeping in sight of one another, to discover the space of two whole degrees. On the fifth day the *Madre de Dios* came in sight, one of the largest carracks belonging to the crown of Portugal. Thomson, who came up with her first, in a ship of Sir John Hawkins's, "again and again delivered his peals as fast as he could fire, and fall astern to load again, thus hindering her way, though somewhat to his own cost, till the others could come up". Burroughs and the *Golden Dragon* came up next, and the former received a shot under water in the bread-room, which made him bear up to stop the leak. Sir Robert Cross then "coming to give his broadside, came so near, that, becalming his sail, he unwillingly fell aboard the carrack, which lashed his ship fast by the shrouds, and sailed away with her by her side". The earl's ships, being the worst sailers, came up last, about eleven at night, and Captain Norton had no intention to board the enemy before daylight, if there had not been a cry from the *Foresight*, "An you be men save the queen's ship!" Upon this he laid the carrack aboard on one side, while the *Tiger* boarded her on the other, through the *Foresight*. That ship took the opportunity to free herself. A desperate struggle ensued when the men had entered into the forechains, "the forecastle being so high, that without any resistance the getting up had been difficult; but here was strong resistance, some irrecoverably falling by the board, and the assault continued an hour and half, so brave a booty making the men fight like dragons". But when the forecastle was won, the Portuguese sought where to hide themselves. The English turned to pillage, "and were ready to go to the ears about it, each man lighting a candle"; and by this they had nearly lost their prize, for by their carelessness they fired a cabin, in which were some hundred cartridges, and they were as eager then to forsake the carrack as they had been to board her, if Norton and some others had not "adventured the quenching of that flame".

When the prisoners were secured, the general "first had presented to his eyes the true proportion of the vast body of this carrack, which," says the writer in Hakluyt, "did then, and may still, justly provoke the admiration of all men not formerly acquainted with such a sight. But albeit this first appearance of the hugeness thereof yielded sights enough to entertain our men's eyes, yet the pitiful object of so many bodies slain and dismembered could not but draw each man's eye to see, and heart to lament, and hands to help, those miserable people, whose limbs were torn with the violence of shot. No man could almost step but upon a dead carcass or a bloody floor, but especially about the helm; for the greatness of the steerage requiring the labour of twelve or fourteen men at once, and some of our ships beating her in at the stern with her ordnance, oftentimes with one shot slew four or five labouring on either side of the helm; whose room being still furnished with fresh supplies, and our artillery still playing upon them with continual volleys, it could not be but that much blood should be shed in that place. Whereupon our general, moved with singular commiseration of their misery, sent them his own chirurgeons, denying them no possible help or relief that he or any of his company could afford them." It may be feared that such humanity, at that time, deserved this special commendation; but Sir John Burroughs acted towards his prisoners with a generosity which was not less rare; for, "moved with compassion of human misery, and not to add too much affliction to the afflicted, he dismissed the captain and most of his followers freely to their own country, and for that purpose bestowed them in one of the earl's vessels, furnished with all things necessary". The captain, Don Fernando de Mendoza, was "a gentleman of noble birth, well stricken in years, well spoken, of comely personage, of good stature, but of hard fortune. Twice he had been taken prisoner by the Moors and ransomed by the king; and he had been wrecked on the coast of Sofala, in a carrack which he commanded, and, having escaped the sea danger, fell into the hands of infidels on shore, who kept him under long and grievous servitude." The prisoners who were thus released were not searched: so rich a prize, indeed, might well content the captors; and they who had lost so much might be permitted to carry with them such of their own valuables as they could. They had, however, the ill hap to fall in with other English cruisers, who took from them, "thus negligently dismissed," says our narrator, "900 diamonds, besides other odd ends".

About 800 black men (if that number be not overstated) were landed on the Island of Corvo. "Having thus disposed of their prisoners, contention about the prize was "well-nigh kindling in the commanders, being so many and so diversely employed". But Burroughs, "to cut off the unprofitable spoil and pillage," to which he saw that many were inclined, promptly and prudently took charge of the whole in the queen's name, the others consenting; for, indeed, it appeared, upon "a slender rummaging of such things as first came to hand, that the wealth would arise nothing disanswerable to expectation, but that the variety and grandeur of all rich commodities would be more than sufficient to content both the adventurer's desire and the soldier's travail. And here," says our narrator, "I cannot but enter into the consideration and acknowledgment of God's great favour towards our nation, who, by putting this purchase into our hands, hath manifestly discovered those secret trades and Indian riches, which hitherto lay strangely hidden and cunningly concealed from us; whereof there was among some few of us some small and imperfect glimpse only which now is turned into the broad light of full and perfect knowledge. Whereby it should seem that the will of God for our good is (if our weakness could apprehend it) to have us communicate with them in those East Indian treasures, and, by the erection of a lawful traffic, to better our means to advance true religion and His holy service. The carrack being in burden, by the estimation of the wise and experienced, no less than 1600 tons, had full 900 of those stowed with the gross bulk of merchandise; the rest of the tonnage being allowed, partly to the ordnance, which were thirty-two pieces of brass of all sorts, partly to the passengers and the victuals, which could not be any small quantity, considering the number of persons, —between 600 and 700,—and the length of the navigation. To give you a taste, as it were, of the commodities, it shall suffice to deliver you a general particularity of them, according to the catalogue taken at Leadenhall, the 15th of September, 1592. (It is remarkable that this should have been the place where an account was taken of the first East Indian cargo that was ever brought to England.) Upon good view it was found that the principal wares, after the jewels (which were no doubt of great value, though they never came to light), consisted of spices, drugs, silks, calicoes, quilts, carpets, and colours, etc. The spices were pepper, cloves, maces, nutmegs, cinnamon, green ginger. The drugs were benjamin, frankincense, galingale, mirabolans, aloes, socotrina, camphire. The silks, damasks, taffatas, sarcenets, altobassos, that is, counterfeit cloth of gold, unwrought China silk, sleaved silk, white twisted silk, curled cypress. The calicoes were book calicoes, calico-lawns, broad white calicoes, fine starched calicoes, coarse white calicoes, brown broad calicoes, brown coarse calicoes. There were also canopies and coarse diaper towels, quilts of coarse sarcenet and of calico, carpets like those of Turkey; whereunto are to be added the pearl, musk, civet, and ambergris. The rest of the wares were many in number, but less in value, as elephants' teeth, porcelain vessels of China, cocoa-nuts, hides, ebon wood as black as jet, bedsteads of the same, cloth of the rinds of trees, very strange for the matter, and artificial in workmanship. All which piles of commodities, being by men of approved judgment rated but in reasonable sort, amounted to no less than 150,000*l*., which being divided among the adventurers, whereof her Majesty was the chief, was sufficient to yield contentment to all parties." *

* Hakluyt, ii., 198.

But, in truth, the parties were not contented: they had expected far too much, and they received somewhat too little. The Earl of Cumberland's share had been estimated by his friends, "according to his employment of ships and men," to two or three millions, so extravagant were their notions! "But because his commission, large enough otherwise, had not provided for the case of his return, and substituting another in his place, some adjudged it to depend on the queen's mercy and bounty."* The queen's adventure in this voyage was only two ships, one only of which, and that the least, was at the capture, and would have been carried off by the carrack, like a lark in a hawk's talons, if the earl's ships had not come to the rescue; yet of this title, "joined with her royal authority," she made such use, that the adventurers were fain to submit themselves to her pleasure, and "she dealt but indifferently with them," says Monson;† —rather, indeed, anything but indifferently. The lioness took her share; and the jackals also helped themselves well, as well at her cost as that of the other claimants. The queen had not "the account of the fifth part of her value, by reason of some men's embezzling, and the earl was fain to accept of 36,000*l.*, for him and his, as out of gift".‡

The size of the carrack excited great admiration. She had nearly been wrecked on the Scilly rocks, and having put into Dartmouth, was unladen there, and the goods sent to London in ten vessels. "But to the end that the bigness, height, length, breadth, and other dimensions, of so huge a vessel might by the exact rules of geometrical observations be truly taken, both for present knowledge and derivation also of the same unto posterity, one M. Robert Adams, a man, in his faculty, of excellent skill, omitted nothing in the description which either his art could demonstrate, or any man's judgment think worthy the memory. After an exquisite

---

* Purchas, 1145.   † P. 165.   ‡ Purchas.

survey of the whole frame, he found the length from the beak-head to the stern (whereupon was erected a lantern) to contain 165 foot. The breadth in the second close deck (whereof she had three), this being the place where there was most extension of breadth, was forty-six foot ten inches. She drew in water thirty-one foot at her departure from Cochim in India, but not above twenty-six at her arrival in Dartmouth, being lightened in her voyage by divers means some five foot. She carried in height seven several stories, one main orlop, three close decks, one fore-castle, and a spar-deck of two floors apiece. The length of the keel was 100 foot, of the main mast 121, and the circuit about at the partners ten foot seven; the main yard was 106 foot long. By which perfect commensuration of the parts appeareth the hugeness of the whole, far beyond the mould of the biggest shipping used among us either for war or receit."* "Being so huge and unwieldy a ship," says another writer, "she was never removed from Dartmouth, but there laid up her bones."†

The success of this last voyage encouraged the earl to more adventures; and he imputed his former failures more to the negligence or unfaithfulness of those whom he had employed to lay in his stores, than to any other cause. His objections to the queen's ships seem to have been removed by the bravery with which the *Foresight* had run aboard the great *Madre de Dios;* and planning now two expeditions at the same time, he obtained two ships royal, which he victualled himself, and with seven others in company sailed for the coast of Spain, from whence he despatched three of these to the West Indies. On the Spanish coast he had the good fortune to fall in with two French vessels from St. Maloes: that port held for the League; the ships therefore were accounted Spaniards, and they were rich enough to repay the costs of

* Hakluyt, 199.   † Purchas, 1145.

his voyage more than threefold. One day, being separated from the rest of his fleet, off Peniche, he met with twelve hulks in the same place where Monson had been captured by the galleys exactly two years before on the same day. He required from them that respect which was due to her Majesty's ship; and they, presuming upon the strength of twelve against one, not considering how much better that one was prepared for war, refused to render it. After two hours' fight he brought them to his mercy; and they to obtain it delivered up a great quantity of ammunition which they carried for the King of Spain's service. And here the earl committed an error that might have cost him dear; for, standing out to sea with some of these hulks, he left Monson in his long boat with fifty men to rummage the others. Towards evening, those which he had under his custody gave him the slip, and returned to their comrades; and Monson would again have been made prisoner in his turn if he had not leaped out of the vessel into his boat on one side as they boarded him on the other; and in so doing he received a hurt in the leg, which annoyed him during the remainder of his life.

The earl, upon the intelligence which he obtained here, made for the Western Islands, hoping to fall in with the carracks before they should meet the Portuguese fleet which had been ordered thither to convoy them. One of that fleet he captured off the Isle of Flores; but being far too weak to encounter their whole force, of which he obtained sight the next day, he stood off to avoid them, and hovered about for three weeks, till he learned that the carracks had passed safely. By this time he had been taken ill; and life is said to have been saved by cow's milk, Monson having ventured ashore in Corvo, and there obtained a milch cow, what with threats and what with promises of reward. They then made homeward; and the whole fleet were so parted during a calm, which lasted several days, that they never saw each other again till they met in England some four or five weeks afterwards. This was the most gainful voyage that the earl made "before or after".*

Meantime the three ships which had been despatched to the West Indies reached St. Lucia, refreshed themselves there, and made for the pearl fishery at Margarita. That fishery was carried on in four *rancheries,* or assemblages of huts: six or seven such villages were erected on different parts of the coast, though only one at a time was occupied; and when the fishery failed in one place, the persons engaged in it removed to another, the empty huts being always ready for them. The pearls, for safety, were carried monthly to Margarita, which stood about three leagues from the shore. Langton, who commanded the privateers, having taken a Spaniard, and learned from him the situation of the inhabited *rancheria,* surprised it by a night march with twenty-eight men, and carried off about 2000*l.* worth of pearls. Afterwards, he brought the ships there, and compelled the inhabitants to ransom their huts and canoes for as many pearls as were valued at 2000 ducats. The alarm had now been given, and when they tried a landing at Cumana they were fain to retire, not without loss. They had no better fortune on any part of the Spanish main. Making then for Hispaniola, they were glad to provide themselves with water upon the little Island of Savona, procured by digging a hole not twenty paces from the wash of the sea, and setting a hogshead therein with the head knocked out, by which means, water, "losing its saltness in that passage," was plentifully taken. They now coasted along, exacting contributions from the different *estancias* and *ingenios,* that is to say, breeding farms and sugar works, as they went. After eight months spent to little profit in hovering about Hispaniola, Jamaica, and Cuba, they made for the Bay of Honduras, and within four leagues of

* Monson, 166. Purchas, 1146.

Porto Cavallo descried seven ships in the road. Though they were then only two in company they anchored within caliver shot, moored their ships head and stern, and bent their broadsides unto them, and there fought all that day with those seven ships, and all night now and then a shot. The next day they brought a vessel of twenty tons from the shore, set her on fire, and endeavoured with their boats to bring her across the *Admiral;* but when the Spaniards saw their intent they got into their boats and made for the land, carrying the rudders with them, that none should sail away with the ships. The English laded the *Admiral* with the best out of the other vessels, and sent ashore to ask if the Spaniards would ransom the rest; and as the answer was delayed, they first fired one which was laden with hides and logwood, and then another with a cargo of sarsaparilla; but all such ransoming had been forbidden by the king, and the privateers were left to take their own course. Nothing more is related of their proceedings, except that they heaved the ordnance overboard, saving two or three brass pieces, in hope some Englishmen might be the better for them afterwards, brought away the *Admiral* of 250 tons, and carried this prize safely to Plymouth.*

In the ensuing year, the earl set forth on his eighth voyage, at his own charge, with the help of some adventurers. The force consisted of the *Royal Exchange*, 250, Captain George Cave; the *May Flower*, of the same burden, Vice-Admiral Captain William Antony; the *Samson*, Rear-Admiral Captain Nicholas Downton; a caravel, and a small pinnace. Early in April they sailed from Plymouth, came in sight of St. Michael's at the beginning of June, and ten days afterwards they descried a great Indian ship, whose burden they estimated at 2000 tons; and which, indeed, was one of the largest ships ever employed in the Indian trade.† The fate of this

* Purchas, 1147. † *Ibid.*

unhappy ship has been fully recorded by the Portuguese as well as by the English.

The name of this carrack was the *Cinco Chagas*, or Five Wounds, in reverential honour of which it had, with the usual Romish ceremonies on such occasions, been named. The Capitam Mor Francisco de Mello embarked in her from Goa, in 1593, at the same time that the other ships of the fleet sailed from Cochim; all, according to the customary and fatal improvidence of the Portuguese, deeply overladen. After vainly endeavouring to make the Cape, the *Chagas*, with much difficulty, put back to Mozambique, and wintered there. Thither also the *Nazareth* put back, arriving in such a state that it was found impossible to repair her. She had been built of ill-seasoned timber, and, in consequence of over-freight, had suffered so much in bad weather that her reaching the island was considered little less than miraculous; and there also arrived 117 Portuguese and 65 slaves, being the remainder of the crew of the ship *St. Alberto:* that ship had been wrecked upon the Penedo dos Fontes; and Nuno Velho, formerly commandant at Sofala, taking command of the people, directed their course so well, that, by an inland journey of 300 leagues, he brought them in three months to the Isle of Inhaca, and from thence found means of embarking them for Mozambique. Of all the other Portuguese ships, many as they were, which had been wrecked upon that fatal coast, the people, though in very many cases they got to shore, had always perished; and there are no tales of shipwreck more deeply distressful than the faithful relations which have been preserved respecting their sufferings. Many of these people deemed it better to return to India than pursue a voyage which had so miserably begun. For others who persevered room was made in the *Chagas;* and that ship, taking on board the jewels of the other two vessels (for this part of the *St. Alberto's* treasures had been saved), and the whole lading of the *Nazareth*, sailed once more for Europe, her crew consisting of about 1400 persons, of whom 270 were slaves.*

Before this ill-fated vessel passed the Cape it encountered long and frequent storms, which compelled it to throw overboard much of its cargo, and some of its provisions also. All on board expected that they should have made for St. Helena, when the captain produced his instructions, whereby, upon a report that the English would be there, he was forbidden to touch at that place; and ordered, in case his food or water ran low, to put into St. Paulo de Loanda. These orders, though against his own judgment, he thought it his duty to obey: to Loanda therefore he went, remained there a few days, took many slaves on board, and meeting soon afterwards with the usual calms in that pestilential region, the fatal disease known by the name of the mal de Loanda carried off about half the crew, and left the survivors in a state of miserable weakness. His further instructions were to make for the Isle of Corvo, where there would be a fleet to protect him: but at Mozambique he had learnt the destruction of the *Santa Cruz,* and the capture of the *Madre de Dios;* and having held a council when they came in the latitude of the Azores, it was resolved that they should avoid those islands altogether. Before, however, three days had elapsed, a mutinous representation against this determination was got up among the soldiers; and upon inquiring into the state of the stores the report was, that it was absolutely necessary to touch at the islands, and there take in provisions and water. Accordingly they steered for Corvo; and being fully aware that privateers would be cruising in that direction, they prepared, as well as their debilitated state would permit, for

* *Historia Tragico-Maritima,* ii., 507-511. In the same volume (pp. 217-313) there is a full and most interesting relation of the shipwreck of the *Santo Alberto,* and the subsequent march of the crew, till they embarked for Mozambique: the account was drawn up by Joam Baptista Lavanha, the king's chief cosmographer.

battle. A little while fortune favoured them. They came in sight of Corvo; but the wind prevented them from coming to anchor there: they stood therefore for Fayal, and off that island fell in with the Earl of Cumberland's squadron.*

"The *May Flower* first got up to her, and received an unwelcome salutation. In the night, the *Samson* came in, and continued the fight, and at last the admiral. They agreed that the admiral should lay the carrack aboard on the prow, the vice-admiral on the waist, and the rear-admiral on the quarter; but it fell out that the admiral, laying her aboard at the loof, recoiled astern, the vice-admiral being so near that she was fain to run with her bolt-sprit between the two quarters, which forced the rear-admiral to lay her aboard on the bow." The Portuguese had pledged themselves to each other that they would defend the ship to the last, and rather perish with her in the sea or in the flames, than surrender so rich a prize to the heretics. There were many brave and honourable men on board of the old Portuguese stamp, capable of adhering to such a resolution; but those who had no honour to lose, and lives at stake, were so greatly the majority that if there had been an alternative they would not have been allowed to choose. One of the most distinguished persons, Don Rodrigo de Cordoba, had both his legs shattered; and, as he was carried below in a dying state, he exclaimed: "Sirs, I have got this in the discharge of my duty. Be of good heart: let no one forsake his post; and let us be consumed rather than taken." According to the Portuguese, the privateers twice boarded the carrack, and were twice driven out: a third time they boarded, one of them bearing a white flag, as expecting that the Portuguese would gladly accept the proposal of surrendering: in fact they had begun to waver; but the Englishman who carried this flag, was the first of that party who was killed; and when a second pilot

* *Historia Tragico-Maritima*, ii., 511-514.

hoisted another flag at the poop, Nuno Velho threw it overboard, and would have killed the man if he had not escaped by speedy flight. The English, indeed, suffered considerable loss: they had one and twenty slain. Antony, their vice-admiral, was killed; Downton, the rear-admiral, crippled for life; and Cave, who commanded the earl's ship, mortally wounded by a shot through both legs. But the privateers, in the heat of action, seem to have forgotten that booty was their object, and, instead of endeavouring to take possession of the carrack, aimed at destroying her. "After many bickerings," says the writer in Purchas, "fire-works flew about interchangeably. At last, the vice-admiral, with a culverin shot at hand, fired the carrack in her stern, and the rear-admiral her fore-castle, by a shot that gave fire to the mat on the beak-head, from thence turning to the mat on the bolt-sprit, and so ran up to the topsail-yard; they plying and maintaining their fires so well with their small shot that many of those which came to quench them were slain. These fires increased so sore, that the vice-admiral's fore-sail and fore-topsail were both burnt; the rear-admiral being in like predicament; while the admiral, with much danger and difficulty, quenched the fires thrown into her from the carrack. To save themselves in this heat and fury, the admiral and vice-admiral fell off, leaving the rear-admiral foul of the carrack's spritsail-yard, in great danger to have been consumed with her, had they not helped her off with their boats." *

A scene more dreadful than the action itself ensued. P. Frey Antonio, a Franciscan, was seen, with a crucifix in his hand, encouraging the poor wretches to commit themselves to the waves and to God's mercy, rather than perish in the flames. The greater part threw themselves overboard, clinging to such things as were cast into the sea for them to float by. The English boats, it is said, made no endeavour to save any

---

* *Historia Tragico-Maritima*, ii., 515-519. Purchas, 1147.

of them : it is even affirmed that they butchered in the water those who came near and entreated to be taken on board. The rear-admiral's boat must, however, be exempted from this atrocious charge ; for by that boat Nuno Velho was picked up, Braz Correa, the captain of the *Nazareth*, and three other persons : ten more, it appears by the Portuguese account, were in like manner saved. Among the passengers in this unfortunate ship were two Portuguese ladies of high birth, Doña Isabel Pereira, a widow, whose father had been chief captain of the Island of Goa, and whose husband, Diogo de Mello Coutinho, had held the command in Ceylon : her daughter, Doña Luiza de Mello, a young and beautiful damsel, was with her. They had been wrecked in the *Santo Alberto*, and had performed a journey of nearly 1000 miles after that wreck, through Caffraria, on foot ; and when many of their fellow-sufferers returned from Mozambique to India, they had resolved on resuming their voyage, because the young lady was going to take possession of her entailed property at Evora. Mother and daughter, when they saw that no help was to be hoped for from the privateers, and that they had to choose between the fire and the water, fastened themselves together with a Franciscan cord ; and their bodies, thus fastened, were cast ashore upon the Island of Fayal. According to the Portuguese statement, about 500 persons perished in the ship; according to the English, there were more than 1100 on board when she left Loanda, of whom only fifteen were saved! Nuno Velho and Braz Correa were brought prisoners to England, where the earl is said to have treated them well, and to have entertained them a whole year as his guests: they were then ransomed for 3000 cruzados, which Nuno Velho paid for both.*

It was not, however, immediately after this deplorable action that the earl sailed homeward : he continued cruising

---

* *Historia Tragico-Maritima*, ii., 520-526. Purchas, 1148.

among the islands about a month longer, when they came in sight of another carrack of 1500 tons, homeward bound from India. They took her for a Spanish ship of war, and under that mistake began a more cautious action. After a while a boat was sent to summon her to surrender to the Queen of England's ships under the Earl of Cumberland's command, unless she would undergo the same fate as the *Chagas;* to bear testimony of which two prisoners were put in the boat, and, the Portuguese say, bound. The Portuguese captain returned a brave answer: he acknowledged Don Philip, King of Spain, he said, not the Queen of England; and if the Earl of Cumberland had been at the burning of the *Cinco Chagas,* so had he, D. Luis Coutinho, been at the defeat and capture of Sir Richard Grenville in the Queen of England's ship the *Revenge.* Let the earl do what he dared for his queen, and he, D. Luis, would do what he was able for his king: his ship was homeward bound from India, laden with riches, and with many jewels on board; let the English take her if they could! The fight was then renewed,* but intermitted by the calm, and remitted (as the English relater allows) by the remisser company, their captains being slain and wounded; "whereupon they gave over," and sailed for England, "having done much harm to the enemy, and little good to themselves".†

"The earl, not liking his ill partage in the *Madre de Dios,*

---

* The Portuguese account states, that the English attempted to destroy this ship, by converting the earl's vessel, which was an old one, into a fire-ship; but that they were prevented from grappling the carrack, first, by a shot that carried away the earl's foremast, and then by a thunderstorm, during which Coutinho got so much ahead of the disabled ship, that the other two dared not pursue them farther (p. 527). This is less probable than the English account. It is unlikely that the earl would have sacrificed his own ship; and still more so, after the recent fate of the *Chagas,* that he should have sought to destroy the carrack, instead of attempting to capture it.

† Purchas, 1148. *Historia Tragico-Maritima,* ii., 526-528.

nor this unhappier loss of two carracks for want of sufficient strength to take them, built a ship of his own of 800 tons * at Deptford, which the queen, at her launching, named the *Scourge of Malice*,† the best ship that had ever before been built by any subject." In this, with three other vessels in company, he would have made what is called his ninth voyage ; but when he had reached Plymouth, the queen recalled him ; and the ships took only three Baltic vessels laden with Spanish property of little value. He set forth again in the ensuing year, but sprung his mainmast, and was forced to return. His next enterprise was upon a smaller scale ; for Essex and the lord admiral going to the coast of Spain with a large fleet of the queen's, together with a squadron of Flemish men of war, "his lordship thought good to await some gleanings in so great a vintage". So he sent out Captain Francis Slingsby, in the *Ascension* of 300 tons, carrying thirty-four guns and 120 men, "chiefly to look for such ships as should come from Lisbon". The captain got sore wounded

* Purchas says 900; but Monson is better authority ; she was "proportioned in all degrees to equal any of her Majesty's ships of that rank, and no way inferior to them in sailing, or other property or condition of ships". Monson states the earl's motives for building her. "At last my lord," he says, "began discreetly to consider the obligation he had to the queen for the loan of her ships from time to time ; and withal weighed what fear of danger he brought himself into, if unluckily any of those ships should miscarry ; for he valued the reputation of the least of them at the rate of his life. Upon these considerations, no persuasions being of force to divert him from attempting some great action on the sea, where he had spent much time and money ; and thinking thereby, as well to enrich himself, as to show his forwardness to do his prince and country service, he resolved to build a ship from the stocks, that should equal the middle rank of her Majesty's : an act so noble and so rare, it being a thing never undertaken before by a subject, that it deserved immortal fame " (p. 189).

† The *Malice-Scourge*, Monson calls it ; "for by that name, it seems he tasted the envy of some that repined at his honourable achievement" (p. 189).

in a vain attempt made with his boats against a caravel: after which the Spanish admiral set forth six ships against him; and himself and another ship, falling in with the *Ascension*, laid aboard, one on the bow and the other on the quarter; "and now the mouths of the great ordnance, being near in place to whisper, roared out their thunders, and pierced thorow and thorow on all hands; which ended, the Spaniards leaped into the fore-chains and main-chains, thinking to have entered the ship, but were bravely repelled. And the English, seeing many together under the admiral's half-deck, discharged among them a fowler laden with case shot, to their no small harm, so that the Spaniards were content to fall off. Of ours, two and twenty were slain and hurt; which loss lighted as much on them which hid themselves, as those which stood to the fight. To prevent the like afterwards, they put safe in hold the chirurgeon, carpenter, and cooper, for the public dependence on them; and made fast the hatches, that others should not seek refuge. But the Spanish admiral tacked about and went in for Lisbon; and the *Ascension*, continuing till they had but a fortnight's provision left, returned, with hurt to themselves and loss also to his lordship."

From the conduct of the men in this action, and from other instances, it appears that an English sea captain could not, in those days, rely with that perfect confidence upon his crew, which has uniformly been felt within our remembrance. The national character was always brave; but that national spirit had not yet been formed among our sailors, which renders courage as much a moral principle as an animal impulse.

The earl's success in so many adventures had not been such as would have encouraged a prudent man to repeat them; but a prudent man would not have engaged in them at first. He now obtained letters patent authorising him to levy sea and land forces, and prepared for the greatest expedition that had ever been undertaken by a subject without the assistance of the sovereign, both in number of ships and land forces.

The force consisted of eighteen sail; and the earl "having by several voyages before attained to a perfect knowledge in sea affairs," took the command in person. "Besides his general design to take, destroy, or any way else to impoverish and impeach the King of Spain or his subjects, he grounded his voyage upon two hopes." The first was that of intercepting the outward-bound East Indiamen as soon as they should sail from the Tagus. The time of their departure was certain; it could not be later than April; and as in burden they exceeded all other European ships, and went out full freighted with commodities for the East Indies, and much money also was sent out in them, they would have abundantly enriched him and the other adventurers. This was his first hope. His other was, if this should fail, to make an attempt with his land forces upon some island or town "that would yield him wealth and riches, being the chief end of his undertaking," —a most unworthy one for one born of such a line, in such a station, and to such an inheritance! The success of his first object depended greatly upon the secrecy of the expedition; and if he had done well and providently, "his fleet," says Monson, "should have been furnished, without rumour, noise, or notice, in several harbours; and the men should not have known the design of their voyage, nor that they were to meet and compose a main fleet". The whole fleet, however, assembled at Plymouth, and sailed from thence on the 6th of March.

The wind being prosperous, though there was much of it, their passage was so fair as to put him in hope that God had prepared them an unlooked-for fortune, if it were well handled, and that he might get sure intelligence concerning the departure of the carracks; "the doing of which undiscovered," says he, "though hard, yet I knew was not impossible for him that could well work"; and considering the mighty importance, he resolved to do it himself, taking with him two other ships; which two only he meant should be seen on the coasts; and accordingly he left the rest of the fleet, appointing them where to lie till he should rejoin them. "But God," says he, "whose will is beyond man's resolutions, forced me to alter this; for my masts, not made so sufficiently as I expected, both now began to show their weakness, especially my mainmast, which I continually looked would have gone overboard. My mariners were at their wits' end; and I protest I would have given 5000*l*. for a new one; the greatest part of my strength both by sea and land having been lost, if that ship had returned in this extremity. Hearing all that would, I heard many opinions to little purpose." So he resolved for himself (though many thought it dangerous, lest the wind should with a storm come up at W.N.W.) to go to the Berlings, and there ride till his masts were fished. He knew the road, which no one else in the ship did; and his fear was not of the wind, but lest he should be discovered, being within three leagues of Peniche, from whence caravels came off to fish. "Go thither," says he, "I must, hopeless otherwise to repair those desperate ruins. My ship was black, which well furthered my device; and though she were great, yet showed not so afar off. Wherefore I came in about eight of the clock at night upon Thursday, when I was sure all the fishermen were gone to sell their fish at Lisbon, and from the main they could not make me. Before the morning I had down my topmasts, my main yard unrigged, and all things ready for my carpenters to work. The small ships with me I made stand off to sea all day, that, not having any in my company, I should be the less suspected; and thus with a strange flag dancing upon my poop, I rid, without giving chase to any, as though I had been some merchant, every day divers ships coming by me that were both good prize, and had been worth the taking." By working night and day, he was ready to sail on Saturday night. The fishermen would return to their fishing ground on the night following; and his hope was to get away undiscovered by them, and rejoin his fleet, which he had appointed to wait for him in the same latitude, between twenty and thirty leagues off.*

At night, however, he heard firing between him and the shore, and rightly guessed that it was his own small ship and little pinnace in action with a vessel which they had seen them chasing to windward before the night closed; and judging, also, that she was above their strength, he slipped his anchor, and "soon came to help the poor little ones, much over-matched". He took her for a Biscayan, and therefore concluded that she would fight well; and, in fact, she returned such an answer to his broadside, that he had three men killed, six or seven hurt, and his ship shot in six or seven places, some of them very dangerous. But, upon boarding and taking her, she proved to be a Hamburgher laden with prohibited commodities. Much as this action exposed him to discovery, he got out of sight of land by daybreak; succeeded, by stratagem, in capturing a fishing-boat from the Tagus; and learned from the men, that, with the next fair wind, five carracks would sail, "with more treasure on board than ever went in one year for the Indies, and also twenty-five ships for Brazil. This welcome news," says the earl, "was accompanied with the meeting again of my whole fleet, which at that very instant I descried: so now being joined, I wished for nothing but a happy hour to see those long-looked-after monsters, whose wealth exceeds their greatness, yet be they the greatest ships in the world." Not doubting to meet them now, and well knowing the way they would come, and being made restless by the joy of such hope, the earl and his fleet "continued gazing for that which came not," till disappointment stared them in the face; then the commander stood for the Tagus in one of his smaller vessels, captured a boat, and learned, that at the time he took the first fishing-boat, a ship, with Spaniards on board, from

* Purchas, 1150.

England, had arrived at Lisbon, which ship was in Plymouth *
when he sailed from the sound, and had given intelligence
that he was at sea, and that his object certainly was to
intercept the Indian fleet. He learned, also, that caravels
had been sent out to search everywhere for him; one of
which, when he returned to his fleet, he understood had
come by them to windward, and discovered them all. †

It was now evident, that the carracks would alter their
course, if they put to sea at all; and, in despair of winning
them by any other means, the earl went again to the Tagus,
to see whether they were come so low down the river that
it might be possible to board them in the night. The wind
favoured him; he got in between the Cachopos,‡ and saw
them riding in the Bay of Oeyras. "Here," says he, "had I
too much of my desire, seeing what I desired to see, but
hopeless of the good I expected by seeing them; for they
were where no good could be done upon them, riding within
the Castle of St. Julian, which hath in it above 100 pieces of
great ordnance; so as though I could have got in (which I verily
believe I could), it had not been possible to have returned, the
wind being ever very scant to come forth withal, and hanging, for
the most part, so far northerly, as that, for fear of the Cachopos,
I must of force have run close by their platforms. With this

---

* Monson might justly censure the earl for want of secrecy in his preparations; but the earl's own narrative shows that another part of his censure was undeserved. "He worthily deserved blame," says Monson, "to present himself and fleet in the eye of Lisbon, to be there discovered, knowing that the secret carriage thereof gave life and hope to the action. By a familiar example of a man that being safely seated in a house, and in danger of an arrest, knows that catchpoles lie to attack him, so fared it with the carracks at that time, who rather chose to keep themselves in harbour, than venture upon an unavoidable danger" (p. 190).

† Purchas, 1151.

‡ The Cat-ships they are called in Purchas, and Oeyras is called Weirs.

unpleasant sight I returned for my fleet." * Here ended his hope of enriching himself by this enterprise. To the Spaniards, however, or rather to the Portuguese, the injury was very great; for rather than put themselves in hazard of him and his fleet, "they chose to give over their voyage, and lose the excessive charge they had been put unto in furnishing their ships; and these carracks lay at home without employment the whole year after". Sanguine adventurers had carried their hopes at this time very far: they thought that the Indians, or rather the Portuguese in India, could not subsist without those commodities which they received from Portugal; and that, if the outward-bound fleet were intercepted, or prevented from sailing for three or four years, the Portuguese Indians must have been compelled to trade with England, rather than endure the want of European goods; and that in time the Indies might have been divided from Portugal, especially if a younger son of the Prior D. Antonio had been carried out, "whom, no doubt," says Monson, "they might have been forced to accept as king".

The earl sailed now for the Canaries; and having been informed by some Spaniards, and by some of our own people who had been prisoners there, that there dwelt a marquis on the Island of Lancerota, whose ransom would be worth 100,000*l.*, he determined upon attempting to surprise him. But these persons, who undertook to pilot him into the road, and then guide him to the castle, even in the darkness, had nearly carried him upon a ledge of rocks in the road; so he was fain to cast anchor till the morning; and then, though he had "no hope left to catch the marquis," unless he were to shut himself up in the castle, yet the earl thought it meet to set all his soldiers on shore, seeing that he had never till then given them any training, and "well knew many of them to be very raw, and unpractised to service at land". The

* Purchas, 1151.

day selected for the service was Good Friday. The earl, in fear of an ague from the cold which he had taken in the last night's watching, confined himself to his cabin, "took some strong physic, and was let blood"; and Sir John Berkeley was sent in command of the men, it being certain that the place could make no resistance against such a force. They landed near Porto de Naos. The guide said the chief town upon the island, Cayas, or Rubicon (from whence the bishops of the Canary Islands were styled Bishops of Rubicon, till the Island of Gran Canaria was conquered), was but three miles from the landing-place; it proved more than three leagues, and of "the most wicked marching for loose stones and sand". The town was abandoned before they reached it; only, as they marched, "the mountaineers would watch if any straggled, and desperately assault them with their lances,* being so swift of foot that none could come near them". The castle was about half a mile from the town, within and about which were now some four or five score men; but they retired without fighting, and the privateers took possession of it. They found within it twelve or more brazen guns, . . . "the least bases, the most culverins and demi-culverins, and an innumerable company of stones laid in places of greatest advantage. The house itself, built of squared stones, flanked very strongly and cunningly both for offence and defence; the entrance thereunto not, as in our forts, of equal height with the foundation ground, but raised about a pike's length in height, so that, without the use of a ladder, there could be no entering. Some of our wisest commanders said, that if

---

* " When a piece is presented to them, so soon as they perceive the cock or match to fall, they cast themselves flat to the ground, and the report is no sooner heard, but they are upon their feet, their stones out of their hands, and withal they charged with their pikes; and this in scattered encounters, or single fight (for either they knew not, or neglect orderly battalion), oftener giveth than receiveth hurt" (Layfield in Purchas, 1156).

they had drawn in their ladders, and only shut the door, twenty men might have kept it against 500." *

Lancerota was the first of the Canary Islands upon which the Europeans established themselves. A party of Norman adventurers, under Jehan de Betancour, landed there in 1400; and their history is the exact prototype of Columbus's. They were hospitably received; they took advantage of that hospitality to construct a fort; they left a garrison there; and that garrison behaved "in such a licentious and cruel manner towards the king and the nation," that their commander and many others were deservedly cut off, and the survivors reduced to the last extremity when the conquerors returned there.† We know not enough of the Canarians, to perceive how far they deserved the misery which the Spaniards brought upon them; but for the Spaniards here, as in the West Indies, and along the coast of America, the sins of the fathers were visited upon the children; and the English, the buccaneers, and the Algerines,‡ were to them what they had been to the indigenous inhabitants. The Earl of Cumberland's object in touching at these islands was no better than that of the Algerines; but it was not worse than what the warfare of the age, by common consent, allowed of; and nothing occurred here to fill him with compunction in his latter days. "No further harm was done to the town or castle, than that of borrowing some necessaries,"—for which no payment was intended. The town is described as consisting at that time of somewhat more than 100 houses, rudely built, and commonly of one story; the roofs with just sufficient sloping to cast off the rain, "covered only with canes or straw laid upon

---

* Purchas, 1151, 1155, 1156. Glas., 219, 220.

† Glas., iv., 11, 12.

‡ In 1618, the Algerines carried off above 1600 persons, being nearly the whole population of the island. They were ransomed by the King of Spain, and sent back (Glas., 218, 219).

a few rafters, and very dirt cast upon them, which, being hardened by the sun, becometh shower-proof". There was an old church,—which was, indeed, the mother church of those islands,—a poor structure, having "no windows, nor admitting light otherwise than by the door; it had no chancel, but was one undivided room, with stone seats along the side, and at the one end an altar, with the appurtenants". There was also an unfinished convent, which was a neat quadrangular building, "with more commodities of fresh water and garden than any other place in the town, even the marquis's house". "Nothing, in a manner," says the chaplain, "was left in the town, saving bulls, and pardons, and divers houses, and good store of very excellent wine and cheese." Of the quality of the wine, Dr. Layfield was probably a more competent judge than the earl, who upon that Good Friday kept an involuntary fast: his lordship says, that "some little wine only was found, which little was too much; for it distempered so many, that if there had been a strong enemy to have attempted, they should have found drunken resistance; the meaner sort being most overthrown already; and the commanders, some distempered with wine, some with pride of themselves, or scorn of others; so as there were very few of them but that fell to most disorderly outrage one with another. It was, in fact, a mutinous disorder of drunkenness"; * and Sir John Berkeley, "with much grief, told the earl that if he took not some severe course to remedy these things, it would be the ruin of their voyage". The earl, therefore, went out here the next day to see the men trained, the greater part of whom he found "both rude and raw"; and calling all the commanders before him, he rebuked them for their yesterday's conduct, and gave articles both for their courses at land and sea, reading to them his commission, that they might know he

* Monson, 192.

had full power to execute the punishment which he had set down for every offence, and assuring them he would not be slow in so doing if they offended.

One of the fleet, which had not been ready to sail with them from England, joined company between Gran Canaria and Teneriffe, and brought some English prisoners who had escaped in a fishing-boat from Lisbon. These men reported that the carracks, in consequence of his departure from the coast, were to sail in a few days; and some days accordingly were spent in waiting for them, till it became certain either that they had gone by, or (as was afterwards ascertained) had given up the voyage for that year. The captains and masters then having agreed that it was not fit to tarry any longer upon that hope, counsel was held concerning their further proceedings, and some were for an attempt upon Pernambuco, which had been so far contemplated from the beginning, that the earl had brought with him his old Portuguese pilots, well acquainted with the Brazilian ports. These pilots thought the season too far spent, for they had often at that season been obliged to put back to Lisbon, and, "on their last passage, had been six or seven weeks in getting one degree": some of the adventurers, however, replied, "that it might fall out otherwise, and that though they might be long in getting thither, yet they were sure of winning the place easily, and gaining wealth enough by the conquest". The earl felt it was now time to disclose his own intentions, being "so far shot to the southward, that he was sure not to meet with any going to the northward, so that no news of him could reach Spain till it came from the Indies". "Then laid I before them," said he, "how our men were already many of them sick, and that undoubtedly the crossing the line would keep them from recovering, although the passage were as good as man could wish. Besides, I remembered them of intelligence given us, both upon the coast of Spain and the island, that the king had sent thither, to defend the place against me, 600 soldiers; and also it was likely he had given order, that if they saw themselves not strong enough to resist, they should flee with their portable goods into the mountains, and set their sugar and Brazil wood on fire; then were we sure to have nothing. And lastly, if we beat long under the line, undoubtedly most of our men would fall sick, and then should we be forced to return without doing anything; for to no other place could we go, once bearing up upon that occasion." Perceiving by their silence that what he said had produced the desired effect, he proceeded to say, that, not to conceal longer what hitherto had been kept secret for the good of all, the truth was, he had "never any intention to go for Brazil, after he found that they could not leave England before Christmas; but that the West Indies was his object," where there were many probabilities to make a voyage by,—as, first, the sacking of Margarita, which they knew was rich; then Puerto Rico; after that St. Domingo; then, in July, the outward-bound fleet would be in the Acoa, where we could not miss them; and if these gave us not content, in the end of July or August we should meet the fleet at Cape S. Antonio. Some of these projects, he mentioned, " more," he says, "to carry the men with good liking thither, than for any thought he had of them himself".

All entering unto his views "with greedy desire and hopeful expectation, he directed them each to make the best of his way for Dominica, thinking it better to go straggling thither, there being possibility to meet some purchase by the way, which they were most in likelihood of when they spread furthest". There they had all arrived on 23rd of May, and then they carried their sick on shore. The island was inhabited only by Indians, who hated the Spaniards, and liked the French no better, but were well pleased with English visitors. They brought great store of potatoes, plantains, pines, pepper, and tobacco, for which they most desired to have swords, hatchets and knives in exchange;

clothes, also, were very much in request with them; but if they could get none, beads or any gaudy baubles were accepted. They spoke some Spanish words, . . . probably enough for all the intercourse that was required. They showed a great desire to obtain the same sort of acquaintance with the language of their new friends: "some of them," says the chaplain, "would point to most parts of his body, and having told the name of it in the language of Dominica, he would not rest till he were told it in English; which having once heard, he would repeat, till he could either name it right, or at least till he thought it was right; and so commonly it would be, saving that to all words ending in a consonant they always set the second vowel; as, for chin they say *chin-ne*, so making the monosyllables dissyllables". The chaplain thought their "wits were able to direct them to things bodily profitable"; he describes them as using either a broad sheet of basket-work, or a very broad leaf in its stead, to shelter them against the rain, because it washed off their red paint, which was so laid on, he said, that if you touched it, you found it on your fingers. They made a drink of the cassava or mandioc root; "better of their pines (and it should seem, says Layfield, that might be made an excellent liquor); but the best, and reserved for the king's cup only, was of potatoes". The earl brought the squadron into a goodly bay, able to receive a greater navy than had been together in the memory of that age: it was at the north-west end of the island; and his information directed him to seek for a hot spring there, which he found fast by the side of a very fine river. "The bath," says Layfield, "is as hot as either the Cross Bath or the King's Bath in the city of Bath in England; and within three or four yards runneth into the river, which, within a stone's cast, disburdeneth itself into the sea. Here the sick men specially found good refreshing;" and here they remained till the 1st of June. It was thought convenient to take a muster of their companies here, "and something better to acquaint every one with his own colours"; but the weather proved so unfavourable that this could not be done.

But notwithstanding the ill weather, the beauty of the country made a strong impression upon those whose hearts were not wholly set upon schemes of plunder. It is "so mountainous," says Layfield, "that the valleys may better be called pits than plains; and withal so unpassably woody, that it is marvellous how those naked souls can pull themselves through them, without renting their natural clothes. Some speak of more easy passages in the inland of the island, which makes it probable that they leave those skirts and edges of their country thus of purpose for a wall of defence. Their hills are apparelled with very goodly green trees, of many sorts. The tallness of these unrequested trees makes the hills seem more hilly than of themselves happily they are; for they grow so like good children of some happy civil body, without envy or oppression, as that they look like a proud meadow about Oxford, when, after some irruption, Thames is again couched low within his own banks, leaving the earth's mantle more ruggy and flakey than otherwise it would have been; yea, so much seem these natural children delighted with equality, and withal with multiplication, that, having grown to a definite stature, without desire of overtopping others, they willingly let down their boughs, which, being come to the earth again, take root, as it were to continue the succession of their decaying progenitors; and yet they do continually maintain themselves in a green good-liking, through the liberality, partly of the sun's neighbourhood, which provideth them, in that nearness to the sea, of exceeding showers; partly of many fine rivers, which, to requite the shadow and coolness they receive from the trees, give them back again a continual refreshing of very sweet and tasty water." *

* Purchas, 1158.

The weather, and the difficulty of finding an open piece of ground of sufficient extent, having rendered it impossible for the earl to muster his people here, he sailed, on the 1st of June, for the Virgin Islands, and on the afternoon of the 3rd, came to an anchor. A fit place having been discovered on one of these uninhabited islands that evening, the land forces went ashore betimes on the following morning, being Whitsunday. There he took a perfect muster of them. The companies, indeed (though after much sickness), were " goodly in number, one might well say, not so few as a thousand". When they had been trained "into all sorts and faces of fights," the earl, who found it, he says, "for many respects meet to speak to them, commanded the drums to beat a call; and the troops being drawn in the nearest closeness that conveniently they might be, that he might be heard of all, his lordship, standing under a great cliff of a rock, his prospect to the seaward, stepped upon one of the greater stones, which, added to his natural stature, gave him a pretty height above the other company ; and so commanding audience, made a speech to them ". We have the harangue preserved, as nearly as he could remember it, in his own unfinished relation. " Kind countrymen and fellow-soldiers," said he, "I am sure there is none here but have marked, and the wisest wonder at my light regarding the many gross faults committed among you, suffering every man to do what he would, and urging no man further than he listed. Many courses drew me to this patience ; only one I will now utter, the rest being fitter to conceal to myself than to make so many acquainted with. The great hope of meeting the carracks made me hope for a short journey; which, if it had happened, I thought it better to return with every man's good word, than by punishing of any to have their ill word at my return. But that hope is altogether past; and now we are settled to another course, which, though it may be will not prove altogether so rich, and must of force keep us longer abroad, yet I assure you, upon my honour and conscience, I do constantly believe there will spring out of it more glory to God, more service to our prince and country, and more honour to ourselves, than could have been done by the carracks if we had taken them all. For the better performance we must fall to another course; I in governing, you in obeying; I in directing you what to do, you in following my directions; to which end I have already delivered you certain articles. And though these twenty days at the least you have had them amongst you, yet fear I there are some which wish they could but light upon so much as they would conceal from me. Base conditions be hateful things in men professing arms; there is none baser than theft, and no theft so base as for a man to steal from his own companion: and he that concealeth anything gotten in this journey, stealeth from every man in it, . . . all going to have their part of whatsoever is gotten. This I thought not unfit particularly to touch, because the speech hath given great offence to the whole army, and no doubt may encourage some of lewd and base humours among us to do the like. But let the warning I now give you drive these thoughts out of their thoughts that hold them; and be also a warning that they heedfully observe the rest of the articles. For, I assure you, my over-patient and forced sluggish humour is shaken off; and I will neither oversee, nor suffer to pass unpunished, ill deservers." *

As they were now within a day's sail of Puerto Rico, he appointed officers for the field. Twelve companies were made up, whereof if any "wanted the full number of eighty, they were plentifully supplied by a large overplus of gallant gentlemen that followed his lordship's colours, borne by Captain Bromley; and Sir John Berkeley also had another eighty; so that the whole army appointed to land was near upon a

* Purchas, 1158, 1159.

thousand, especially seeing that the officers of several companies were not reckoned in these numbers". It was now debated whether to pass through the Virgins, which many of the masters and sea captains would have preferred as the nearer way, and there were divers on board, both soldiers and mariners, who had gone this way with Drake; or to hold the old course through the Passages. The first was the nearer but more dangerous way, being, says Layfield, very narrow, about the breadth of the Thames near London, and they durst not promise themselves the continuance of a leading wind. The earl, however, determined upon the farther and safer course; more desiring, he said, to be the first that took Puerto Rico, than the second that passed through the Virgins. On the morning of the 5th, two small pinnaces were sent forward to explore the landing, Captain Knotsford, who was in one of them, having been Sir John Hawkins's pilot, and esteemed to be very expert in those countries. The fleet lingered till it was dark, and then putting out all sails, came to them undiscovered a little after midnight. But the pinnaces had found the distance more than had been supposed; it was dark before they reached the place which they went to discover, and for fear of carrying the earl to leeward, they had tarried for him and done nothing. He stood off and on till morning, and then descried what appeared to him a smooth landing-place; but all who had been with Drake insisted that it was impossible to get there, "the wind over-blowing all day out of the sea". The earl, however, and Sir John Berkeley rowed thither, and found it not only smooth but a most goodly sandy bay, and that they might march all along by the sea-side till they came to the town. Well pleased with this, he gave orders that every captain and ship should put their men in boats, and follow his bloody colours, which he would have presently landed. But some of the commanders objected that the march seemed to be great, that none knew the way, and that if the town, as they had often heard, stood on an island, they should be forced to return to their ships, not having means to get unto it. "Gentlemen," said the earl, "a willing mind makes long steps with great ease. I have been sick, and am not now strong; you shall go no farther nor faster than I will do before you. For guides, we need no better than our eyes; the town standing by the sea-side, and we landing from the sea, see no other but fair sandy bays all the way thither. We might land much nearer, if we were sure there were anywhere to leeward such a headland as this, that maketh smooth landing within it; but that being uncertain, I mean to take this, which I do assuredly believe God hath directed us unto; for I am sure it is better than any ever told me of. And for your last argument, that if it be an island we shall not get into it, that reason is nothing; for you see our boats may row by us; and when we shall come to any water, they may set us over if it be deep; in shallow places we shall pass ourselves. So all you have said or can say being thoroughly answered, let me have no more speaking, but get your men all into your boats and follow in order as I have directed you." Further, he told them, that in taking Puerto Rico, they should possess the keys of all the Indies, and that though there were not so many millions in the town as when a greater force failed to take it, it was nevertheless rich, and there were gold mines in the island. And if men of judgment thought it was too strong for their strength to carry, because it had already resisted a much stronger force, that consideration ought to encourage them, seeing the more cause would they have to be proud of taking it; "and believe me," he pursued, "assured we are to take it, now we see where to land quietly; the Indian soldiers live too pleasantly to venture their lives; they will make a great show, and perhaps endure one brunt, but if they do any more, tear me to pieces!" *

* Purchas, 1153, 1154.

By eight in the morning the whole force was landed, about a 1000 men, "in a most fine place," says the earl, "where not any wet his furniture nor saw an enemy; by which means all our troops were put in good order, and were made much stronger than a small resistance before we were marshalled would have made us". The landing was about four leagues from the town, toward which they marched in the extreme heat of the day; this, and the way being sandy, would, he says, "no doubt have tired many, but that going all along by the sea, they marched at pleasure in it when they listed; and besides, had the place whither they were going still in sight, which, standing upon the top of a hill, showed much nearer than it was". Commonly on firm, sometimes on loose sand, yet it was a fair march for three leagues, when a few horsemen who had been sent to view their strength, came near enough to reconnoitre them, then turned their horses and galloped away. They soon fell in with a negro who was willing enough to be their guide, but he neither spoke good English nor good Spanish; and moreover was in great fear, as well he might be, at finding himself exposed to imminent danger on one side or the other, whether he led them right or not. "Through most unpassable rocks and cliffs," he brought them to the entrance of an arm of the sea, by which the little island on which the capital stands is separated from the main one. The earl had expected to get over in his boats, but this he saw was hindered by a bulwark on the island side, close at the mouth of the entrance, with five pieces of great brass ordnance. The entrance was not above sixty yards over, and a little within stopped quite across with piles; so that while the Spaniards occupied this fort it was not possible to get in there. There were some who proposed to plant musqueteers among the rocks, that they might beat those in the fort from their guns; but though this was thought feasible, it was not determined on, because, if the fort had been silenced, they were ignorant of the depth; and the boats had not yet found any landing-place. "And here," the chaplain says, "we were at a flat bay, even at our wits' end." The earl, however, was sure there must be some good passage by which the horsemen had come; "and with much ado the negro, being something comforted, and partly with threatening, partly with promises, brought to the little wits he had," was made to understand whither they wanted to be guided. "When," says the earl, "I perceived he understood me, I followed him through the most wickedest wood that ever I was in in all my life." The troops went on "with as nimble minds as weary bodies, for they had marched from morning till it was even on the edge of the evening, but they would not be weary; and, at length, through such untrodden paths, or rather no paths, as would have taught," the chaplain observes, "the most proud body to stoop humbly," they came upon the footing of the horsemen, and following their beaten track, came just at sunset to a long and narrow causeway, leading to a bridge, which connected the great island with the lesser one. The causeway was wide enough for three persons abreast, and the bridge was drawn up: on the opposite bank was a strong barricade, and a little beyond it a fort with ordnance. They learnt from another negro, that at low water the passage was fordable beside the causeway; "but their own sailors could say little to the ebbing and flowing here;" and the only way to know the fit time of assault was to set a continual watch, to give present information of the ebb. Two in the morning was the time which the negro stated. The troops, therefore, were ordered to rest and refresh themselves, for the better enabling them to fight in the morning.*

* Purchas, 1154, 1160. Thus far the earl's own narrative of the voyage extends. "The same honourable hand," says Purchas, "hath been our actor and author; but here, when he comes to doing, he breaks off speaking, and (*tam Marte quam Mercurio*) exchangeth words for

They retired to a piece of open ground over which they had passed. The negro guided them to some fresh water; some had brought bread with them, and the earl "was no niggard of what he had". His lodging that night was his target. "I," says the chaplain, "lay at his head, and to my remembrance never slept better. Two hours before day the alarum was given very quietly, and was readily taken, for we needed not but to shake our ears." There grew a question concerning the command that day, between Berkeley and the earl, arising from an honourable desire on both sides to have the post of danger. The earl yielded to a fair plea, becomingly urged, and to the representation that, being the general, it behoved him, for the sake of the army, to consider his own preservation; nevertheless he persisted in being at the service in person, though he left Sir John with the command; and he put himself in armour, as did all the com-

swords, and mercurial arts into martial acts." He then often declares the reason which induced him to leave out a political discourse, and state-moral mystery of this history, written by the same noble commander. "The times," he says, "are altered, and howsoever planets have their peculiar course, fixed stars must move with their orb, and follow the first movable. The men of Bethshemesh bought dearly their prying into the ark; and I know not how I may be tolerated to utter now in public those state mysteries which he then in private counselled for his country's good. I could also be willing, as I know the world would be greedy of such morsels; but Æsop's dog, snatching at the shadow of a morsel in the water, lost that which he had in his mouth; and his crow, gaping to sing to please the fox, displeased herself with loss of all her other wealth and purchase. Everywhere in this vast work we have been wary, and yet scarce wary enough of this danger in our wariest wariness; wherein yet (if any such fault be) it is not an itching finger, busy in things above us, but store of business in so multiform a task, perhaps, hath occasioned oversight to eyes, otherwise dim enough. Once whatsoever the king and state disclaim, I disclaim also as not mine, because I and mine are theirs, and no further desire to be, or see mine own than in the public; of which, and for which (under God) I am, have, can, write, do, speak, acknowledge all things. I will pry in the East and West Indies, rather than state it at home" (p. 1154).

manders, and who else had armour, for they looked that the service should be hot. So, indeed, it proved; the enemy's sentinels discovered them as they approached; the Spaniards were perfectly prepared; and the member of the Church militant, when he declares it may be well said that it was well fought by his comrades, says also, that if it had been day, and every one could have seen what he did, so many would probably not have deserved so much commendation. The assault continued about two hours; and "though the assailants left no way in the world unattempted, yet no way could they find to enter the gate". The causeway, he says, had been purposely made so rugged, that the adventurers, in order to keep their feet, chose to wade in the water beside it. The earl's shield-bearer stumbled, and falling against the earl overthrew him into the water, where, being by reason of his armour unable to rise, he was in great danger of drowning. It was not till a second attempt, that the sergeant-major, who was next him, succeeded in getting him out, and not till he had swallowed so much salt water as to cause such extremity of sickness, that he was forced to lie down in the very place upon the causeway, till, being somewhat recovered, he was able to be led to a spot of more ease, where the bullets made him threatening music on every side; and there he remained till the end of the action, lying upon the ground, "very exceeding sick," in a place so perilous that it would have been as safe to be at the entry of a breach by assault.*

The assailants had the advantage of numbers, but they were in a position where that advantage could not avail them. "Not less than 3000 English bullets were sent among the Spaniards, who, on their part, were not much behind the invaders in sending these heavy leaden messengers of death; for besides six pieces of great ordnance which played just upon the causeway, and some pretty store of musqueteers,

* Purchas, 1161.

at a port fast by the gate there lay a fowler, or cast piece, that did more scathe than all the rest, for this shot at once many murdering shot, wherefore the piece is also called a murderer." Yet the English came to the gate, and some two or three began to hew at it with bills, for want of fitter instruments; others meantime were at the push of the pike at the ports and loop-holes, and having broken their own pikes seized those of their enemies with their naked hands and broke them. With all these exertions they could not force an entrance, and Berkeley, attempting to discover if a passage could be found on either side of the gate, twice waded so far that he got into deep water, and must have perished if he could not have swam. The end was that the tide came in; and when day began to break, the water, which had been knee-deep, was up to the waist; daylight would have enabled the Spaniards to sweep the causeway with their guns, and the English were brought off in good time to the place where they had passed the night. "God," the chaplain says, "would not have more bloodshed, nor our troops as yet to have their wills." The loss in killed and wounded was something less than fifty. As soon as the surgeons had looked to the wounded, the men were marched to the sea-side, where the boats had been ordered to meet them with food.*

While they refreshed themselves there, the earl went on board, being still so sick that some danger was apprehended. His intention had been to rest on board that night, but his thoughts were so busied and restless that in a few hours he had digested another plan of operations, and came on shore again to put it in execution. The resolution was to attack the fort at the entrance of the channel; and believing it necessary to carry this, at whatever cost, he ordered one of the ships to bear in close to the shore, though the danger of

* Purchas, 1161.

her driving upon the rocks was apparent. Some fifty musqueteers were stationed upon the broken ground opposite; from whence it had before been noted that they might beat the enemy from their guns. At the same time 200 men were embarked in boats, that they might effect a landing between the forts and the town. In the course of an hour, the ship and the musqueteers had so beaten the fort that the boats landed at leisure, and this advantage was gained with the loss of only one man killed and three wounded; but as it had been apprehended, the ship went upon the rocks, and finally was cast away. The Spaniards met them after they were landed, and skirmished awhile gallantly, till, finding themselves the weaker party, they effected an honourable retreat into a wood, on the skirt whereof they had made their stand: the invaders then advanced to the fort, which had been forsaken, and there they established themselves for the night. By the time the boats returned for a second embarkation it was late at night, and the water so low that there could be no passage till the next flood; so the companies were again marched to the safe ground on which they had taken up their lodging before; there they rested and refreshed themselves, waiting for the tide, crossed there as soon as it served, and being thus in the smaller island, they now made little doubt of complete success. The distance was about a mile and half from the town, the way woody on either side, and so narrow that not more than three men could march abreast; yet though the ground was so fit for ambuscades, "or," says Layfield, "for the Irish manner of charging, by sudden coming on and off," no attempt was made to oppose or annoy their march. By day-break they reached the town, and found none but women there, and men whom either age or infirmity or wounds had disabled; the rest had betaken them to one of their forts to the seaward, called Mora.*

* Purchas, 1161, 1162.

The city of San Juan de Puerto Rico is described at that time as less in circuit than Oxford, "but very much bigger than all Portsmouth within the fortifications, and in sight much fairer". There was not much lost ground within that space, the buildings having increased one-fourth within the three preceding years. The streets were large, the houses built after the Spanish manner, of two stories height only, but very strongly, and the rooms "goodly and large, with great doors, instead of windows, for receipt of air". "The cathedral was inferior to the poorest of our cathedral churches; and yet," says the chaplain, "it is fair and handsome; two rows of proportionable pillars make two aisles, besides the middle walk, and thus all along up to the high altar. It is darker than commonly country churches in England, for the windows are few and little, and those indeed without glass (whereof there is none to be found in the town) but covered with canvas, so that the most of the light is received by the doors." The earl, as soon as he had taken full possession of the town, set sufficient guard, and quartered his companies, summoned the fort, requiring the governor to deliver it up to him for the Queen of England, who had sent him thither to take it; the governor returned for answer that the King of Spain had sent him thither to keep it, and keep it he would as long as he was able. It was now a great object with the earl to reduce it with the least possible loss, for he considered that he was to leave a strong garrison, and yet must himself go home well guarded. His first care was to cut off all their means of supply; and for this purpose boats were stationed between the fort and the main; two batteries also were provided, in case the enemies' food should last longer than he wished. They were ready on the ninth day after the capture of the town too late to be then opened; and the morrow being Sunday, he would not begin on that day; so it was deferred till the next morning.*

* Purchas, 1162, 1164.

"The noise of war meantime was not so great, but that the still voice of justice was well heard." "It is no news," says Layfield, "that in such companies there will be outrages committed." One very good soldier the earl publicly disgraced for "over-violent spoiling a gentlewoman of her jewels". But as this example did not prove terrible enough to the rest, he called a court-martial, that justice might be armed with the authority of all the commanders; and two were condemned to death upon the article of defacing churches and offering force to women. "He that did violence to a Spaniard's wife, was a soldier, and had given very good proof of his valour; so far, that his lordship had taken special notice of him; but, being convicted of this crime, there was no place left for mercy; but hanged he was in the market-place, the Spaniards, as many as would come, being suffered to be present at the execution. The other, who had defaced a church, was a sailor; great intercession was made for him by the importunity of the sailors." *
According to Monson, "there was occasion at that time to please them above the soldiers: twice he was taken from the gallows, while endeavours were used in vain to obtain his pardon, but when he was brought out the third time the earl allowed himself to be entreated". It was, indeed, a case in which the feelings of his people went with the offender, for the soldiers "could not be held from defacing unorderly the images of the saints. They were, however, brought by these examples to much better terms of rule and obedience." †

On Monday "the batteries began to speak very loud; and whereas till then four or five soldiers could not appear within reach of the fort, but that a shot of great ordnance would be sent to scatter them, scarce a Spaniard was now to be seen upon any part of their wall". In the course of one day it was perceived that the cavalier was sufficiently beaten, and

* Purchas, 1165. Monson, 193.   † Purchas, 1164, 1167.

that with the next rain (which at that season was neither seldom nor little) it would fall; being of a sandy earth, it did but crumble into dust. The cannoneers were directed therefore to "beat the other point nearer the sea, for that so flanked the gate and the breach already made, that without great danger there could not any approach be made, and his lordship was grown exceedingly niggardly of the expense of any one man's life". By the middle of the ensuing day the Spaniard demanded a parley, and proposed to give up the fort, on condition that "with colours flying, match in their cocks and bullets in their mouths, they should be set without the point of the bridge, and go whither they would; that all prisoners should be delivered without ransom, and no man's negroes or slaves be detained". The earl utterly refused any such composition; but told him that because he took no pleasure in shedding Christian blood, he would deliver them terms, which if they liked, he would receive them to mercy. These articles were sent to the governor in the earl's own hand, and in these characteristic words:—

"A resolution which you may trust to.

"I am content to give yourself and all your people their lives: yourself with your captains and officers to pass with your arms; all the rest of your soldiers with their rapiers and daggers only.

"You shall all stay here with me, till I give you passage from the island, which shall be within thirty days.

"Any one of you which I shall choose shall go with me into England, but shall not stay longer there than one month, but being well fitted for the purpose, shall be safely sent home into Spain without ransom."

It was doubted whether there were any in the fort who understood English, and therefore some advised that the articles should be translated into Spanish: "but his lordship peremptorily refused to seek their language, but would have them to find out his". He gave them respite for deliberation till eight the next morning, and at that time the conditions were accepted, the Spaniards only desiring further, that they might have two colours left them, in lieu of which they promised that nothing should be spoiled in the fort. The governor and his company dined with the earl: after dinner he returned to the fort, brought out the men, nearly 400, and delivered the keys to the earl, who immediately brought in his own colours and Sir John Berkeley's, and placed them upon the two points of the fort. Everything hitherto had been conducted not only honourably but courteously on either side: the Spaniards took all their property with them, and were secured in Fortaleza, a strong castle in the city, which they had not attempted to defend. On the following day the fleet entered the harbour, the fort Mora "being to the sea very strong, and fitted with goodly ordnance, and bestowed for the most advantage to annoy an enemy that possibly could be devised, insomuch that it was thought impossible for any vessel to pass that point if its passage were opposed by her guns. Yet was it very dangerous to ride without, as the invaders found by the loss of many anchors and cables, and one of their ships."

The prisoners were sent to Carthagena, as a place so far to the leeward that they neither, in haste, could make any preparation for the recovery of Puerto Rico, nor send news to Spain. The governor and some few others who deserved some respect, were put on board the ships that convoyed them, and were permitted to proceed in those ships to England. The earl's "honourable resolution and intendment," as the chaplain called it, "was not to come so far for the sake of taking and spoiling some place in the new world, and then run home again, but to keep Puerto Rico, by God's leave, if it pleased God to give it into his hands. That was the place he meant to carry, whatsoever it might cost him, being the very key of the West Indies, which locketh and shutteth all the gold and silver on the continent, and America, and Brazil:" such was his* opinion of its importance. He knew, says Layfield, that St. Domingo might, with much less loss, be taken, and would bring much greater profit for the present; in regard thereof, and of the desire he had his adventurers should become gainers, his thoughts sometimes took that way, but finally they stayed at Puerto Rico, and there settled themselves. As this was his resolution before he had it, so was it also after he had it, and then not only his, but every man of worth or spirit saw such reason in his lordship's designment, that some thought themselves not graciously dealt with in being passed over, while others were named to stay. He was indeed persuaded that though the "eminent and known profits" of the place were ginger, sugar and hides,† yet the island was rich in gold mines, and that the

---

* Sir William Monson had formed a very different opinion. "Whereas," he says, "all men's actions have a reasonable show of likelihood of good to redound to them in their intended enterprises, yet cannot I conceive how a land attempt upon towns could yield my lord any profit, or the merchants that adventured with him. For my lord by experience well knew, having been himself at the taking of some towns, that they afforded little wealth to the taker, because riches of value will be either burned or secretly conveyed away. And for merchandises of great bulk which that poor island yielded, it was only some few hides, black sugar and ginger, which would not amount to any great matter, to countervail the charge of so costly a journey. Commonly that island sends out two or three ships of a reasonable burden to transport the yearly commodities it yieldeth; for though it bears the name of being in the Indies, yet it is a place remote and unfrequented with traffic, either from the Indies or any other place; or though the island should be surprised at such a season of the year as their commodities were ripe and ready for transportation, yet the value is not to be esteemed, where so many people that adventured with my lord were to look up for a dividend according to their adventure" (p. 191).

† "There is so incredible abundance of horses," says the chaplain, "that it is lawful for any man to kill what he needeth for his use, if only he be so honest as to bring the skins to the proper owners. Now these hides must rise to a huge sum of riches, considering that their cattle are far larger than any country that I know in England doth yield; for

King of Spain, in his policy, had ceased to work them, because of their very productiveness; "the sweetness he found made him unwilling to have any co-partners;" and seeing that this island lay nearest the Indies to those people of whose interloping he stood most in fear, "he would not lay such a bait" to attract them, lest having once set foot there, "they should not only gild their fingers, and pay their soldiers for the present with his treasure," but "make it their halting-place on the longer journey to the other islands and continent, which were the coffers from whence his wars were fed". Another view of recondite policy was imputed to the Spanish king, who was supposed to reason thus,—that if in a shorter voyage and less time his subjects were sure to make themselves masters of as much gold as if they went farther, few would fetch it from Peru, or the other more inland parts of the Indies. Moreover, it was reported to the conquerors as a certain truth, that Joachin de Luyando,* formerly a

their kine that I have seen here are for goodliness, both of heads and bodies, comparable with our English oxen. And I wot not how that kind of beast hath specially a liking to these southerly parts of the world above their horses, none of which I have seen by much so tall and goodly as ordinarily they are in England. They are well made and well mettled, and good store there are of them; but methinks there are many things wanting in them which are ordinary in our English light horses. They are all trotters; nor do I remember that I have seen above one ambler, and that a very little fiddling nag" (p. 1171).

* This man, says Layfield, may be judged to have been of no great either wit or care; for it is certainly reported, that oftentimes meeting his own slaves coming out of the country to his house in Puerto Rico with store of gold, he did not know them to be his own, till themselves told him so; and yet this man died so very rich, that he left every of his three sons 100,000 ducats. Insomuch, that the youngest of them being in Spain upon the despatch of some business which his father had left unsettled, was there thought of state so good that a marquis thought his daughter well bestowed upon him in marriage. But see how nothing will last where God, with His preserving blessing, doth not keep things together. For at this day scarce is there any remainder left

mint master in the island, had sent the king a mass of pure gold, which was found to be worth 3500 ducats; and "divers times he had found such pieces of pure ore, that only by splitting them he made himself trenchers of gold to eat his meat on".* Perhaps the military chaplain was as little likely as any of those who were under his spiritual care to consider how much happier this rich Joachin might have been if he had remained in his own country, where he might have eaten from a wooden trencher with as good an appetite, and a better conscience.

The English apprehended no ill from the climate. From three in the morning till six was the coolest part of the day; "a man might then well endure some light clothes upon him; from six till about eight it was very 'sweltering';" then a fresh breeze usually sprung up and continued to blow till four or five in the afternoon, during which time the houses were comfortably cool: the hottest hours were from thence till midnight; and it was thought dangerous to be abroad then because of the *sereno*, which Layfield translates, "the rainy dew": the soldiers who lay abroad in the fields awoke wet with it. "Books had their glued backs melted and loosened by the heat: flowers or fruits candied in England lost their crust there, and English comfits grew liquid;" but after some little acquaintance he thought it likely to prove a very healthful place, for they found hale people there who were eighty or ninety years old. The report of some mortality that had lately prevailed there seems not to have disquieted them. "What place," said the chaplain, "is always free from that scourge of God?" But

of all his riches; and this now most poor though great lady, not being able to proportion herself to the lowness of her fortune, and besides vexed with her husband's ill condition, hath, by authority, left him; and having entered religious profession, is at this present in a nunnery in St. Domingo (p. 1170).

* Purchas, 1165, 1170.

he soon discovered that the great rains in July and August "must needs be very dangerous to bodies already rarefied by the heat of the sun then over them, and yet rather where vehement exercise hath more opened the pores whereby inward heat is exhaled". Early in July more than 200 had died, there were twice as many sick, and "no great hope to recover the most of them". The disease was a flux, "sometimes in the beginning accompanied with a hot ague, but always in the end attended by an extreme debility and waste of spirits, so that for some two days before death the arms and legs would be wonderful cold, and this was held for a certain sign of near departure". From this mortality the earl "saw it was not God's pleasure that this island as yet should be inhabited by the English"; and as soon as he became conscious that it was not in his power to keep the city which he had taken, he made overtures to the Spaniards for ransoming it. They entertained these overtures without any intention of coming to an agreement, but in hope of prolonging the time, till the prevailing distemper should have so far weakened the invaders, that they should be unable to destroy the place before they abandoned it. This, the chaplain affirms, had never been his lordship's purpose; and it appears that on his part he had not much expectation of obtaining the ransom: but he thought such a negotiation the likeliest way of deluding the islanders, "whom he could not so well rule with any other bit, his own strength being now grown weak".*

Meantime all the hides, ginger and sugar which could be collected were forthwith shipped, and so was all the ammunition in the city and all the ordnance which had been taken; "which amounted," says Layfield, "in all and of all sorts very near the full number of fourscore cast pieces, some of them the goodliest that I ever saw". He also put on board

* Purchas, 1167, 1168.

some specimens of the sensitive plant in pots, hoping that he might succeed in conveying to England what appeared to him and his people the most extraordinary production of the island.* This done, he left the strength of the navy with Sir John Berkeley, to follow him as soon as they were ready, and sailed himself with two of the larger ships and seven smaller ones. "The true reason of his desire to be gone from Puerto Rico quickly was a desire he had to be at the Azores, for he had so plotted the voyage, that still he would have a string left in store for his bow, and he hoped to be there before the Mexican fleet. The instructions which he left with every ship, under his own hand, were in these words: 'You shall steer in with the southward part of Flores. If you find me not in that course, then seek me between ten and fourteen leagues of Fayal, west-south-west. If there you find me not, then come through betwixt Fayal and the Pike, and seek me in the road at Graciosa. If you find me at none of these places, you may be assured I am gone from the islands to England.' He left order with

* "This herb," the chaplain says, "is a little contemptible weed to look upon, with a long wooden stalk creeping upon the ground, and seldom lifting itself above a handful high from the ground. But it hath a property which confoundeth my understanding, and perhaps will seem strange in the way of philosophers who have denied every part of sense to any plant; yet this certainly seemeth to have feeling. For if you lay your finger or a stick upon the leaves of it, not only that very piece which you touched, but that that is near to it, will contract itself, and run together as if it were presently dead and withered; not only the leaves, but the very sprigs being touched, will so disdainfully withdraw themselves as if they would slip themselves rather than be touched; in which state both leaf and sprig will continue a good while before it return to the former green and flourishing form. And they say that so long as the party which touched it standeth by it, it will not open, but after his departure it will; this last I did not myself observe, and if it be so, it must be more than sense whence such a sullenness can proceed; but for the former, I have myself been often an eye-witness, to my great wonder, for it groweth in very many places in the little island" (p. 1174).

Berkeley to leave the city undefaced, saving only that Fort Mora should be rased to the landward." Both the earl's division and Berkeley's were scattered in a storm; the earl, however, when he came off Flores, met with enough of his ships to form a respectable force; but he learnt that the homeward-bound carracks were passed by, and that the Mexican fleet was not expected: and upon this disappointment a council was held, and it was determined to return to England without delay. They would probably have all been wrecked upon Ushant and the rocks, if the earl had not, in opposition to his master, judged from the soundings that they were near the coast of France, and given orders therefore to take a more northerly course; for the next morning that coast was seen.*

This was his last expedition. No other subject ever undertook so many at his own cost; and Fuller gives him the distinction of being "the best born Englishman that ever hazarded himself in that kind"; adding, that his fleets were "bound for no other harbour than the port of Honour, though touching at the port of Profit in passage thereunto; I say *touching* (says the old worthy), for his design was not to enrich himself, but impoverish the enemy. He was as merciful as valiant (the best metal bows best), and left impressions of both in all places where he came." Fuller eulogises him as "a person wholly composed of true honour and valour". There were some other ingredients in his character; and when the Earl of Cumberland bore "next to his paternal coats three murdering chain shots," such an addition to his armorial bearings was more significant than he intended it. The desire of gain must have influenced him in his privateering speculations as much as the desire of honour; for a prodigal expenditure, and losses in horse-racing (which species of gaming had in his days begun to be one of the

* Purchas, 1168, 1176.

follies of the great) had embarrassed his affairs. Next to his voyages, this passion, and the display which he made at tilts, and in all other expensive sports, "were the great occasion of his selling land"; and he is said to have "consumed more than any one of his ancestors".* The large expenditure which his station required his own ample means could amply have supported; but no means are adequate to the demands of prodigality.

When James came to take possession of his new kingdom, this nobleman "attended him with such an equipage of followers, for number and habit, that he seemed rather a king than Earl of Cumberland. Here happened a contest between the earl and the lord president of the north, about carrying the sword before the king in York: the office, upon due inquiry, was adjudged to him; and whilst Clifford's Tower," says Fuller, "is standing in York, that family will never be therein forgotten." He died in the forty-eighth year of his age, and was buried at Skipton. His armour may still be seen in Appleby Castle. His two sons died in infancy; and the only daughter whom he left experienced little of his love, for bequeathing to her 15,000*l.* he cut off the entail of his estates and settled them upon his brother. She contested the settlement without success; but on the death of that brother without issue the estates reverted to her. This daughter, by her second marriage Countess of Pembroke, was one of the most high-minded and remarkable women of her age; and seems to have been the last person in England by whom the old baronial dignity of feudal times was supported. All the good connected with it was manifested in this instance without any of the evil. Daniel was her tutor,—and she had the honour of erecting Spenser's monument.

* *Hist. of Westmoreland*, 290.

HAWKINS AND DRAKE

SIR JOHN HAWKINS, the second son of Master William Hawkins and Joan Trelawny his wife, was born at Plymouth. His father is said to have been much esteemed by Henry VIII. as a principal sea-captain, and is the first Englishman who is known to have traded to Brazil, having made two voyages thither in his own ship, the *Paul* of Plymouth, in the years 1530 and 1532.* Plymouth was already a port so famous that the biographer of Devonshire extols it as presenting "a kind of invitation from the commodiousness thereof to maritime noble actions"; † and the youth was brought up to his father's calling, and gained much experience by making early in life several voyages to Spain, Portugal, and the Canaries, "which were, in those days, extraordinary adventures". Being "grown in love and favour" with the Canarians by his good and upright dealing, and inquiring from them concerning the state of the West Indies, he was assured that, "negroes were very good merchandise in Hispaniola; and that store of them might easily be had upon the coast of Guinea". He resolved upon trying his fortune in this trade; and having communicated that desire with his worshipful friends in London, Sir Lionel Ducket, Sir Thomas Lodge, his father-in-law, Master Gunson, Sir William Winter, and some others, they liked so well of his intention that they became liberal contributors and adventurers in the action.

Three good ships were accordingly provided, the *Solomon*

* Hakluyt, iii., 700. † Prince's *Worthies*.

of 120 tons, the *Swallow* of 100, and the *Jonas* of 40, "in which small fleet Hawkins took with him not above a hundred men,* for fear of sickness and other inconveniences, whereunto men in long voyages are commonly subject". He sailed in October, 1562, touched at Teneriffe, where he received friendly entertainment, and proceeded to Sierra Leone; which place is said to have been called Taggarin by the natives. There he stayed some time, "and got into his possession, partly by the sword, and partly by other means, to the number of 300 negroes at the least, besides other merchandise which that country yieldeth". With this prey (so it is properly denominated) he sailed for Hispaniola, and arrived first at the port of Isabella, "where he had reasonable utterance of his English commodities, and of some part of his negroes, trusting the Spaniards no further than that by his own strength he was able to master them". At Puerto de Plata he made "like sales, standing always upon his guard"; and at Monte Christo, on the north side of the island, "made vent" of the remainder of his negroes, receiving for them, at these places, by way of exchange, some quantity of pearls, and hides, ginger, sugar, and "other like commodities," enough not only to load his own vessels, but for freighting two other hulks; † and so "with prosperous success, and much gain to himself and the aforesaid adventurers, he came home, and arrived in September, 1563".

It is now no honour to have been the first Englishman who engaged in the slave trade. ‡ But it is not generally known

---

* "Such," says Campbell, "were the beginnings of Britain's naval power!" With how little reflection must that inapt observation have been written!

† Hakluyt, iii., 500.

‡ This is ascribed to Hawkins; but a sentence in Camden's history (honourable to the historian) seems to throw some doubt upon it. "Blackmoor slaves," he says (108), "were now commonly bought in Africa by the Spaniards, and, from their example, by the English, and sold again in America; *how honestly I know not.*"

how so iniquitous a trade grew up without being regarded as in the slightest degree repugnant either to natural justice, or to the principles of Christianity. At a time when European warfare had been mitigated by the courtesies of chivalry, and by the frequent changes of political relations, more than by any growing sense of humanity, the wars between Mahommedan and Christian were carried on with as much ferocity as in the days of Cœur de Lion: only where the contending parties, as in Spain, were continually opposed to each other, such unrelenting butchery was disused by mutual though tacit consent, because it would have reduced the land to a desert; and there those who fell into the hands of their enemies were made slaves. The Portuguese, having cleared their own territory, invaded the Moors in Barbary; the same system was there pursued with the same people. Their first discoveries were made as much in the spirit of conquest as of adventure; and the same treatment which usage had allotted to the captured Moors was extended, as of course, to the negroes who were taken along the same line of coast. To so great an extent did this prevail, that negro slavery was almost as common in Portugal in the early part of the sixteenth century as it afterwards became in the sugar islands. And so entirely were all persons possessed with the opinion that slavery was the condition to which this unhappy race was destined, that Las Casas, when he proposed the substitution of negro for Indian slavery, as a measure of humanity, never suspected himself of acting inconsistently, nor dreamed that the injustice and cruelty were as great to the one race as to the other.

Hawkins, then, is not individually to be condemned if he looked upon dealing in negroes to be as lawful as any other trade, and thought that force or artifice might be employed for taking them with as little compunction as in hunting, fishing, or fowling: this was the common opinion of his age, and not a solitary voice had been raised against it. In the ensuing year he sailed upon a second trading voyage, with the *Jesus* of Lubeck, which was a queen's ship of 700 tons, the *Solomon* of 140, and two barques, the one of 50, and the other of 30, well stored, and manned with 170 men. They fell in and joined company with another queen's ship, the *Minion*, Captain David Carlet, and the *St. John Baptist*, of London, bound for Guinea. Their consort, the *Minion*, was blown up by the carelessness of a gunner; but most of the people were saved. Hawkins' instructions were thought worthy of being recorded as " good orders for a fleet on a long voyage ". They were in these words : " The small ships to be always a-head and a-weather of the *Jesus*, and to speak twice a day with the *Jesus* at least. If in the day the ensign be over the poop of the *Jesus*, or in the night two lights, then shall all the ships speak with her. If there be three lights aboard the *Jesus*, then doth she cast about. If the weather be extreme, that the small ships cannot keep company with the *Jesus*, then all to keep company with the *Solomon*, and forthwith repair to Teneriffe, to the northward of the road of Sirroes. If any happen to any misfortune, then to show two lights, and to shoot off a piece of ordnance. If any loose company, and come in sight again, to make three yawes, and strike the mizen three times. Serve God daily ; love one another; preserve your victuals; beware of fire, and keep good company." *

They touched at the Canaries,† " the fruitfulness of which island," says the historian of this voyage,‡ " doth surely exceed far all other that I have heard of. For they make wine better than any in Spain : they have grapes of such bigness

---

* Hakluyt, iii., 501.

† " Here we took fishes with heads like conies, and teeth nothing varying ; of a jolly thickness, but not past a foot long ; and is not to be eaten without flaying, or cutting off his head " (Hakluyt, 503).

‡ John Sparke.

that they may be compared to damsons, and in taste inferior to none: for sugar, suckets, raisins of the sun, and many other fruits, abundance; for rosine and raw silk there is great store: they want neither corn, pullets, cattle, nor yet wild fowl. They have many camels, also, which, being young, are eaten of the people for victuals, and being old they are used for carriage. About this island are certain flitting islands, which have been oftentimes seen, and when men approached near them they vanished; as the like hath been of these islands now known, by the report of the inhabitants, which were not found of long time one after the other; and therefore it should seem he is not yet born to whom God hath appointed the finding of them." From thence they made Cape de Verd, where the natives are described as "more civil than any other, because of their daily traffic with the Frenchmen," and as being "of nature very gentle and loving". This they had shown by their treatment of some shipwrecked Frenchmen a little before. Yet, though Hawkins knew the disposition of these people, and had taken on board one of the men who had been so kindly used, that he was not, without difficulty, persuaded to leave them, he endeavoured to kidnap some for slaves, and laid snares for them accordingly. But the crew of the ship which had been blown up revealed the intended treachery, and thereby frustrated it: perhaps, having lost their ship, they were not entitled to share with the rest; for it is not to be supposed that they had any better sense of right and wrong than their comrades.*

Hawkins could not enter the Rio Grande, as he wished, for want of a pilot; he proceeded, therefore, to "one of the islands called Sambula," and staying there certain days, went "every day on shore to take the inhabitants, with burning and spoiling their towns". It is no extenuation of this conduct that it appeared to the natives as legitimate a con-

* Hakluyt, 502, 503.

sequence of the law of the strongest as it did to themselves: nevertheless, when we contemplate the course of history, it is a consolatory consideration, that the evil produced by invasions and conquest is not all additional evil; but that, as in this case, barbarous tribes or nations have endured from strangers such miseries as they would otherwise have inflicted upon each other. A people whom the relater of this voyage calls Samboses, and whose own country was beyond Sierra Leone, had conquered these islands three years before from the Sapies, a tribe who inhabited about Rio Grande. "These Sapies," he says, "be more cruel than the Samboses; for whereas the Samboses live most by the spoil of their enemies, both in taking their victuals, and eating them also, the Sapies do not eat man's flesh, unless in the war they be driven by necessity thereunto; which they have not used but by the example of the Samboses, but live only upon fruits and cattle, of which they have great store. This plenty is the occasion that the Sapies desire not war, except they be thereunto provoked: whereas the Samboses, for want of food, are enforced thereunto, and are not wont only to eat them that they kill, but also keep those that they take until such time as they want meat, and then they kill them." The desire of gold was another motive; for the Sapies buried the dead with their golden ornaments, and the fiercer tribe plundered the graves, the use of gold, as a medium of exchange, being almost the sole practice of civilised society "in which the Portuguese had instructed the natives of the coast".*

The Sapies were in appearance the more barbarous people of the two: they filed their teeth, "for a bravery to set out themselves" (a fashion, however, which is likely to have originated in manners as ferocious as those of their neighbours); and "they do jagg their flesh," says the writer, "both legs, arms, and bodies, as workmanlike as a jerkin-maker with us

* Hakluyt, 504.

pinketh a jerkin". These people were kept by their conquerors to till the ground; and by their labour it had been brought into a more productive state than any other part of the country. Poor wretches, the arrival of the English brought with it nothing but evil to them, for upon them it was that the whole evil fell: their habitations were burnt, their plantations wasted; and, while the Samboses escaped in their canoes to the main, they fell into the invaders' hands, and exchanged the easiest of all states of slavery for the worst. "We took many in that place," is the statement of one of these freebooters, "and as much of their fruits as we could well carry away." This booty was obtained at the cost of a single life: a man, at their departure, having tarried rashly to gather pompions, was watched by the negroes, who came behind him, overthrew him, and cut his throat; thus taking no undue vengeance upon the only white man that fell into their hands.*

Flushed with this "prosperous success," Hawkins was easily persuaded by some Portuguese whom he fell in with after leaving the island, to attack a negro town called Bymeba, where, they told him, there was great quantity of gold, and not above forty men, and 100 women and children; so that if he would "give the adventure, he might get 100 slaves". He was provoked by his ruling motive, the desire of gain; and also by a determination "that the Portuguese should not think him to be of so base a courage, but that he durst give them that, and greater attempts". Accordingly, forty well-appointed men set forth upon this adventure, guided by certain Portuguese, "who brought some of them to their deaths". A marginal note in the original narrative says, here, "Portugals not to be trusted"; but the narrative itself shows, that misconduct, and not treachery, brought upon this party what they well deserved. They dispersed, contrary to the

* Hakluyt, 505.

captain's orders, every one thinking to secure what gold he could for himself: the negroes took advantage of this, attacked the stragglers, and drove the whole party to their boats, pursuing them to the water. Seven of the kidnappers were killed, including Master Field, captain of the *Solomon*, and twenty-seven wounded. The people were somewhat discomforted at this; but Hawkins, "in a singular wise manner, carried himself with countenance very cheerful outwardly, as though he did little weigh the death of his men, nor yet the great hurt of the rest; although his heart inwardly was broken to pieces for it". "But he assumed this cheer to the end, that the Portugals, being with him, should not presume to resist against him, nor take occasion to put him to further displeasure." *

After this the two ships anchored at Taggarin, while the smaller crafts went up "a river called the Casserroes," about their traffic. There they learnt from the Portuguese that a great battle was about to be fought; the people of Sierra Leone having prepared 300 canoes to invade them of Taggarin. A day was appointed for the battle, "which we would have seen," says the narrator, "to the intent we might have taken some of them, had it not been for the death and sickness of our men, which came by the contagiousness of the place". The canoes carried threescore men apiece, and the towns up the river were large, so that they had looked for a good booty in prisoners; but the fatal climate compelled them to make haste away; and they were informed by a Portuguese that they had narrowly escaped from the King of Sierra Leone, "who had made all the power he could" to take some of them, partly for the desire he had to see what kind of people they were. An attempt to surprise them failed, for they took alarm at him, though not thinking there had been such a mischief pretended towards them as there was indeed. "If

* Hakluyt, 506.

these men," says the writer, "had come down in the evening, they had done us great displeasure, for that we were on shore filling water: but God, who worketh all things for the best, would not have it so, and by Him we escaped without danger, His name be praised for it." *

These adventurers resembled the Spaniards as much in their sense of religion as in their want of any sense of justice or humanity. Making for the West Indies, they were becalmed for the space of eighteen days, "having now and then," says the writer, "contrary winds and some tornados, amongst the same calm; which happened to us very ill, being but reasonably watered for so great a company of negroes and ourselves. This pinched us all; and, that which was worst, put us in such fear that many never thought to have reached the Indies without great death of negroes and of themselves; but the Almighty God, which never suffereth His elect to perish, sent us the ordinary breeze." The first land which they made was Dominica, happening fortunately upon the most desolate part of the island; whereby they escaped all danger from the cannibals, whom the Spaniards represented as the most desperate warriors in the Indies, and "very devils in respect of men". Proceeding to Margarita, the alcayde entertained them hospitably, and gave them both beeves and sheep for refreshing their men; but the governor would neither speak with Hawkins, nor permit him to traffic, nor allow him to engage a pilot. He despatched notice of their arrival to the viceroy at St. Domingo; and the viceroy sent orders, in consequence, to Cape de la Vela, and to other places along the coast, that no man should trade with these interlopers, but that they were to be resisted with all the force that could be brought together.†

Obtaining no trade here, and finding no opportunity to take in water, Hawkins departed and came to Cumana.

* Hakluyt, 506. † *Ibid.*, 507.

The Spaniards whom he found there, said "they were but soldiers newly arrived, and were not able to buy his negroes," and they directed him to a commodious watering-place two leagues off called Santa Fé. Next day the Indians came down, "presenting meal and cakes of bread, made of a kind of corn called maize, in bigness of pease, the ear whereof is much like to a teazel, but a span in length, having thereon a number of grains. Also they brought down hens, potatoes, and pines, which we bought," the relater proceeds, "for beads, pewter whistles, glasses, knives, and other trifles. These potatoes be the most delicate roots that may be eaten, and do far exceed our parsnips or carrots. Their pines be of the bigness of two fists, the outside whereof is of the making of a pine apple; but it is soft like the rind of a cucumber, and the inside eateth like an apple, but it is more delicious than any sweet apple sugared." The opinion formed of the Indians here was, that they "surely were gentle and tractable, and such as desire to live peaceably, or else it had been impossible for the Spaniards to have conquered them as they did, and the more to live now peaceably, they being so many in number and the Spaniards so few".*

Having passed between Tortuga and the main, Hawkins sailed along in his pinnace to discern the coast. The Caribs, of whom he saw many on shore, and some in their canoes, showed him gold, invited him by friendly tokens to trade, and were very importunate with him to land; which, "if it had not been for want of wares to traffic with, he would not have denied them, because the Indians which he had seen before were very gentle people, and such as do no man hurt; but, as God would have it, he wanted that thing, which, if he had had, would have been his confusion: for these were no such kind of people as he took them to be, but more devilish a thousand parts, and are eaters and

* Hakluyt, 508.

devourers of any man they can catch,—bloodsuckers both of Spaniards, Indians, and all that light in their laps; not sparing their own countrymen, if they can conveniently come by them". This Hawkins learnt at Borburata, where he anchored and went ashore to speak with the Spaniards, declaring himself to be an Englishman, who came thither " to trade with them by the way of merchandise," and requiring licence so to do. They made answer that they were forbidden to traffic with any foreigner, on penalty of forfeiting their goods; "wherefore they desired him not to molest them farther, but to depart as he came, for other comfort he might not look for at their hands, because they were subjects, and might not go beyond the law". To this he replied, that being in a queen's armada, with many soldiers on board, he was in need both of refreshment for them, and food and money also, without which he could not depart. Their princes were in amity one with another: the English had free traffic in Spain and Flanders; and he knew no reason why they should not have the like in all the King of Spain's dominions. Upon this the Spaniards said they would send to their governor, who was threescore leagues off; ten days must elapse before his determination could arrive: meantime he might bring his ships into the harbour, and they would supply him with any victuals he might require.*

The ships accordingly went in, and received all things according to promise. Hawkins then "advised himself, that to remain there ten days idle, spending victuals and men's wages, and, perhaps, in the end, receive no good answer from the governor, it were mere folly". So he requested licence for the sale of certain lean and sick negroes, who were like to die upon his hands if he kept them ten days, having little or no refreshment for them; whereas, if they were disposed of, they would be recovered well enough: and this request,

* Hakluyt, 509.

he said, he was forced to make, because he had not otherwise wherewith to pay for the necessities which he wanted. This request being put in writing was deemed reasonable, and they granted him a licence to sell thirty slaves. But though some eagerness to purchase had previously been shown, no one came now to buy. Hawkins knew not whether they sought to protract the time till the governor's answer should arrive, that they " might keep themselves blameless," or if some other policy were in view: upon demanding the cause, he was told that the licence had been granted only to the poorer people to buy negroes of small price ; their money was not ready like rich men's ; and, moreover, as soon as they saw the ship, they had sent away their money and their wives to the mountains for fear, and it would take two days to bring them back. Some, however, came to cheapen, but showed such a disposition to bring down the price, that Hawkins sent for the principal of the town, and made show as if he would depart, saying he was sorry that he had troubled them, as also that he had sent for the governor. For it was not only a licence to sell that he sought, but profit also, which he saw was not to be had there ; and, therefore, he would seek farther. And he showed them his papers, that they might see what he had paid for his negroes ; and declared, also, "the great charge he was at in his shipping and in wages". The Spaniards, who wanted slaves, and hoped to get them cheap, did not like to hear of his departure: they "put him in comfort to sell better there than in any other place "; and went so far as to say that, if licence were refused, he should not lose his labour in tarrying, for they would buy without it.*

The details are curious, because this voyage led the way to those hostilities in the New World, which made the English name so formidable there, and so odious, and which

* Hakluyt, 509.

first called forth the character of the English seaman in its whole strength; and because with these transactions at Borburata that illicit trade commenced, which continued as long as Spain retained its colonies upon the American main. That Hawkins might be induced to stay, the Spaniards bought some of his lean negroes; but when the purchasers paid the duty, and required from the officers of the customs the customary discharge, the officers refused to give it, and, instead of carrying the money to the king's account, distributed it to the poor " for the love of God". He could not have acted more wisely with a view to his own exculpation; but this caution put a stop to the sale, the purchasers fearing that they might be called upon for payment of the duties a second time. So trade was suspended till the fourteenth day, when the governor arrived. To him Hawkins repeated his petition: he had come thither in a ship of the queen's majesty of England bound to Guinea; but, driven here by wind and weather, he had great need not of necessaries alone, but money for the payment of his soldiers to whom he had promised it; and, indeed, they would not depart without it, though he were willing to do so. Further, he represented that, notwithstanding the prohibition, it would be well taken at the governor's hands if he granted a licence in this case, seeing that there was a great amity between their princes, and that the thing pertained to our queen's highness. This petition was taken into consideration by the governor in council, and the licence was granted; but any abatement of the king's custom, being thirty ducats upon every slave, was refused.*

But as Hawkins had little scruple how he obtained his negroes, or what papers he exhibited, or what story he told, so he was determined that the king's duties should not stand in his way, and that if he could not obtain his price by fair

* Hakluyt, 510.

means, he would extort it from his customers by fear. With this resolution, he landed 100 men, well armed with bows and arrows, harquebusses and pikes, and marched toward the town. Speedy messengers came out to know his demands. "So our captain," says his honest chronicler, "declaring how unreasonable a thing the king's custom was, requested to have the same abated, and to pay 7½ per cent., which is the ordinary custom for wares through his dominions there; and unto this if they could not grant, he would displease them." Answer was returned, that all things should be to his content: the soldiers and mariners, however, insisted upon having hostages; when these had been given, the traffic was begun, and went on without disturbance; and Hawkins, it seems, found no further difficulty in obtaining what he thought a fair price. By mere accident, however, his presence, unwelcome as it must have been to the persons in authority, proved to be of singular benefit to the town. A party of Caribs having obtained a guide, came in their canoes by night to burn the place and massacre the inhabitants; and their purpose was likely to have succeeded, if the Spaniards had not been upon their guard against the English.* Before they left this place, a French vessel from Havre arrived from the coast of Guinea, having been beaten off from St. Jorge da Mina by the Portuguese galleys, and bringing to Hawkins tidings "most sorrowful for him to understand," that the captain of his consort the *Minion*, with a merchant and twelve mariners, had been betrayed by the negroes on their first arrival there, and were detained prisoners by the Portuguese; so that there was great doubt of bringing home the ship.

Having ended their dealings at Borburata, they proceeded to the Island of Curaçoa, where they had "traffic for hides, and found great refreshing both of beef, mutton, and lambs; whereof there was such plenty that, saving for skins, they

* Hakluyt, 510, 511.

had the flesh given them for nothing; and the worst in the ship thought scorn, not only of mutton, but also of sodden lamb, which they disdained to eat unroasted". But, notwithstanding this sweet meat, the narrator says, "they had sour sauce there; and after nine days' tarriance, were rejoiced when they departed: for by reason of riding so open at sea, what with blasts, whereby their anchors being aground there, three at once came home, and also with contrary winds blowing, whereby, for fear of the shore, they were fain to haul off to have anchor-hold, sometimes a whole day and night they turned up and down; and this happened not once, but half a dozen times in the space of their being there". Hawkins made next for Rio de la Hacha: there he spoke with the king's treasurer of the Indies, resident there; told him of his quiet traffic in Borburata; produced a certificate from the governor in confirmation of this statement; requested licence to trade here also in like manner; and when he was told that this could not be granted, the viceroy having sent express commission from St. Domingo to resist him with all the force they could, he repeated his story of having been forced by contrary winds to come into these parts. "But seeing they would, contrary to all reason, go about to withstand his traffic, he would not it should be said by him, that, having the force he had, he was driven from his traffic perforce, but would rather put it in adventure whether he or they should have the better; and, therefore, he called upon them to determine, either to give him licence to trade, or else stand to their own defence." In reply to this, they gave him the licence which he asked, but offered a price less by one-half than what he had obtained at Borburata. "Whereupon the captain, weighing their unconscionable request, wrote to them a letter, saying, that they dealt too rigorously with him, to go about to cut his throat in the price of his commodities, which were so reasonably rated, as they could not by a great deal have the like at any other man's hands;

but seeing they had sent him this to his supper, he would in the morning bring them as good a breakfast." *

Having given this hint that he intended to settle the price of his commodities in his own way, Hawkins accordingly fired a culverin, in the morning, "to summon the town," and prepared to land with 100 men, having two brass falcons in his great boat, "and in the other boats double bases in their noses". The townsmen, "incontinent, in battle array," marched from the town, making semblance as if they would resolutely have opposed the landing; and he, "perceiving them so to brag, commanded the two falcons to be discharged at them; which put them in no small fear to see, as they afterwards declared, such great pieces in a boat". At every shot they fell flat to the ground; and at last, for fear of these guns, they broke their array, and dispersed. Still their horsemen, being about thirty, made a brave show, coursing up and down, their white leather targets in one hand, and their javelins in the other: but as soon as Hawkins marched towards them, they sent a flag of truce; and the treasurer, in a cautious interview with this ugly merchant, acceded to all that he asked. Hostages were demanded, as before, on the alleged determination of the men; and these having been given, "we made our traffic quietly". Nevertheless, as the Spaniards seemed to be collecting, Hawkins thought a second display of his strength necessary; and when the final settlement was to be made, he went with his three boats, as before, "with bases in their noses, and his men with weapons accordingly". All, however, passed off peaceably; and though some displeasure had arisen concerning money due by the Governor of Borburata, which was to have been paid by the treasurer here, and of which the treasurer refused payment, Hawkins "would not molest him" for a debt which was not his own, but was content to remit it until another time.

* Hakluyt, 512.

They parted with a show of friendship: the captain demanded a testimonial of his good behaviour: it was not given till he was under sail, ready to depart: then having received it, he very courteously took his leave, shooting off the bases of his boat for his farewell; and the townsmen returned this parting salute with four falcons and thirty harquebusses,—glad to be sped of such traders.*

He now made for Hispaniola; but was driven so far to leeward, that he fell in with the "middle of Jamaica, though the clouds, which lay upon the land two days together, made it appear like a headland. There was a Spanish merchant in Hawkins' ship, who, trading in Guinea, and being by treason taken of the negroes, and afterwards bought by the Tangomangos, was by our captain brought from thence, and had his passage to go into his own country." Poor man! he was little benefited by this act of humanity. Deceived by the appearance of the land, he pointed to the objects which, as his hopes and imagination shaped them, seemed to him well known. This was such a place; yonder was such a man's ground; behind that point was the harbour. Before he went into the pinnace to go ashore, "he put on his new clothes, and for joy flung away his old. But in the end," says the angry narrator, "he pointed so from one point to another, that we were a-leeboard of all places, and found ourselves at the west end of Jamaica before we were aware of it; and being once to leeward, there was no getting up again: so that, by trusting of this Spaniard's knowledge, our captain sought not to speak with any of the inhabitants, which, if he had not made himself sure of, he would have done as his custom was in other places." But this man was a plague not only to our captain, whom he made lose, by overshooting the place, 2000*l*. by hides, which he might have gotten, but also to himself; for having been three years out of his country, and in

* Hakluyt, 513.

great misery in Guinea, and now in hope to come to his wife and friends, as he made sure account, he could not find any habitation neither there nor in Cuba, which we sailed all along; but it fell out ever, by one occasion or other, that we were put beside the same, so that he was fain to be brought to England; and it happened to him as to that Duke of Samaria, when the Israelites were besieged; "for not ever thinking to have seen his own country, he did see the same, and went upon it; and yet it was not his fortune to come to it, nor to any habitation, whereby to remain with his friends according to his desire ".*

This unfortunate Spaniard, as he had at first been mistaken in the part of the coast, fell into a greater mistake concerning the island itself, and concluded that it was Hispaniola; in which erroneous opinion Hawkins concurred, because, being ignorant of the force of the current, he could not believe that he had been so far driven to leeward. He set his course, therefore, for Jamaica, as he supposed; and this further error "came to as ill a pass" as the first; "for by this did he also overpass a place in Cuba called Santa Cruz, where, as he was informed, was great store of hides to be had"; and missing, thus, two of the ports "where he thought to have raised great profit by his traffic, and also to have found refreshing of victuals and water for his men, he was now disappointed greatly". The latter necessary he found upon the Isle of Pinas; and "although it were neither so toothsome as running water, by the means it is standing, and but the water of rain, and, moreover, being near the sea, was brackish, yet did not they refuse it, but were more glad thereof, as the time then required, than they should have been another time with fine conduit water". After wandering in these seas three weeks longer, they overshot the Havannah, "which," says Sparke, "is an harbour whereunto all the fleets of the Spaniards come,

* Hakluyt, 514.

and do there tarry to have one the company of another". Hawkins meant to have watered there, if he had hit the port. He seems not to have entertained any apprehension that, if he had fallen in there with any ships of greater strength, they might have been disposed to put a stop to his trading by just such cogent means as he had employed in carrying it on. At length, in great want of water, he made for the coast of Florida, and there ranged along, anchoring every night, because he would miss no place where this want could be supplied, and entering every creek in search for the Huguenot colony which Admiral de Coligni had sent thither under René de Laudonnière. He found them not where he expected, but on the river May; where Laudonnière had erected a fort about two leagues from the sea, which he named La Caroline. They had been reduced, by war, desertion, and mutiny, from 200 to about 40; and Hawkins heard from them the sad history of their misfortunes and their misconduct. Little as was the sense of religion that either party manifested in their general dealings, on this occasion it became a bond of sympathy and a security for good faith. No precautions were thought necessary in their intercourse. Hawkins supplied them out of his ship with such stores as he could spare; and, to help them the better homeward, spared them also one of his barques of fifty tons; * when Laudonnière could not be persuaded to accept of a passage to Europe for himself and his people, though he had determined upon returning thither without delay, after destroying the fort, lest the Spaniards or English should occupy it.†

* Hakluyt, 516-518.

† "Fort honnête homme," Charlevoix calls Hawkins on this occasion; "et que, bien loin," he adds, "d'abuser du triste état ou il trouva les François, fit au contraire tout ce qu'il put pour les soulager. Surtout quand il eut reconnu qu'ils etoient Protestans." Of this, however, Hawkins could not have been ignorant. "Il vint seul et sans armes lui rendre visite." And for the stores which he spared them, Charlevoix

He now sailed for England; and contrary winds prolonged the voyage "till victuals scanted, so that they were in despair of ever reaching home, had not God," as they truly said, "provided for them better than their deserving". "In which state of great misery," says Sparke, "we were provoked to call upon Him by fervent prayer; which moved Him to hear us": and they arrived, at length, at Padstow, in Cornwall, through His mercy, in safety, "with the loss of twenty persons in all the voyage, and with great profit to the venturers, as also to the whole realm, in bringing home gold, silver, pearls, and other jewels great store. His name, therefore, be praised for evermore. Amen!"* Thus piously the writer of this narrative concludes his relation, as if utterly unconscious that he had been engaged in anything iniquitous. Contrariwise, it was considered that Hawkins had rendered good service to his country by opening for it a new branch of trade; insomuch that, "by way of increase and augmentation of honour, a coat of arms and crest were settled upon him and his posterity, by a patent thus worded: He bears sable on a point wavee, a lion passant gold, in chief three besants. Upon his helm a wreath argent and azure, a demi-Moor, in his proper colour, bound and captive, with annulets on his

says: "Non seulement Hawkins lui en avoit fait un bon prix, mais il y avoit ajouté quantité de présens" (*Hist. de la N. France*, c. lxxxix., xc.).

De Morgues confirms the account of this fair dealing, *æquo admodum pretio*, and that some stores were given to the French (De Bry, 21).

Hawkins' historian thought there were means to reap a sufficient profit in Florida and Virginia; though it might seem unto some that, because gold and silver were not so abundant as in other places, the cost would not quit the charge. For breeding cattle, he thought no country could be more favourable; and the profit from hides was very great. But as to forming a settlement there, "because," he says, "there is not the thing we all seek, being rather desirous of present gains, I do, therefore, affirm the attempt thereof to be more requisite for a prince, who is of power able to go through with the same, than for any subject" (p. 520).

* Hakluyt, 521.

arms and ears, or mantelled gules double argent." * "A worthy symbol," Campbell observes, † "of the infamous traffic which he had opened to his country."

After an expedition in 1567, for the intended relief of the Huguenots at Rochelle, he prepared for a second adventure to Guinea and the Spanish Indies; ‡ and sailed from Plymouth, in October, 1567, with his old ship the *Jesus* of Lubeck, the *Minion*, and four other vessels. Arriving at Cape de Verd, he landed 150 men, "hoping to obtain some negroes, where he got but few, and those with great hurt and damage to his own men; chiefly, it was thought, proceeding from poisoned arrows: for although, in the beginning, the hurts seemed to be but small, there hardly escaped any that had blood drawn of them, but died in strange sort, with their mouths shut some ten days before they died, and after their wounds were whole". Thence they proceeded, "searching with all diligence the rivers from Rio Grande to Sierra Leone"; when, having "gotten together" not so many as 150 slaves, sickness and the lateness of the season, says Hawkins, "commanded us away, thus having nothing wherewith to seek the coast of the West Indies". While the commander was holding counsel whether to make for St. Jorge da Mina, and there obtain gold for their wares, so to defray their charges, a negro king sent to desire their aid against his neighbours, promising them for their pains all the prisoners who should

---

* Prince's *Worthies of Devon*.   † Vol. i., 405.

‡ Herrera says, that two Portuguese offered to conduct this fleet to a place where they might load themselves with gold and other riches: that upon this allurement the queen supplied Hawkins with two ships, he and his brother fitting out other four and a pinnace, that the force on board amounted to 1500 soldiers and mariners, who were to be paid by a third of the profits (*que yvan al tercio de la ganancia*); and that, when the expedition was on the point of sailing, the Portuguese deserted from Plymouth, and got to France: but as the cost of the outfit had been incurred, it was thought proper to proceed (*Historia General*, l. xix., c. xviii., p. 718).

be taken. Without regard to anything but the prospect of gain, the offers were accepted, and 120 men sent to assist this barbarian. They assaulted a town containing 8000 inhabitants, strongly paled and fenced after their manner, and so well defended, that the English, having had six slain and forty wounded, sent to Hawkins for more help; "whereupon," says he, "considering that the good success of this enterprise might highly further the commodity of our voyage, I went myself; and, with the help of the king of our side, assaulted the town both by land and sea; and very hardly, with fire (their houses being covered with dry palm leaves), obtained the town, and put the inhabitants to flight; where we took 250 persons, men, women, and children. And by our friend, the king of our side, there were taken 600 prisoners, whereof we hoped to have had our choice; but the negro (in which nation is seldom or never found truth) meant nothing less: for that night he removed his camp and prisoners, so that we were fain to content us with those few that we had gotten ourselves." *

Having, however, now obtained between 400 and 500 negroes, he hoped, by carrying them to the West Indies, to countervail the charges of this expedition with some gains. Having made the Island of Dominica, he "coasted on from place to place, making his traffic with the Spaniards as he might; somewhat hardly, because the king had straightly commanded all his governors in those parts by no means to suffer any trade to be made with them". Notwithstanding,

---

* Hakluyt, 521, 522. "When they were about to land in the river Bambo," Herrera says, "a sea-horse (*cavallo marino*) gave the boat a blow, which would have swamped it if it had not speedily got to shore: the creature," he adds, "sprang upon the prow at the same time, and with its tail and arm, or paw, carried off a trumpeter" (p. 718). "Here, too," he says, "Hawkins took on board twelve Frenchmen, the miserable remains of fifty, who had put off in their boat from a sinking ship, and remained at the mercy of the waves, subsisting upon four figs a day till these alone survived."

he had "reasonable trade and courteous entertainment" from the Isle of Margarita unto Carthagena, except at Rio de la Hacha, "from whence came all the pearls". The treasurer, who had the charge, would by no means agree to any trade, or suffer us to water; he had fortified his town with divers bulwarks in all places where it might be entered, and furnished him with 100 harquebusiers; so that he thought, by famine, to have enforced us to put a-land our negroes; "of which purpose," says Hawkins, "he had not greatly failed, unless we had by force entered the town: which, after we could by no means obtain his favour, we were enforced to do. So, with 200 men, we brake in upon their bulwarks, and entered the town, with the loss only of two men,* and no hurt done to the Spaniards, because, after their volley discharged, they all fled. Thus having the town, with some circumstances, as partly by the Spaniards' desire of negroes, and partly by friendship of the treasurer, we obtained a secret trade, whereupon the Spaniards resorted to us by night, and bought of us to the number of 200 negroes. In all other places where we traded, the Spaniard inhabitants were glad of us, and traded willingly."†

Carthagena was the last town which they thought to have seen on the coast. There the governor was so straight—that is, he observed his orders so properly—that Hawkins could have no dealings with any Spaniard; and, because his trade was nearly finished, he neither thought it prudent to venture a landing, nor to "detract further time," but departed in peace, hoping to escape the hurricanes, for "the time of these storms" was approaching. But passing by the west end of Cuba, towards Florida, there "happened to them" a storm, which continued four days, and "so beat the *Jesus* that they cut down all her higher buildings; her rudder also

* Herrera says: "He lost his *sargento mor* here, and three others" (p. 719).
† Hakluyt, 522.

was sore shaken, and withal the ship was in so extreme a leak," that they were "rather on the point to leave her than to keep her any longer". Yet, hoping to "bring all to good pass," they made for the coast of Florida, and there found no place nor haven for their ships because of the shallowness of the coast. "Thus being in greater despair, and taken with a new storm, which continued other three days," Hawkins thought that his only resource was to take for his succour "the port which serveth the city of Mexico, called St. Juan de Ulloa; in seeking of which port," he says, "we took on our way three ships, which carried passengers to the number of 100; which passengers we hoped should be a mean to us the better to obtain victuals for our money, and a quiet place for the repairing of our fleet".*

That port they entered on the 16th of September. The Spaniards of Vera Cruz mistook them for a fleet from Spain which was daily expected; and under that mistake the chief officers came aboard to receive the dispatches, † and "being deceived of their expectation," were greatly dismayed; "but when they saw our demand was nothing but victuals, they were recomforted. I found in the same port," says Hawkins, "twelve ships, ‡ which had in them, by report, 200,000*l.* in gold and silver; all which being in my possession, with the king's island, as also the passengers before in my way thitherward stayed, I set at liberty, without the taking from them the weight of a groat." He had good reason for being upon his good behaviour at this juncture; and, detaining two persons of estimation for his own security, he sent post to Mexico, representing to the viceroy that he had put in here by stress of weather, in want of victuals, and his ships in

---

* Hakluyt, 522.

† " Fue tanto el recato de Juan de Aquines, que nunca los oficiales conocieron los navios, hasta que los tomaron, y se los llevaron " (Herrera, 719).

‡ Herrera says six, with a great quantity of silver on board.

great need of repair: these wants the English, as friends to King Philip, requested they might be supplied with for their money; they requested, also, that, with all convenient speed, order might be taken for preventing any cause of quarrel on the arrival of the Spanish fleet. This message left the port on the night after their entrance: "on the morrow," says Hawkins, "we saw open of the haven thirteen great ships. I sent immediately to advertise the general of the fleet of my being there, giving him to understand, that, before I would suffer them to enter the port, there should some order of conditions pass between us for our safe-being there and maintenance of peace.

"Now it is to be understood that this port is made by a little island of stones, not three foot above the water in the highest place, and but a bowshot of length any way: this island standeth from the mainland two bowshots or more. Also it is to be understood that there is not in all this coast any other place for ships to arrive in safety, because the north wind hath there such violence, that, unless the ships be very safely moored, with their anchors fastened upon this island, there is no remedy for these north winds but death. Also the place of the haven was so little, that of necessity the ships must ride one aboard the other, so that we could not give place to them, nor they to us. And here I began to bewail that which after followed: 'For now,' said I, 'I am in two dangers, and forced to receive the one of them'. That was, either I must have kept out the fleet, the which, with God's help, I was very well able to do; or else suffer them to enter in with their accustomed treason, which they never fail to execute, when they may have opportunity to compass it by any means. If I had kept them out, then had there been present shipwreck of all the fleet, which amounted in value to six millions, which was in value of our money 1,800,000*l.*; which I considered I was not able to answer, fearing the queen's majesty's indignation in so weighty a matter. Thus with myself revolving the doubts, I thought rather better to abide the jutt of the uncertainty than the certainty : the uncertain doubt, I account, was their treason, which, by good policy, I hoped might be prevented ; and, therefore, as choosing the least mischief, I proceeded to conditions." *

The fleet, which was commanded by Francisco de Luxan, brought out a new viceroy, Don Martin Henriquez ; and his presence rendered it unnecessary to wait for instructions from Mexico.† Indeed the circumstances admitted of no delay ; for the fleet, being advised from Vera Cruz that the English were in the port, kept off at a distance of some three leagues, and were in danger of the north winds, which are as frequent on that coast as they are perilous. Upon receiving Hawkins's overtures, the viceroy, therefore, desired him to propose his conditions, promising that, for the better maintenance of amity between the two crowns, they should on his part be favourably granted and faithfully performed : he added "many fair words, how, passing the coast of the Indies, he had understood of our honest behaviour towards the inhabitants where we had to do; the which," says Hawkins, " I let pass. We required victuals for our money, and licence to sell as much ware as might furnish our wants ; and that there might be of either part twelve gentlemen as hostages; and that the island, for our better safety, might be in our own possession during our abode there, and such ordnance as was planted on the same island, which were eleven pieces of brass ; and that no Spaniard might land on the island with any kind of weapon." These conditions the viceroy " somewhat disliked " at first ; as well he might, coming from one whom he could regard as nothing better than an armed

---

* Hakluyt, 523.

† According to Herrera, the English had been some days in the port, and the permission for which they had applied had arrived from Mexico. But these are points upon which Hawkins must be the best authority.

contrabandist. Chiefly he objected to the demand that the English should have the island in their own keeping: this, however, Hawkins justly regarded as an indispensable condition, seeing that "if they had had it, we should soon have known our fare; for with the first north wind they had cut our cables, and our ships had gone ashore". The negotiations, not being expedited by any dangerous weather, continued three days. At last, the viceroy consented to all that was required, reducing only the number of hostages to ten: these, with all speed on either part, were exchanged; the viceroy gave a writing, "signed with his hand, and sealed with his seal, of all the conditions; and forthwith commandment was made, by sound of trumpet, that none should violate the peace on pain of death. The two generals met and pledged their faith each to the other; and all having been, as it seemed, concluded, the Spaniards entered the port, the fleets saluting one another as the manner of the sea doth require. Thus, Thursday, we entered the port, Friday we saw the Spanish fleet, and on Monday, at night, they entered. Then we laboured two days placing the English ships by themselves, and the Spanish ships by themselves; the captains of each part, and inferior men of their parts, promising great amity; which even as with all fidelity it was meant on our part, so the Spaniards meant nothing less on theirs." *

Hawkins soon had reason to suspect that the Spaniards were secretly furnishing their ships with men from the shore: indeed, on the very night after the Spaniards had entered, 120 soldiers had been conveyed on board. The viceroy, who, by permitting this, clearly consented to the intended treason, left things in this state, and departed for Mexico. On the morning of Thursday there were manifest indications of some intended treason; such as "shifting of weapons from ship to

* Hakluyt, 523, 524.

ship; planting and landing of ordnance from the ships to the island; passing to and fro of companies of men, more than required for their necessary business, and many other ill likelihoods, which caused him and his people to have a vehement suspicion. Therewithal he sent to the general to inquire what was meant. The answer was, that he would be their defence against all villainies;* and commandment was given, accordingly, to unplant all things suspicious." Hawkins's apprehensions were not removed by these fair words and fair appearances: he had reason to believe that not less than 300 men had been secretly conveyed on board a ship of 900 tons, which was moored next the *Minion*; and, as the master of the *Jesus* spoke Spanish, he sent him to the viceroy, and required to be satisfied if any such thing were or not. "The viceroy now seeing that the treason must be discovered, forthwith stayed our master, blew the trumpet, and of all sides set upon us. Our men which warded ashore, being stricken with sudden fear, gave place, fled, and sought to recover succour of the ships. The Spaniards, being provided for the purpose, landed in all places in multitudes from their ships, which they might easily do without boats, and slew all our men ashore without mercy; a few only escaping on board the *Jesus*. The great ship immediately fell aboard the *Minion*; but, by God's appointment, in the time of the suspicion we had, which was only one half-hour, the *Minion* was made ready to avoid; and so leesing her head-fasts, and

* On the faith of a viceroy, Hawkins says: but it was the general, Luxan, who was now acting on his own authority, and on the avowed principle that faith was not to be kept with freebooters: *Que aquellos Ingleses eran cossarios y que no se les devia guardar la fe dada*. Indeed the story, as told by the Spanish historian, has a blacker character than in Hawkins's relation. Herrera says, that Luxan sent a good number of Spaniards on shore, armed only with daggers, who feigning good fellowship with the English, invited them to drink, and when they had drank enough, and the signal was given, suddenly attacked them, the ships at the same time opening their fire.

hauling away by the stern-fasts, she was gotten out: thus, with God's help, she defended the violence of the first brunt of these 300 men. The *Minion* being passed out, they came aboard the *Jesus;* which, also, with very much ado, and the loss of many of our men, kept them out. Then were there also two other ships that assaulted the *Jesus* at the same instant, so that she had hard getting loose; but yet, with some time, we had cut our head-fasts, and gotten out by the stern-fasts. Now, when the *Jesus* and the *Minion* were gotten about two ships' length from the Spanish fleet, the fight began so hot on all sides, that, within one hour the admiral of the Spaniards was supposed to be sunk, their vice-admiral burnt, and one other of their principal ships supposed to be sunk; so that the ships were little able to annoy us." *

Had the English maintained the island long enough after the first manifestation of hostility, to have spiked the guns there, the whole action would have been as glorious to them as it was dishonourable to the Spaniards; but they had made no preparation against an attack, and when it was made the men who were ashore lost all courage and with it all presence of mind. Their ordnance being thus in the Spaniards' hands, "did us," says Hawkins, "so great annoyance, that it cut all the masts and yards of the *Jesus*, in such sort that there was no hope to carry her away; also it sunk our small

* Hakluyt, 524. The Spanish account differs from this: it says that Hawkins, having fought all day, and seeing twelve of his men killed by the fall of a mast, and that his other vessels were in bad plight, went on board the *Almeranta*, and ordered his own ship to be set on fire, and so put to sea. The ship, however, was not burnt; and the Spanish hostages who were left in it said that he had always treated them well. The Spaniards say that they sunk one vessel, and that another with sixty men got out, but afterwards was driven on the coast of Panuco, where the people were made prisoners by the inhabitants of S. Luis de Tampico and sent to Mexico, and there, by the viceroy's orders, treated well (p. 720).

ships (the *Judith* only, a small barque of fifty tons, excepted) : whereupon we determined to place the *Jesus* on that side of the *Minion*, that she might abide all the battery from the land, and so be a defence for the *Minion* till night ; and then to take such relief of victuals and other necessaries from the *Jesus* as the time would suffer us, and to leave her. As we were thus determining, and had placed the *Minion* from the shot of the land, suddenly the Spaniards fired two great ships which were coming directly with us ; and having no means to avoid the fire, it bred among the men a marvellous fear, so that some said, ' Let us depart with the *Minion* ' ; others said, ' Let us see whether the wind will carry the fire from us '. But to be short, the *Minion's* men, who had always their sails in readiness, thought to make sure work ; and so, without either consent of the captain or master, cut their sail." Hawkins himself was "very hardly" received on board. Most of the men who were left alive in the *Jesus* made shift and followed the *Minion* in their boat; the rest, whom the boat could not hold, were enforced to abide the mercy of the Spaniards, "which," he says, "I doubt, was very little ".*

Thus only the *Minion* and the *Judith* escaped ; and Hawkins complains that the latter that same night forsook him in his great misery. Having removed about two bowshots from the Spanish ships, the *Minion* rode until morning, and then gained the Isla de Sacrificios, about a mile off : there a north wind took them ; and being left only with two anchors and as many cables,—for in the conflict they had lost three

---

* Hakluyt, 425. Little, indeed; "for it is a certain truth," says Miles Philips, "that whereas they had taken certain of our men ashore, they hung them up by the arms upon high posts, until the blood burst out of their fingers' ends: of which men so used there is one Copstowe, and certain others yet alive, who, by the merciful providence of the Almighty, arrived here at home in England, carrying still about with them (and shall to their graves) the marks and tokens of those their inhuman and more than barbarous cruel dealings " (Hakluyt, 473).

cables and two anchors—they thought always upon death, which ever was present; "but God," says the commander, "preserved us to a longer life. [That north wind prevented the Spaniards, according to their own account, from pursuing him: but they might have done this when the wind changed, and, doubtless, would have done so, had they not been so roughly handled in the action.] The weather waxed seasonable, and the Saturday we set sail; and having a great number of men and little victuals, our hope of life waxed less and less." Some were for yielding to the Spaniards; some rather desired to reach a place where they might give themselves to the infidels; and some had rather abide, with a little pittance, the mercy of God at sea. "So, thus, with sorrowful hearts, we wandered in an unknown sea by the space of fourteen days, till hunger enforced us to seek the land; for hides were thought very good meat: rats, cats, mice, and dogs, none escaped that might be gotten; parrots and monkeys, that were had in great price, were thought then very profitable if they served the turn one dinner. Thus on the 8th of October we came to land in the bottom of the same Bay of Mexico, in $23\frac{1}{2}°$, where we hoped to have found inhabitants of the Spaniards, relief of victuals, and place for the repair of our ship, which was so sore beaten with shot from our enemies, and bruised with shooting off our own ordnance, that our weary and weak arms were scarce able to keep out water. But all things happened to the contrary; we found neither people, victuals, nor haven of relief; only a place where, having fair weather, with some peril we might land a boat." *
This was on the coast of Tabasco.

Here some of his people desired to be set ashore, making their choice rather to submit themselves to the mercy of savages than longer to hazard themselves at sea, where they very well saw that should they remain together, if they per-

* Hakluyt, 524, 525.

ished not by drowning, hunger must enforce them in the end to eat one another. Desperate as the request was, he could not but consent to it. About a hundred took this resolution, and about as many more resolved, at all risks, to take the chance of reaching their own country.* The former were

* Thus Hawkins relates the story: a very different one is told by Miles Philips: he says that to this request "our general did very willingly agree, considering with himself that it was necessary for him to lessen his number, both for the safety of himself and the rest; and thereupon being resolved to set half his people ashore that he had then left alive, it was a world to see how suddenly men's minds were altered; for they which a little before desired to be set on land were now of a different mind, and requested rather to stay. By means whereof our general was enforced, for the more contentation of all men's minds, and to take away all occasions of offence, to take this order. First, he made choice of such persons of service and account as were needful to stay; and that being done, of those which were willing to go, he appointed such as he thought might be best spared, and presently appointed that by the boat they should be set on shore; our general promising us that, the next year, he would either come himself, or else send to fetch us home. Here, again, it would have caused any stony heart to have relented to hear the pitiful moan that many did make, and how loth they were to depart. The weather was then somewhat stormy and tempestuous, and, therefore, we were to pass with great danger; yet, notwithstanding, there was no remedy, but we that were appointed to go must of necessity do so: howbeit, those that went in the first boat were safely set on shore; but of those which went in the second, of which I myself was one, the seas wrought so high, that we could not attain to the shore, and, therefore, we were constrained, through the cruel dealing of John Hampton, captain of the *Minion*, and John Sanders, boatswain of the *Jesus*, and Thomas Pollard his mate, to leap out of the boat into the main sea, having more than a mile to shore, and so to shift for ourselves, and either to sink or swim; and of those that so were (as it were) thrown out, and compelled to leap into the sea, there were two drowned" (pp. 473, 474). Those who were landed, he says, had only one caliver, and two old swords among them.

The relation of Job Hortop, another of the party, is more in conformity with Hawkins. "Our general," he says, "was forced to divide his company into two parts, for there was mutiny among them for want of victuals; and some said that they would rather be on the shore, to shift for themselves amongst the enemies, than to starve on shipboard.

landed; Hawkins determined to water there, and then with his "little remain of victuals to take the sea". He was on shore with fifty of his remaining crew expediting this work, when there arose an extreme storm; during three days they could not regain the ship, and the ship was in such peril that every hour they expected to see it wrecked. But "God again had mercy on them," and with fair weather they got clear of the coast of the Indies and the Gulf of Bahama. After this, his men, oppressed with famine, began to sink and die, till the few survivors grew into such weakness that they were scarce able to manage the ship. The wind "being always ill for them to recover England," they made for the coast of Galicia, and on the last day of December put into Pontevedra. There, "by excess of fresh meat, the men grew into miserable diseases". Most of them died; and Hawkins perceiving that, notwithstanding all endeavours to conceal his weakness, the Spaniards had discovered it, and were planning some treachery, removed with all speed possible to Vigo. Some English ships which were lying there assisted him, and spared him twelve of their men, with which help he arrived at last in Mount's Bay. He concludes his relation with these

He asked them who would go on shore, and who would tarry on shipboard? those that would go on shore, he willed to go on fore-mast, and those that would tarry, on baft-mast. Fourscore and sixteen of us were willing to depart. Our general gave unto every one of us six yards of Roan cloth, and money to them that demanded it. When we were landed he came unto us, where, friendly embracing every one of us, he was greatly grieved that he was forced to leave us behind him; he counselled us to serve God and to love one another, and thus courteously he gave us a sorrowful farewell, and promised if God sent him safe home, he would do what he could, that so many of us as lived should by some means be brought into England; and so he did.

"Since my return into England, I have heard that many misliked that he left us so behind him, and brought away negroes. But the reason is this, for them he might have had victuals, or any other thing needful, if by foul weather he had been driven upon the islands, which for gold nor silver he could not have had" (Hakluyt, 491).

words: "If all the miseries and troublesome affairs of this sorrowful voyage should be perfectly and thoroughly written, there should need a painful man with his pen, and as great a time as he had that wrote the lives and deaths of the martyrs".*

It is remarkable that the Spanish character, honourable as it had formerly been, and as it afterwards again became, should at this time have been stained by so many instances of bad faith. The perfidy of some of their kings, especially of Ferdinand, first brought upon the nation this disgrace. He acted upon the Machiavellian principle, that in policy whatever is expedient is right; and the Romish Church consecrated that principle for his successors, when it pronounced that no faith was to be kept with heretics,—a principle which no Church but that which styles itself infallible has ever proclaimed, and which can be held by none but those whose conscience is not in their own keeping. The treachery with which Hawkins had been treated excited a strong feeling in England, especially among military and seafaring men. They exclaimed against the Spaniards for breach of treaty in this case, inasmuch, they said, as it had been agreed between Charles V. and Henry VIII. that there should be free com-

* Hakluyt, 526. Hawkins little knew, when he penned that sentence, that some of his unhappy companions would be entitled in the strictest sense to that appellation! George Rively, Peter Momfrie, and Cornelius, an Irishman, were burnt at Mexico; Robert Barret and John Gilbert at Seville. Many others, who saved their lives by renouncing the opinions which they had been compelled by torture to avow, though they would have professed anything to have escaped persecution, were flogged on horseback through the streets of Mexico, and condemned there or in Seville to the galleys, and to different terms of imprisonment. The narratives which Miles Philips and Job Hortop published of their adventures and sufferings must have contributed greatly to that abhorrence of the Spaniards which so long prevailed in this country. The first effected his escape after sixteen years, the latter after three and twenty. Both accounts bear every mark of veracity. It appears that the Spaniards would have been disposed to treat them with great kindness, if it had not been for the Inquisition.

merce between the subjects of both princes, in all and singular their dominions and islands,—not excepting America, which already at that time belonged to Charles; and on this ground they wished that war might be declared against Spain.* Both parties were in the wrong. An infraction of that treaty, by closing the American ports, was a point for discussion between the two Governments, and if the English Government had thought fit, a ground of war, if any wrong in consequence had been offered to one of the queen's subjects; but it was not for a subject to take the matter into his own hands, and declare his determination of trading in those ports amicably if the authorities pleased, but otherwise, arms in hand, whether they would or not. After he had thus declared, and acted up to that declaration, there could have been no just cause of complaint on the part of England, if he and his fleet had been fairly taken or destroyed. But by acting basely the Spaniards gave the English the advantage of a fair quarrel; and though the queen, because she was at that time perplexed with the troubled state of affairs in Scotland, for that cause, and for other weighty considerations, gave no ear to those who would at once have engaged the nation in a war with Spain, there were adventurers who resolved to prosecute the quarrel at all risks.

The *Judith*, which made part of Hawkins's fleet, and was the only vessel except the *Minion* that escaped, was commanded by Francis Drake, a name that soon became terrible to the Spaniards. The cottage in which Drake was born, on the beautiful banks of the Tavy, was demolished some thirty years ago, till which time it had remained unchanged; a stall for cattle belonging to the farm-house hard by now stands upon its site. By his own account, as repeated by Camden, he was born of mean parentage, but his name was given him in baptism by his godfather, Francis Russel, afterwards Earl

* Camden, 108.

of Bedford ; and he is said to have been akin to Hawkins, at whose cost and under whose care it is also said that he was brought up, being the eldest of twelve sons. That cost, however, could have been little ; and the care, perhaps, little more than such countenance as gave him consideration in the eyes of his employers, if Camden's statement be correct, which in the main it must needs be, having been derived from Drake himself. His father being likely to be called in question* for his religion as a Protestant, in the days of persecution fled from Devonshire into Kent. When better days arrived, he obtained an appointment " among the seamen in the king's navy to read prayers to them " ; and soon afterwards was ordained deacon, and made vicar of Upnor Church upon the Medway ; the road, says Camden, where the fleet usually anchoreth. Here, " by reason of his poverty, he put his son to the master of a barque, his neighbour, who carried on a coasting trade, and used sometimes to transport merchandise to Zeeland and to France ". This master " held Drake hard to his business " ; and " pains with patience in his youth," says Fuller, " knit the joints of his soul, and made them more solid and compacted ". The master was so satisfied with his conduct, and pleased with him, that, being unmarried, he bequeathed him the barque at his death. With this he continued his active and thriving way of life ; and had got together some

* Camden says he was called in question by the law of the six articles ; but Campbell observes, that, if Drake was born some time before, Sir Francis Russel could have been but a child, and, therefore, not likely to be his godfather : moreover, he says this account makes him ten years older than he was. But Drake was two and twenty when he obtained the command of the *Judith :* this carries back his birth to 1544, at which time the six articles were in force, and Francis Russel was seventeen years of age. Fuller says, upon this occasion, that " the sting of Popery still remained in England, though the teeth were knocked out," and that Drake was born in Devonshire and brought up in Kent ; " God dividing the honour betwixt two counties, that the one might have his birth, and the other his education " (*Holy State*, 123).

little money, when, hearing that Hawkins was fitting out an expedition for the New World, he sold his vessel, and, repairing to Plymouth with some other "stout seamen," embarked himself and his fortunes in the adventure.*

In this unfortunate voyage Drake lost all that he had accumulated by his former industry; but a divine,† belonging to the fleet, comforted him with the assurance that, having been thus treacherously used by the Spaniards, he might lawfully recover in value of the King of Spain, and repair his loses upon him wherever he could. "The case," says Fuller, "was clear in sea divinity; and few are such infidels as not to believe doctrines which make for their own profit. Whereupon Drake, though a poor private man, undertook to

---

* Camden, 248. Fuller's *Holy State*, 123. Prince's *Worthies of Devon*. Campbell. It is certain that Hawkins was displeased with Drake for "forsaking him in his great misery, and shifting for himself". Herrera says that Drake escaped from the island by a ship's cable; that Hawkins ordered him into a French ship (which he had taken from some Portuguese who had captured it off Cape Blanco, and in which was most of the gold which they had obtained), and that Drake, instead of obeying his further orders and waiting for him off the port, made all speed for England, reported there that Hawkins was lost, and rose up with the gold himself, saying he had distributed it among the men. "This," says Herrera, "was his beginning; and though the queen kept him three months in prison, she pardoned him upon intercession, and so the matter rested" (p. 720). Camden says that Drake hardly escaped with the loss of what he had. The charge of peculation is no doubt a calumny; for his imprisonment, if it really took place, breach of orders, and the desertion of his commander, would be sufficient cause. Drake, according to Job Hortop, was made master and commander of a Portuguese caravel, captured on the way from the Canaries to Cape Blanco.

† These are Camden's words, from whence it may be surmised that possibly that divine was Drake's own father. Fuller and subsequent writers who have followed Fuller say it was the minister of his ship. "The doctrine, however rudely preached, was very taking in England; and, therefore, he no sooner published his design than he had numbers of volunteers ready to accompany him, though they had no such pretence even as he had to colour their proceedings" (Campbell, i., 418).

revenge himself on so mighty a monarch, who, not contented that the sun riseth and setteth in his dominions, may seem to desire to make all his own where he shineth." * Two or three voyages he made to gain intelligence, it is said, in the West Indies; and in these he got some store of money " by playing the seaman and the pirate ".† Some reputation now he had by this time acquired as a skilful and adventurous mariner; for now, it is said, he got a commission, and sailed from Plymouth, in 1570, with two ships, the *Dragon* and the *Swan;* and the year after in the *Swan* alone. In these voyages he acquired certain notice of the places to be aimed at.‡ Thus prepared with all needful information, he sailed from the Sound on Whitsun Eve, 1572, in the *Pascha* of Plymouth, of seventy tons, and his brother, John Drake, in the *Swan,* of twenty-five, with three handsome pinnaces, taken asunder and stowed aboard, to be put together upon occasion. He was well provided with a year's victuals, and with all necessary ammunition; but the force with which he commenced this first hostile expedition against the Spanish Indies consisted of no more than seventy-three men and boys. With these he sailed§ for Nombre de Dios, which " was then the granary of the West Indies, wherein the golden harvest brought from Panama was hoarded up till it could be conveyed to Spain".‖

On the 2nd of July he came in sight of the high land of America, and directed his course to Port Pheasant, so named by him on a former voyage, because of the number of those

---

* " And now," he adds, " let us see how a dwarf, standing on the mount of God's Providence, may prove an overmatch for a giant."

  † Camden.   ‡ Prince.

§ " With all speed and secrecy, as loth to put the town to too much charge, which he knew they would willingly bestow, in providing beforehand for his entertainment " (Fuller).

‖ Fuller. Nombre de Dios " then served the Spaniards for the same purposes, though not so conveniently, as those for which they afterwards used Porto Bello " (Campbell, i., 418).

birds which he had there seen. Landing here, they found this warning newly inscribed on a plate of lead, and fastened to a tree of such conspicuous magnitude that four men could not enclasp its girth : " Captain Drake, if you fortune to come into the port, make haste away, for the Spaniards which you had with you here last year have betrayed this place, and taken away all that you left here. I departed hence this present 7th of July, 1572. Your loving friend, John Garret."
—This Captain Garret was of Plymouth; and was probably, like his friend, one of those persons who made war against the King of Spain and his subjects upon their own account. Drake, however, was not induced to alter his plans by this unfavourable information, but employed seven days in putting together his pinnaces in that convenient port. " As they had completed this business, an English barque from the Isle of Wight, James Rowse,* captain, with thirty-eight men aboard, came into the port, and being made acquainted with his design, joined company with him." Some of the men had been there with him the year before.

Sailing from hence for Nombre de Dios, they kept close to the shore, and lay quiet all night, intending to attempt the town at break of day. But he was forced to alter his resolution, and assault it sooner; for he heard his men muttering among themselves about the strength and greatness of the place : † wherefore he roused them from their rest before

---

* In Sir William Davenant's opera upon this part of Drake's history, one of the sailors says, or sings,—

> " The lion Rowse is landed here,
> I'll run to meet him at the pier;
>   A ton of yellow gold
>   Conceal'd within our hold,
> For half my share I scorn to take,
> When he is joined with dragon Drake ".

† " And when men's heads are once fly-blown with buzzes of suspicion, the vermin multiply instantly, and one jealousy begets another " (Fuller).

they had hatched their fears, and persuaded them it was dawn when the moon rose. The town was unwalled, and they entered it without difficulty in two companies, with trumpet sounding and drum beating, and with "fire-pikes divided between both companies, which no less affrighted the enemy than gave light to the English, who thereby discovered every place as if it had been broad day ".* But the Spaniards were not unprepared, and saluted them in the market-place with a volley of shot. Drake returned the greeting with a flight of arrows, "the best ancient English compliment," and drove them from the ground; but not without receiving a severe wound in his leg. This he dissembled, "knowing that, if the general's heart stoops the men's will fall; and that, if so bright an opportunity once setteth, it seldom riseth again ". They made their way to the house where the bars of silver were deposited,† Drake telling them "he had brought them to the mouth of the treasury of the world, which if they did not gain, none but themselves were to be blamed". He bade them break it open; but as he stepped forward to encourage them by his example, his strength, sight, and speech failed him, and he began to faint for loss of blood. They bound up his wound with his scarf; and when he would not be persuaded, they "added force to their entreaties, and so carried him to his pinnace ".‡ It was time to retreat,

---

* Prince.

† "They discovered," says the relation, "a vast heap of wealth in the lower room, consisting of bars of silver, piled up against the wall, seventy foot in length, ten in breadth, and twelve in height, each bar between thirty-five and forty pounds' weight" (Prince). They might have looked into the room through the grating, but certainly had neither time nor opportunity for measuring it.

‡ Fuller. "Thus victory sometimes slips through their fingers who have caught it in their hands." Lopez Vaz, whose brief account of this expedition fell into the hands of the English, and is published (in a translation) by Hakluyt (vol. iii., p. 525), says, that Drake landed about 150 men, left seventy of them in a fort which was there, and, with the rest,

for the Spaniards had discovered their weakness; and the adventurers, many of whom had got good booty before they retired, found it necessary to re-embark, and put off to an island some two leagues distant, where they remained two days. Several men were wounded in this affair, but only one slain. While they lay off the island, one of the garrison came off to them, trusting, as it seems, to their honour; and declaring that he came for no other purpose than to see those whose courage was such that, with such inconsiderable forces, they had ventured upon so incredible an attempt. He asked, however, whether their captain were the same Captain Drake who had been on this coast the two preceding years? and as

marched into the town, without doing any harm till he came to the market-place. There he discharged his calivers, and sounded a trumpet; and "the people hereupon, not thinking of any such matter, were put in great fear, and, waking out of their sleep, fled all into the mountains, inquiring one of another what the matter should be,—remaining as men amazed! But some fourteen or fifteen of them," he says, "went to the market-place, and seeing the English to be but few, fired their harquebusses at them with such fortune as to kill the trumpeter, and shoot one of the principal men through the leg, upon which he retired towards the fort. Meantime they in the fort, hearing the firing in the town, and finding when they sounded their trumpet that it was not answered, concluded that their comrades had all been cut off, and thereupon fled to their pinnaces. And the captain and his people, finding the fort forsaken, were in so great fear, that, leaving their furniture behind them, and putting off their hose, they swam and waded to their pinnaces, and so went with their ships out of the port."

Except as to the numbers, and the manner of the retreat, this relation is in the main confirmed by the English account, Drake having been thus wounded, and the only Englishman who was slain (though many were hurt) being the trumpeter. Herrera makes no mention of this expedition. A notice relating to it, but under the erroneous date of 1568, occurs in the "Compendio Historial y Indice Chronologico Peruano y del Nuevo Reyno de Granada," annexed to the very rare work of P. Manuel Rodriguez, entitled *El Marañon y Amazonas*. It is in these pithy words: "Tubose noticia en las costas de Indias, que las infestaba el Draque, Cosario, que fue muy prejudicial, como se dize despues".

many of the Spaniards were wounded with arrows, he asked also whether the arrows were poisoned, and how the wounds might be cured? The captain made answer he was the same Drake concerning whom they inquired; that it was never his custom, nor that of his countrymen, to poison their arrows; that their wounds might be cured with the ordinary remedies; and that he only wanted some of that gold and silver which they got out of the earth and sent into Spain to trouble all the world.*

Having been disappointed here, Drake made toward Carthagena, and took several vessels on his way laden with provisions and goods. What was of more eventual importance, he opened a communication with the Cimarrones, or Maroons, negroes who had escaped from slavery, and established themselves in freedom in the interior of the Isthmus of Darien. "They had towns of about sixty families, in which the people lived cleanly and civilly," and their chief was able to raise 1700 fighting men. By these people he was informed that the treasure was brought from Panama to Nombre de Dios upon mules, a *recua* or party of which, consisting as might happen of from thirty to seventy, he might probably intercept. On this adventure, his leg having been healed, Drake set forth. One of the chief Cimarrones, as they were on the way, led him to a height, where from a great tree, it is said, that both seas might be seen. The story says that steps were cut in the trunk of this huge tree for ascending it, and that almost in the top "a convenient arbour had been made, wherein twelve men might sit". Into this Drake mounted; and, obtaining a full sight from thence of that ocean, concerning which he had heard such golden reports, besought God to grant him "life and leave once to sail an English ship in those seas".†

* Prince.

† Prince.—Camden's is a less circumstantial but more likely account: " that, after having burnt the rich receptacle or storehouse of merchandise

The rashness of one of his own men, "who had taken a little too much aqua-vitæ," marred this enterprise: through this man's folly the Spaniards were alarmed, and Drake had

upon the river Chirage, called the Cross, roving for a time up and down in the parts adjoining, he descried from the mountains the South Sea. Hereupon the man, being inflamed with ambition of glory and hopes of wealth, was so vehemently transported with desire to navigate that sea, that falling down there upon his knees, he implored the Divine assistance, that he might at some time or other sail thither, and make a perfect discovery of the same; and hereunto he bound himself by a vow. From that time forward his mind was pricked on continually, night and day, to perform his vow" (p. 249).

Balboa expressed similar feelings in precisely the same situation. When his Indian guides pointed out to him the height from whence "he might see the other sea so long looked for, and never seen before of any man coming out of our world, approaching to the top of the mountain, he commanded his men to stay, and went himself alone to the summit, as if it were to take the first possession thereof; where falling prostrate upon the ground, and raising himself again upon his knees, as the manner of the Christians is to pray, lifting up his eyes and hands toward heaven, and directing his face toward the new-found South Sea, he poured forth his humble and devout prayers before Almighty God, as a spiritual sacrifice with thanksgiving, that it pleased His Divine Majesty to reserve unto that day the victory and praise of so great a thing unto him, being a man but of small wit and knowledge, of little experience and base parentage. When he had thus made his prayers after his warlike manner he beckoned to his companions to come to him, showing them the great main sea heretofore unknown to the inhabitants of Europe, Africa, and Asia. Here again he fell to his prayers as before, desiring Almighty God and the blessed Virgin to favour his beginnings, and to give him good success to subdue those lands to the glory of His holy name, and increase of His true religion. All his companions did likewise, and praised God with loud voices for joy. Then Vasco, with no less manly courage than Hannibal of Carthage showed his soldiers Italy from the promontories of the Alps, exhorted his men to lift up their hearts, and to behold the land even now under their feet, and the sea before their eyes, which should be unto them a full and just reward of their great labours and travails now overpast. When he had said these words he commanded them to raise certain heaps of stones, in the stead of altars, for a token of possession" (Peter Martyr. Eden's translation, 97).

at first to encounter not a party of muleteers, but of men prepared for defence. He put them to flight, however, and got possession of Venta de la Cruz, which seems to have been a station between the two ports on each side of the isthmus. Here the English account says, that both the Maroons and his own people were strictly ordered not to hurt any woman nor unarmed man, and that this order was faithfully obeyed. In the Spanish relation it is said that six or seven merchants were killed here, and no gold or silver found, but much merchandise, to the value of 200,000 ducats, which he burnt, together with the place. He had better fortune soon in hearing "the sweet music of the mules coming with a great noise of bells"; and presently he got sight of two *recuas* or companies, under no other care than that of the muleteers, who mistrusted nothing. Taking from these as much treasure as they could carry, they buried several tons of silver; but one of his men fell into the Spaniards' hands, and was compelled by torture to discover the place, so that, when Drake's people returned for a second lading, it was almost all gone. Upon returning to the coast where his pinnaces had been appointed to meet him, they were not to be seen, but in their stead seven Spanish pinnaces which had been searching all the shore thereabouts. Being now in great fear that his ships also were lost, he constructed a raft of the trees which the river brought down, mounted a biscuit sack for a sail, and "with an oar shaped out of a young tree, for a rudder," he with three others, it is said, ventured out of the mouth of the river. If this account be true, his motive must have been to obtain a better view of the coast from the water, than he could in a country covered with woods. Having sailed upon this raft about six hours, always up to the waist in water, and at every wave up to the arm-pits, they had sight of their own pinnaces, which, not perceiving them, were making behind a point for shelter from the wind and night. Drake then ran his raft ashore, got round the point by land, and there joyfully found them. They went about to the Rio Francisco, took in their comrades with the treasure that they had secured, and rejoined the ships. Nothing now remained but to dismiss their Maroon allies. Pedro, one of the chief and most serviceable of them, had taken a fancy to Drake's sword, and was so delighted when it was presented to him, that he desired him to accept four wedges of gold as a grateful return. Drake accepted them as courteously as they were proffered, but threw them into the common stock, saying it was just that they who bore part of the charge in setting him to sea, should enjoy their full proportion of the advantage at his return. He now sailed homeward with so prosperous a gale that in twenty-three days he passed from Cape Florida to the Scilly Isles; and arriving at Plymouth on a Sunday, the news was carried into the church during sermon time, and "there remained few or no people with the preacher," all running out to welcome one who was already regarded as the hero of that place and of that county.*

Though Drake had enriched himself in this expedition, success served only to excite him to a greater enterprise. But while he was "brooding privately over this new design," it was in part forestalled by one who had served under him in the various capacities of soldier, sailor, and cook. This person, whose name was John Oxenham, is said to have obtained the good opinion both of his captain and comrades in no ordinary degree. Drake, when he beheld from "that goodly and great high tree" of the Maroons the sea of which

---

* Prince. "There want not those," says Fuller, "who love to beat down the price of every honourable action, though they themselves never mean to be chapmen. These cry up Drake's fortune herein, to cry down his valour; as if this his performance were nothing, wherein a golden opportunity ran his head, with his long forelock, into Drake's hands, beyond expectation. But certainly his resolution and unconquerable patience deserved much praise, to adventure on such a design, which had in it just no more probability than what was enough to keep it from being impossible" (*Holy State*, 126).

he had heard such golden reports, communicated especially to Oxenham his purpose of one day sailing upon it, "if it would please God to grant him that happiness"; and Oxenham, in reply, protested that unless Drake were to beat him from his company, "he would follow him by God's grace". On one occasion, when a party was to be sent on shore, and the people would not consent that Drake should venture his person, John Oxenham and Thomas Sherwell were put in trust for the service, "to the great content of the whole company, who conceived greatest hope of them next to the captain, whom, by no means, they would condescend to suffer to adventure".* Oxenham "had gotten among the seamen the name of captain for his valour, and had privily scraped together good store of money"; and, having now been some time at home, and becoming impatient of idleness, he determined no longer to wait for Drake,† but undertake, on his own account, the adventure which that enterprising commander had projected. Following, therefore, the course which his late commander had so successfully pursued, he sailed for the isthmus with one ship and seventy men, revisited his old acquaintance the Maroons, and learned from them that the treasure which he had hoped to intercept on its way from Panama was now protected by a convoy of soldiers. Disappointed in this hope, he determined upon a bolder adventure. He drew his ship aground in a retired and woody creek, covered it with boughs, buried his provisions

---

* Burney's *Hist. of Discoveries in the South Sea*, i., 294, 295. *Sir Francis Drake Revived*, 54, 81.

† "Drake," says Prince, "being prevented from setting forth, partly by secret envy at home, and partly by being employed in his prince and country's service in Ireland. 'Tis true Oxenham had formerly promised him to assist him in that noble undertaking; but having already waited his leisure for so doing two years, and not knowing how much longer it would be, if at all, ere his occasions would permit him so to do, he might think himself disobliged from his promise, and so he undertook something himself."

and his great guns, and taking with him two small pieces of ordnance, went, with all his men and six Maroon guides, about twelve leagues into the interior, to a river which discharges itself into the South Sea. There he cut wood and built a pinnace, "which was five and forty foot by the keel"; embarked in it, and secured for himself the honour (if so it may be called, under such circumstances) of being the first Englishman that ever entered the Pacific. In this vessel he went to the Isla de Perlas, five and twenty leagues from Panama, and there lay in wait for the appearance of a vessel from Peru. After lurking ten days, he captured a small barque bringing gold from Quito; and, six days afterward, another with silver from Lima.

Not satisfied with this, he searched the islands for pearls; and having found a few, returned to his pinnace, made for the river in which he had embarked, and, when he was near the mouth, dismissed his prizes, thus incautiously allowing them to perceive where he was entering. The alarm was soon given; first, by some negroes from the island, who, as soon as he had left them, hastened in a canoe to Panama.* Juan de Ortega was immediately dispatched with 100 men, beside negro rowers, in four barques; and he falling in with the prizes on his way was by them directed to the river. Here,

---

* There is a more romantic but far less likely story (Prince calls it "another guess account"), that in one of the prizes Oxenham found "two pieces of especial estimation; the one a table of massy gold set with emeralds, sent for a present to the king; the other, a lady of singular beauty, married and the mother of children. The latter grew to be his perdition; for he had capitulated with these Symerons, that their part of the booty should be only the prisoners, to the end to execute their malice upon the Spaniards for their cruelty to them; showing their revenge by roasting them, and eating their hearts. John Oxenham was taken with the love of the lady, and to win her good-will, what through her tears and detestation of this barbarous action, breaking promise with the Symerons, he gave the prisoners their liberty, except the lady; and they, making haste to Panama, sent out forces to intercept him,"

however, he was at fault; for the river discharged itself by three channels: he had made his choice to ascend the greatest of these streams, when feathers were observed coming down one of the smaller channels, from whence it was inferred that the pirates had plucked some fowls upon its banks. Here, therefore, he entered; and, after four days' search, discovered the pinnace, with six Englishmen on board. These men leaped ashore, and ran for their lives: one was killed in his flight, the others escaped. Ortega, leaving twenty men in his boats, entered the country with the rest of his force; and, pursuing such traces as were to be found, came upon a hut or barrack, from whence the English, upon the alarm given them by their comrades, had fled, but where they had left their booty, and whatever else might have encumbered them. He removed the treasure to his barques, and thought it more prudent to wait awhile for the chance of events, than to enter upon a painful and uncertain pursuit.

In this he judged wisely. There had been a dispute between Oxenham and his men when they had got their plunder ashore: he had required them to carry it to their ship, promising them their shares; the sailors, however, demanded a present division of the spoil: he was angry that his word should be doubted, and they were incensed that he made any difficulty in satisfying their claim. His life was threatened: the matter, however, seems to have been compromised, and Oxenham went in search of negroes to act as carriers. These he procured among the Maroons; and returning with them, met his men who had escaped from the pinnace, and those who were fleeing from the barrack. The loss of their booty at once completed their reconcilement: he promised larger shares if they should succeed in recapturing it; and marched resolutely in quest of the Spaniards, relying upon the Maroons as well as upon his own people. But Ortega was prepared for such an attempt: the Spanish were experienced in bush-fighting, and made such advantage of their experience, that, with the loss of seven killed and wounded, they slew five of the negroes and eleven Englishmen, and took seven of Oxenham's men prisoners. Thus defeated, he made for his ship with the remainder of his men; and Ortega, having buried his dead, returned with the treasure, the pinnace, and the prisoners to Panama. Advice had been sent from thence to Nombre de Dios: vessels were despatched to search along the coast for the Englishman's ship; and when Oxenham and his people reached the spot where they had, as they hoped, concealed it, it was gone. Nothing remained to them but to trust to the friendship of the Maroons, till they could build canoes, in which it was their intention to try their fortune upon the Northern Sea, if they could surprise some vessel there. But in this, which, if time had been given them for attempting it, would have been no forlorn hope, they were prevented. The Spaniards, who knew how insecure they must be while fifty such adventurers were at large in the country, sent 150 men under Diego de Frias to hunt them out: some who were sick fell into his hands; and the others, whom he failed to take, Oxenham being one, were, after a while, delivered up by the negroes. They were brought to Panama; and Oxenham was then asked whether he had his queen's authority for entering the King of Spain's dominions? This could not be produced, nor was it pretended: summary condemnation followed, and the prisoners were executed as pirates, except Oxenham, the master, the pilot, and five boys, who were sent to Lima, the latter as fit subjects for mercy and conversion beeause of their youth; the three former as being the chiefs of the crew, of whom it was expedient that an example should be made in the Peruvian capital. In that city Oxenham and his two companions suffered death * as common enemies of

---

* Prince says: " There is a family of considerable standing of this name (Oxenham) at South Tawton, near Okehampton, of which is this strange and wonderful thing recorded; that at the deaths of any of them a bird

mankind; "thus miscarrying," says Camden, "in this great and memorable adventure".*

Another freebooter followed Drake's course the ensuing year. This was Master Andrew Barker, of Bristol, who,

with a white breast is seen for a while fluttering about their beds, and then suddenly to vanish away ".

Howell has this account in one of his letters, written from London in 1632: "As I past by St. Dunstan's, in Fleet Street, the last Saturday, I stepped into a lapidary or stonecutter's shop, to treat with the master for a stone to be put upon my father's tomb, and, casting my eyes up and down, I spied a huge marble, with a large inscription upon it, which was this, to my best remembrance :—

"' Here lies John Oxenham, a goodly young man, in whose chamber, as he was struggling with the pangs of death, a bird, with a white breast, was seen fluttering about his bed, and so vanished.

"' Here lies also Mary Oxenham, the sister of the said John, who died the next day, and the same apparition was seen in the room.'

" Then another sister is spoken of. Then,—

"' Here lies hard by James Oxenham, the son of the said John, who died a child in his cradle a little after; and such a bird was seen fluttering about his head a little before he expired, which vanished afterwards.'

" At the bottom of the stone there is,—

"' Here lies Elizabeth Oxenham, the mother of the said John, who died sixteen years since, when such a bird with a white breast was seen about her bed before her death.'

" To all these there be divers witnesses, both squires and ladies, whose names are engraven upon the stone. This stone is to be sent to a town hard by Exeter, where this happened. Were you here I could raise a choice discourse with you hereupon " (*Epistolæ Ho-Elianæ*, book i., sec. 6, ep. ix.).

* Hakluyt, iii., 526, 527; Camden, 251, 252. The account of this adventure we owe to Lopez Vaz, a native of Elvas, who was taken in the Plata, by one of the Earl of Cumberland's ships, having with him the *Discourse* which he had written concerning Drake's attempt on Nombre de Dios, and the subsequent expedition. The manuscript came into Hakluyt's hand. "The Spaniards of that country (Darien)," he says, " marvelled much at this one thing, to see that, since the conquering of this land, there have been many Frenchmen that have come to those countries, but they never saw Englishmen there, but only these two : and although there have many Frenchmen been on the coast, yet

having traded for some years with the Canaries, left one Charles there, the son of Dominic Chester, a Bristol merchant, as his agent. The said Chester devised means of securing for himself a certain portion of his employer's goods, and this with a good conscience, under favour of his father's patron-saint and namesake. For when Captain Roberts arrived with a cargo, and with charge to bring home returns for Barker, this Charles accused him to the Inquisition, and, on the pretext that he was Barker's partner, the whole property was confiscated to the Holy Office, such portions only excepted as the informer received for his meritorious services, or had previously secured for himself. By means of some humane friar, Roberts was delivered from prison, at the cost of all he had brought with him in his ship; and returning empty, the charges of his voyage were added to Barker's loss, making it amount to nearly 2000*l*. It was in vain to seek redress, " for no suit prevaileth against the Inquisition of Spain ". So Andrew Barker, in recompense of his injury, and also to recover his loss from the Spaniards themselves, fitted out two barques, one called the *Ragged Staff*, himself being captain, and Philip Roche master thereof; the other, named the *Bear*, had one William Coxe for her master and captain. They sailed from Plymouth, on Whitsunday; burnt two villages in the Isle of Maya, in revenge for their trumpeter there treacherously killed by the Portugals, and having reached Trinidad, began their piracies and their fatal disputes among themselves.

never durst they put foot upon land; only these two Englishmen adventured it. All these things coming to the hearing of the King of Spain, he provided two galleys, well appointed, to keep those coasts; and the first year they took six or seven French ships. And after that this was known, there were no more Englishmen or Frenchmen of war that durst adventure to approach the coast, until this present year 1586, that the aforesaid Francis Drake arrived there with a strong fleet. But it is likely that, if the King of Spain live, he will in time provide sufficient remedy to keep his countries and subjects from the invasion of other nations."

In the Bay of Tula (about eighteen leagues south-west of Carthagena), they took a frigate and treasure therein, to the value of 500*l*. in bars of gold and ingots of silver, with some quantity of *corriente*, or coin, in reals of plate, and "certain green stones called emeralds, whereof one, very great, being set in gold, was found tied secretly about the thigh of a friar". The frigate they left; and finding that some Spanish men-of-war were in pursuit of them, passed on to the mouth of the Chagre, and there landed ten men to seek the Maroons, who, it was supposed, were ready to join with the English and French against the Spaniards. The men returned without having discovered them, but brought with them "a disease called there the Calentura, which is a hot and vehement fever"; they infected others, and some eight or nine died.

Between the Chagre and Veragua they took a frigate, in which was some quantity of gold, and where they found also four cast pieces of ordnance which had belonged to Oxenham's ship. This capture was made in good time, the *Ragged Staff*, because of her great leakage, being no longer seaworthy; wherefore they set the Spaniards ashore, removed her crew into the prize and then sunk the vessel. At Veragua, the ill blood between Barker and his master Roche, which had been hardly repressed before, broke out afresh; they fought, and Barker was wounded in the cheek. They made from thence, by the direction of certain Indians, for the Bay of Honduras, and captured on the way a barque with some money and provisions on board, and the Escrivano of Carthagena, "who, being a man of some note, was put to his ransom"; the rest were dismissed freely. The first race of freebooters were in nothing more honourably distinguished from their successors than in this, that they exercised no cruelty upon their prisoners, and committed no murder. Arriving at the Island of St. Francisco, in the mouth of the Bay of Honduras, Coxe, the master of the *Bear*, with a party of mutineers, boarded Barker's ship, took possession of it and of all his booty, and set him ashore upon the island, where he and one Germane Welborne fought, and both were wounded. Barker would then fain have returned to the ship, but this was resisted, and he was told that he should not come on board till they were ready to depart. Whatever may have been their intentions with respect to him, his troubled life was near its close; for, one morning, at daybreak, a party of Spaniards arriving secretly in the island, surprised the English and slew nine of them; of these Barker was one; about twenty escaped by getting on board. Coxe then, with two parties, in a pinnace and a skiff which he had taken at the island, surprised the town of Truxillo in the bay, and took there "wine and oil as much as they would, and divers other good things, but no gold or silver, nor any other treasure which they would confess. But before they could return to their ship, some men-of-war chased her; the pinnace shifted for itself and got safe, leaving for haste those that were in the skiff, being eight persons; what became of them afterwards God knoweth." Their misfortunes did not end here; for having now determined to sail for England, and being in the main sea, homeward bound, about sixty leagues from the isle, the frigate their prize, "wherein was the treasure for the adventurers, and that which pertained to the captain, to the value of 2000*l.*, being over-set with sail, with a flaw of wind was overthrown, and all the goods therein perished". Fourteen men were drowned in her; Coxe and eight others were saved. They had built a frigate upon the shore of the Honduras, in place of the *Bear*, which seems to have followed the fortunes of its old companion the *Ragged Staff;* in this they reached Scilly, when, Roche having died on the passage home, Coxe and Andrew Brown divided the remaining prize money among the survivors, "delivering to some five pounds, to some six, to some seven, to some more, as every man was thought to have deserved": the barque and the guns (Oxenham's among them) were left at Scilly to the use of Brown. "Divers of our company," says the person from whom Hakluyt collected his relation, "were committed to prison upon our arrival at Plymouth, at the suit of Mr. John Barker, of Bristol, as accessories to his brother, our captain's death, and betrayers of him unto the enemy. And after straight examination of many of us, by letters of direction from his Majesty's privy council, the chief malefactors were only chastised with long imprisonment, when, indeed, before God, they had deserved to die: whereof some, although they escaped the rigour of man's law, yet could they not avoid the heavy judgment of God, but shortly after came to miserable end. Which may be example to others to show themselves faithful and obedient in all honest causes to their captains and governors." *

It appears then that the persons who went upon this piratical voyage thought they were engaged in an honest cause. Most men who enter upon unlawful courses, either form a code of convenient morals for themselves, or act upon the accursed opinion that there is nothing to be hoped or feared beyond the grave. But there were circumstances, which made the light in which these precursors of the buccaneers regarded their proceedings, appear plausible to the nation as well as to themselves. During great part of Elizabeth's long reign, Spain and England, though formally at 'peace, were in a state of manifest enmity and of private warfare ; and that enmity was on both sides more acrimonious than could have been generated in any ordinary war. No English subject, while trading with those parts of the Spanish dominions with which the trade was authorised by treaty, was safe, unless he was a Roman Catholic. The Inquisition looked upon all heretics who came within its reach as amenable to its laws, no matter what their country ; they were rebellious subjects of the Universal Roman Catholic

* Hakluyt, iii., 528-530.

Church, and, as such, to be seized and punished, wherever that wicked Church was strong enough to enforce its pretensions. If the confiscation of English property, and the imprisonment and ill usage (even to tortures and death) of English subjects, should have the effect of bringing on hostilities between the two crowns, whatever might be the policy of the Spanish Government, this was what the clergy and the Inquisition desired. The English people resented this before the queen could venture to resent it otherwise than by unavailing remonstrances; and the injured parties took a shorter course, in which some gallant spirits, and many desperate ones, were ready to join. Thus, in Barker's case, he had just cause of complaint against the Spanish authorities, by whom he had been iniquitously deprived of his goods; and if he could have indemnified himself by the forcible seizure of property belonging to the Inquisition, or to the Spanish Government, without injury to any other parties, this would have been nothing more than what by the law of nations might be justified, when national law had been by the other party set at nought: but this was impossible; and what, if so restricted, would have been a just act of reprisal, was an act of piracy when committed against the King of Spain's subjects. So the Spaniards naturally and properly considered it. They knew nothing of the injuries upon which Drake as well as Barker is said to have founded his right of making war upon the King of Spain; nor would they indeed have allowed them to be injuries; nor that, if they had been such, any such right could be derived from them. While, therefore, the private warfare continued, they executed as pirates all whom they made prisoners; and this was conformable to the acknowledged law of nations.

The first adventurers of this stamp did not, however, consider themselves pirates, for two reasons: first, because they professed to carry on hostilities only against the Spaniards, not, like the Vikingar and Vitalians, against all who traversed the seas; secondly, because they had good reason to believe that, although not commissioned by their own Government, they were acting with its connivance, and under its tacit sanction. In this way of thinking, therefore, they were fairly at war, carrying it on at a twofold risk, seeing that, if taken by the enemy, they had no mercy to expect; but also with a prospect of far greater gains than could be obtained in any other service. The danger might have been little different in ordinary wars; for whether war should be what was then termed good or bad, depended in those days upon the temper of an individual commander, not upon any fixed law or general usage. But this formed no part of their consideration. Among such men, those who were not thoughtless of danger were regardless of it. Some were of as heroic a spirit as the greatest of the Spanish conquerors; others were of no better qualities than the worst of them; and perhaps not a few were perfectly aware that they were pursuing a safer course upon the seas at whatever hazard, than if they had been braving the laws at home.

There was another circumstance which undoubtedly entered into the views of the better adventurers, and was not without some influence upon all. A strong feeling of indignation had been excited against the Spaniards for their cruelties in the New World, by a relation ascribed, on no good grounds, to Bartolome de Las Casas, and published in many languages, with engravings, in which the acts of the most atrocious barbarity were represented. In one respect it was, perhaps, well that this impression should have been produced, lest posterity, in astonishment and admiration at the intrepidity, and perseverance, and unparalleled achievements of the conquerors, should have overlooked their crimes. Contemplating the history of their conquests with that religious temper wherewith all history ought to be contemplated, nothing more mournful is to be found in the annals of the human race. We can perceive only that abominations, like those of the

Canaanites, prevailed among all the more civilised nations of the New World; and that the Spaniards, who were the appointed instruments of Divine judgment, substituted other evils in the place of those which they extirpated; sacrificed more victims to avarice than the Mexicans to their idols; and are now suffering from the consequence of their long-continued and unrepented offences. Further than this, the course of Providence is not evolved. The first chastisement which the Spaniards received was from those adventurers who now assailed them in their conquests, and led the way for the buccaneers, the Vikingar of the New World. Even these wretches thought it some justification of themselves that they were taking vengeance for the Indians; and that feeling, in a certain degree, was entertained also by Drake and his contemporaries.

Moreover, the Spaniards founded their right of conquest on Pope Alexander's grant, the validity of which grant was, of course, denied by a people who had thrown off the papal yoke. England acknowledged in the Spaniards no right but that of the strongest to those parts of America which they actually possessed, and none to those extensive regions in which they had formed no settlement. Least of all could the English, in an age when the spirit of maritime enterprise had been excited, submit to an assumption of dominion, which pretended to exclude them from the Caribbean Sea, and from the Great Pacific, on which Vasco Nuñez de Balboa, the first European who ever beheld it, had not looked with a more ambitious eye than the first Englishman by whom it was seen, Francis Drake.

There can be little doubt that the plan of Drake's voyage was communicated to the queen, and by her approved. Sir Christopher Hatton introduced him to Elizabeth, and it is said that she gave him a sword, with this remarkable speech: "We do account that he which striketh at thee, Drake, striketh at us!" It is said, also, which is less credible, that he had a commission from his sovereign. This would have been inconsistent with her cautious policy; it was enough for her at this time to assure him of her secret sanction. The expedition was fitted out at his own cost,* "with the help of divers friends, adventurers; it consisted of his own ship the *Pelican*, 100 tons; the *Elizabeth*, of 80, captain, John Winter; the *Marygold*, a barque of 30 tons, captain, John Thomas; the *Loan*, a fly-boat, of 50, captain, John Chester; and the *Christopher*, a pinnace, of 15, captain, Thomas Moon". These ships he manned with an able and sufficient crew, "to the number of 164, men, gentlemen, and sailors, and furnished with such plentiful provision of all things necessary, as so long and dangerous a voyage seemed to require"; taking out with him the frames of four pinnaces in pieces, to be put together when occasion required. "The smallness of this force," it is remarked by Admiral Burney,† "for an enterprise of such magnitude, is not so extraordinary as that a navigation, which on account of its difficulties and dangers had been many years discontinued, should be undertaken in vessels so diminutive." "Neither did he omit, it is said, to make provision for ornament and delight; carrying to this purpose with him expert musicians, rich furniture (all the vessels for his table, yea, many belonging to the cook-room, being of pure silver), with divers shows of all sorts of curious workmanship, whereby the civility and magnificence of his native country might, among all nations whither he should come, be the more admired." ‡ In this he followed the example of the Portuguese, in their first voyage to the East.

* Herrera says, at the cost of the queen also, and of Sir John Hawkins, and others. He states the number of men at 200 fighting men, besides ten young men of family (*cavalleros mozos*), who went out to learn the art of navigation, and he says that each vessel carried eighteen brass pieces, as if the ships had been all of equal tonnage. That of the admiral's ship, which is the only one he specifies, he states at 120 (t. ii., p. 384).

† i., 305.   ‡ Prince.

Great care was taken to conceal his destination; few of the persons who were embarked were acquainted with his designs; and the better to conceal them, it was given out that they were bound for Alexandria. On the 15th of November, 1577, they sailed from Plymouth; but the next morning the wind falling contrary, they put into Falmouth, and there so terrible a tempest took them, and so vehement, that all their ships were like to have gone to wreck. The admiral was obliged to cut away his mainmast, and the *Marygold* was driven ashore. They put back to Plymouth to repair, and set forth a second time, with better fortune, on the 13th of December. When they were out of sight of land Drake first gave his people some ground for conjecturing what course he intended, by appointing the Island of Mogadore, on the coast of Barbary, for the place of rendezvous, in case any of the fleet should part company. Between that island and the main, from which it is one mile distant, they found a very good and safe harbour, with good entrance, and void of any danger. Here he put together one of his pinnaces. The island was not inhabited. An intercourse was opened with the Moors of the main, by means of one of the crew, who had formerly been a captive among them. Hostages were exchanged the first day, and traffic promised by the Moors for the next; but when they came with camels to the sea-side, as if bringing their wares, one of the men too hastily leaped on shore, meaning to become a hostage as on the yesterday; he was seized, a dagger was held to his throat to deter him from making any resistance:* the boat's crew, seeing a number of armed men start up from behind the rocks, found it prudent to return, and the prisoner was laid on a horse and carried away. The first narrator remarks upon this, that "a man cannot be too circumspect and wary of himself among such miscreants". Drake landed, and marched

* Hakluyt, iii., 730.

a little way into the country, hoping to redeem the man, or obtain some satisfaction; but the Moors neither offered to resist nor approached to treat; he could obtain no intercourse with them, and sailed from Mogadore on the third day after his arrival there. The intention of the Moors was, however, less inimical than it appeared. Their king, Muley Moloc, was then expecting that memorable invasion from Portugal which in the ensuing year took place, under the unfortunate Sebastian; he wanted to know what ships these were, and if anything could be learnt concerning the Portuguese. The prisoner was taken to his presence, and when all that he could communicate had been collected from him, Muley gave orders for conducting him back to the ship, with offers of friendship and assistance to the general. But the fleet had departed; this, however, was no misfortune to the man, who was not long afterwards sent home in an English merchantman.*

At Cape Blanco they remained four days: there Drake mustered his men on shore, and trained them in warlike manner, to make them fit for all occasions; and leaving there the *Christopher*, he took in its stead one of the Spanish barques called canters, being of the burden of forty tons or thereabouts, releasing some other prizes which he had made, after taking out of them such necessaries as he wanted and they could yield. Leaving this place on the 22nd, they anchored off the Isle of Maya on the 28th, when a party was sent to "view the island, and the likelihood that might be there of provision". The inhabitants had been forbidden to trade with any such visitors, and when they saw them, they salted the wells near the landing place, and forsook their houses. It was easy for them thus to spoil the water, salt being produced there without labour, "save only that the people gather it into heaps, which continually in great quantity is

* Burney, 308.

increased upon the sands by the flowing of the sea, and the heat of the sun burning the same, so that of the increase thereof they keep a continual traffic with their neighbours". Marching into the island, they found grapes and cocoa-nuts, and saw goats, which were so chased by the inhabitants that they could kill none of them; but the people, as if to stop the mouths of their uninvited visitors, had laid out some old dried goats' flesh, which being but ill, and small, and few, the English made no account of. Next they sailed by the Island of Santiago, from whence three pieces were fired at them, but at such distance that they could do no harm. The mountains and high places there, they were told, were possessed by Moors, who had escaped from their Portuguese masters, and maintained themselves in great strength. Off this island they espied two ships under sail, gave chase to one, and boarded her from a boat without resistance; she proved to be a Portuguese, bound for Brazil, with many passengers, and among other commodities good store of wine. Drake transferred the prisoners to the pinnace which he had set up at Mogadore, giving them their clothes, provision, and one butt of their own wine, and letting them go, all except the pilot Nuno da Sylva, whom he detained, because it was discovered that he was well acquainted with the coast of Brazil. The prize he committed to Master Thomas Doughtie's custody, with twenty-eight men; but complaint being soon after made against him that he had received things from some of the Portuguese prisoners, and kept them for his own use, he was removed in consequence, and Thomas, the general's brother, was made captain of the prize instead. The wine and provision with which this ship was laden, was the most valuable part of their stores.*

From the Cape de Verds they were nine weeks without the sight of land, "often meeting with unwelcome storms and

---

* Hakluyt, 731, 732. Burney, 309, 310.

less welcome calms, being in the bosom of the burning zone, not without the affrights of flashing lightnings and terrifying claps of thunder; yet, still with the admixture of many comforts, for, being but badly furnished with fresh water, their necessities were, for seventeen days together, constantly supplied with rain; nor was their fleet in all that time dispersed, nor did any ship lose company except the Portuguese prize, for one day, which then came in again, to their great comfort,—for the loss of it, it is said, would have defeated the voyage."* When they were near the equator, Drake, being very careful of his men's health, let every one of them blood with his own hands. † On 5th February, he made the coast of Brazil, in latitude $31\frac{1}{2}$ S.; "and being discovered at sea by the inhabitants of the country, they made upon the coast great fires for a sacrifice to the devils, about which they use conjurations (making heaps of sand and other ceremonies), that when any ship shall go about to stay upon their coast, not only sands may be gathered together in shoals in every place, but also that storms and tempests may arise, to the casting away of ships and men".‡ Thus the sailors were told, probably by the Portuguese pilot, and they were also assured that the efficacy of these conjurations had often been proved. On the 7th they lost the canter, which had been named the *Christopher*, after the pinnace for which she had been exchanged: by Drake's great care in dispersing his ships they fell in with her again; and his pleasure at recovering her was such that he named the place where they met the Cape of Joy: "the name, however, was as little permanent as the feeling with which it was imposed. The country appeared to them very fair and pleasant, with an exceeding fruitful soil, and they saw great store of large and mighty deer," but not being able to chase the deer, they contented themselves with slaughtering seals at an anchorage eighteen leagues within the Plata, thinking them "good and acceptable meat both as food for

* Prince.   † Camden, 250.   ‡ Hakluyt, 732.

the present, and as a supply of provisions for the future". They sailed farther up, till they found but three fathoms depth, and filled their casks with fresh water by the ship's side. On the 27th they left the Plata, pursuing their course towards the south. The ship in which Doughtie was parted company that night, and the *Christopher* two days afterwards.

In latitude 47 S. they saw a bay within a headland, which seemed as if there should be a commodious port there. Drake did not think it prudent to stand in with the ship, till he had examined it: he anchored, therefore, three leagues from the coast, and went to explore it himself the next morning in a boat. As he approached, a native made his appearance, shouting and dancing to the noise of a rattle which he shook in his hand; no doubt this was the maraca, which the savages of South America used in most of their ceremonies from the Orinoco southwards, and far in the interior. It was supposed that he invited them to land, but a fog came on, the weather became bad, and Drake thought it necessary to return to his ships, being three leagues from them: the fog thickened; the ships could no longer be seen, and Captain Thomas in the *Marygold*, being anxious for the general's safety, ventured to stand into the bay, fortunate in both his hopes, for Drake got on board, and he came to anchor in a secure situation. The other ships were obliged to stand out to sea. On the morrow the weather became fine, and Drake kindled fires on the shore as signals for the dispersed ships, none of which were in sight; but they were soon assembled, except the *Swan* and the Portuguese prize, which had been named the *Mary*. The natives kept at distance, answering by gestures and unintelligible speech the signal which was made to them by showing a white cloth. Places were discovered near the rocks, constructed for the purpose of drying the *nandu* or American ostrich, and other birds for food. More than fifty *nandus*, either dried or in a state of preparation, were found there; their thighs were as large as "reasonable legs of mutton ".* The English thought they were intended for a present; they took accordingly what they found, but it seems they left what was accepted as a full compensation, for a friendly intercourse was afterwards established.

According to their account the *nandu* was decoyed by stalking, a practice known in civilised as well as in savage countries. The natives shaped such a resemblance as they could of the bird's head and neck at one end of a staff, and fastened plumes of its feathers at the other; holding this before them, they approached their intended prey, and either decoyed or drove them into some neck of land, across which they stretched a strong net, and then set dogs upon them. That practice, however, is no longer known; and it is said that it is now impossible to take this bird by any snare. † Leaving this place, which was not convenient for the fleet, they found a good port in $47\frac{1}{2}$ S., and having given his orders there, Drake sent out Winter in the *Elizabeth*, to search for the two missing ships to the southward, and went northward in the admiral himself on the same quest. He met with the *Swan* the same day, brought her into harbour and broke her up for firewood, having taken everything out of her that could be of use: this was done to lessen the number of ships and the chance of separation, and that their force might be more compact. Here they "made new provision of seals, whereof they slew to the number of from 200 to 300 in the space of an hour. Some days passed before any natives were seen; they, however, made the first advances by signs from the shore, as if inviting some English who were on a small island opposite. Drake sent a boat and such presents in it as were taken out for such occasions; these, as the Indians manifested some want of confidence, were tied to a pole, and the pole was stuck in the ground a little way from the landing place, and left for them. They in return put some of

* Burney, 312.   † Azara, iv., 172.

their coronals and carved bones on the same place. Some kind of traffic followed upon this opening, but on their part it was still cautious; they would receive nothing by hand; it must be placed on the ground for them, and the words by which they expressed themselves willing or unwilling to accept the things proffered in exchange, were presently understood. Hakluyt's author describes them as naked, saving only about their waist the skin of some beast with the fur or hair on, and something also wreathed on their heads. Their faces were painted with divers colours; some of them had on their heads the similitude of horns, every man his bow, which was an ell in length, and a couple of arrows. They were very agile people, and quick to deliver, and seemed not to be ignorant in the feats of war, as by their order of ranging a few men might appear." Some had one leg, one shoulder, or the whole side, painted white, and the other black, with white moons on the black part, and on the white black suns. It is worthy of notice, that this parti-coloured fashion, as well as that of ornamenting the head with the similitude of horns, is at this time in use among the tribes on the far distant coast of California.

The men who frequented the port were not above fifty in number; no canoes were seen among them. "They fed on seals and other flesh, which they ate nearly raw, casting pieces of four or six pounds weight into the fire, till it was a little scorched, and then tearing it in pieces with their teeth like lions, both men and women." They were a merry race; the sound of the trumpet delighted them, and they danced with the sailors. The chaplain of the fleet, Mr. Francis Fletcher, describes them as of large stature; and that the Austral tribes are so, may be affirmed on the most satisfactory testimony, but the fact has been much exaggerated. "One of the giants," says Fletcher, "standing with our men when they were taking their morning draught, showed himself so familiar that he also would do as they did; and taking a glass in his hand (being strong canary wine), it came no sooner to his lips, than it took him by the nose, and so suddenly entered his head, that he was so drunk, or at least so overcome, that he fell on his bottom not able to stand; yet he held the glass fast in his hand, without spilling any of the wine; and when he came to himself, he tried again, and tasting, by degrees got to the bottom. From which time he took such a liking to the wine, that having learnt the name, he would every morning come down from the mountains with a mighty cry of wine! wine! wine! continuing the same until he arrived at the tent." *

In this place, which he named Seal Bay, Drake remained something more than a fortnight. When he sailed from thence the Portuguese prize was still missing; and it was not long before the canter again parted company, and was absent three or four days. They unloaded her, therefore, when next they came to anchor, and abandoned her, letting her drift to sea. On the 19th, they had the good fortune once more to meet the Portuguese; and on the next day the whole fleet anchored in the "good harborough called by Magellan Port Julian". That some navigator had been there before them was, indeed, certain; for they found a gibbet standing there, † and from that rueful monument supposed it to be the spot where Magellan did execution upon some of his disobedient and rebellious company; some of their bones also were remaining. As soon as the ships were secured, Drake went to search for a watering place, and to see what provisions this ill-omened harbour could furnish. His brother, Captain Thomas, Robert Winter, Oliver the master-gunner, and two others, went in the boat with him. Two of the natives came to them on their landing, received the presents which were offered, and appeared as well pleased as they were familiar. They were armed with bows and

---

* Burney, 315, from Fletcher's MSS.   † Hakluyt, 733, 751.

arrows; and the gunner, to show them how well the English understood the use of that weapon, discharged an arrow from his own bow. The natives tried all theirs, but could not shoot so far; and they seemed pleased at seeing his skill. Presently another Indian came, "but of a sourer sort"; and manifestly disliking the confidence with which his countrymen treated the strangers, angrily made signs to the English to depart. No doubt it was well remembered how treacherously Magellan had kidnapped two of the natives here, and the blood that was now shed was probably in revenge for that wickedness. Robert Winter, whether in mere sport, or that he wished to let this sterner savage behold a specimen of English archery, prepared to shoot as the gunner had done; but in drawing it to its full length, the string broke. While he was busied in refitting it, the savages shot at him so suddenly, that before any mischief was apprehended, one arrow was fixed in his shoulder, and another pierced his lungs. Upon this the gunner took aim at them with his caliver; it missed fire, and he was immediately shot "through the breast and out at back, so that he fell down stark dead". The Indians were now increasing in number; and it appeared that they had commenced this attack, not in a confidence upon their own dexterity alone, but with the assurance of being supported.

Drake upon this ordered his companions to cover themselves with their targets, and approach the enemy, but not in a regular line; and he directed them to break the arrows that were shot at them, observing that the savages had but a small store. At the same time he took the piece which had so unhappily missed fire, aimed at the Indian who had killed the gunner, and who was the man that had begun the fray, and shot him in the belly. An arrow wound, however severe, the savage would have borne without betraying any indication of pain; but his cries, upon being thus wounded, were so loud and hideous, that his companions were terrified and fled, though many were then hastening to their assistance. Drake did not pursue them, but hastened to convey Winter to the ship for speedy help; no help, however, availed, and he died on the second day. The gunner's body, which had been left on shore, was sent for the next day; the savages, meantime, had stript it, as if for the sake of curiously inspecting it: the clothes they had laid under the head, and stuck an English arrow in the right eye for mockery. Both bodies were buried in a little island in the harbour.* No further attempt was made to molest the English, though they remained nearly two months in the harbour, and no after intercourse took place. The lesson which the natives had received was sufficient; perhaps it was the more effectual, because the individual upon whom the punishment fell was the one at whose instigation the fray had been begun.†

A more tragical event followed. Magellan had in this same port quelled a dangerous mutiny, with an intrepidity and promptitude that would have been worthy of all praise, if treachery and assassination had not been among the means which he employed. Drake apprehended a similar danger. It is said, in the earliest relation of his expedition, that he began here to inquire diligently into Master Doughtie's actions, "and found them not to be such as he looked for, but tending rather to contention, or mutiny, or some other disorder, whereby the success of the voyage might greatly have been hazarded; that the company were called together, and made acquainted with the particulars, which, partly by

---

* Cliffe, 751. Burney, 317, 318.

† Admiral Burney thought it might be received as a proof that the dispositions of the Patagonians were not in general mischievous and revengeful, that they attempted no farther injury, nor offered any kind of interruption to the English in their watering, wooding, or other avocations (p. 318). My kind-hearted old friend thought too favourably of savage nature. These Indians would have watched for every opportunity of vengeance, if they had not been deterred by fear or by superstition.

Doughtie's confession, and partly by evidence, were found to be true; which," says the writer, "when our general saw, although his private affection to Master Doughtie (as he then in the presence of us all sacredly protested) was great, yet the care he had of the state of the voyage, of the expectations of her majesty, and of the honour of his country, did more touch him (as indeed it ought) than the private respect of one man; so that the cause being thoroughly heard, and all things done in good order, as near as might be to the course of our laws in England, it was concluded that Master Doughtie should receive punishment, according to the quality of the offence. And he, seeing no remedy but patience for himself, desired before his death to receive the communion; which he did at the hands of Master Fletcher our minister, and our general himself accompanied him in that holy action: which being done, and the place of execution made ready, he having embraced our general, and taken his leave of all the company, with prayer for the queen's majesty and our realm, in quiet sort laid his head to the block, where he ended his life." It is further said that when the execution was over, Drake addressed the whole company, exhorting them to unity, obedience, and regard of the voyage in which they were engaged; for better confirmation whereof he willed every man to prepare himself for receiving the holy communion on the following Sunday, "as Christian brethren and friends ought to do. This," the relator says, "was done in a very reverent sort; and so, with good contentment, every man went about his business." *

A mystery has been thrown over this transaction, and a suspicion, † in consequence, of the darkest kind, has been

---

* Hakluyt, 733.

† Admiral Burney, than whom no man ever desired to judge more equitably and more kindly of others, expresses no opinion on the case,

brought upon the character of Drake, who, in this matter, has been more injured by his friends than by his enemies. It is certain that Doughtie was tried for attempting to raise a mutiny; that he was "found guilty by twelve men after the English manner, and suffered accordingly".* The most indifferent persons in the fleet were of opinion that he had acted seditiously, and that Drake cut him off because of his emulous designs. The question is, how far those designs extended? He could not aspire to the credit of the voyage, without devising how to obtain for himself some more conspicuous station in it than that of a gentleman volunteer: if he regarded Drake as a rival, he must have hoped to supplant, or, at least, to vie with him; and in no other way could he have vied with him but by making off with one of the ships, and trying his own fortune. Considering what such adventurers too often were, and were likely to be, and how frequent mutinies were among them,—considering, too, that Doughtie had been removed from the command of the Portuguese prize upon a charge of peculation, and that resentment,

because he thought the statements too imperfect for forming one. The subject, he said, could not, perhaps, be better closed than by the reflections which they produced in the mind of Dr. Johnson. That great and good man says: "How far it is probable that Drake, after having been acquainted with this man's designs, should admit him into his fleet, and afterwards caress, respect, and trust him, or that Doughtie, who is represented as a man of eminent abilities, should engage in so long and hazardous a voyage, with no other view than that of defeating it, is left to the determination of the reader. What designs he could have formed with any hope of success, or to what actions worthy of death he could have proceeded without accomplices (for none are mentioned), is equally difficult to imagine. Nor, on the other hand, though the obscurity of the account, and the remote place chosen for the discovery of this wicked project, seem to give some reason for suspicion, does there appear any temptation from either hope, fear, or interest, that might induce Drake, or any commander in his state, to put to death an innocent man upon false pretences" (p. 322).

* Camden, 251.

whether for the wrongful charge, or the rightful removal, might be rankling in him,—this is no improbable supposition; and if this were proved, the sentence cannot be deemed unjust.

The enemies of Drake, however, gave out that he sailed from England with secret instructions from Leicester to take off Doughtie upon any pretence whatever, because Doughtie had reported that Walter, Earl of Essex, was poisoned by Leicester's means.* That Essex was not poisoned is as certain as any such fact can be at such a distance of time; and if Leicester had been as bad a man as he has been represented (that is, far worse than he was), it was not thus that he would have taken vengeance for what was a common calumny; nor was Drake one who would have taken upon himself to execute so nefarious a design. This charge may, with perfect confidence, be dismissed; nor would any doubt be entertained upon the subject, if an injudicious advocate had not, in vindication of Drake, attempted to prove too much. In the history of the voyage published under the name of Francis Drake, the admiral's nephew, it is affirmed that Doughtie embarked in the expedition with the determination of overthrowing it, raising a mutiny, and accomplishing his ends by the murder of Drake and his most faithful friends; and that Drake received information of this by letter before he sailed from Plymouth, but could not and would not credit "that a person whom he so dearly loved would conceive such evil purposes against him". When, however, his practices, having been well observed, became too certain, the general, then assembling in Port Julian "all his captains and gentlemen of his company, propounded to them the good parts which were in the gentleman, the great good-will and inward affection, more than brotherly, which he had ever since his first acquaintance borne him, not omitting the respect which

* Camden, 251.

was had of him among no mean personages in England; and afterwards delivered the letters which were written to him, with the particulars from time to time which had been observed, not so much by himself as by his good friends; not only at sea, but even at Plymouth; not bare words, but writings; not writings alone, but actions, tending to the overthrow of the service in hand, and making away of his person". The proofs, this advocate avers, were "so many and so evident, that the gentleman himself, stricken with remorse of his inconsiderate and unkind dealing, acknowledged himself to have deserved death, yea, many deaths, for that he conspired not only the overthrow of the action, but of the principal actor also. The chiefest in place and judgment in the whole fleet, with their own hands," he says, "under seal, adjudged that he deserved death, and that it stood by no means with their safety to let him live; and, therefore, they remitted the manner hereof, with the rest of the circumstances, to the general." The general then gave the condemned party his choice, whether he would be executed in the island? or be set ashore on the main? or return to England, there to answer his deed before the lords of her Majesty's council? Doughtie replied, that he would not endanger his soul by consenting to be left among savage infidels; and as for returning to England, if any could be found to accompany him on so disgraceful an errand, yet the shame of the return would be more grievous than death; therefore he preferred ending his life on the island, desiring only that he and the general might once more receive the holy communion together, and that he might not die other than the death of a gentleman. From this choice he was not to be dissuaded by any reasons that could be urged. Accordingly, on "the next convenient day, a communion was celebrated by Master Fletcher; the general himself communicated in the sacred ordinance with Master Doughtie; after which they dined at the same table together, as cheerfully, in sobriety, as ever in their lives they had done ; and taking their leave by drinking to each other, as if some short journey only had been in hand".* A provost marshal, appointed for the occasion, had meantime made all things ready ; and after drinking this stirrup-cup, Doughtie went to the block.

This statement is so certainly false in its most important part, that it would be entitled to no credit in any of its minor circumstances, even if those circumstances were less improbable at first sight. Fletcher the chaplain's relation of the voyage is still preserved in manuscript. It is there stated, that the same persons whose accusation had brought upon Doughtie his former disgrace (namely, John Brewer, Edward Bright, and other of their friends) laid now more dangerous matter to his charge, for words spoken by him to them in the general's garden at Plymouth, long before their departure ; "which," says Fletcher, " it had been their part or duty to have discovered at the time, and not to have concealed them for a time and place not so fitting. How true it was wherewith they charged him upon their oath, I know not ; but he utterly denied it, affirming that he was innocent of such things whereof he was accused." So far was he from confessing his guilt, that, according to this person, who of all others must have possessed the most clear knowledge on this point. " he utterly denied the truth of the charges against him, upon his salvation, at the time of his communicating the sacrament, and at the hour and moment of his death ".† Mr. Fletcher speaks of Doughtie in terms of more than common regard, and describes him as a man of extraordinary endowments. Neither in his nor in any other contemporary account is it said that he had the choice allowed him of returning to England, there to answer for himself before the lords in council. It is, indeed, most

* Burney, 319, 320. *World Encompassed*, 32.
† Burney, 321, 322.

unlikely that Drake could have spared a ship to convey him; and not to be believed that he, standing upon his innocence, would have rejected such an alternative had it been proposed to him. And the cheerful dinner, and the parting glass, are such embellishments of the story, that the person who devised them could have no expectation of their obtaining belief from any one, except by a reflex supposition in the reader's mind that a circumstance so incredible never would have been invented, and its extreme incredibility was, therefore, an evidence of its truth.

The falsehood of this statement ought not, however, to weigh against Drake, unless he were cognisant of it; but there is no proof of this, nor can it fairly be presumed from the fact that the narrative wherein it was brought forward is said to be the work of Drake's nephew and namesake. A calumny had been raised against the great navigator, and evidently not without some injurious effect: panegyrical biographers have passed over the whole transaction in silence, thereby showing that they did not like to touch upon it: Drake's representative may have fallen into the great folly and greater fault of thinking it allowable to counteract one falsehood by another. Mr. Fletcher's evidence makes it certain that Doughtie made no confession of guilt, but it proves nothing more. The general opinion in the fleet was, that a mutiny had been designed. The Portuguese pilot, who is likely to have been an attentive observer, and must have been an impartial one, says that Doughtie was put to death because he would have returned * (it will presently appear that one of the ships took the first opportunity of doing so). The Spaniards, † willing as they

---

* Hakluyt, 791.
† " En esta baya se quiso amotinar la gente a persuacion de un cavallero llamado Tomas Auter, que se quiso alzar con el armada; y Francisco Draque fué tan diligente que le prendió, y luego le hizò cortar la cabeza y salvó el peligro" (Herrera, *Hist. Gen.*, ii., 384).

were to load Drake with every kind of obloquy, were so far from blaming him on this account, that they extolled him for his vigilance and decision. The sufferer's solemn protestations of innocence are easily accounted for; and he would persist in them till the last, because till the last there was always a possibility that they might be believed; it was truly a case, in which, while he persisted in them, as long as there was life there was hope. Finally, and this consideration may be deemed conclusive, the justice of Drake's proceedings was not called in question on his return.

Doughtie was buried on an island in the harbour: the bodies of Robert Winter and Oliver the gunner were interred at the same time, in the same place; and the chaplain set up a stone upon their graves, whereon he engraved their names, and the day, month, and year of their burial. Here the Portuguese prize, being leaky and troublesome, was broken up;* the fleet was thus reduced to three, the *Pelican*, the *Elizabeth*, and the *Marygold;* and having completed their watering, wooding, and repairs, and remained in Port St. Julian from the 20th of June to the 17th of August, they sailed from that port. On the 20th they made Cape Virgenes,† remarkable, at four leagues' distance, for its high and steep grey cliffs, full of black spots. Here, too, they met with an ill omen, the bones of a corpse "whose flesh was clean consumed". ‡ And here, for a good omen, perhaps, as well as

---

"This port," says Lopez Vaz, "I take to be accursed, for that Magellan likewise put some to death there for the like offence" (Hakluyt, 791).

* Herrera says that this vessel went down in a storm with all on board, before they put into Port St. Julian; and that another vessel was broken up for fuel, because of the extreme cold.

† The eleven thousand had been dropped for shortness. Magellan named the cape in honour of that noble army, having discovered it on the day appropriated for this ridiculous legend in the Romish calendar.

‡ Burney, 323. Hakluyt, 733.

out of respect to his friend Sir Christopher Hatton, he changed the name of his ship, calling her, instead of the *Pelican*, the *Golden Hind*, which Sir Christopher probably bore in his arms. On the following day they entered the straits.

The lateness of the season seems to have been the only thing which prevented Amerigo Vespucci from discovering this passage into the South Sea before that sea had been seen by Balboa, and eighteen years before the famous voyage of Magellan.* He had conceived the hope of making this great discovery, and had nearly accomplished it.† Magellan named it the Patagonian Straits, after the natives, to whom, because they wore ill-shaped sandals, he had given the name of Patagons, *patagon* signifying in Spanish a large, clumsy foot. The inappropriate name has been fixed upon the people, not upon the strait, which is properly called after Magellan himself; though before it obtained that appellation from popular justice there was an attempt to call it the Strait of Victoria, after the name of his ship.‡ Juan Ladrilleros had been sent with two ships from Valdivira to survey the strait in 1558. The ships were separated by a storm. The one put back with few of her crew remaining. Ladrilleros executed his commission in the other with great diligence, and extraordinary perseverance and resolution. When he returned to Chili, two men and himself were all who survived to navigate the vessel, the rest having perished by cold and hunger.§ Other attempts followed from the same quarter: nothing is known of them but that they failed; and Drake was the third person who performed the passage—the second who performed it from Europe.

"We found the strait," says the first narrator, "to have many turnings, and, as it were, shuttings up, as if there

---

* I write the name thus because it is so written in our maps, and so called in common pronunciation; but the proper name is Magalhaens.

† Grynæus, iv., 124. *Hist. of Brasil*, i., 28.

‡ Pigafetta, 26, 40.   § Burney, 249.

were no passage at all; by means whereof we had the wind often against us, so that some of the fleet recovering a cape or point of land, others should be forced to turn back again, and to come to an anchor where they could. There be many fair harbours, with store of fresh water, but yet they lack their best commodity; for the water is there of such depth that no man shall find ground to anchor in, except it be in some narrow river or corner, or between some rocks; so that if any extreme blasts or contrary winds do come (whereunto the place is much subject), it carrieth with it no small danger. The land on both sides is very huge and mountainous; the lower mountains whereof, although they be monstrous and wonderful to look upon for their height, yet there are others which exceed them in a strange manner, reaching themselves above their fellows so high, that between them did appear three regions of clouds. These mountains are covered with snow. The strait is extreme cold, with frost and snow continually; the trees seem to stoop with the burden of the weather, and yet are green continually; and many good and sweet herbs do very plentifully grow and increase under them." * Drake gave the name of Elizabeth to the largest of three islands, "lying triangle-wise," near which they anchored, when, by their own account, they were thirty leagues within the strait. The other two he named St. Bartholomew's (on whose day he anchored there), and St. George's. "There," says Cliffe,† "we stayed one day, and victualled ourselves with a kind of fowl which is plentiful on that isle, and whose flesh is not far unlike a fat goose here in England. They have no wings, but short pinions, which serve their turn in swimming: their colour is somewhat black, mixed with white spots under their belly and about their necks. They walk so upright, that, afar off, a man would take them to be little children. If a man

---

* Hakluyt, 734. † *Ibid.*, 752.

approach anything near them they run into holes in the ground (which be not very deep), whereof the island is full; so that to take them we had staves with hooks fast to the end, wherewith some of our men pulled them out, and others being ready with cudgels did knock them on the head, for they bite so cruelly with their crooked bills that none of us were able to handle them alive." This seems to be the earliest account in our language of the penguin. Three thousand of these birds were slaughtered in less than one day, and the ships "victualled themselves thoroughly therewith".

As they approached the western end they observed a number of channels toward the south, and Drake went in a boat to discover the best passage. They met a canoe as they returned, in which were Indians of a smaller stature, and different from those with whom the affray had occurred. Their canoe was excellently well made of bark; the body being handsomely moulded, and the seams so close, though only stitched with thongs, or perhaps the sinews of some animal, that scarcely any water entered: both the prow and stern were semicircular and high. The tools which they used were made of the large mussel shells which, in the strait, are found sometimes twenty inches in length; these they grind to so sharp an edge that it could cut the hardest wood, and even the bones of which they made fish-gigs. They had a hut on the island near to which the ships had anchored; it was merely formed of a few poles covered with skins. Their vessels were of bark, well shaped and made.* On the seventeenth day after making Cape Virgenes, Drake cleared the strait, and entered the South Sea.

Balboa had taken possession of that sea in the true spirit of a Spaniard. Reaching its shore for the first time during the ebb, he seated himself there, with his companions, and

* Burney, 324.

waited patiently till the tide turned and reached him. Rising then, armed as he was for the occasion, with a sword in one hand and a banner in the other, bearing the Virgin Mary with the arms of Castille at her feet, he advanced into the waves till he was above knee-deep, saying, with a loud voice: "Long live the high and mighty sovereigns of Castille! Thus, in their names do I take possession of these seas and regions; and if any other prince, whether Christian or infidel, pretend any right to them, I am ready and resolved to oppose him, and to assert the just claims of my sovereigns!"* The possession which had thus proudly been taken was now, for the first time, about to be disturbed.

Drake's intention was to steer north, that they might get, as speedily as they could, out of "the nipping cold". The season, however, had not been rigorous; rather, indeed, for that region, it seems to have been unusually favourable. On the second day after clearing the strait, they had sailed about seventy leagues to the north-west, when a gale from the north-east came on, and continued more than a fortnight, with such violence that they could carry no sail, and were driven till they were in 57° S. latitude, and above 200 leagues west of the strait. The wind then became favourable, and, at the end of another week, during which they held a north-east course, they made the land, but the weather would not permit them to anchor. The *Marygold* was obliged to bear away before the gale, and was never heard of more. The two remaining ships a week afterwards stood, under low sail, into a bay, where they hoped to have found shelter, it "being a very foul night, and the seas sore grown". The bay proved "very dangerous, full of rocks". Drake's cable broke, and the *Golden Hind* was driven out to sea. Winter made no attempt to follow him; but the next day,

---

*Quintana, *Lives of Balboa and Pizarro*. Translated by Mrs Hodson (p. 46).

"hardly escaping the dangers of the rocks," entered the strait again, and, anchoring there in an open bay, made great fires on the shore, that if Drake should put into the strait also, he might discover them. After ten days he proceeded farther, and went into a sound, in which he remained three weeks, and named it the Port of Health, because most of his men being "very sick, with long watching, wet, cold, and evil diet," soon recovered here. They found the large mussels "very pleasant meat, and many of them full of seed pearls". Captain Winter now alleged that he stood in despair both of having favourable winds for Peru and of Drake's safety: he, therefore, "gave over the voyage, full sore against the mariners' mind," and sailed for England, where he arrived with the reproach of having abandoned his commander.*

Meantime Drake, from the Bay of Parting of Friends, as he named the place in which he parted company from his last remaining consort, was driven as far as 55° S., and found two days' shelter on the coast of Tierra del Fuego, where he also met with good water and wholesome herbs. But the winds once more returning to their old wont, forced him again from his anchorage, with this additional misfortune, that the shallop, with eight men in it, and provision for only one day, lost sight of the ship. These poor men regained the shore, entered the straits, salted and dried penguins there, and coasted on till they reached the Plata, and put into a small river on the south side. Six of them landed there in unhappy hour, and entered the woods to seek for food. They fell in with a party of Indians, who with their arrows wounded them all, took four, pursued the others to the shore, and, when the wounded men got on board and pushed off, pursued them with their arrows, and wounded those who had been left in charge of the boat.

* Cliffe. Hakluyt, 752.

These unhappy men reached an island about three leagues from the mainland, where two of them died of their wounds, and their boat was beaten to pieces against the rocks. Upon this island, which was about a league in compass, they remained two months, living upon small crabs, eels, and a fruit like an orange; but there was no fresh water, and, unable longer to endure the want of it, they ventured to make for the mainland, on a large plank some ten feet long, having made paddles with which to guide it. The passage was the work of three days and two nights. "On coming to land," says Carter, "we found a rivulet of sweet water; when William Pitcher, my only comfort and companion (although I endeavoured to dissuade him), being before pinched with extreme thirst, overdrank himself, and, to my unspeakable grief, died within half an hour, whom I buried as well as I could in the sand." Carter fell into the hands of some Indians, who had compassion on him, and conducted him, after a while, to a Portuguese settlement; and, after nine years, he was fortunate enough to return to his own country.*

Drake, having lost his pinnace, was driven still farther south, ran in again among the islands, and at length "fell in with the uttermost part of the land towards the south pole,—without which there is no main nor island to be seen to the southward; but the Atlantic Ocean and the South Sea meet in a large and free scope". The storm, which with little intermission had continued fifty-one days, ceased: they found an anchoring place at the southern extremity of the land, since called Cape Horn; and to all the islands which lay without, and to the south of the strait, Drake gave the name of the Elizabethides. He had thus accidentally discovered Cape Horn, and by that displaced the old *terra*

* Burney, 368. Purchas, iv., 1188. Purchas in a marginal note abbreviates the last part of this tragedy into two words, "Pitcher breaks". This is characteristic of Purchas, and it is not less so of Admiral Burney that he has noticed it.

incognita from a large portion of the space which it occupied in the map : "We altered the name," says Mr. Fletcher, "to *terra nunc bene cognita*". Drake went ashore, and, sailor-like, leaning over a promontory, as far as he safely could, came back, and told his people that he had been farther south than any man living.* On 30th of October, the wind came fair, and "departing from the southernmost part of the world known, or (as they thought) like to be known," they sailed to the north-west, stored themselves with birds and seals from some islands, and coasted for nearly four weeks along the American shore, till they arrived at the Island of Mocha, and anchored there. The Portuguese pilot describes it as small and low land, full of Indians, and altogether possessed by them. The English supposed that the cruel and extreme dealings of the Spaniards had forced these people, for their own safety and liberty, to flee from the main and fortify themselves here,—an erroneous supposition, for they would have been more secure in the wild parts of their own country. The general landed: the Indians came to the water side, "with show of great courtesy, bringing potatoes, roots, and two fat sheep, for which they received a suitable return; and, as it was then late, it was agreed that the ship should take water there on the morrow". Drake accordingly went in the boat with twelve men, and set two of them, with their vessels, ashore: the Indians lay in ambush by the watering place, sprang upon them, and either seized or slew them; and when the boat was hastening to their succour, a flight of arrows was discharged at it with such effect as to wound every one of the crew,—the general himself under the right eye. It was not without difficulty that the boat escaped from this imminent danger, for the Indians pursued their advantage with such resolution that they seized four of the oars, and kept possession of them. None of the assailants

---

* This he himself told to Sir Richard Hawkins.

were hurt, for the English had not time to use a harquebuss. No attempt was made to take vengeance for this unprovoked attack : it was supposed to have been made under a mistaken notion that they were Spaniards ; and it seems Drake admitted that, in that case, the Indians would have acted rightly, and, therefore, that it did not behove him to punish the offence. He sailed the same day, and, happily, none of the wounded died, though they had lost their principal surgeon.

A hope still remained of meeting with the two missing ships. It had been appointed that in case of separation they should look for each other on the coast of Peru, about the latitude of 30° S., and Drake accordingly made diligent search as he sailed along. On the last of November an Indian was found fishing, and brought on board : he was made to comprehend that the ship wanted provisions, and would pay for them, and was then dismissed with gifts. This man's report pleased the natives so well that they brought to the seaside a fat hog, poultry, and other food ; and an Indian, of some apparent consequence, went on board. He spoke Spanish ; told them that they had passed the Port of Valparaiso six leagues ; that a Spanish ship was then lying at anchor there, and that he would pilot them thither, which he did accordingly, having no suspicion that they were enemies to the Spaniards, who had never yet seen an enemy in those seas. Felipe, as this civilised Indian was called, did the English good service in conducting them to this port. They found the ship riding at anchor, with eight Spaniards and three negroes aboard : who, taking the new comers for friends, saluted them with beat of drum, and made ready a jar of Chili wine to drink with them. The pirates (they are entitled here to no better name) were no sooner aboard, than one of them, Thomas Moon, struck at a Spaniard, exclaiming : "'*Abaxo perro!*' down dog! and began to lay about him ". "One of these Spaniards, seeing persons of that quality in these seas, all-to-crossed and blessed himself." Another leaped overboard, and swam ashore to give the alarm; the rest were secured under hatches. The town was not more prepared for resistance than the ship, and less capable of it. It consisted of some nine families, who took flight before the English landed and fell to spoil. Little booty was found there: a small chapel contained nothing that was thought worth taking, except a silver chalice, two cruets, and an altar cloth, which Drake transferred to the use of his own chaplain; but there was store of Chili wine in a warehouse, which, with other provisions and some cedar planks for fuel, was carried on board. The prisoners were set ashore, one man excepted, who, being a Greek by birth, was called Juan Griego, and whom they detained to serve as a pilot to Lima. The prize they rifled when they got out to sea: they found in her 1770 jars of Chili wine, 60,000 pieces of gold, some pearls, and some merchandise. Well pleased with this adventure, they rewarded Felipe the Indian, and landed him at that place which was most convenient for him.

From hence they ran along the coast, looking anxiously for their lost consorts; and because the ship was too large to examine close in-shore, and a boat not strong enough in case of an attack, they put together a pinnace, which might safely look into every bay and creek. A fortnight after their departure from Valparaiso they anchored about cannon-shot from the mouth of the Coquimbo, and sent a party to get water. Not far to the north was a Spanish town, of which they were not aware, and a considerable body of horse and foot came down upon the men while they were filling their casks. The English, however, who were keeping good watch, retreated to their boat, and pushed off in time; one Richard Minivy only, in a fit of fool-hardiness, refused to escape, killed one of their horses, and was himself killed, and his body thrown upon a horse, and carried off. This place not suiting their purpose, nor the entertainment being such as they desired, they weighed anchor. The next day Drake, having anchored in a bay in 27° 55' S., embarked in the pinnace, and turned back in it to make one more search for the lost ships: the wind baffled him, and after one day's trial he gave up the attempt; yet, in apparent hope that as much diligence would be used in seeking him as had been manifested on his part, he remained in this bay more than four weeks, then proceeded slowly along the coast.

They landed next at a place called Tarapaca, and, while looking for water, found a Spaniard lying asleep, and thirteen bars of silver lying by him, which were worth 4000 ducats. No personal injury was offered to the man; nor to another, whom, on a second landing not far off, they met with an Indian in his company, driving eight llamas, each carrying a hundredweight of silver, divided equally in two leathern bags. The llamas as well as their freight were taken on board. From this part of the coast many Indians came off to exchange fish for knives and glasses; and even at an Indian town, where two Spaniards resided as governors, they obtained some llamas in the way of traffic. At Arica they found two ships at anchor, one of which yielded some 40 bars of silver, weighing about 20 lbs. each; the other 200 jars of wine. Only a negro was on board: the people, mistrusting no danger, were gone to the town; "which," says one of the adventurers, "we would have ransacked, if our company had been better and more in number". The sight of certain horsemen ready to have attacked them if they had landed deterred them from the attempt. But they learnt from the negro that there was a ship not far before them richly laden. Taking with him one of his prizes, Drake went in pursuit, he himself in the pinnace close along shore, the ships keeping their course a league to seaward; and having proceeded thus about five and forty leagues they saw the vessel at anchor. But the tidings that a sea-rover was in pursuit had reached the Spaniards a few hours before, and they had landed 800 bars of silver belonging to the king; everything else of any value had been removed in time. Here, too, there was a muster on the shore, which it would have been rash to encounter. Drake, therefore, held on his way: but taking this vessel and his other prizes with him, one excepted, which he had burnt at Arica, when they were about a league out at sea, he ordered all their sails to be set, and then let them drive before the wind; while he with only his own ship and the pinnace proceeded to Callao, the port of Lima.

Leisurely as Drake had proceeded, he arrived in sight of the capital of Peru before it was known there that an enemy's ship had entered those seas. When he landed at Valparaiso, the Governor of Chili was in the interior, prosecuting that war against the Araucans which has given so great a celebrity to their name; and the authorities did not venture to take upon themselves the responsibility of sending a vessel with despatches to Peru.* A few leagues off that harbour, Drake boarded a barque laden with silks and other goods, which the owner, a Portuguese, was glad to redeem by engaging to pilot the English into Callao.† He brought them in after night-fall, "sailing in between all the ships that lay there, seventeen in number," twelve of which were moored, and had all their sails ashore, "for the master and merchants were here most secure, having never been assaulted by enemies". They rifled these ships, and found in one of them a chest of silver *reales*, and good store of silk and linen. Their inquiry was for the ship that had the silver on board: the silver, it was replied, was on shore; but they were likewise informed that a richly laden treasure ship called the

---

* The viceroy, D. Francisco de Toledo, states this in his letter to the Governor of the Rio de la Plata: if such advice had been sent, he says, "Se habieran escusado hartas perdidas y gastos que se han recaecido á S. M. y à los particulares" (*Viage al Estrecho por Pedro Sarmiento*, lxxx.).

† Herrera, 385.

Cacafuego (a name not to be translated) had lately sailed for Payta. They cut the cables of these ships, and the masts of the two greatest, and let them drive, not for wantonness, but in provident foresight, that they might be disabled from pursuing him. While he was thus employed, a vessel from Panama, laden with Spanish goods, entered the harbour, and anchored close by the *Golden Hind*. A boat came from the shore to search it; but because it was night they deferred the search till the morning, and only sent a man on board. "The boat then came alongside Drake's vessel, and asked what ship it was? A Spanish prisoner answered, as he was ordered, that it was Miguel Angel's from Chili. Satisfied with this, the officer in the boat sent a man to board it; but he, when on the point of entering, perceived one of the large guns, and retreated into the boat with all celerity, because no vessels that frequented that port, and navigated those seas, carried great shot." The speed with which the boat made off upon this discovery alarmed the Panama ship, which forthwith cut her cable, and put to sea. Drake's men manned their pinnace, and pursued. The Spainards, instead of striking at their summons, shot one of the crew, upon which the pinnace returned. But the *Golden Hind* presently set sail, and gained so fast upon the Panama ship, that the men took to their boat, and escaped ashore, leaving the ship with everything on board.*

Drake's great object was now to overtake the *Cacafuego*: the wind failed, and boats were put out to tow the ship. Meantime the alarm had been given in Lima; and the viceroy, Don Francisco de Toledo, hastened instantly to Callao, and exerted himself through the remainder of the night with such success that two vessels, with 200 men in each, were despatched in pursuit before Drake was out of sight of the port. Their orders were to board the rover if

---

* Nunho da Sylva. Hakluyt, 746.

they could come up with her,—for they had no artillery. The wind, however, sprung up, of which the English made eager use; and the Spaniards were as little desirous of coming up with them as they were of being detained by an action in which nothing was to be gained. So manifest, indeed, was this unwillingness, that though there were persons of some distinction on board, the viceroy punished many for cowardice,* not allowing the excuse they had devised for themselves by following the Panama, which Drake dismissed with Juan Griego and his other pilot on board. Drake now made all speed to the north, the pinnace keeping close inshore, the ship about a league and half from land. After some days they stopped a vessel bound for Callao, from which they "took a lamp and a fountain of silver," and learnt that she had seen the treasure ship three days before. At Payta they boarded another, and were told that the *Cacafuego* had left that port two days ago. Neither of these vessels did they detain, but taking from the latter some provisions and a negro, hastened on. On the morrow† they captured a ship bound for Panama, and sent the crew and passengers, among whom were two friars, ashore. In this prize they found forty bars of silver, eighty pounds weight of gold, and a golden crucifix, "set with goodly great emeralds". This booty cost one of the men his life; he had secreted two plates of gold, denied it when accused, and was hanged when they were found upon him.

They crossed the line on 24th February; and Drake promised to give his chain of gold to the man who should have the good fortune first to descry the golden prize, for which all eyes were eagerly looking out. On St. David's Day they

---

* "Aunque yvan en ellos gente honrada, de miedo se bolvieron, y Don Francisco de Toledo castigó por ello a muchos" (Herrera, 385). Nunho da Sylva relates the excuse, and says nothing of the cowardice.

† Hakluyt, 735, 747. Burney, 336.

made Cape St. Francisco in latitude 0° 40′ N., and if Drake had been a Welshman, the day would have been rendered doubly dear to him, for at three in the afternoon a certain John Drake, going into the top, espied the object of their long chase about four leagues to seaward. And here the Portuguese pilot describes what Hakluyt calls "a pretty device to make their ship sail more swiftly". "Because the English ship was somewhat heavy before, whereby it sailed not as they would have it, they took a company of *botijas*, or Spanish pots for oil, and filling them with water, hung them by ropes at the stern of the ship to make her sail the better." The device was not wanted; for the Spanish captain, Juan de Anton,* made towards the English ship† to know what she was, thinking her to be one of the ships that used to sail along the coasts and traffic in the country. When they were near enough Drake hailed them to strike, and the other refusing, "with a great piece he shot her mast overboard, and having wounded the master with an arrow, the ship yielded". They took possession, sailed with her further into the sea all that night, and the next day and night, making all the way they could. Being then at safe distance from the coast, they stopped, and lay by their prize four days, taking out her cargo and transferring it to their own ship. They found in her great riches, as jewels and precious stones, thirteen chests full of *reales* of plate, eighty pounds weight of gold, and twenty-six tons of silver: 300 bars of the silver belonged to the king, and the rest was the property of private merchants. The whole value was estimated at 360,000 pieces of gold, that of the silver alone being 212,000*l*.; and the captors congratulated themselves that their ship might now well be called the *Golden Hind*. A little of the ex-

* Santona?
† Herrera says that had it not been for this mistake the English would not have captured her, because the South Sea ships were excellent sailers, better than any others in the world (385).

ultation of success was shown upon this occasion. Among other plate, two very fair gilt bowls of silver were found, belonging to the pilot, to whom Drake said, "Sennor pilot, you have here two silver cups, but I must needs have one of them!" The pilot, who knew that need has no law, and that the adventurer who addressed him had just then as little, assented, "because he could not otherwise choose," and gave the other also to the steward of the general's ship. In a better spirit Drake called for the register of the treasure on board, and wrote a receipt in the margin for the whole amount.*

Many a witticism was passed upon the unseemly name † of their unfortunate prize, which, at the end of four days, was dismissed, and three men put on board, whom Drake had taken on the way for pilots. Drake gave the captain

---

* C. Suarez de Figueroa, 209: Lope de Vega also relates this, and says that the Spaniards themselves were amused at it.

—tomaste la rica presa opima
De un millon y seyscientos mil ducados;
Donde España ha tenido en mas estima
Aquellos tus donayres celebrados,
Quando al maestre y del navio ministro
Pediste de la plata el gran registro.

Las margenes del qual por recibidas
Satisfaciendo con estrañas veras,
Firmaste de tu nombre las partidas,
Como si dueño de la plata fueras.
Hasta las letras oy estan corridas
De que esta burla a su registro hizieras,
Bolviste el libro, que fue en tanto estrago
Para el dueño gentil recibo y pago.
                            Dragontea, canto 1.

† "When this pilot departed from us, his boy said thus unto our general: 'Captain, our ship shall be called no more the *Cacafuego*, but the *Cacaplata*, and yours shall be called the *Cacafuego*'; which pretty speech of the pilot's boy ministered matter of laughter to us, both then and long after" (Hakluyt, 736).

a letter of safe-conduct, in case he should fall in with the *Elizabeth* or the *Marygold*. This letter, which has been preserved by the Portuguese pilot, is remarkable for its kindness and religious feeling. The contents, as retranslated in Hakluyt from the Portuguese or Spanish version, were these:—

"Master Winter, if it pleaseth God that you should chance to meet with this ship of Señor Juan de Anton, I pray you use him well, according to my word and promise given unto them; and if you want anything that is in this ship of Señor Juan de Anton, I pray you pay them double the value of it, which I will satisfy again; and command your men not to do her any hurt; and what composition or agreement we have made, at my return into England I will, by God's help, perform; although I am in doubt that this letter will never come to your hands. Notwithstanding I am the man I have promised to be,—beseeching God, the Saviour of all the world, to have us in His keeping, to whom only I give all honour, praise, and glory. What I have written is not only to you, Master Winter, but also to M. Thomas, M. Charles, M. Caube, and M. Anthony, with all our other good friends, whom I commit to the tuition of Him that with His blood redeemed us; and am in good hope that we shall be in no more trouble, but that He will help us in adversity; desiring you, for the passion of Christ, if you fall into any danger, that you will not despair of God's mercy, for He will defend you, and preserve you from all danger, and bring us to our desired haven: to whom be all honour, glory, and praise, for ever and ever. Amen.*

"Your sorrowful captain,

"Whose heart is heavy for you,

"Francis Drake."

* Hakluyt, 747.

The general had now no other object in these seas;* how to make his way home with this great booty was the next consideration. To return by the strait was, on many accounts, unadvisable; the season was unfavourable, and they knew the difficulties and dangers of that passage: moreover, the Spaniards expecting them to take that course, would be likely both to have despatched ships in quest of them, and a force to intercept them there. This was no vain surmise: the whole coast of Chili and Peru was in such alarm, that a stop was put to all maritime trade; for it was known that Drake expected to be joined by his two consorts, and in every port the people were under arms to resist them. All the consequences of such an invasion, and more than all, were apprehended by the Spanish authorities: they thought that nothing less than the King of Spain's dominion in those seas, and the properties and lives and souls of the inhabitants, were at stake.† It was not Drake's business now to encounter any danger that could be avoided; but greater proof of his ability as a seaman, and of his enterprising genius, was never given than at this time; for instead of at once resolving to follow the course of Magellan, and so compass the globe, he conceived the hope of rivalling that great navigator by exploring a passage between the two great seas, at the opposite extremity of America.‡ This he propounded to his ship's company. "All of us," says one, who writes as if he had been present, "willingly hearkened and consented to our general's advice; which was, first, to seek out some convenient place to trim our ship, and store ourselves with wood

* "Thinking himself, both in respect of his private injuries received from the Spaniards, as also of their contempts and indignities offered to our country and prince in general, sufficiently satisfied and revenged, and supposing that her majesty, at his return, would rest satisfied with this service" (Hakluyt, 736).

† *Viage del Sarmiento*, 4.

‡ *World Encompassed.* Burney, 339.

and water, and such provisions as we could get; and thence forward to hasten on our intended journey for the discovery of the said passage, through which we might with joy return to our longed homes." *

They now sailed for the coast of Nicaragua, which they made on 16th March, "near a small island named Canno," two leagues from the mainland; there they found a small bay, wherein they anchored, at five fathom deep, close by the land, and near a fresh water stream. On the 20th, a vessel was seen attempting to pass close by. The pinnace was sent in chase, and brought her in. She was laden with sarsaparilla, butter, and honey, and other things. The sarsaparilla they threw ashore; and used the vessel as a receptacle for their stores, while they laid their own ship down to examine her bottom. The island afforded them wood and fish, and would have supplied alligators and monkeys if they had chosen to take any on board. While they remained here they felt the shock of an earthquake. In eight days the repairs, wooding and watering were completed, and they sailed westward, taking with them their prize; which, however, after keeping two days longer, they dismissed, detaining some of the men to serve as pilots, and taking " the sea cards, wherewith they should make their voyage, and direct themselves in their course ".† And so sailing until 6th April, about evening, they discovered a ship that held two leagues to seaward from the land; and before the next day, in the morning, they were hard by her, and suddenly fell upon her while her men slept. She was apparently from Manilla,

* Camden (p. 252) is mistaken in saying that the viceroy had at this time sent ships to fortify the strait. He could not do this till the Panama fleet arrived; and the expedition appointed for this service was not ready to sail from Callao till Oct. 11 (*Viage del Sarmiento*, pp. 4, 40).

† Admiral Burney says: "Whether these were charts of those seas or only the cards of steering compasses was not explained". I have no doubt that the former are intended.

laden with "linen cloth (which probably means muslins), fine China dishes of white earth, and great store of China silks; of all which," says the relater, "we took as we listed". He adds, that the owner of the ship was on board, who was a Spanish gentleman; and that the general took from him a falcon of gold, with a great emerald in the breast thereof. They took a negro out of this vessel, and dismissed her with all her crew, one man excepted, whom they detained to show them some watering place. He brought them into the haven of Guatulco. They landed there, in happy hour for some negroes, upon whom the criminal court was then sitting in judgment for having conspired to set the town on fire. Judges and prisoners were conveyed on board; and the chief judge was made to write to the inhabitants, ordering them to leave the town, while the English might remain here. There were but seventeen Spaniards residing here; and neither they nor the coloured population had much to lose, for the adventurer who tells us that the town was ransacked boasts of no other plunder than a pot as big as a bushel full of silver *reales*, and a gold chain and some jewels which one "Thomas Moon took from a Spanish gentleman, whom he caught as he was flying out of the place".

Drake remained here nearly a fortnight; and before he departed he released all his prisoners, and put the Portuguese, Nunho da Sylva, on board a ship in the harbour, to find his way to Portugal as he could.* From Guatulco they steered

* This is injuriously represented, as if the poor man had been left in an enemy's country. It was hardship enough for him to lose his ship and his goods, and be carried from the Cape de Verds through the strait and to the coast of Nicaragua. But he could not have been dismissed at any point which would have been more convenient for himself; and in the relation which he drew up for the viceroy of New Spain, he makes no complaint of his treatment. It is very much to his honour, and something to that of Drake and his men, that there is not in this plain and evidently faithful relation the slightest expression of prejudice or resentment against the English.

"directly off to sea," and sailed (the accounts say) 500 leagues in longitude to get a favourable wind. On 3rd June, having sailed in different directions 1400 leagues, without seeing land, they had arrived in latitude 42° N. A great change in the temperature was now felt; the people were benumbed with the piercing cold, which increased to that extremity on sailing two degrees farther north, that meat, as soon as it was removed from the fire, would presently be frozen, and the ropes and tackling of the ship were quite stiffened. Contrary winds forced them to run in with the land, which they then unexpectedly descried; for they had not supposed that America in that latitude extended so far to the west. "They stood toward the shore, and anchored in an open ill-sheltered bay. The wind was strong and in gusts; upon any intermission, there came a thick stinking fog, in which they were enveloped, till it was dispersed by the renewed strength of the wind. They could not remain here; and the direction of the wind, with the severity of the cold, not only discouraged them from persisting in the attempt to go farther north, but commanded them to the southward, whether they would or no." So they drew back from latitude 48°, to which they had advanced, ten degrees, "in which height it pleased God to send them into a fair and good bay, with a good wind to enter the same". There can be little doubt that this bay was that which is now called Port San Francisco.*

There were huts close to the water side. The day after they anchored many natives showed themselves on the shore, and a single man was sent off in a canoe. Immediately he began to speak, though at a considerable distance from the ship, and continued to do so as he paddled on, till having drawn as near as he thought fit upon this first advance, he stopped, made a long and earnest address accompanied by

* Burney, 343. Hakluyt, 440.

gesticulations not more intelligible than the harangue; and when he had finished, returned with great show of reverence to the shore. Soon after he repeated the same ceremony in the same manner; and presently a third time, but he then brought a bunch of feathers, resembling those of a crow, neatly fastened together, clean and handsomely cut; and also a small basket made of rushes, and filled with an herb which they called *tabah* :* these he tied to a short stick, and cast them into the ship's boat. In return Drake directed some presents to be put on a plank in the water, and pushed towards him; but he refused to touch them, and would receive nothing except a hat, which being thrown from the ship, he took up. No intercourse followed upon this ceremony; both parties, however, seemed to consider that a good understanding had been established by it, and to have acted accordingly in good faith. The natives were not distrustful, because they had only once been visited by Europeans, thirty-seven years before, when Joam Rodrigues Cabrillo,† a Portuguese by birth, was sent by the viceroy of New Spain to explore that coast : he happened to be a humane good man, as well as a skilful navigator; and the whole of his intercourse with the natives had been of the most friendly kind. Drake knew not that any such earlier discovery had been made of these parts; but he felt the beneficial consequences of his predecessor's conduct; and neither he nor his people did anything during their tarriance to counteract the favourable impression which Cabrillo had made.

* The author of the "famous voyage" says tobacco (Hakluyt, 441). I have followed Admiral Burney in using the name by which the natives called it; but that it was tobacco I have no doubt. For the Californians, though they had not discovered the art of preparing any fermented liquor, used to intoxicate themselves at their feasts with the smoke of this wild herb (*Noticia de la California*, t. i., p. 79).

† Burney, i., 220-224. Herrera, Dec. 7. 1. 5. c. 3, 4. *Noticia de la California*, i., 181-183.

He was not, however, unmindful of that caution which ought always to be observed among any people whose character is not well known, and especially among savages. It was necessary to lighten the ship in order to come at a leak which she had sprung. She was anchored, therefore, close to the shore, and Drake landed his men, with tents, and such things as were necessary for fortifying their temporary encampment. The natives upon perceiving this collected in arms, and in large companies; yet their demeanour was that of men who had prepared themselves to resent wrong, not to offer it; and when signs were made to them to lay aside their bows and arrows they did so, accepted the gifts which were offered, and in return presented the general with feathers, nets, and skins. They retired at evening, to all appearance, well satisfied; but when they had reached their dwellings loud lamentations were distinctly heard from thence, though the distance was not less than three parts of a mile, and the voices of the women were distinguished, whose miserable shrieking rose above the deep and doleful outcries of the men. During the two following days no one came near the tents, and Drake is said to have fortified them by building a stone wall round. On the third day, a more numerous assemblage than had yet been seen convened on the nearest eminence, from whence one of their orators delivered with violent enunciation a long speech, his words falling " so thick one on the neck of the other, that he could hardly fetch his breath again ". When he had ended, all the natives bowed their heads, and sung out *oh* in a solemn and lengthened tone, whereby it was supposed that they signified their assent to all that had been said. The men then left their bows on the ground, descended to the encampment, and offered bunches of feathers and baskets of tobacco to the general, which he accepted, and made them presents in return. But the women, meantime remaining on the hill, " tormented themselves lamentably " : they tore their cheeks and bosoms, uttered pitiable cries, threw off their upper garment, and holding their hands over their heads, dashed themselves on the ground, repeating this till they were covered with blood. The English did not behold this miserable sight without compassion, and Drake felt the more, because he and his people were persuaded that the natives took them for gods, and meant this as a religious act of propitiation. A proper sense of piety prompted him to the wisest measure that could have been taken. He ordered all his people to prayers, and divine service was performed with an earnestness which the natives understood. The effect which he had hoped for was produced, a stop was put to their self-lacerations and other acts of violence: they "seemed to be greatly affected at what they witnessed"; that is, they regarded it with awe, and at every pause in the service they chanted out their solemn *oh*. When it was over, and they rose to depart, they restored all the presents which had been made them, and no one could be persuaded to take away with him a single thing.*

The news having spread into the country, more natives flocked to the place, and two heralds made the general understand that their chief, or *hioh*, as he was called, was coming to visit him, but that he desired to have some token sent him that his coming might be in peace. They were dismissed with what they asked for; and forthwith the hioh, who was "of a goodly stature and comely personage," advanced toward the fort with a princely majesty, the people crying continually after their manner, and as they drew near so did they strive to behave in their actions with comeliness. One "of a large body and goodly aspect" led the way, bearing a club of dark-coloured wood, to which were fastened two coronals, "a less and a bigger, made of network, and artificially wrought with feathers of many colours".

* Burney, 345-348. Hakluyt, 441.

Three chains also were suspended from it, "of a marvellous length, and made of a bony substance,* every part thereof being very little, thin, finely burnished, with a hole pierced through the middle, the number of links making one chain being in a manner infinite. Few be the persons that are admitted to wear them, and those persons are stinted in the number, by which it seems their rank was denoted." Next came the hioh, wearing a coronal like those which were borne before him, and a cloak of what the English took for rabbit skins. About 100 "tall and warlike men accompanied him, with similar cloaks but of different skins". Some wore feathered coats, others had their heads "covered with a very fine down, which grows in that country upon an herb much like our lettuce". All had their faces painted, each after his own fashion. Each brought something for a present. "The naked, common sort of people followed," every one having his face painted, some with white, some with black, and other colours, "and having feathers in their hair, which they gathered up in a bunch behind. Women and children brought up the train, each bringing a round basket or two with bags of tobacco, broiled fish, and a root called *petah*, of which meal was made, to be either baked or eaten raw. Even the children carried each a present."†

Drake, seeing so numerous a body of natives, drew up his men within the "fenced place, making against their approach a very warlike show". The Californians, "being trooped

---

* A marginal note in Hakluyt says, "These are like chains of Esurnoy in Canada and Hochelage," that is, strings of wampum. Langsdorff says, that the Indians at this place still retain the art of making the pieces of which these strings are composed with marvellous exactness, all of the same size, and boring them without an iron instrument. They are cut from the shell of a kind of mussel, which he did not see. One of them is represented in the plates to the German edition of Langsdorff's work (*Reise um die Welt*, ii., 143).

† Burney, 348-350. Hakluyt, 441.

together in their order," first made a general salutation, which was followed by a general silence. The club bearer then pronounced with a loud and manly voice, after the dictation of one who stood close to him, an oration which seemed to the English to continue half an hour, and at its conclusion the whole train chanted that long *oh*, which was interpreted to signify amen, so be it! Men and women then descended the hill (leaving the children), and advanced in order towards the camp; their demonstrations were so peaceful that Drake allowed them to enter; the club or sceptre bearer (as he is dignified by the relater) "began a song, observing his measures in a dance, and that with a stately countenance; the hioh with his guard, and every degree of persons following, did in like manner sing and dance, but the women only danced and kept silence". When they were within the camp, they continued their song and dance a reasonable time. Then, in the words of the earliest account, "they made signs to our general to sit down, to whom the king and divers others made several orations, or rather supplications, that he would take their province and kingdom into his hand and become their king, making signs that they would resign unto him their right and title of the whole land, and become his subjects. In which to persuade us the better, the king and the rest with one consent, and with great reverence, joyfully singing a song, did set the crown upon his head, enriched his neck with all their chains, and offered unto him many other things, honouring him by the name of hioh,* adding thereunto, as it seemed, a sign of triumph; which thing our general thought not meet to reject, because

---

* "These honours," says Admiral Burney, "paid to a stranger, have more than a shade of resemblance to the custom which has been found among so many Indian nations, of exchanging names with those whose alliance or friendship they desire. The general, to have manifested an equal return of consideration, might have decorated his visitor with some ornament, and have saluted him by the name of Drake" (p. 350).

he knew not what honour and profit it might be to our country. Wherefore, in the name and to the use of her majesty, he took the sceptre,* crown, and dignity of the said country in his hands; wishing that the riches and treasure thereof might so conveniently be transported to the enriching of her kingdom at home, as it aboundeth in the same." † The natives accompanied this act of surrender with a song and dance of triumph, "because (says another relater) they were not only visited of gods (for so they still judged us to be), but the great and chief god was now become their god, their king and patron, and themselves the only happy and blessed people in all the world". ‡

That the natives meant to make a surrender of their country by these ceremonies is what none but men prepossessed with notions which were common to all Europeans in that age could have supposed; but that they regarded the English as beings, if not of superior nature, yet of such superior knowledge and power, that it was necessary to propitiate them by circumstances approaching to idolatry, must be inferred from the scene which immediately ensued. "The common sort of people, leaving the king and his guard with our general, scattered themselves together with their sacrifices among our people, taking a diligent view of every person; and such as pleased their fancy (which were the youngest), they, enclosing them about, offered their sacrifices unto them with lamentable weeping, scratching, and tearing

---

* The invariable custom adopted by Europeans, of claiming and taking formal possession of every new land they meet with (whether it is inhabited or uninhabited never entering into the consideration), no doubt disposed Drake to credit, if it is true that he did credit it, that these people, simply, and for no cause, value received, or other consideration, made a voluntary gift of themselves and their country to him, a perfect stranger (Burney, 354).

† Hakluyt, 441.

‡ *World Encompassed*, 76.

the flesh from their faces with their nails, whereof issued abundance of blood. But we used signs to them of disliking this, and stayed their hands from force, and directed them upwards to the living God, whom only they ought to worship." Such, too, as had sores, craved help of the strangers, as of persons who assuredly they thought could heal them. Whereupon, the writer says, "we gave them lotions, plasters, and ointments, agreeing to the state of their griefs, beseeching God to cure their diseases. Every third day they brought their sacrifices unto us, until they understood our meaning that we had no pleasure in them. Yet they could not be long absent from us, but daily frequented our company to the hour of our departure, which departure seemed so grievous unto them, that their joy was turned into sorrow. They entreated us that, being absent, we would remember them, and by stealth provided a sacrifice, which we misliked."*

The Californians were in a ruder state than many of the North American nations. The people whom Drake saw were a burrowing tribe: their houses or dens were circular, roofed with timber, the centre forming a kind of spire,† near which "an opening that resembled the scuttle of a ship served the double purpose of door and chimney". They were not so far advanced as to use the hammock; but slept, like our British ancestors, upon rushes, around a central fire. Most of the men were nearly naked; the women wore a loose garment round the waist, made of bulrushes, "combed after the manner of hemp": over the shoulders they had a deer skin. Deer were very numerous: in an excursion which Drake made to some of their villages in the interior, he saw herds of a thousand in a company, "being most large

---

* Hakluyt, 442.

† "Their houses," says the old relation, "are digged round about with earth, and have from the uttermost brims of the circle clefts of wood set upon them, joining close together at the top like a spire steeple, which by reason of that closeness are very warm" (p. 441).

and fat of body ". " The whole country was like a warren of a strange kind of conies, their bodies in bigness as be the Barbary conies, their heads as the heads of ours, the feet of a wunt (or mole), and the tail of a rat, being of great length; under her chin on either side a bag, into the which she gathered her meat, when she hath filled her belly abroad." The skins of these creatures were much esteemed, "for their king's coat was made of them". Drake named the country New Albion, "in respect of the white banks and cliffs which lie towards the sea," and also for old England's sake. He set up a monument of the queen's "right and title to the same, namely, a plate nailed upon a fair great post, whereupon was engraven her majesty's name, the day and year of our arrival there, with the free giving up of the province and people into her majesty's hands, together with her highness's picture and arms in a piece of sixpence of current English money under the plate, where under was also written the name of our general". Nova California is still named New Albion in English maps; but no consequences, either evil or good, have resulted from the possession thus confidently taken.* That part of the Americas has even to this time escaped from all the evils of conquest, and the attempts that have been made to civilise it have been in the spirit of that religion which was proclaimed with the announcement of peace on earth, good will towards men. The Jesuits, who were as beneficially employed in America as they were mischievously in Europe, established missions there, in which,

---

* " It seemeth that the Spaniards hitherto had never been in this part of the country, neither did they ever discover the land by many degrees to the southwards of this place" (Hakluyt, 442). The English knew nothing at that time of Cabrillo's voyage, nor indeed of anything that the Spaniards had done in that direction. They too were dreaming of Eldorados, and thought there was "no part of the earth here to be taken up wherein there is not some special likelihood of gold or silver" (*Ibid.*).

though they attempted, and consequently effected, less than in Paraguay and among the Chaquitos, they reclaimed very many hordes from a savage life, and reduced them to a state of contented pupilage, in which their bodily wants were amply provided for. Upon the abolition of that order the Franciscans were substituted for them in these parts, and the Californian missions appear to have been the only ones that were not either utterly ruined or miserably deteriorated by the change.

After remaining five weeks in port Drake took his departure, and as long as the ship continued in sight, the natives kept fires on the tops of the hills. The design of seeking for a passage by the north of America was, with general consent, given up, seeing that the northern summer was so far advanced, and that the wind was then blowing from the northwest; and it was determined to follow the example of Magellan, and steer for the Moluccas. After taking "good store of seals and birds" from the Farellones, which are near the entrance of Port St. Francisco, they sailed sixty-eight days without seeing land, and then fell in with some inhabited islands, which, from the conduct of the natives, they named the Island of Thieves,—another remarkable coincidence with the circumstances of Magellan's voyage. These people began by fair trading: then took the English articles and would make no return; and, lastly, when the English refused to deal any more with such customers, attacked the ships with stones, wherewith they had come well provided. A great gun was fired over their heads: it frightened them away; but when they found that they were not hurt, they returned more audaciously to the unprovoked attack, and "could not be got rid of till they were made to feel smart as well as terror". There is little doubt that these were the Pelew Islands. Drake was not clear of them till 3rd of October. On the 16th he made the Philippines, and on 3rd of November had sight of the Moluccas, and steered for Tidore,

18

where it was his intention to anchor; but a boat came off from the Island Motir, and Portuguese enough was spoken by those who came in it to make him understand that the Portuguese had been driven out from Ternate, and had taken up their quarters in Tidore, and to invite him to change his destination and go to Ternate, when they understood that he was not a friend to the Portuguese. Thither, accordingly, he went; and sending a velvet cloak as a present to the king, requested to be furnished with provisions, and to trade for spices.*

The king, who had already been told "what good things he might receive by traffic," prepared forthwith to visit the ship. He sent before him "four great and large canoes, in every one whereof were certain of his greatest states that were about him, attired in white lawn of cloth of Calicut, having over their heads from the one end of the canoe to the other a covering of thin perfumed mats, borne up with a frame made of reeds for the same use, under which every one did sit in his order, according to his dignity, to keep him from the heat of the sun; divers of whom being of good age and gravity did make an ancient and fatherly show. There were also divers young and comely men attired in white, as were the others. The rest were soldiers, which stood in comely order, round about on both sides; without whom sat the rowers in certain galleries, which being three on a side all along the canoes did lie off from the side thereof three or four yards, one being orderly builded lower than another, in every of which galleries were the number of fourscore rowers. These canoes were furnished with warlike munition, every man, for the most part, having his sword and target, with his dagger, besides other weapons, as lances, calivers, darts, bows and arrows; also every canoe had a small cast base (or cannon) mounted at the least one full yard upon a stock set

* Burney, 356-358.   Hakluyt, 739.

upright. Thus coming near the ship in order they rowed about it, one after another, and passing by, did their homage* with great solemnity, the great personages beginning with great gravity, and fatherly countenance, signifying that the king had sent them to conduct the ship into a better road." The king soon arrived, and was received with a salute of great guns, with trumpets sounding, and such politic display of state and strength as Drake knew it was advisable to exhibit. He and his suite were "passing well contented with the presents which were made them; and taking his leave, as the ship anchored, he promised to repeat his visit the next day, and said that provisions should be supplied ".†

That same night provisions were sent, consisting of rice, fowls, "unperfect and liquid sugar," sugar canes, "a fruit which they call figo," cloves, and "meal, which they call sagu, made of the tops of certain trees, tasting in the mouth like sour curds, but melting like sugar, whereof they make certain cakes, which may be kept the space of ten years, and yet then good to be eaten". But instead of repeating his visit, as he had promised, the king sent his brother on the morrow to invite the general ashore, and remain on board as hostage for his safe return. The breach of promise made Drake "mislike" this invitation, and his whole company utterly refused to let him accept it. Not, however, to express any suspicion, that should it prove needless might justly give offence, he sent some of his officers with presents in his stead. They were received in great state, in a large and fair house, near the castle which this prince had taken from the

* Here, too, Drake's people were possessed with the notion of an intended surrender of the rights of sovereignty. The first relater says, "the king was moved with great liking toward us, and sent to our general with special message, that he should have what things he needed and would require, with peace and friendship; and, moreover, that he would yield himself, and the right of his island, to be at the pleasure and commandment of so great a prince as we served" (p. 739).

† Hakluyt, 739. Burney, 358.

Portuguese. About 1000 persons were assembled, among whom were seven ambassadors* from different countries. The king came in, after a while, with twelve guards, and under a rich canopy, embossed with gold. "From his waist down to the ground was all cloth of gold, and the same very rich; his legs were bare, but on his feet were shoes of Cordovan skin. In the attire of his head were finely wreathed hooped rings of gold; and about his neck he had a chain of perfect gold, the links whereof were great and one fold double. On his fingers he had six very fair jewels; and sitting in his chair of estate, at his right hand stood a page with a fan in his hand, breathing and gathering the air to the king. The fan was in length two feet, and in breadth one, set with eight sapphires, richly embroidered, and knit to a staff three feet in length, by which the page did hold and move it." No treachery had been intended: the interview ended well; and the English were offered an exclusive trade with Ternate and its numerous dependent isles,† if they would enter into engagements of amity and commerce with him.

Sultan Baboe, or more properly Baab-Ullah, by whom this proposal was made, was a more politic and powerful prince than any of the twenty-four sultans who had preceded him in the sovereignty of those islands. His father, Sultan Hairun, had been assassinated in his own palace by the Portuguese,

---

* Two Turks, liegers, the old relation says, and one Italian, and "four grave persons, apparelled all in red down to the ground, and attired on their heads like the Turks, and these were said to be Romans, and liegers there to keep continual traffic with the people of Ternate" (p. 740). Who these may have been it is impossible to guess, farther than that they were Mahommedans.

† Seventy they are said to be in Hakluyt. They were commonly accounted seventy-two, but Valentyn enumerates twenty more, besides more than a hundred uninhabited ones, of which the birds and turtles are in full, but not peaceful, possession.

mutual wrongs and mutual intolerance having exasperated them against each other. The history of the Portuguese in the Moluccas, far unlike that of the mother-country and its other conquests or colonies, may be described as a series of crimes, with little to mitigate them, and nothing to redeem the perpetrators from abhorrence and execration.* They cut the body of Hairun in pieces, salted them, and when Baab-Ullah offered even to become a Christian if they would give him the dishonoured remains of his murdered father, they cast them into the sea. The sultan had his revenge, but it was that of a brave and honourable man : he besieged them in their fort St. Paulo, compelled them, by famine, to surrender, received the keys in a casket of finely wrought silver, and made the army hut themselves upon the beach till opportunity might offer of a passage to their own country. A galleon arrived ; but those on board regarded the capitulation as so shameful, that they refused to take their countrymen on board, and there they must have remained, if the people of Tidore had not, in hatred to the Ternatans, transported them to their island, and allowed them to construct a fortress there ; and though Baab-Ullah pursued them thither, and defeated them and their allies in battle, they maintained themselves there. † These events occurred only six years before Drake's arrival, and they explain the readiness with which the sultan proposed to enter into an alliance with the English. Powerful as he then was, he knew that he might possibly one day stand in need of European aid ; and in the eastern islands the sultans seem always to have been merchant princes. But the English did not yet extend their views of commerce so far, and Drake had not come there "to spy the land," even with mercantile intentions.

* My knowledge of it is derived from their own historians ; and if there is a wickeder history than that of the Portuguese in the Moluccas, it has not come within the course of my reading.

† Valentyn, *Beschryving der Moluccas*, i., 206, 207.

His first object was to discover the weakness of Peru; having succeeded in that, to go round the world was not only a point of ambition but his best way home.

Among the persons who came on board the *Golden Hind* during the six days that she remained at Ternate was a Chinese, who informed Drake, through an interpreter, that he was related to the family of the reigning emperor, but had been unjustly accused of a capital crime, and was afraid that if it came to trial, innocent though he was, he should not be able to make his innocence appear. He had, therefore, solicited and obtained leave to expatriate himself, upon condition that if he could bring home any important intelligence, he should be allowed to live in his native country, otherwise he must pass his life in exile. Now, he said, he accounted himself a happy man, in that he had seen and spoken with the English, thinking this was a thing for which, perhaps, he might find favour in China; and he endeavoured to persuade Drake to go thither, not doubting but that it would be a means to obtain him advancement and honour. But Drake's business was to secure both the wealth and the glory which he had acquired, by returning home with as little delay as possible; and the poor Chinese departed sorrowfully, when he found that his persuasions did not succeed.*

Having stored himself with provisions, and laid in as large a quantity of cloves as convenient stowage could be found for, Drake sailed on 9th of November; and on the 14th anchored at a small uninhabited island near the eastern part of Celebes. There he erected tents, intrenched them to be prepared for unwelcome visitors if any should arrive, set up a forge, and repaired the ship carefully. Four weeks were passed in this occupation without molestation of any kind. They had to provide themselves with water from an adjacent

---

* *World Encompassed*, 93. Burney, 359.

island; in all other respects this was most commodious. It was covered "with wood of a large and high growth, straight, and without boughs, save only in the head or top, whose leaves are not much differing from our broom in England. Amongst these trees, night by night, through the whole land, did show themselves an infinite swarm of fiery worms flying in the air, whose bodies being no bigger than our common English flies make such a show and light, as if every twig and tree had been a burning candle." Such is the exaggerated description which one of these adventurers has given of a very striking and beautiful sight. "In this place breedeth also wonderful store of bats, as big as large hens"; and, better than such ugly poultry, "a kind of cray fish, of such a size that one was sufficient to satisfy four hungry men". These, which seem to be exaggerated in size, were land crabs, and "very good and restoring meat". "They are," says another relater, "as far as we could perceive, utter strangers to the sea, living always on the land, where they work themselves earths; or rather they dig huge caves under the roots of the largest trees, where they lodge by companies together. Sometimes, when we come to take them, for want of other refuge, they would climb into the trees and hide themselves, where we were enforced to follow them."*

From hence they sailed toward the west, and thereby got entangled among the islands and shoals near the coast of Celebes. With the hope of escaping from these, they held a southern course; but on 9th of January, when they thought themselves in a clear sea, early in the first watch, the ship running under full sail, with the wind large, and blowing moderately fresh, came at once upon a rocky shoal, and stuck fast. "Boats were got out to examine if an anchor could be placed in any direction, by which they might

---

* Hakluyt, 740. Burney, 361.

endeavour to draw the ship off into deep water; but at the distance of only a boat's length no bottom could be found with all their lines. The ship had not become leaky in consequence of the shock; but she remained all night fixed, and another examination after daylight was as fruitless as the former." There she continued till four in the afternoon. The general, "as he had always hitherto shown himself courageous, and of a good confidence in the mercy and protection of God, so now he continued in the same; and lest he should seem to perish wilfully, both he and his men did their best endeavour to save themselves. Those endeavours were all vain; and it was to God's special mercy that they were alone beholden for their preservation, when no human effort could avail. In a state which was hopeless, as well as helpless, the crew were summoned to prayers; and when that duty was performed they tried what could be done by lightening the ship. Three tons of cloves were thrown out, eight of the guns, and a quantity of meal and pulse; but none of the treasure, though that was the heaviest part of the cargo.*

* Fuller says otherwise in a most characteristic passage. The ship, he says, struck twice on a dangerous shoal, " knocking twice at the door of death, which no doubt had opened the third time. Here they stuck, having ground too much, and yet too little to land on; and water too much, and yet too little to sail in. Had God, who, as the wise man saith, holdeth the winds in His fist, but opened His little finger and let out the smallest blast, they had undoubtedly been cast away; but there blew not any wind all the while. Then they, conceiving aright that the best way to lighten the ship was first to ease it of the burthen of their sins by true repentance, humbled themselves by fasting under the hand of God; afterward they received the communion, dining on Christ in the sacrament, expecting no other than to sup with Him in heaven. Then they cast out of their ship six great pieces of ordnance; threw overboard as much wealth as would break the heart of a miser to think on't; with much sugar, and packs of spices, making a caudle of the sea round about. Then they betook themselves to their prayers, the best lever at such a dead lift indeed, and it pleased God that the wind, formerly their mortal enemy, became their friend" (*Holy State*, 127).

No visible benefit was produced. The ship had grounded on a shelving rock; where she lay there was on one side only six feet depth at low water, and to float her it required thirteen. The wind blowing fresh directly against the other side kept her upright during the time she was left by the tide; but when it was nearly at the lowest the wind slackened, and the ship losing this prop fell toward the deep water: her keel with the shake was freed from the rocks; and, not less to the surprise than to the joy of every one aboard, she was once more afloat. Thus were they delivered at the very time when the tide was least favourable, and when all efforts were thought useless."*

"Having suffered many dangers by winds and shoals," they fell in, on the 8th of February, with "the fruitful island of Barateva," of which they say that, "to confess a truth, since the time that we first set out of our country of England, we happened upon no place, Ternate only excepted, wherein we found more comforts, and better means of refreshing". The people they found comely, just in dealing, and courteous to strangers. From thence they set their course for Java; which island, according to them, "was governed by five rajahs, living at that time in such unity, as if they had one spirit and one mind". The people, by their account, dwelt together as harmoniously as their chiefs. "They have a house in every village for their common assembly; every day they meet twice, men, women, and children, bringing with them such victuals as they think good; some fruits,

* Burney, 363. This excellent seaman follows the author of the *World Encompassed* in this detail, wherein I have followed him—safe always with such a guide. The account in Hakluyt (p. 741) says, that they lightened the ship; "and then the wind (as it were in a moment by the special grace of God) changing from the starboard to the larboard of the ship, we hoisted our sails, and the happy gale drove our ship off the rocks into the sea again, to the no little comfort of all our hearts, for which we gave God such praise and thanks as so great a benefit required".

some rice boiled,* some hens roasted, some sagu; having a table made three feet from the ground, whereon they set their meat, that every person sitting at the table may eat, one rejoicing in the company of another." It is a mournful reflection that in proportion as we become acquainted with the real condition and character of distant nations, the more there is to subtract from the first favourable opinion that is formed of them.

Here Drake was informed that not far off there were ships as large as his own, and he was warned to beware of them; though he must previously have known his danger as he drew near the Portuguese settlements, this warning is said to have made him hasten his departure from Java. From thence he steered for the Cape of Good Hope, which his men thought "a most stately thing, and the fairest cape they had seen in the whole circumference of the earth". They landed on the west side in search of water, and finding no spring must have been distressed if they had not providently collected rain water in good time. They supplied themselves at Sierra Leone, and concluded their prosperous voyage at Plymouth after two years and nearly ten months; arriving on Monday by their own reckoning, they found that it was Sunday in England. Drake immediately repaired to court, and was graciously received there, though the treasure

* They boil their rice in an earthen pot, made in form of a sugar loaf, being full of holes, as our pots which we water our gardens withal; and it is open at the great end, wherein they put their rice dry, without any moisture. In the meantime they have ready another great earthen pot, set fast in a furnace, boiling, full of water, whereinto they put their pot with rice, by such measure that the grains, swelling, become soft at the first, and by their swelling, stopping the holes of the pot, admit no more water to enter; but the more they are boiled the harder and more firm substance they become, so that in the end they are a firm and good bread; of the which with oil, butter, sugar, and other spices, they make divers sorts of meats, very pleasant of taste, and nourishing to nature (Hakluyt, 741).

which he brought home was placed in sequestration, in case it should be found necessary to answer such demands as would be made for it. Her own right of navigating the ocean in all parts Elizabeth firmly asserted to the Spanish ambassador, and as firmly denied any right which the Spaniard laid claim to in the Indies by virtue of the pope's grant. And though she yielded so far as to pay a considerable sum of money to an ostensible procurator of certain merchants who claimed it, enough seems to have been retained to make it a profitable adventure for the captors. Drake was rewarded with such honours as he had well deserved. The queen gave orders that his ship should be drawn up in a little creek near Deptford, and there preserved as a monument of the most memorable voyage that the English had ever yet performed. "Having, as it were, thus consecrated it, she honoured it and him by going on board to partake of a banquet there; and on that occasion * Drake knelt to her, and rose up Sir Francis. The good fortune which had attended the *Golden Hind* on her voyage round the world did not forsake that

---

* On this occasion also the Westminster scholars set up the following verses upon the mainmast:—

      "PLUS ULTRA, Herculeis inscribas, Drace, columnis,
        Et magno, dicas, Hercule major ero".

On Hercules' pillars, Drake, thou may'st *plus ultra* write full well,
And say, I will in greatness that great Hercules excel.

      "Drace, pererrati novit quem terminus orbis,
        Quemque semel mundi vidit uterque polus,
        Si taceant homines, facient te sidera notum,
        Sol nescit comitis non memor esse sui."

Sir Drake, whom well the world's end knows, which thou didst compass round,
And whom both poles of heaven once saw which north and south do bound,
The stars above will make thee known if men here silent were;
The sun himself cannot forget his fellow-traveller.

ship when laid up in this its last harbour. The bridge of planks by which the queen and her retinue went on board broke under the crowd of people who stationed themselves upon it; about 100 persons fell, and yet no one suffered any serious injury.* The ship remained at Deptford till it decayed: it was then broken up; and from one of its planks a chair was made, and presented to the University of Oxford.

It was, probably, about this time that Sir Francis assumed the arms of the Drakes of Ash, near Axminster, which, as he was not able to make out his descent from that family, was, "in those days, when the court of honour was in more honour, a matter not so easily digested". Bernard Drake, the representative of that family, was a sea-rover like himself; and instead of feeling that the tree of his pedigree would be rendered more illustrious by having the name of Sir Francis Drake pendent from it than by any fruit that it had ever before borne, resented the assumption angrily; high words ensued, and he gave Sir Francis a blow within the verge of the court: worse consequences might have followed had this outrage been offered in any other place; and the queen, it is said, not leaving the laws to take cognisance of the offender, terminated the dispute by bestowing upon Sir Francis "a new coat of everlasting honour to himself and posterity for ever". "The field," says Gwillim,† "is diamond, a fess wavy between the two pole stars, Arctic and Antarctic, pearl. Such was the worth of this most generous and renowned knight, as that his merits do require that his coat-armour should be expressed in that selected manner of blazoning that is fitting to noble personages, in respect of his noble courage and high attempts achieved." The crest given him was a ship on a globe, under ruff, held by a cable with a hand out of the clouds, and a wivern gules, his wings displayed, and tail nowed (being the Drake arms), hung by the

---

* Camden, 253, 254.   † P. 81, ed. 1679.

heels in the rigging,—marking thereby the queen's displeasure towards the bearer of that coat. He, however, according to the tradition in his family, told the queen, with no unbecoming spirit, that though she might give his competitor a nobler coat of arms than his, she could not give him an ancienter. * Elizabeth's displeasure was but for a time; and sparing as she was in the distribution of honours, it was not long before she rewarded the services of this gentleman, as they well deserved, with knighthood.

Whether this expedition were justifiable or not upon those principles by which all Christian states ought to hold themselves bound, Drake's conduct in it, as a navigator and a commander, is entitled to the highest praise. It has been said of him that he was a willing hearer of every man's opinion, but commonly a follower of his own, and this is the highest praise that can be bestowed upon a man so competent to form an opinion for himself. The next great enterprise in which he was engaged was planned after Elizabeth had openly entered into an alliance with the United States. Philip had then laid an embargo upon all English ships, goods, and subjects in his dominions; and the queen authorised such as sustained loss by this measure to indemnify themselves by taking and arresting all ships and merchandise belonging to the subjects of Spain wherever they could find them.† Not waiting for the war at her own doors, she fitted out an expedition, consisting of twenty-five sail of ships and pinnaces. Drake was appointed admiral, Martin Frobisher vice-admiral, Christopher Carleill, "a man of long experience in the wars as well by sea as land," general of the land forces. The soldiers and seamen amounted to 2300. They sailed from Plymouth on the 14th of September, 1585, for the coast of Spain; and after a few days, "for lack of favourable wind," put in within the isles of Bayona. No sooner had part of the fleet anchored than Drake ordered the pinnaces and boats to be manned, got into

* Prince. † Monson, in Churchill, iii., 155.

his galley, and rowed toward the town of Bayona, then a considerable place, his intent being, says the historian of the voyage, "with the favour of the Almighty, to surprise it". They were presently met by a messenger from the governor; the communication ended in Drake's despatching Captain Sampson, one of the two corporals of the field, to demand of the governor, "first, if there were war between Spain and England; and, secondly, why the English merchants and their goods were embargoed?" The governor replied, that he knew of no war between the two nations, and it lay not in him to make any: the embargo had been the king's pleasure, but not with intent to injure any man; and, in fact, it had been taken off by the king's counter order a week ago, to certify which he sent the English merchants then resident there. But it was with no pacific intention that this armament had been set forth. The troops landed, and quartering themselves as well as they could, and setting good guard upon every approach, thought to rest themselves there for the night. Wine, fruit, and other refreshments were sent from the town to their unbidden and unwelcome visitants, as if they had been friends. But about midnight the weather began to overcast: it was deemed wiser to repair aboard than make any longer tarriance, and before they could recover the fleet a storm arose; many of the ships drove from their anchorage, some were forced out to sea in great peril, and one was driven to England. "The extremity of the storm lasted three days." *

When the fleet had re-assembled, Carleill was sent with part of it "to see what he could do above Vigo". He intercepted many boats and caravels, in which the inhabitants were removing their property up into the country, except one boat, in which were the plate and ornaments of the high church. The booty was of little value to the captors, yet the loss of the people was computed at more than 30,000

* Cates, in Hakluyt, iii., 535.

ducats, the ducat being 5s. 6d. The next day Drake joined Carleill in a station above the town, chosen "as well for the more quiet riding of his ship as also for the good commodity of watering, which the place afforded full well". Meantime the Governor of Galicia, having collected some 2000 foot and 300 horse, hastened to this point, and demanded a parley with the English commander. Drake consented, "so it might be in boats upon the water". Hostages were given on both sides; and an agreement was concluded that the English "should furnish themselves with fresh water, to be taken quietly by their own people, and with all other such necessaries as the place would afford, paying for the same". This done, the fleet sailed for the Canaries.*

The parties had regarded each other here with respect; and humiliating as it was for the governor of such a province to have consented to such an agreement, his presence prevented greater evil, the disposition of the English being to burn and destroy, or to extort a ransom as the price of their forbearance. Great and not unreasonable alarm was excited by their appearance. Their force was estimated at 5000 troops, with 30 ships, besides many pinnaces and oared shallops: it was feared that they were designed for the South Sea; and the mischief which they might effect upon the way was forecast by the Marquis of Santa Cruz. In eighteen days from Bayona, at this season, Drake might sack Madeira, the Canaries, and the Cape de Verds; forty days more might carry him to Rio Janeiro: he might take possession of the mouth of that fine harbour, which commands the entrance, fortify it, and maintain it by leaving a garrison of 500 men there: he might then pass the strait, enter the South Sea, and attack Lima. The population of that city consisted of 2000 families, but they were neither a warlike people, nor had they been trained to arms; and as the place

* Cates, in Hakluyt, iii., 536.

was open, and had no artillery for its defence, the English might take and sack it, and proceed to make themselves masters of the land; in furtherance of which views it was very probable that they would get possession of Panama. If this were not Drake's design, it might be to sack St. Domingo, Puerto Rico, and the coast of Tierra-Firma to Carthagena and Nombre de Dios, and by way of Venta de Cruz attack Panama from that side. The Havannah, also, was in great danger, the fortress being but small and weak. The marquis advised, therefore, that despatches should be sent off with all possible diligence to the viceroys and governors in the Indies; that a fleet should be ordered out to sail in pursuit of the English, and give them battle; that 1000 Catalonian and Genoese sailors should be distributed in this fleet, and 6000 soldiers levied for it, a greater number being raised, to the end that those who were chosen might be able men.*

Drake, meantime, was on his way to the Canaries, and made first for the Isle of Palma, "with intention," says Cates, "to have taken our pleasure of that place, for the full digesting of many things into order, and the better furnishing our store with such several good things, as it affordeth very abundantly". But he complains "we were forced by the vile sea-gate, which at that present fell out, and by the naughtiness of the landing-place, being but one, and that under the favour of many platforms, well furnished with great ordnance, to depart with the receipt of many of their cannon shot; but the only or chief mischief was the dangerous sea surge, which at shore all along plainly threatened the overthrow of any boats as should have attempted landing". They then tried the Island of Hierro, and landed about 1000 men: the inhabitants came to them; and, by means of a young Englishman who resided there, represented "their state to be so poor, that they were all ready to starve".

* Hakluyt, 530, 534.

This poverty was their defence; and the expedition, thus a second time disappointed, proceeded for the Cape de Verds.*

Arrived at the principal of those islands, they anchored between the towns of Playa and Santiago. Carleill was landed there with 1000 men, marched toward the latter place, being the capital, during the night, halted at some two miles' distance till break of day, and then advancing "hard to the walls" saw no enemy to resist him, the inhabitants having, at sight of the fleet, fled into the interior. Two companies of thirty men each were then sent to enter the town, the whole of which, being in a valley, was completely seen from the high ground on which the troops had arrived; the great ensign was also sent, "which had nothing on it but the plain English cross, to be placed toward the sea, that our fleet might see St. George's cross flourish on the enemy's fortress. Order was given that all the ordnance throughout the town, and upon all the platforms, which were about fifty pieces, all ready charged, should be shot off in honour of the queen's majesty's coronation day, being the 17th November, after the yearly custom of England, which was so answered again by all the ships in the fleet, being now come near, as it was strange to hear such a thundering noise last so long together." The town was in form like a triangle, having cliffs, "as it were, hanging over it," on the east and west; both heights were fortified, though no attempt had been made to defend the works. On the south was the sea; and at the north end the valley, in which the town is built, becomes so narrow, that it was estimated not to be above ten or twelve score over. A stream came down the valley, and formed a pond near the sea-side, at which the ships were watered with great ease. Above the town the valley expanded, and was wholly converted into gardens and orchards. Carleill remained on the heights till the deserted town was quartered out for the lodging of the whole army; that done,

* Hakluyt, 536.

he took possession, and set such sufficient guard in every part that there was no cause for any present fear.*

Here the English continued a fortnight, finding no treasure nor any booty of greater value than provisions, and "trash for the Indian trade". None of the inhabitants came near them, till one day a Portuguese approached with a flag of truce; and being received by Captains Sampson and Goring, first asked what countrymen they were, and then put the pithy question, whether there was war between England and Spain? Their answer was, that they knew not; but that if he would go to the general he could best resolve him of that particular. This he refused, as having no such commission from the governor. They then told him that if the governor desired to take a course for the good of the place and the people, "his best way was to present himself unto our noble and merciful general, Sir Francis Drake, whereby he might be assured to find favour both for himself and the inhabitants; otherwise, within three days, we should march over the land, and consume with fire all inhabited places, and put to the sword all such living souls as we should chance upon". Some cause of complaint the English had against the people of this island, for having broken their promise to "old Master William Hawkins of Plymouth," a few years before, and murdered many of his men; and to this they imputed the fear which prevented the authorities from opening any negotiation, and the inhabitants from holding any communication with them. A week after their arrival, Drake marched with 600 men to a village called St. Domingo, twelve miles inland, where he had heard that the governor, the bishop, and all the chief inhabitants, had retired: it was deserted before they arrived; but when, after waiting awhile, not only to rest themselves, but to see whether any would come to confer with them, they marched back, the islanders showed themselves with

* Hakluyt, 537.

some force both of horse and foot, yet not in such strength as to venture or abide an attack; "so in passing some time at gaze with them, it waxed late before the men reached Santiago". The invaders had expected that either the governor or the bishop, whose authority they believed to be great, or the people either of town or country, would entreat them to leave some part of their needful provision, "or at least to spare the city at their departure"; that is, they expected that a ransom would be offered, and they took "great discontentment and scorn" at a conduct which disappointed their hopes. The wisest course that the islanders could take with such enemies was thus to disappoint them, it being better to suffer any immediate havoc that might be made than, by purchasing a respite, to attempt a repetition of such visits. But they provoked the invaders by murdering a boy, whom they caught straggling, and by mutilating his body "in a most brutish and beastly manner". In revenge for this the invaders burnt every house in the town, and every house which they saw in their incursions, except the hospital: that they left uninjured; and there and in other places affixed a paper, declaring the reason why they had exercised this vengeance. Having thus inflicted upon the islanders all the evil they could, they re-embarked leisurely, but cautiously, and set sail, not having suffered the slightest loss.*

Unpunished, however, they did not depart; for though, till then, not a man had been lost by sickness, there now began among them such mortality, that in the course of a few days between 200 and 300 died. "The sickness," says Cates, "showed not his infection till we were departed thence, and then seized our people with extreme hot burning and continual agues, whereof very few escaped with life, and those for the most part not without great alteration and decay of their wits and strength for a long time after." Upon

* Hakluyt, 537, 538.

some of the dead marks appeared which were taken for plague spots. The first land which they made after a passage of eighteen days was Dominica: not thinking it safe to make any tarriance there, because of the character of the Caribs, though they exchanged beads and such trifles which they had brought from Santiago for "great store of tobacco and cassavi bread," they proceeded to St. Christopher, which at that time was uninhabited, and there spent some days of Christmas, to refresh the sick, and to cleanse and air the ships. There a counsel was held; and it was determined that they should make for the great Island of Hispaniola, "as well for that they knew themselves then to be in their best strength, as also the rather allured thereunto by the glorious fame of the city of St. Domingo, being the ancientest and chief inhabited place in all the tract of country thereabouts".

The city of St. Domingo is the oldest, and was once the most considerable Spanish city in the New World. Bartolome Columbus founded it so early as the year 1496, and called it Nueva Isabella, removing to it the inhabitants of the earlier settlement named after the Queen of Castille. He placed it on the eastern side of the river Ozama, where a copious fountain supplied it with good water, that of the river being salt or brackish for some leagues up. The first inhabitations were hastily constructed with wood and reeds, and were nearly destroyed in 1502 by a hurricane. Shortly afterwards Ovando removed it to the opposite side of the Ozama. In the first years of the conquest a city was moved almost as easily as a camp; and such removals were sometimes made with no worthier motive than the desire of a new governor to gain reputation at the expense of his predecessors. By this motive Ovando is thought to have been influenced* when he aban-

---

* Oviedo, lib. iii., c. 10, f. 31. Yet, in an earlier part of his most valuable work (lib. ii., c. 13, f. 19), Oviedo says that the foundations were not originally laid on the present site, because Bartolome Columbus was

doned a well-chosen and commodious site for one which was exposed to morning fogs, and where fresh water was wanting. That want he meant to supply by bringing an aqueduct from the river Haina; and the foundations of the city were laid by him in a manner and upon a scale worthy of the Spaniards in their best days. In the next generation it was said, that, space for space, no city in the mother country was better built, Barcelona alone excepted; that the emperor Charles V. was often lodged in Spain in worse houses than were to be found in this capital; that the palace of the viceroy, Diego Columbus, far exceeded that of any subject in Spain; and that the streets having been built, according to a regular plan, upon convenient ground, and laid out by cord and compass, excelled those of any other place that its earliest historian Oviedo had ever seen.* The first cross which Columbus— in evil hour for the Indians—planted on the island was preserved in the cathedral, enclosed in a silver case, richly inlaid, and secured in a tabernacle with three locks, the keys of which were kept by three of the dignitaries of the church. To that cathedral, also, the remains of Columbus, pursuant to his will, were translated from Seville, and there they rested on the right of the high altar till, upon the scandalous cession to France of the Spanish part of Hispaniola, the brazen coffin wherein they were deposited was removed to the Havannah by the direction of his representative the Duque de Veragua, who, on that occasion, manifested a feeling in which the miserable Charles IV. and his profligate ministers were wanting.†

unwilling to disturb the cacica Catalina and the Indians who were settled on that side of the river. "The city was called St. Domingo," he says, "not only because the adelantado came to found it on a Sunday (*Domingo*), which Sunday also was St. Domingo's day, but, moreover, because his father's name was Domenico *y en su memoria el fió llamar Sancto Domingo a este ciudad.*"

* *Historia, Natural et General,* f. 31. Sommario (in Ramasio, iii., 46).
† Walton's *Spanish Colonies,* i., 144.

Proceeding with the determination of attacking this city, and not knowing how greatly it was fallen from its high estate, Drake came up with a small frigate, on the way, bound for the same port; and having "duly examined the crew, learnt from them that it was a barred harbour, commanded by a strong castle; but that, about two miles to the westward of it, there was a convenient landing-place," to which one of the men offered to pilot him. The troops, accordingly, embarked in pinnaces and boats,—Drake going in his namesake, the barque *Francis*, as admiral: thus they lay all night at sea, bearing small sail; and on the morrow, being New Year's Day, safely * disembarked about daybreak. Having seen them landed, Drake returned to the fleet, "bequeathing them to God and the good conduct of Master Carleill". About noon they approached the city, from whence some 150 brave horse began to present themselves. But the invaders played upon them with small shot, and supported that fire "with good proportion of pikes in all parts"; and the Spaniards, having viewed the very superior force which threatened them all round, found it necessary to let them proceed toward the two sea-ward gates: both gates were manned, and ordnance planted there, and some troops of small shot in ambuscade by the wayside. Carleill divided his force, consisting of some 1200 men, into two bodies, giving Captain Powell the command of one: they were to enter both gates at the same time; and he swore to Powell, "that, with God's good favour, he would not rest till they met in the market-place".†

The artillery was discharged with some effect, though not much: the first man that fell was very near Carleill, who "began forthwith to advance both his voice of encourage-

---

* "At that time," says Cates, "nor yet is known to us any landing-place where the sea surge does not threaten to overset a pinnace or boat" (p. 539).

† Hakluyt, 539.

ment and pace of marching," hastening all he could to prevent the Spaniards from reloading their guns; and, notwithstanding the ambuscade, his men "marched, or rather ran, so roundly into them, that pell-mell they entered the gates, and gave them more care every man to save himself by flight than reason to stand any longer to their broken defence". Forthwith the victorious adventurers made their way to the Plaza Mayor, or market-place; "a place of very fair, spacious, square ground:" there Powell, with the other detachment, met them. They strengthened it and its avenues with barricadoes, and secured themselves there as the most convenient position, thinking the city "far too spacious for so small and weary a troop to undertake to guard. The castle was abandoned that night; some of the garrison being made prisoners, and others fleeing, by the help of boats, to the other side of the haven, and so into the country. Next day, the English quartered a little more at large, but not into the half part of the town; and so, making substantial trenches, and planting all the ordnance that each part was correspondent to other," they held the town a month. *

It was a great marvel and no less disappointment both to the adventurers and the sleeping partners of the concern, that such a famous and goodly built city, so well inhabited of gallant people, should afford no greater riches than was found there; for at that time it was not understood, in England, that, as the conquests on the main became of more importance, Hispaniola had declined; and that its native population had been consumed, and, consequently, that its mines had ceased to be productive. The colonists had opened a surer source of prosperity in the cultivation of their fertile soil; but gold and silver money had disappeared (as at this time in Brazil), the only currency which was found was in copper, and that in great quantity. "We found

---

* Hakluyt, 540.

here," says Cates, "great store of strong wine, sweet oil, vinegar, olives, and other such like provisions, excellent wheat meal, packed up in wine pipes and other casks, and other commodities, as woollen and linen cloth, and some silks; all which were brought out of Spain, and served us for great relief. (Good store of brave apparel our soldiers also found for their relief.) There was but little plate, or vessel of silver, in comparison of the great pride in other things of this town; because, in these hot countries, they use much of those earthen dishes, finely painted or varnished, which they call porcellana, which is had out of the East India; and for their drinking they use glasses altogether, whereof they make excellent, good and fair, in the same place. But yet some plate we found, and many other good things, as their household garniture, very gallant and rich, which had cost them dear, although unto us they were of small importance." *

The Spaniards here were more ready to treat † for the ransom of their city than the Portuguese had been in the Cape de Verds. There was, in the gallery of the governor's palace, "painted, in a very large scutcheon, the arms of the King of Spain; and in the lower part of the scutcheon a terrestrial globe, whereon a horse was represented as in the act of leaping from it, with a scroll proceeding from his mouth, and displaying these words, *Non sufficit orbis*,—The world sufficeth not". The invaders, who looked upon this "as a very notable mark and token of the unsatiable am-

---

* Hakluyt, 541.

† Faria y Sousa ascribes this to the pusillanimity of Christoval de Ovalle, president of the audience there. He had been advised of the danger (according to this historian) in time to have provided for defence; but disbelieving or disregarding the information, he was half dead with fear when he saw the English in the island, and actually died when told that they were making search for him (*Europa Portugueça*, t. iii., p. l., c. 2, § 27).

bition of the Spanish king and nation," could not refrain from pointing it out to the Spaniards who came to negotiate with them, nor from sarcastically inquiring what was intended by such a device; at which they "would shake their heads, and turn aside their countenance in some smiling sort, without answering anything, as greatly ashamed thereof. For by some of our company," says Cates, " it was told them, that if the Queen of England would resolutely prosecute the war against the King of Spain, he should be forced to lay aside that proud and unreasonable reaching vein of his, for he should find more than enough to do to keep that which he had already, as by the present example of their lost town they might, for a beginning, perceive well enough." *

This was in no commendable spirit of bravery; and the enmity with which the Spaniards and English then regarded each other needed nothing to exasperate it. Drake had sent out a negro boy, with a white flag: there could be no mistake concerning it, for the same flag was used, in like manner, by the Spaniards themselves; but some of their officers fell in with the bearer and ran him through the body with a horseman's spear. The poor boy returned to the general, wounded as he was, told his story, and died in his presence. Upon this Drake, " being greatly passioned," ordered the provost marshal to take two friars, who were among his prisoners, under a guard, to the place where the boy had been hurt, and there hang them both. Another Spaniard he set at liberty to declare to the authorities wherefore this execution was done; and to tell them, farther, that until the party who had thus murdered his messenger were delivered into his hands for condign punishment, there should no day pass wherein there should not two prisoners be hanged, until all who were in his hands were consumed. This terrible message, and the dreadful proof which had been

* Hakluyt, 540.

given of Drake's determination to carry his words into effect, made them send the offender, on the following day, to be delivered into his hands; " but it was thought a more honourable revenge to make them there, in his sight, perform the execution themselves;" and this was done.*

The treaty concerning the ransom proceeded slowly, and "upon disagreements," the invaders still spent the early mornings in firing the houses without their intrenchment; and they found it " no small travail to ruin them ; being very magnificently built of stone, with high lofts". For many successive days, 200 sailors, from daybreak till nine o'clock, when the heat began, did nothing but labour to fire these houses; the same number of troops being drawn out to protect them during this work of devastation. " Yet," says Cates, " did we not, and could not, consume so much as one third part of the town ; and so in the end,—what wearied with firing, and what hastened by some other respects,—we were contented to accept of 25,000 ducats, of 5s. 6d. each, for the ransom of the rest." †

The expedition then stood over to the main, and kept along the coast till they came in sight of Carthagena. That city, which was then the principal fortress in all that country, and contained about 450 families, was built upon a sandy peninsula, formed by the sea on one side, and on the other by a great lake, which communicates with the harbour. The mouth of the harbour lay some three miles westward of the town, and the fleet entered, about three in the afternoon, without any resistance, or meeting with any impediment. In the evening, Carleill landed, toward the harbour mouth ; the plan being that the land forces should advance about midnight, "as easily as foot might fall," along the sea-wash of the shore, while the fleet drew the attention of the Spaniards by a false attack upon a little fort at the entrance of the

* Hakluyt, 540. † *Ibid.*

inner haven. When the troops were within two miles of the town, some hundred horsemen fell in with them; but the ground being bushy, even to the water-side, was unfavourable for these enemies, and upon the first volley they turned about, and hastened back to give the alarm. At the same time the English heard a firing in the harbour, where, if anything more than a feint was intended, nothing was done : the place was strong, and a chain drawn across the narrow entrance; but little or no harm was received. The troops, meantime, advanced till they came to the neck of the peninsula, about half a mile from the town. The strait was about fifty paces over; "fortified clean across with a stone wall, well and orderly built, with flanking in every part, and a ditch". There was only so much space left as might serve for ordinary passage; but this opening was now fortified with a good barricado of barrels " filled with earth, full and thick, as they might stand on end one by another; some part of them standing even in the main sea. This place of strength was furnished with six great pieces, demi-culverins and rakers, which shot directly in front upon the assailants; and without the wall, on the inner side of the strait, they had brought two great galleys, with their prows to the shore, and eleven pieces of ordnance, thus flanking the approach. On board these the English estimated that there were from 300 to 400 harquebussiers, and, to defend the barricado, 300 shot and pikes." *

The Spaniards, being thus ready to receive their sturdy visitors, spared not their shot; but they expended most of it in vain; for they were too eager to wait till they could see the enemy; and while they fired in the darkness, Carleill advanced along the lowest ground, close to the water's edge, where the tide, too, had somewhat fallen. He had ordered his men not to fire till they should come to the wall-side; so, " with pikes roundly together," they approached, and finding

* Hakluyt, 541.

the barricado of barrels, strongly as it was manned, the best place where to make their assault, they assailed it. "Down went the butts of earth, and pell-mell came our swords and pikes together, after our shot had given their first volley, even at the enemy's nose." The English pikes were somewhat longer than theirs, and the English were also better armed, for very few of the Spaniards wore any defensive armour: this want, and the disadvantage of their pikes, was felt when it came thus to the push. Their standard-bearer, fighting manfully to the last, fell by Carleill's hands: they gave way; and the assailants, giving them no time to breathe, followed them into the town. At every street's end they had raised barricadoes of earth-work, with trenches in front, which were better made than defended; the little resistance which they attempted there being soon overcome, with trifling loss. They had stationed many Indian archers "in corners of advantage, with their arrows most villainously empoisoned; so that if they did but break the skin, the party so touched, unless it were by great marvel, died". Some were likewise "mischieved to death by small sticks, sharply pointed, of a foot and a half long, fixed in the ground, with the points poisoned, right in the way from the place where they landed toward the town; but by keeping the shore, the invaders escaped the greater part of these". The chief commander of the Spaniards was wounded and taken by Captain Goring; and when the English had established themselves in the market-place no farther opposition was attempted, the Spaniards retiring into the interior, whither they had previously removed their families and their treasure. They had been warned of their danger twenty days before, and had employed the time diligently in preparing both for defence and for the consequences of defeat. *

Having taken the city, the adventurers pursued the same course as at St. Domingo; and though, "upon discontent-

* Hakluyt, 542, 545.

ments, and for want of agreeing in the first negotiations for a ransom, they touched the town in its outparts, and consumed much with fire," yet some of the humanities of war were observed here. "There passed divers courtesies," says Cates, "between us and the Spaniards, as feasting and using them with all kindness and favour"; so that the governor and the bishop, and divers other gentlemen of the better sort, came to visit the general. One day the sentinel on the church tower descried two small barques standing in for the harbour; upon which Captains Moon and Varney embarked, with a party of sailors, in two pinnaces, thinking to take them before they came so near the shore as to be apprised, by signals, that the town was in possession of an enemy. The alarm, however, was given in time; the barques ran ashore; the men hid themselves among the bushes, where they were presently joined by those who had made signals to them, and from thence fired upon the English, who, without any regard of danger, had boarded the vessels, and were "standing all open in them". Varney was killed by this discharge, and some five or six others mortally wounded, Captain Moon among them, who was the same person that struck the first blow at a Spaniard in the South Sea.*

This was the only loss which the English sustained from the enemy while they occupied Carthagena; but the disease which they had brought with them from the Cape de Verds still continued; and, though its ravages were not so great as at the first, it reduced their numbers, and, in a still greater degree, their strength; few or none of those who escaped with life remaining fit for service.† In consequence of this

* Hakluyt, 544.

† "Yea, many of them were much decayed in their memory; insomuch that it was common, when one was heard to speak foolishly, to say he had been sick of the calenture. The original cause thereof is imputed to the evening, or first night air, which they term *la serena;* wherein they say, and hold very firm opinion, that whoso is then abroad in the open air shall

mortality, Drake consulted his land captains what course they thought most expedient now to be undertaken. The first question proposed to them was touching the keeping of the town against the present force of the enemy, or that which might come out from Spain. Upon this their opinion was, that, though they had not above 700 men who could answer present service, the residue (some 150) being altogether unable to stand them in any stead; yet, being victualled and munitioned, they might well keep the town. But it was for the sea captains, they said, to give their resolution how they would undertake the safety and service of the ships upon the arrival of any Spanish fleet.

The second point was, "whether it were meet to go presently homeward, or make farther trial of their fortune, thereby to seek after that bountiful mass of treasure, for recompense of their travails, which was generally expected at their coming forth from England". To this they replied, "that it was well known how they, both officers and soldiers, had entered into this action as voluntary men, without any imprest or gage from her majesty, or anybody else; and that, hitherto, they had discharged the parts of honest men; for, by the great blessing and favour of their good God, they had taken three notable towns, wherein all men thought very great treasures would have been found: for Santiago was the chief city of all the islands and traffic thereabouts; St. Domingo was the chief city of Hispaniola, and the head government not only of that island, but of Cuba, and all the islands about it, and all such inhabitations of the firm land as were next unto it,—a place, too, magnificently built, and which entertained great trade of merchandise: lastly, this city of Carthagena, which could not be denied to be one of the chief places of most especial importance to the Spaniards

certainly be infected to the death, not being of the Indian or natural race of that country. Our men were thus subjected to the infectious air" (Hakluyt, 543).

of all on this side the West India. All these cities, with the goods and prisoners taken in them, and the ransoms of them all put together, were found far short to satisfy the expectations which, by the generality of the enterprisers, were first conceived. They considered the slenderness of the strength to which they were reduced; as well in respect of the small number of able bodies, as not a little in regard of the slack disposition of the greater part of those which remained, very many of the better minds and men being either consumed by death or weakened by sickness and hurts. And, lastly, seeing that no enterprise was laid down convenient to be undertaken with their reduced strength, and withal of such certain likelihood as might, with God's good success, which it might please Him to bestow, promise to yield them any sufficient contentment, they concluded that it was better to hold sure the honour already gotten, and return with it to their gracious sovereign and country, from whence," said they, "if it shall please her majesty to set us forth again, with her orderly means and entertainment, we are most ready and willing to go through anything that the uttermost of our strength and endeavour shall be able to reach unto: but, therewithal, we do advise and protest, that it is far from our thoughts either to refuse, or so much as seem to be weary of anything which for the present shall be farther required or directed to be done by us from our general." *

Being thus convinced that, in all prudence, they must give over the intended enterprise against Nombre de Dios, and so overland to Panama, where they "should have stricken the stroke for the treasure and full recompense of their tedious travails," they took into consideration the third and last point, which was touching the ransom of the city. Their demand had been 100,000*l.*: an offer had been made of 27,000*l.* or 28,000*l.*, and they thought it better to accept this than to break off by standing upon the first demand, "which,"

* Hakluyt, 543, 544.

said they, "seems a matter impossible for the present to be performed by them; and, to say truth, we may now, with much honour and reputation, better be satisfied with that sum offered by them at first (if they will now be contented to give it) than we might at that time with a great deal more, inasmuch as we have taken our full pleasure, both in the uttermost sacking and spoiling of all their household goods and merchandise, as also, in that we have consumed and ruined a great part of their town with fire". Farther, they considered that there were in that voyage a great many poor men who had ventured their lives, and divers of them spent their apparel and such other little provision as their small means enabled them to prepare; "which being done upon such good and allowable intention as this action carried with it against the Spaniard, our greatest and most dangerous enemy, so (said they) we cannot but have an inward regard to help toward the satisfaction of this their expectation, and by procuring them some little benefit to encourage them, and to nourish their ready and willing disposition both in them and in others by their example, against any other time of like occasion. But because it may be supposed that herein we forget not the private benefit of ourselves, and are thereby the rather moved to incline ourselves to this composition, we declare hereby, that what part or portion soever it be of this ransom for Carthagena, which should come unto us, we do freely give and bestow the same wholly upon the poor men who have remained with us in the voyage, meaning as well the sailor as the soldier, and wishing with all our hearts it were such, or so much, as might seem a sufficient reward for their painful endeavour." *

This paper was signed by Carleill as lieutenant-general, and by all the land captains; and conformably to their opinion, a ransom of 110,000 ducats was accepted. Carthagena, though not half the size of St. Domingo, yielded so

* Hakluyt, 544.

much larger a sum, because its harbour and its position rendered it a most important place, and it was inhabited by rich merchants; whereas St. Domingo was chiefly inhabited by lawyers and "brave gentlemen," being the seat of that court before which all appeals were brought from the islands and from the neighbouring main. The officers had dealt generously towards their own people in the affair of this ransom; but in their subsequent conduct toward the Spaniards they cannot be held free from reproach: for after they had received the money, and evacuated the town, they stationed some of their soldiers in the convent of St. Francisco, which was a little way off on the harbour side, and told the Spaniards that neither that building nor a block-house at the mouth of the inner harbour was included in the composition: thus they extorted from the convent another thousand crowns, and demanded as much more for the block-house; the townsmen declared that they were not able to pay them, "having stretched themselves to the utmost of their power; and Drake, therefore, undermined the fort, and blew it up".*

They sailed from Carthagena on the last of March, and after two or three days put back; a great ship which they had taken at St. Domingo, and laden with ordnance, hides, and other spoil, having sprung so great a leak, that she was hardly kept from foundering. Several days were spent in distributing the cargo of this vessel among the other ships: then they departed once more; and on the 27th of April reached Cape St. Antonio, the westernmost part of Cuba. Failing to find fresh water there, they made for Matanzas, which is to the east of the Havannah. But in the course of a fortnight, through lack of favourable weather, they were brought again to Cape St. Antonio. By this time their want of water was such, that they made more careful search, and found in sufficient quantity what they supposed to be rain water

* Hakluyt, 545.

newly fallen and collected in pits made in marshy ground, some 300 paces from the shore. " Here," says Cates, " I do wrong if I should forget the good example of the general, who, to encourage others, and to hasten the getting water aboard, took no less pains himself than the meanest. Throughout the expedition, indeed, he had everywhere shown so vigilant a care and foresight in the good ordering of his fleet, accompanied with such wonderful travail of body, that, doubtless, had he been the meanest person, as he was the chiefest, he had deserved the first place of honour. And no less happy do we account him for being associated with Master Carleill his lieutenant-general, by whose experience, prudent counsel, and gallant performance, he achieved so many and happy enterprises, and by whom also he was very greatly assisted in setting down the needful orders, laws, and course of justice, and the due administration of the same upon all occasions." No difference of any kind, indeed, seems to have occurred between Drake and any of his officers during this expedition. From thence they made for the coast of Florida, not touching anywhere, but keeping the shore in sight, till on 28th of May they descried a scaffold raised upon four high masts, for a lookout to the seaward. Upon this Drake manned the pinnaces and landed, "to see what place the enemy held there, no one in the armament having any knowledge of it ". *

Having marched about a mile up the river St. Augustine, they saw the Fort of San Juan de Pinos on the opposite side, newly erected by the Spaniards, and not yet completed. Carleill would fain have crossed with four companies, and intrenched himself so near the fort as to play upon it with his muskets, till a battery could be planted; but, because the sailors were not at hand to make trenches at this time, the intention was abandoned. Not to be inactive, however, he crossed during the night with a few chosen men in a small

* Hakluyt, 546.

skiff, to espy what guard the enemy kept, and to explore the ground. Though he did this as covertly as might be, the Spaniards took the alarm; and supposing that the whole force was approaching to the assault fired off some of their pieces, and then with all speed abandoned the work, and made the best of their way to the city (so called) of St. Augustine, where there was a garrison of 150 men. Carleill returned, knowing nothing of their flight. He was presently followed by a French fifer, who, having been prisoner in the fort, gladly seized the opportunity to escape, and came over the river in a small boat, playing "the tune of the Prince of Orange's song". When the guard called out to him, he told them who he was and what had happened, and offered either to remain in the hands of the English, or return to the fort with those who chose to believe him and go thither. There was no reason to doubt his tale: both Drake and Carleill crossed forthwith with as many boats as were at hand, leaving orders for the rest to follow. A few Spaniards, "bolder than the rest," had remained after their companions, and fired two guns at them; but on shore the English went, and entered the place without finding any man there. When the day appeared, they saw that it was built entirely of timber, "the walls being none other than whole masts or bodies of trees set upright, and close together in manner of a pale". "The ditch had not yet been made, nor was the work in other respects finished; so as to say the truth, the Spaniards had no reason to keep it, being subject both to fire and easy assault. There were fourteen great pieces of brass ordnance planted on a platform, which was constructed of large pine trees, laid across, one on another, and some little earth between. The garrison, who were 150 in number, had retired in such haste, that they left behind them the treasure chest containing about 2000*l.*" *

* Hakluyt. Gabriel de Cardenas, *Ensaio Chronologico a la Historia de Florida*, 161, 162.

Drake, no doubt, felt some satisfaction when he learnt from the Frenchman that the Governor of Florida, at this time, was D. Pedro Menendez, Marquez de Aviles, nephew of that Menendez whom he erroneously supposed to have been the general of the fleet by which Hawkins had been so treacherously attacked at St. Juan de Ulloa, and from which he had at that time himself so narrowly escaped. An opportunity for taking vengeance upon one nearly related to the imagined offender seemed now to be afforded him; and he would, without delay, have marched to attack the adelantado in his capital, the city of St. Augustine, if the march had been practicable; but, by reason of rivers and broken ground between the two places, it was necessary again to embark in the pinnaces and ascend the great river. When they landed, as it appears not far from the city, some of the Spaniards showed themselves, fired a few shot, and presently withdrew. They were pursued, and the sergeant-major, Anthony Powell, leaping upon one of their horses which they had left, advanced rashly beyond his company in pursuit, over ground which was overgrown with a species of high grass: seeing this, a Spaniard laid wait for him, and shot him through the head; and before any could come to his rescue his body had been pierced with many wounds, as if in insult and hatred. He was much lamented, "being in very deed an honest, wise gentleman, and a soldier of good experience, and of as great courage as any man might be". This was the only loss that the English experienced in their descent. The adelantado had prudently withdrawn in time to collect the whole of his forces at St. Matheo, and the city was left without a single inhabitant. It is described as being then a prosperous settlement, with its council-house, church, and other edifices and gardens all round about, all which were burnt and laid waste by the invaders in vengeance. *

* Hakluyt, 547. Cardenas, 162.

About twelve leagues to the north, the Spaniards had another settlement called St. Helena, with a garrison of equal force, maintained "for no other purpose than to keep all other nations from inhabiting any part of all that coast,"—a purpose deemed as important by them as it was judged to be arrogant and unreasonable by the English. It was resolved, "in full assembly of captains," to attack this place also, and from thence proceed in search of Raleigh's recently planted colony in Virginia. But when they came opposite St. Helena, the shoals were found too dangerous for them to attempt an entrance without a pilot, and under unfavourable circumstances of wind and weather. Abandoning, therefore, this design, they kept coasting on till, on 9th of June, "upon sight of one special great fire," Drake sent his skiff to shore, and found, as he had hoped, some of his countrymen there, by whose direction he reached the place which they made their port, and wrote from thence to their governor, Master Ralph Lane, who was then in his fort at Roanoak. On the morrow, Lane came with some of his company; and Drake, understanding the state of their affairs, liberally proposed, with the consent of his captains, to leave them a ship, a pinnace, boats, men, and a month's provision, for prosecuting their discovery of the country and coasts, and as much more provision as might suffice for their voyage home, if, at the month's end, they thought good to return; or, if they were satisfied that they had already sufficiently explored the land, he offered them all a passage, being 103 persons. They thankfully accepted the first of these proposals, and a ship was delivered to them; but, before the provisions could be put on board, a storm came, to the great danger of the whole fleet, while some of the ships being of too great draught to enter the harbour, were at anchor in a wild road, about two miles from shore. Many cables parted, many anchors were lost; and some vessels, which had lost all, were driven out to sea, and never again joined company till they met in

England: that which should have been left with the colony was one. Drake, notwithstanding the loss which had been thus sustained, offered them another ship, but one which, being considerably larger, was not so well suited to their purposes. For this reason, and because no small part of his stores, and some of the persons on whose services most reliance had been placed, were in the ship of which he had been thus deprived, Lane, and those with whom he advised, thought the only course that remained for them was to accept the proffered passage, as a providential deliverance, "by the very hand of God, as it seemed, stretched out to take them thence". They were taken on board; and, after a passage of thirty days, the fleet in good safety arrived at Portsmouth.*

The booty obtained in this expedition was valued at 60,000*l.*, "whereof the companies which travelled in the voyage were to have 20,000*l.*, the adventurers the other forty; and of the 20,000*l.* it was computed that some six pounds would come to a single share": 240 pieces of artillery, the far greater number brass, were part of the spoil. The loss of men in the voyage amounted to about 750,—three parts of them by sickness. It is said that tobacco was first † brought into England by the men who returned from Virginia with Drake at this time. The expedition was more creditable to the resolution with which it was conducted than to the councils wherein it was concerted. Little hurt was done to the King of Spain, who was rather awakened than weakened by it, but great and cruel injury was inflicted upon individuals: they were thereby made to hate the English, not as heretics only, but

---

* Hakluyt, 264, 548.

† Camden, 324. "Certainly," he says, "from that time forward it began to grow into great request, and to be sold at a high rate; whilst, in a short time, many men everywhere, some for wantonness, some for health's sake, with insatiable desire and greediness, sucked in the stinking smoke thereof through an earthen pipe, which presently they blew out again at their nostrils; insomuch as tobacco shops are now as ordinary in most towns as tap-houses and taverns."

as a people who were the vikingar of the age; and the Spanish government received a lesson which taught it the necessity of fortifying its distant ports, and increasing its maritime strength.* Drake, however, suffered no loss of

* Monson says: "The fleet was the greatest of any nation, except the Spaniards, that had ever been seen in those seas since the first discovery of them; and if the action had been as well considered of before their going from home, as it was happily performed by the valour of the undertakers, it had more annoyed the King of Spain than all other actions that ensued during the war" (p. 155). In his opinion, the queen had then "a notable opportunity to annoy and weaken the Spaniards by keeping the three towns which had been taken: she was rich in those days, and her subjects no less able than willing to contribute to what she proposed, they were so much devoted to her in their hearts"; she might have bound the States of Holland to any conditions she pleased against the Spaniards at that time; whereas, from that time till her death, "notwithstanding we were drawn into the war by them, yet they traded peaceably into the King of Spain's dominions, and never offered to annoy the Spaniards by any act of hostility at sea, but supplied them with ships and intelligence against us". He thought, also, that, in point both of reputation and profit, the places ought to have been maintained, as a motive and mean for prosecuting the victories thus begun (p. 240).

Monson was mistaken, both in his opinion and on the grounds upon which he founded it. At no time during her reign was Elizabeth rich. How greatly the measures of her otherwise vigorous government were crippled by necessary parsimony was, perhaps, not so well known to him as it now is; but he might have seen that if Drake had attempted to keep possession of those places, which are among the most unwholesome for Europeans of any in the world, the consequences would have been as fatal as they were at Puerto Rico. I have elsewhere explained the conduct of the Dutch. But Monson felt and thought rightly when he said: "Whosoever makes an enterprise on a town in America, with an intention not to keep it, will do no more than a malicious person that seeks the destruction of his neighbour in setting his house a-fire, without any other prospect in so doing but mischief and revenge. I confess we shall damnify the inhabitants of the town so sacked and spoiled, as the owner of a house burnt will be damnified; but it is no more loss or prejudice to the King of Spain, or to the bordering countries, than to the neighbour of the man that shall have his house burnt; for every bears his own particular loss" (p. 241).

reputation in this voyage : he had bravely and ably executed the service on which he was sent, overcoming the enemy everywhere, and yielding only to an evil against which the skill of man was of as little avail as his strength. When, therefore, Elizabeth, in the year 1587, was assured that preparations were making upon a great scale in the Spanish ports, for the invasion of England, and thought it wiser to prevent the danger than wait for it, she appointed Drake to command the fleet which was equipped for that intent. It consisted of four ships of the navy royal, namely, the *Bonaventura*, in which he went as general; the *Lion*, Captain William Borough, who was comptroller of the navy; the *Dreadnought*, Captain Thomas Venner; and the *Rainbow*, Captain Henry Bellingham; to these two of the queen's pinnaces were "appointed as handmaids". Certain tall ships of the city of London were added, and the whole armament amounted to some thirty sail.*

Sailing from Plymouth early in April, they met on the 16th, in latitude 40°, two Middleburg ships coming from Cadiz, from whom they learnt that great store of warlike provision had been collected in that and the adjacent ports, ready for transport to Lisbon. For Cadiz, therefore, Drake made with all possible speed, and on the 19th entered the road. Sixty ships and many other small vessels were lying there, little expecting such an attack, and yet not unprepared for defence, having the fortresses to protect them, and also some galleys. Six of these vessels assailed the invaders in front of the town, but were soon compelled to retire under the fortress. Two from St. Mary's, and two from Puerto Real, came boldly to the fight and shot freely, "but altogether in vain," so that they hastened back with no little loss. A great Ragusan ship of 1000 tons, carrying 40 guns, and very richly laden, was sunk early in the action. Before night Drake was master of the road, and there he

* Hakluyt, ii., part ii., 121.

continued till the morning of the 21st, with so little loss as to be thought at the time "not worth mentioning"; with little ease, "by reason of their continual shooting from the galleys, the fortresses, and the shore, where continually at convenient places they planted new ordnance"; but also with no little triumph, for never was daring service more resolutely performed. Drake had two objects in view, which were not very compatible at this time: to sink, burn, and destroy for the public good; and, on the other hand, to secure as much as he could for the benefit of the merchant adventurers, who bore by much the larger part in this adventure. The labour which lay upon the sailors day and night during the six and thirty hours after the action, in discharging the stores from their prizes, was so great, that it was a pleasant sight to them when the Spaniards set fire to the ships which they could no longer defend; though the greatest danger to which the conquerors were exposed was when the ships thus fired were drifted toward them in flames by the tide.

About thirty vessels were burnt, sunk, or taken in this daring enterprise. Among them were four large Biscayans, taking in stores for the armament at Lisbon, and another of 1000 tons, laden for the West Indies. Some twenty French ships, and some Spanish ones that could pass the shoals, escaped to Puerto Real, where about forty others were lying in sight of the English. When Drake left the road, satisfied as he well might be with the success of his attempt, ten galleys came out after him, "as it were in disdain, to make some pastime with their ordnance": the wind just at this time scanted, so that the fleet cast about, stood in with the shore, and anchored within a league of the town; but the galleys, alert as they had seemed to be, suffered them to ride quietly there; and thus brought themselves into disrepute with the English sailors. * The loss which had been inflicted

* The author of the relation in Hakluyt says: "We now have had

upon the Spaniards was great: the insult and humiliation were greater; and Philip pursued his plans of vengeance with exacerbated hatred. Drake, having despatched advice of his triumphant proceeding to England, turned back along the coast, and captured and burnt nearly 100 vessels before he came to Cape St. Vincent's, dealing "favourably with the men, and setting them ashore"; but he destroyed all the fishing boats and nets, "to their great hindrance," and in the hope of spoiling the tunny-fishery for that year. Near the Cape a landing was made; and that he might ride there in harbour at his pleasure, he assaulted the Castle of Sagres, and took that fortress with three others, some by force, some by surrender. He then entered the mouth of the Tagus, anchored near Cascaes, sent to the Marquis of Santa Cruz, who, as general of the armada, was with his galleys in the river, preparing for the invasion of England, told him who he was, and said he was then ready to exchange bullets with him. The marquis, according to the English account, replied that he was not then ready for him, nor had any such commission from his king. But the insult here, and at Cadiz, is said to have "bred such a corrosion in his heart, that he never enjoyed good days after," and within few months died of chagrin, happy in thus being removed before the invincible armada went to its destination. *

What Drake had done delayed the sailing of that armament for the current year. The public service had been

experience of galley-fight; wherein I can assure you, that only these four of her majesty's ships will make no account of twenty galleys, if they be alone, and not busied to guard others. There were never galleys that had better place and fitter opportunity for their advantage to fight with ships: but they were still forced to retire; we riding in a narrow gut (the place yielding no better), and driven to maintain the same, until we had discharged and fired the ships, which could not conveniently be done but upon the flood, at which time they might drive clear of us" (p. 122).

* Hakluyt, 122, 123.

thus effectually performed; but he knew that if nothing more were done, it would not give satisfaction to the merchant adventurers, who expected some immediate and tangible profit upon their disbursements. He shaped his course, therefore, toward the Azores, having obtained intelligence that the *San Philipe*, a Portuguese carrack from India, had wintered at Mozambique, and was expected to reach Lisbon in the passing month. His stores were becoming low, and his people importunate to return; but he with fair speeches, of which no man was more a master, persuaded, and prevailed with them to cruise yet a few days longer off the islands. And on this occasion fortune made him large amends for all former losses and disappointments, for he fell in with and easily captured the prize he looked for. This, says the writer of the voyage, was the first carrack that ever was taken coming from the East Indies, which the Portugals took for an evil sign, because the ship bore the king's own name. The whole company assured themselves now, that every man would have a sufficient reward for his travail, and thereupon they all resolved to return home, with the willing consent of their general. He dismissed the prisoners in certain vessels, with all the courtesies and humanities of war; and sailing then for England, the whole fleet arrived safely with their prize at Plymouth,* " to their own profit and

* "And here, by the way, it is to be noted, that the taking of this carrack wrought two extraordinary effects in England: first, that it taught others that carracks were no such bugs but that they might be taken (as since, indeed, it hath fallen out in the taking of the *Madre de Dios*, and firing and sinking of others); and, secondly, in acquainting the English nation more generally with the particularities of the exceeding riches and wealth of the East Indies; whereby themselves and their neighbours of Holland have been encouraged, being men as skilful in navigation, and of no less courage than the Portugals, to share with them in the East Indies, where their strength is nothing so great as heretofore hath been supposed" (Hakluyt, 122).

Lediard says: "The taking of this ship was of a greater advantage

due commendation," says one of the happy company, "and to the great admiration of the whole kingdom ". *

The service which in this voyage he had performed at Cadiz, and all along the coast to the Tagus, Drake called singeing the King of Spain's beard. This was said in the mirthful spirit of a sailor; and with that spirit of local patriotism, from which so many great and good actions have arisen, he expended no trifling part of the riches which he had won in supplying Plymouth with fresh water: the inhabitants had till then been enforced to fetch it from a mile's distance. The head of the spring from which it was now to be brought is between seven and eight miles distant in a direct line; but by indentings and circlings it was to be conveyed twenty-four miles, † through valleys, wastes, and bogs; and what was most troublesome, through a mighty rock, thought to be impenetrable. He, nevertheless, "made the way he could not find, and overcoming the difficulty, finished the enterprise to the continual commodity of the place, and his own perpetual honour". "And fine would have been the diversion," says the good old vicar of Berry Pomeroy, "when the water was brought somewhat near the town, to have seen how the mayor and his brethren, in their

---

to the English merchants than the value of her cargo to the captors; for, by the papers found on board, they so fully understood the rich value of the Indian merchandises, and the manner of trading into the eastern world, that they afterwards set up a gainful trade and traffic, and established a company of East India merchants " (i., 229).

* Hakluyt, 123. Monson, 156. Lediard, i., 228.

† Prince says thirty. "Various mills were erected on the stream for the use of the town at Sir Francis's expense. He vested the property in the mayor and commonality, and their successors for ever. The water is brought to a reservoir above the town, and from thence distributed by leaden pipes. The lessee pays a fine of 3*l*. 13*s*. 6*d*. for twenty-one years of the water, and an annual quit-rent of 12*s*. Persons who use more water than private families pay a double quit-rent, and brewers a fourfold one " (*Beauties of England and Wales*, iv., 148).

formalities, went out to meet it, and bid it welcome thither; and being thus met, they all returned together; the gentlemen of the corporation, accompanied with Sir Francis Drake, walked before, and the stream followed after into the town, where it has continued so to do ever since." Perhaps the day of that peaceful triumph was the happiest of Drake's public life.

His next service was as vice-admiral in that fleet by which, with the aid of the elements, the mighty preparations of the Spaniards were frustrated, their invincible armada dispersed, and England providentially saved from a most formidable invasion. In the ensuing year he was employed as admiral in an expedition sent to Portugal, in the vain hope of establishing the claim of a pretender to that kingdom. In this adventure the government took little part, acting upon a system of parsimonious policy, as if it risked nothing, so it avoided the risk of expense, and considered not how greatly the national interests and national character must be affected by the issue, and that that issue could not be fortunate unless adequate means were applied. The journey of Portugal (as this expedition was at the time called) was undertaken chiefly at the charge of Drake and Sir John Norris, grandson of that Norris who was unjustly executed with Anne Boleyn. Elizabeth always rightly regarded his family as entitled to more than ordinary favour on that account; and this Sir John and his brethren (six in all) were " men of haughty courage, and great experience in the conduct of military affairs;—persons," says Sir Robert Naunton,* "of such renown and worth, as future times must out of duty owe them the debt of an honourable memory". No English soldier in that age had seen more service than this Sir John. He had been trained under Coligny in the religious wars in France, served in Ireland while yet very young under Walter, Earl of Essex, held various commands in the Low Countries till he became

* Scot's *Somers Tracts*, i., 267.

general of the English forces there; and in the year of the armada, when an invasion was expected, was made "marshal of the field in England". There were others who engaged in the charge of the expedition, but fewer than had been expected; and some of those who subscribed their names, thinking that the scheme would never be brought to bear, but that they might gain credit by displaying a readiness to encourage it, withheld their money when they saw that serious preparations were made, and 10,000*l*. was thus withdrawn from the sum on which the leaders had calculated. And this was not the only nor the most serious defalcation from the means which had been looked for. Six hundred English horse from the Low Countries were withheld for other service, and seven out of thirteen old companies from the same school of war: the Dutch, instead of supplying six men of war and ten companies, sent only four companies;* and the government, which had promised twelve pieces of cannon, gave only a third part of that number. †

When the expedition sailed from Plymouth it consisted of 11,000 troops and 1500 seamen. There had been some weeks' previous delay; and when all was ready contrary winds detained them a whole month, living upon provisions which they could ill afford to consume in inaction. The generals at length, weary of these cross winds, "thrust to sea in the same, choosing rather to attend the change thereof there, than by being in harbour to lose any part of the better, when it should come, by having their men on shore".

---

* Camden (429) says the estates joined some ships, although they were somewhat discontented with the English, because Wingfield, Governor of Gertruydenberg, and the English garrison in it, had betrayed that town to the Spaniards. But these could not have been ships of war, or their failure in this point would not have been distinctly stated, as it is in the relation ascribed to Colonel Anthony Wingfield (Hakluyt, ii., part ii., 133).

† Hakluyt, 123. Camden, 429.

Two days the wind continued cross; and some of the fleet, having twenty-five companies on board, parted company during that time, "either not being able or not willing to double Ushant". Nearly 3000 men thus forsook the expedition at sea, "whereof some passed into France, and the rest returned home". The weather then became favourable; and in five days more, on the evening of 20th of April, the troops disembarked in a bay something more than a mile from Corunna.* No attempt was made to prevent or impede their landing; † but as they presently marched toward the town, they were encountered on the way: the Spaniards, however, retired within their walls, and the invaders took up their lodging for the night in the "villages, houses, and wind-mills next adjoining, and very near round about the town". They were not disturbed there by the garrison: but the galleon *San Juan*, one of the few which had escaped from the general wreck of the armada, was lying in the harbour; and with two galleys, and three smaller vessels, fired upon their lodgings during the night, and as they passed to and fro. ‡

Before day, Norris reconnoitred the base town: this, which

---

* This place is called the Groine in Hakluyt, as it still is by the sailors,—an easy corruption from Cruna, the name bestowed upon it at the beginning of the thirteenth century, when Alonso IX. founded it, and removed thither the inhabitants of Burgo Viejo. *Cruna* is the Galician word for *coluna*, a column or pillar; and it is supposed that the town took its name from the Torre de Hercules at the entrance of the port, that well-known lighthouse having this appearance when seen from a distance (Cornide, *Investigaciones sobre la Torre de Hercules*, etc., p. 17, n.).

Joshua Barnes tells us that Logroño also was called Groing by the English (*Hist. of Edward III.*, 705).

† Faria y Sousa says, however, that the marquis made more resistance than could be made, "fortificóse lo major que pudo, y mas de lo que se podia resistió la desembarcacion" (p. 94).

‡ Hakluyt, 138.

retains the name of La Pexaria, or Pescaderia, from the days when it was only of importance as a fishing station, stands upon a small tongue of land, and contained at that time 1500 houses. On the land side it was protected by a wall and a dry ditch, but on neither of the water sides were there any defences, and Norris resolved upon attempting it by escalade, in two places. As a preliminary measure it was necessary to silence the enemy's ships. Some artillery was landed: as soon as it opened, the galleys retired to Ferrol, and the other vessels ceased their fire. The rest of the day was spent in preparing for the attack. Twelve hundred men under Colonel Huntley, and the vice-admiral, Captain Fenner, were to be landed on one side the peninsula on which Corunna stands, and the long boats and pinnaces which landed them were to keep up a fire as they approached. On the other side, Captain Wingfield, who was Norris's lieutenant-colonel, and Captain Sampson, who held the same rank under Drake, were to enter with 500 men at low water, if they found it passable: otherwise they were provided for the escalade; and on the land side 300 men, under Colonels Bret and Umpton, were to set up their ladders and scale the wall. The three attacks were to be made at the same time. In strict obedience to this part of their orders, Wingfield and Sampson began the assault as soon as the signal was given: they found good resistance, and were twice beaten from their ladders, yet persevered in the attempt. Huntley and Fenner landed, meantime, with no great difficulty, and but little loss; and some of this party, under Captain Hinder, having effected an entrance, scoured the wall, clearing the way for Bret and Umpton to enter without resistance, and passed on till he came in the rear of those who were resisting Wingfield and Sampson: upon this the defence was abandoned. The Spaniards, indeed, knowing that if attacked from the water it was not tenable, had determined upon withdrawing the garrison and the inhabitants into the high town, should this be the plan of the assailants; but in the confusion and fear which prevailed, the signal for recalling the troops from the land side was not made; and men whose courage deserved a more generous treatment than they underwent were sacrificed through this error.*

Upon the English having thus entered in three places, "with a huge cry," the inhabitants, they who could, betook themselves to the high town, which they might with less peril do, because the assailants, being strangers, knew not the way to cut them off. "Some," says one of the expedition, "fled to the rocks in the peninsula; some hid themselves in chambers and cellars; some found favour to be taken prisoners; but the rest, to the number of about 500, falling into the hands of the common soldiers, had their throats cut"; and this seems to have been perpetrated and related equally without compunction. The cellars were found full of wine, 2000 pipes having been collected there, toward the provision for a second armada; and the men, by inordinate drinking, becoming reckless of danger, or incapable of perceiving it, exposed themselves to the shot from the upper town, whereby many were hurt.† It was thought that by their excesses at

---

* Hakluyt, 139.

† In the only Spanish account of these transactions which I have been able to consult, it is said that the wine was purposely left; and that the Spaniards, taking advantage of the drunkenness and consequent disorder thus produced, killed as many as 800 stragglers, whom the succours, as they arrived from the interior, fell in with and found drunk and sleeping. This writer says: "Bebieron bellamente los Ingleses, como valientes bebedores; y pareciendoles que ya eran señores de la tierra, lo que menos cuidado les daba era la guerra" (*P. M. F. Felipe de la Gandara, Armas y Triunfos del Reino de Galicia.* 1672, p. 470).

The author was chronista general of that kingdom. The first part of his account cannot be reconciled with the English statements. According to him the invaders landed more than 10,000 men, and took possession of Burgo, an open village (*lugar*), without walls or castle, more than a league from Corunna: there they began to visit the drinking

this time they brought on the subsequent sickness and mortality. From the few prisoners who were taken, they learnt that there were in the town when they arrived 500 soldiers, the poor remains of seven companies who had returned from "the journey of England," and that money and stores had been sent thither for a second attempt at invasion. *

The Spaniards had been taken by surprise, which they ought not to have been in any of their great ports on this side the Straits. But the governor, who was the Marquez de Zerralbo don Juan Pacheco Osorio, prepared now with a Spaniard's determination for defence. His first object was to prevent the enemy from taking possession of the galleon; and as this could by no other means be effected, he gave orders for destroying it; the crew, accordingly, overcharged the guns, set the ship on fire, and left her in flames, "which burnt in terrible sort for two days together". When she had burnt to the water's edge, and the English came to search her hull, they found only sixteen whole cannon out of fifty: the rest had burst in their discharge, as had been designed, and were taken out in broken pieces and molten lumps. Every exertion was made for improving the fortifications, which were strong but old. All hands were employed at this, and in carrying earth for the ramparts, which were now made; and so intent were they upon these operations,

houses, instead of making any attempt to occupy the bridge (at the head of the harbour, over the mouth of the Mandeo), and take a position, to prevent succours from arriving. "They might have done this easily," he says, "*sin que pudiera entrar gente por parte alguna.*" Afterwards they attempted to insulate the fortress by cutting across the isthmus; but there were rocks in the way, large reinforcements had already entered, and the fire from the walls put an end to their operations. He makes no mention whatever of the storming the base town, nor of the subsequent carnage, but simply says that they burnt the suburb called La Pescaderia, which contained 1500 houses.

* Hakluyt, 140.

that they left the Puerto Real, or royal gate, open, and Corunna, according to the Galicians, would have been lost, if a greater personage than the governor had not taken upon himself the defence in this emergency. For the English entered not only without resistance, but without any one speaking to them or giving the alarm: so strange a circumstance made them apprehensive of some stratagem; still, however, though with all possible circumspection, they advanced up the street, at the end of which stood the parochial church of the upper town; and to whom should that church be dedicated but to the peculiar patron of Spain and especial glory of Galicia—Santiago? He did not indeed appear in person: short as the distance was from Compostella, the occasion was not of sufficient importance for him to leave his shrine and mount his celestial white horse; but out of his church there issued a great darkness, and in the midst of that darkness a great light; and the light dazzled, and the darkness confused, and both terrified them: they made their way out of the gate with more alacrity than they had entered it; and Santiago achieved for his faithful devotees the only one of all his numerous victories in which no blood was shed.*

This was a modest miracle for the saint, the country, and the religion. Another and not less thaumaturgic saint worked none upon the occasion, though he might seem to have been more especially invited or provoked to manifest his power. Without the Puerta de los Aires, and fronting it, was a convent of St. Domingo: the invaders occupied it; and from the upper windows and other parts of the edifice fired into the town. These things passed on the day after the escalade. On the morrow some 2000 men from the adjacent parts approached the gates as confidently as if they had been resolved to enter: but they advanced without order; and losing a few men in the first encounter took to flight, and

* Gandara, 471.

outstripped their pursuers. A party following up this success foraged round about, and brought back kine and sheep in abundance, to the great relief of the army, whose provisions when they landed * were well nigh exhausted. Norris meant in the ensuing night to take a " long munition house built upon the wall "; but the Spaniards apprehending this, and knowing how advantageous a position it would be for the enemy, burnt it before the attempt could be made. At the same time a fire broke out in the lower end of the town, "which, had it not been by the care of the general heedily seen unto, and the fury thereof prevented, by pulling down many houses which were most in danger, had burnt," says Wingfield, " all the provisions we found there, to our wonderful hindrance ".†

Two demi-cannons and two culverins were now planted under the garden of the convent, but with little skill or foresight, for the first or second fire shook down the cross wall by which this battery was " defended or gabioned "; it then lay open to the enemy. They did not overlook their opportunity; and the lieutenant of the ordnance, with some of the cannoneers, were slain there. The battery was secured during the night. When it was ready to open, the general sent to summon the place: the man who bore it was fired at from the town. Presently a Spaniard was hanged over the wall, and a signal for parley made, the object of which was to let the English see that this summary punishment had been inflicted upon the person who fired at the messenger; and they took the opportunity of requesting to have " fair

---

* Wingfield says: " What extremity the want of that month's victuals which we did eat during the month we lay at Plymouth for a wind might have driven us unto, no man can doubt of that knoweth what men do live by, had not God given us, in the end, a more prosperous wind and shorter passage into Galicia than hath been often seen, where our own force and fortune revictualled us largely " (Hakluyt, 135).

† Hakluyt, 141.

war," promising it on their part. They made inquiry concerning what prisoners were in the hands of the English, but would not listen to any proposal for surrendering.*

Norris had now sufficiently reconnoitred the walls to see that they were almost everywhere built upon a rock: one place, however, he thought mineable, and men were presently set to work there, who, after three days' labour, and on the seventh after their entrance of the base town, had bedded their powder,—but, as afterwards appeared, not far enough into the wall. The breach by that time was thought assaultable, and companies were drawn out for a simultaneous attack there, and at the point where it was expected that the mine would make an opening. But the mine failed, "by reason the powder brake out backward in a place where the cave was made too high". Nothing therefore could be attempted that day. The miners resumed their work, and by the second day after had wrought well into the foundation of the wall. The first failure drew after it no ill consequence; not so the partial success of the second attempt. The explosion brought down half the tower under which the mine had been made, and opened a practicable breach: it was immediately assaulted; and when the men had gained the summit, the other half fell on them; some twenty or thirty were crushed, and the men were "so amazed, not knowing whence that terror came, that they forsook their commanders, and left them among the ruins of the mine". The two ensigns were shot in the breach, but their colours were rescued; among those on whom the tower fell "was Captain Sydenham pitifully lost, who having three or four great stones upon his lower parts was held so fast that neither himself could stir nor any reasonable company recover him; notwithstanding the next day, being found to be alive, there were ten or twelve lost in attempting to relieve him". It

---

* Hakluyt, 141.

is the most honourable incident on the part of the English, during their descent in Galicia, that so many should have exposed and lost their lives in endeavouring to perform this act of forlorn humanity toward their suffering countryman;* and the least honourable on that of the Spaniards that they should have fired on men who were exposing themselves for such a motive.

Meantime a breach which had been made by the poor battery in the convent garden was attempted; and the officers brought their men to the push of the pike at the summit. But the Spaniards had prepared all means of defence, and they were encouraged by the masculine exertions of the wife of an alferez,—Maria Pita was her name. With a spirit which women have more often displayed in Spain than in any other country, she snatched up sword and buckler, and took her stand among the foremost of the defendants; and so much was ascribed by the people to the effect of her example, that she was rewarded for this service with the full pay of an ensign for life, and the half pay was settled upon her descendants in perpetuity.† The defence, however, was not difficult; for the rubbish over which the assailants mounted "slid outward from under their feet; and it then appeared that half the height of the wall had received no injury".‡

---

* Hakluyt, 141.

† Gandara, as chronista mayor of Galicia, is good authority for a circumstance like this. The story gained something by travelling in its own country. Faria y Sousa says, that this virago lost none of her courage at seeing her husband killed before her eyes, and that she wounded an English standard-bearer, mortally, with a lance (p. 95. Gandara, 472).

‡ " For let no man think that culverin or demi-cannon can sufficiently batter a defensible rampire. And of those pieces which we had, the better of the demi-cannons, at the second shot, broke in her carriages " (Hakluyt, 141).

The writer argued, that if the battering pieces which were promised for the armament, but not supplied, had been there, the place would have been taken.

Thus, had there been more spirit for renewing the assault, the breach no longer appeared practicable. From both points of attack the retreat lay through a narrow street or lane, and many were hurt there.* Whatever the loss may have been, the failure was so complete, that it determined † the general to abandon an enterprise which he now considered hopeless. But to secure his embarkation it was necessary to disperse a considerable force with which the Conde de Andrade was encamped behind the Puente de Burgo, waiting there to be joined by the Conde de Altamira, and then, with united strength, to advance for the relief of the town. Norris accordingly, leaving Drake, with five regiments, to guard their quarters, marched, with nine, to meet the enemy. His brother, Sir Edward Norris, who commanded the van, came in sight of them some half mile from their camp, and beat them from place to place (though " they had good places of defence, and cross walls which they might have held long "), till they came to the bridge, " on the foot of the farther side whereof lay their camp, strongly intrenched ". Sir Edward followed at the point of the pikes, through a heavy fire: the enemy's shot flanked both sides of the bridge, and at the end was a barricado of barrels. They who should have guarded it forsook their station, seeing this " proud approach ". Sir Edward entered, and charging the first who opposed him, pike in hand, fell, " with very earnestness, in over-thrusting," and received a grievous sword wound in the head. The general, and some other officers,

---

* Gandara, in his exaggerated statement, says, that the English held out a signal for burying their dead, who were found to be 1500; and that the loss of the Spaniards, from the time that the expedition landed, till it re-embarked, amounted only to thirty-five. I wish Wingfield's account of the slaughter in the base town rested on no better authority, or could be suspected of equal exaggeration.

† The expression in Hakluyt is, " it made him grow to a new resolution " (p. 141).

"most honourably" rescued him; and overcoming, not without a severe struggle, the brave resistance that was made, obtained then an easy victory over the rest of the army. The standard was taken, and the fugitives hotly pursued for some three miles. "How many," says Wingfield, "2000 men (for of so many consisted our vanguard) might kill in pursuit of four sundry parties, so many you may imagine fell before us that day. And to make the number more great, our men having given over the execution, and returning to their stands, found many hidden in the vineyards and hedges, whom they despatched." Two hundred, also, were found in a convent, and were there put to the sword, and the convent spoiled and burnt. This was not the "fair war," for which the Spaniards had asked, and which, by their honourable conduct at the time of asking, they had deserved. The contrary system can be justified only when reprisals become necessary, as the sole means of putting a stop to it; but in that age fair war seems, almost, to have been the exception. *

After what is called "the fury," and might better have been termed the wickedness † "of the execution," the vanguard was sent one way, and the main body the other, "to burn and spoil, so that you might have seen the country, more than three miles' compass, on fire". The next day was spent in shipping their artillery, ‡ and whatever booty could be transported; and they attempted, during the last night of their tarriance, to burn that part of the upper town where

---

* Hakluyt, 142. Camden, 430.

† Such a carnage after the action well deserves to be so qualified, especially if the relater in Hakluyt is to be believed when he says, that "there were slain in this fight, on our side, only Captain Cooper, and one private soldier".

‡ Their own and those taken in the base town, "which," says Wingfield, "had it been such as might have given us any assurance of a better battery, or had there been no other purpose of our journey but that, I think the general would have spent some more time in the siege of the place".

the houses were built upon the wall by the water side; but the Spaniards were vigilant, and made so good a defence that they frustrated this intention. At their departure, however, the invaders, by their own account, set fire to every house of the base town, so that not one was left standing there.* Putting then to sea, after contending nine days with contrary winds, they reached the Berlings, having a little before fallen in with Essex, who, with some other volunteers of note, had followed the expedition in a single ship. By this time, the troops had suffered much by sickness, aggravated by their own excesses at Corunna; and the loss during the siege had been considerable.† But this was not the only evil ‡ during the eighteen days of their continuance there; troops had been sent to Lisbon, and all persons of any influence, who were suspected of favouring Antonio, were removed from that city, and sent into Spain. Antonio, indeed, had been considered of so little consequence in this first act of the expedition, that he seems not to have been

---

* Gandara confirms this, but represents it having been done before the attempts on the upper town; and he avoids all mention of the action at the Puente de Burgo.

† El Peregrino Español (Antonio Perez) whose *Tratado Parænetico* was translated into French and English, and widely circulated by the Portuguese emigrants, says that the greater part of the troops died there, and all the best artillerymen: but he seems to refer this loss rather to the mortality than the siege; and his object was to show that the expedition failed wholly through the misconduct of the English, and not owing to the weakness of Antonio's partisans.

‡ Sir William Monson says: "The landing at the Groyne was an unnecessary lingering and hindrance of the other great and main design; a consuming of victuals and weakening of the army by the immoderate drinking of the soldiers, which brought a lamentable sickness amongst them; a warning to the Spaniards to strengthen Portugal; and (what is more than all this) a discouragement to proceed farther, being repulsed in the first attempt" (160). This is true, except as to the waste of provision. Monson himself says, that "divers of the ships had not four days' victuals when they departed from Plymouth".

consulted concerning it, nor, indeed, is he noticed in the accounts of it till the fleet arrived at Peniche. The troops landed there, about a mile from the town, with much difficulty, owing to the wind and the surf, and with the loss of one boat, carrying twenty-five men. Essex commanded this party; and when men enough had been disembarked for forming two troops, he left one to protect the landing, and advanced with the other against some companies who sallied from the town to oppose him. The Spaniards fled when it came to the push of the pike: he entered the open town, and summoned the castle, which the commandant, Antonio de Araujo, readily surrendered to Antonio, acknowledging him as his king. *

Here it was agreed that the army should proceed overland to Lisbon, and the fleet meet them in the Tagus. When the army was marshalled and ready to act, Drake, " to make known the honourable desire he had of taking equal parts in all fortune with them, stood upon the ascent of a hill by which the battalions marched, and, with a pleasing kindness, took his leave severally of the commanders of every regiment, wishing them happy success, with a constant promise, that if the weather did not hinder him, he would meet them at Lisbon with the fleet". The non-performance of this engagement brought a reproach upon Drake, who may, with more cause, be censured for having made it. While the army proceeded with little encouragement from the Portuguese, whose eager co-operation they had been led to expect, Drake sailed for Cascaes and took possession of the town. The inhabitants, who abandoned it upon his landing, returned upon his assurances of all peaceable kindness if they would acknowledge Antonio for their king, and supply the fleet with necessaries; but the castle, having a Spanish garrison, was maintained against him. Here he remained, till the army, weakened by sickness, unable for want of artillery (the little

* Hakluyt, 144.

which they had being in the fleet) to make any serious attempt upon Lisbon, knowing themselves far inferior in number to the Spanish troops who were collected against them, and undeceived as to the influence and strength of the pretender's adherents, gave up this ill-planned and worse conducted attempt, and came to join him at Cascaes. Whatever blame was afterwards imputed to the admiral, those who were on the spot, and were capable of forming a dispassionate opinion, must have admitted the validity of the motives which had withheld him from entering the river. The fleet must have passed within culver shot of St. Julian's, which was then accounted "one of the most impregnable forts to seaward in Europe: this and the other two forts between Cascaes and Lisbon Drake might have passed with a reasonable gale"; but once in the Tagus, the coming out again was uncertain: there were galleys in the river ready at any advantage to have assailed him: he would have been exposed to fire ships; and if a fleet had been brought against him at the mouth of the river, he had neither the hope of victory nor of escape, and the destruction of the army must have followed upon the loss of the ships.*

The emigrants whose expectations had been so cruelly disappointed, imputed Drake's breach of promise to his regarding the interests of the merchant adventurers rather than those of the expedition, because while he remained at Cascaes many prizes were brought in there. Most of these were easterlings, of which not fewer than three scores belonging to the Hanse towns, and laden with naval stores, as was supposed for another armada, were captured. Some were of great burden, with little on board, and evidently built as ships of war: it could not be doubted that these were for the Spanish navy. The embarkation of the troops was secured by forcing the Castle of Cascaes to surrender, the commandant requiring only such a display of force as

* Camden, 431, 432. Monson, 160.

might justify him in offering no farther resistance. It was occupied then by English troops, till the armament was ready to sail, and partially blown up at their departure. One company had been left at Peniche, together with the sick and wounded: some vessels were sent to bring them away, and advices were despatched to the commanding officer overland: the advice arrived in time, but not the ships; for the commander, then apprised of what had happened, and learning also that an enemy's force was hastening against him, embarked in barques which were on the spot, and with such haste that he neither brought away the artillery nor all his men. *

Nine galleys from Andalusia had entered the Tagus some days before the departure of the English: these, with the twelve which were stationed there, followed the fleet; and on the following morning, taking advantage of a dead calm, cut off some stragglers, and ran down some who endeavoured to escape from them in their boats. One hulk had Captain Minshew and his company on board, and he was seen fighting to the last after his ship was on fire: the calm meantime was such, that none of the great ships could approach to assist him, though every effort was made by towing them. In this and in another action with a straggler the galleys were so roughly handled, that they discontinued the pursuit. The expedition had been instructed to ply for the Azores if the wind were northerly; but if it blew from the south, then for the Isles of Bayona. The fleet was dispersed in a gale; but after seventeen days the two commanders and good part of the ships were united off Vigo. In that interval many men had been cast overboard; for not only was the sickness raging among them, but many died of hunger, and more must have perished for lack of sufficient food, if the mortality which carried off their comrades had not left a

* Hakluyt, 149.

more competent allowance for the survivors. Not more than 2000 effective men were now left. They were landed in two bodies : they approached the town on two sides ; and though a strong barricado had been constructed at the end of every street, no defence was attempted. The inhabitants deemed it prudent to withdraw in time, and had removed with them everything of value, except good store of wine. It was thought too hazardous to make a movement upon Bayona, whither they had fled, and where they knew, from one of their Corunna prisoners, that there was a strong garrison. The English contented themselves with spoiling the country for some seven or eight miles, burning the villages and the standing corn : then, after setting fire to every house in the town, they re-embarked. *

Still the commanders clung to the hope of returning with some booty that might compensate for the loss incurred in this luckless expedition. It was agreed that Drake should draft the able men into twenty of the best ships, and sail for the Azores for the chance of falling in with the Indian fleet, while Norris with the rest of the armament should return home. They parted with this understanding : on the second night there arose a greater storm than any they had encountered since they left England ; both squadrons were dispersed ; and when Norris, twelve days afterwards, reached Plymouth, he found that Drake had arrived there, and all the queen's ships, and many others ; but every vessel had taken the opportunity, which the storm afforded, of going its own way, " some led by a desire of returning whence they came, and some," says Wingfield, " being possessed of the hulks (the Hanse towns' prizes), sought other ports, from their general's eye, where they might make their private commodity of them,—which they did to their own great advantage ". At Plymouth the army was dissolved, eight companies

* Hakluyt, 150.

only being retained : every soldier received five shillings, and "the arms he bare to make money of, and this was believed to be more than could by any means be due to them".* It appears, however, that some of the men who compared their wages with their pains, murmured against this distribution, and that this increased the unpopularity, † which in some

* "For they were not in service three months; in which time," says Wingfield, "they had their victuals, which no man will value at less than half their pay, for such is the allowance in her majesty's ships to her mariners; so as there remained but ten shillings a month more to be paid: for which there was not any private man but had his apparel and furniture to his own use; so as every common soldier discharged received more in money, victuals, apparel, and furniture than his pay did amount to" (Hakluyt, 151).

† "As our country," says Wingfield, "doth bring forth many gallant men, who, desirous of honour, do put themselves into the actions thereof, so doth it many more, who, though their thoughts reach not so high as others, yet do they listen how other men's acts do pass; and, either believing what any man will report unto them, are willingly carried away into errors, or, tied to some greater man's faith, become secretaries against a noted truth. The one sort of these take their opinions from the highway side, or, at the farthest, go no farther than Paul's, to inquire what hath been done in this voyage; where if they meet with any whose capacity before their going out could not make them live, nor their valour maintain their reputation, and who went only for spoil, complaining on the hardness and misery thereof, they think they are bound to give credit to these honest men who were parties therein, and, in very charity, become of their opinions. The others, to make good the faction they are entered into, if they see any of those malcontents (as every journey yieldeth some), do run unto them, like tempting spirits, to confirm them in their humour, with assurance that they foresaw, before our going out, what would become thereof.

"Be ye not, therefore, credulous in believing every report; for there have been many more beholders of these things that have passed than actors in the same; who, by their experience not having the knowledge of the ordinary wants of war, have thought that to be hard, not to have their meat well dressed, to drink sometimes water, to watch much, or to see men die and be slain, was a miserable thing; and not having so given their minds to the service as they are anything instructed thereby, do, for want of better matter, discourse ordinarily of these things" (p. 151).

degree is generally attached to the leaders of an unsuccessfu expedition. *

A very rich booty is said to have been brought home, and 150 pieces of great ordnance ; but the loss of lives had been very great, of 12,500 men little more than 6000 returning : the Spaniards exaggerated the loss to 16,000 ; and, tracing to the disease which the survivors brought home a great mortality which ensued, they said that England suffered more for having sent an armada against Spain, than Spain for having sent an armada against England. † Yet the result of the expedition was to confirm the English people in that opinion of their superiority to the Spaniards, whether at sea or in the field, which they had now begun to entertain ; and the spirit of adventure became more general. Elizabeth's conduct toward the Hanse towns encouraged that spirit. She had warned those towns against carrying provisions or military stores into Spain or Portugal, upon peril of losing ships and lading, according to special treaty in this case, and to the acknowledged practice and law of nations. Conscious that they were violating that treaty, and amenable to that law, the easterlings took the perilous course, north about, rather than risk passing the Channel ; but when their ships were captured off the mouth of the Tagus, they complained as if their privileges had been violated, and called for restitution. The queen replied, that their ships, being employed in carrying warlike stores to the enemies of England, she had lawfully taken them, and could not have done otherwise, unless she would wilfully bring destruction upon herself and her people. Privileges, to which they appealed, might neither be claimed nor allowed to the prejudice of the public safety, which is the highest law : nor was the appeal maintainable in itself; for in the privilege granted by Edward I. to the Hanse towns, it was expressly provided that they

* Hakluyt, 151, 152.   † Faria y Sousa, 197.

should not carry any merchandise into the dominions of the declared enemies of England. More than once had their ships been detained heretofore, when, during war with France, they had supplied the French with stores; and this had been done not by England only, but by Charles V., the Kings of Sweden, Denmark, and Poland, and recently by the Prince of Orange, according to the law of nations; for neutrality must so be used, that the neutrals while they help one party hurt not the other. Referring then to the tone of their demands, she reminded them that it did not become cities and towns to use menaces to kings; for her part she feared not the threats of the greatest monarchs, much less of particular cities; and as for the due and just rights of neighbourhood, she punctually observed them with all men. *

Whatever murmurs had been raised against the conduct of the Portugal voyage, Drake's character was too well established both in the estimation of the court and of the people to be seriously affected by them: the failure of that expedition was sufficiently accounted for by want of means, † want of co-operation on the part of Antonio's party, and the mortality among the troops. And when, in the year 1594, in conjunction with Sir John Hawkins, he proposed to the government to set on foot an armament against the West Indies, the project was readily entertained.

Hawkins, after his unhappy adventure at St. Juan de Ulloa, seems to have given up the career of enterprise. In 1573 he had been appointed treasurer or comptroller of the navy, a high and arduous office, which he discharged so ably that he is said to have introduced more useful inventions into the navy, and better regulations, than any of his predecessors. He acted as rear-admiral against the armada, and received,

* Camden, 433.

† Monson says, that, in his opinion, the two generals never overshot themselves more, than in undertaking so great a charge with so little means.

on that occasion, the honour of knighthood, which he had well deserved. During a long course of service, he had obtained a great name in his profession, and, notwithstanding his loss in the Gulf of Mexico, no inconsiderable fortune, for he and his elder brother were at one time owners of thirty good ships.* The queen, no doubt in consequence of his representations, resolved upon putting her navy upon a better and more regular footing than it had before been, and assigned a yearly sum of 8970*l*. † for keeping it in repair; and in the same year, 1590, she sent ten of her own ships, under Hawkins and Sir Martin Frobisher, to threaten the coast of Spain, and intercept the Indian ships. But the Spaniards obtained intelligence of this in time to send despatches out, and order the homeward-bound fleet to winter in India, rather than run the hazard of falling in with this force; others, which were on their way, either meeting with timely advice, or warned by their own forethought, kept at a distance from the islands, and by that unsuspected course reached Lisbon safely. Hawkins, therefore, cruised about in vain, and with such singular ill success that not a single prize fell into his hands. A landing which he attempted at Fayal was not more fortunate; and after seven months he returned, without loss indeed, but without any apparent advantage, though it was known afterwards that the delay of a year in their expected returns had proved most injurious to the Spanish merchants, and that the ships as well as their owners suffered greatly. No blame could be imputed to the commanders. Sir John, however, thought it necessary to offer some apology in the report of his voyage: this he did at considerable length; and concluded by reminding the queen that Paul planteth and Apollos watereth, but it is God who giveth the increase. This ill-applied allusion to Scripture is said to have provoked from Elizabeth a characteristic

* Campbell, i., 415. † Camden, 439. Lediard, 274.

burst of anger :—" God's death ! " she exclaimed : " this fool went out a soldier, and is come home a divine ".*

This was but a momentary feeling ; and when Drake and Hawkins, " presuming much upon their own experience and knowledge," proposed that a West Indian voyage should be undertaken, and offered to engage deeply in it, the queen concurred in a project, of which, in the opinion of all men, the most promising expectations were entertained. Much had been done to impede the preparations of Philip for a second attempt at invasion, much to injure the Spaniards, and more to irritate them ; but Philip was both a determined and a powerful enemy. Till the forced union with Portugal, Spain had made little account of its navy, its only maritime war having long been what was carried on with the Mahomedan powers within the Straits ; but the spoil committed by the English expeditions, far and near, not upon the seas alone, but in the islands, in the West Indies, upon the coasts of Chili and Peru, and even in its own most important and best fortified ports, made the government feel the necessity of raising a maritime force, wherewith at once to be protected and revenged. This object had been pursued with such diligence, that within three years after the failure of the armada, the Spaniards had a formidable fleet; and in three years more 69 ships, built at the king's charge, had been added to it, most of them of 1000 tons' burden and upwards. When hostilities begun, the Spanish ships were " huge and mighty in burden, weak and ill-fashioned in building, lame and slow in sailing, and fitter for merchandise than war," having indeed " been more intended for it " : old seamen, like Hawkins, used to maintain that one of the queen's ships could beat four of them. They were now constructed for war, and were so superior to the English ships in strength and weight of metal, that nothing but English seamanship and

* Monson, 162, 247. Lediard, 274.

English courage could have contended against such superiority. But the Spaniards also had good sailors, though only from their northern ports; for the Catalans no longer supported their ancient reputation. Most of their officers, from the rank of captain downward, were Biscayans, with whom (it is the testimony of an English admiral than whom none of his age had seen more service) there were few that could be compared for knowledge, hardiness, and valour. But the Biscayans made but a small part of the sailors: the discipline of the navy was bad; and the naval service was regarded with contempt by the military.

Rumours were abroad that a second and more formidable armada had been completed, and intelligence came from many quarters that the conquest of England would again be attempted. Upon this, men were levied in all the maritime counties, and watch and ward appointed to be kept upon the sea coast. The apprehension was as general as it had been in 1588; and now, too, as then, the sense of danger brought with it nothing like dismay. It was, indeed, lamented, that so much brave blood and so much treasure had been lost in France, wasted, as it were, in aid of insincere allies; but "all men," says Camden, * "buckled themselves to war; and wailing women, with renewed grief, lamented that their sons and brethren who had fallen in that thankless service had not been reserved for these times". On this account the West Indian voyage was delayed, to the great cost of the adventurers: it was deemed unfit to send away so many good ships and men while there was reason to think they might be wanted in our own seas, and on English ground. The Spaniards, however, effected no more than what sufficed to show that however vigilantly the Channel might be guarded, partial descents were always possible. They had possession at that time of Blavet in Bretagne, a small but strong place

P. 497.

upon the river of that name, from the ruins of which Port Louis was afterwards constructed. From thence D. Diego Brochen, with four galleys, under favourable opportunity of weather, crossed the mouth of the Channel, and effected a landing at Penzance. They sacked and burnt that place, with the two poor fishing towns of Mousehole and Newlin; but the inhabitants had taken flight. No life was lost, and no prisoner taken; and the galleys returned as safely as they came.*

If the object of this descent was to impress the English with the belief that a great invasion was to follow, it not only failed, but produced an opposite effect. Tyrone, indeed, induced by Romish instigations, and relying upon Spanish support, commenced a rebellion in Ireland, which added new horrors to the barbarous history of that most barbarous island. But though this disquieted Elizabeth's councils, so little apprehension was entertained of any danger from the Spaniards at home, that Hawkins and Drake were allowed to begin their voyage. Their force consisted of 26 sail, and about 2500 men. Six were queen's ships, Drake sailing in the *Defiance*, and his colleague in the *Garland*. Sir Thomas Baskerville was the commander by land, and Sir Nicholas Clifford his lieutenant-general. The first intent of this expedition was, that they should land at Nombre de Dios, march across the isthmus to Panama, and seize what treasure might be there, which it was supposed would be much, and, if they thought it feasible, keep possession of that place. But a few days only before they sailed from Plymouth letters came from the queen, informing them, upon sure intelligence from Spain, that the West Indian fleet had arrived, but that one treasure ship, having lost a mast, had

---

* Camden, 499. Monson, 167. Lediard, 310. "These," says Camden, "were the first and last Spaniards that ever made any hostile landing in England." It seems that Pero Nino's name was never so well (or, rather, so ill) known here, as that of his contemporary, Arripay, in Spain.

put back to Puerto Rico; wherefore she ordered them to take the good opportunity thus presented, and make for this great prize,—a course which was the more advised, because it was not much out of their way to Nombre de Dios. *

They "brake ground" (in the phrase of their own journalist) "out of Plymouth Sound on the 28th of August, 1595, and at the end of four weeks arrived off the Isle of Grand Canary. Drake and Baskerville were for landing here, for the honour of conquering it, as well as for the sake of victualling the fleet. Hawkins was for obeying the queen's instructions, and losing no time in accomplishing the main enterprise; but the sailors represented their need of a supply of provisions: this is said to have been a pretence on their part, who had the hope of plunder before their eyes; and when Baskerville engaged to take the place within four days, Hawkins consented. This having been determined, they found at daybreak that they had overshot their mark; so they stood about, and by nine o'clock were at anchor before the fort, about a league eastward of the city of St. Anna, and at one, 1400 men were in readiness to land in a sandy bay between the city and the fort. But the hours which had elapsed since the fleet first hove in sight had been well employed in erecting a bulwark, and planting ordnance to command the landing-place; seeing which, and that a heavy surf was then breaking on the beach, the generals perceived that they could not make the attempt without too great and manifest a risk. After a vain demonstration, therefore, in which some of the smaller ships riding at anchor within musket shot of the shore were in some danger, they went to the western side of the island, and there watered. A few men venturing rashly to some distance from the shore were set upon by the herdsmen, who with their dogs and staves killed most of them, and took prisoner the surgeon of one of

* Monson, 167.

the ships, from whom they learnt all that he knew concerning the objects of the voyage. And upon this the governor despatched a caraval to all those places which were threatened. This warning, however, had been anticipated by advices from the Spanish Government which reached the West Indies before the expedition sailed from England, —such early and sure intelligence had that government obtained. *

A month afterwards, when they were near Martinico, Drake, being ahead with four or five other ships, was separated from the rest of the fleet in a gale. They made for Dominica, he for Marigalante, and they joined company again at Guadaloupe. Some traffic had been carried on at Dominica, where great store of tobacco was grown, which " most of the English and French used to purchase from the Caribs, with knives, hatchets, saws, and such like iron tools," —no slight indication of improvement in the Indians, if beads, hawk-bells, prisms, and other toys had ceased to be received in payment. It is said that these Indians had plantations of various fruits in Marigalante, which they kept like gardens; but there seems no assignable reason why they should have made their plantations on another island instead of their own. Having reached Guadaloupe, the expedition watered there, washed the ships, set up the pinnaces, the materials of which they had taken out, and landed the men that they might refresh themselves on shore. †

The day after Drake's arrival there, five Spanish *zabras* were seen, ships of 200 tons; from which, as their course was by Dominica toward Puerto Rico, Drake rightly concluded ‡ that the treasure was still in that island, and that this force had been ordered thither to convoy it: they belonging to a squadron of eight, which had been sent for that purpose, under Don Pedro Tello. Captain Wignol in the *Francis,* a barque of thirty-five tons, being the last

* Hakluyt, 583. † *Ibid.*, 584. ‡ Purchas, iv., 1171.

straggler of Hawkins's fleet, fell in with them, and was captured in sight of a caraval that escaped, and carried tidings of the capture to the commanders. It is said that Hawkins, foreseeing but too clearly the consequences of this misfortune, immediately sickened. Tello, in fact, put his prisoners to the torture,* and thus extracted from them a declaration of what he might, with sufficient certainty, have inferred from the appearance of an English force in those seas. The expedition tarried at Guadaloupe three days after this mishap, and for this the commanders have been censured; but it may be doubted whether any haste which they could now have made would have been attended with better speed. Sailing once more on the 4th of November, they came to anchor, on the morning of the 8th, within the Virgin Islands: this had

---

* Lope de Vega relates this in lines, some of which are as atrocious as the others are characteristic:—

" Siguiendo pues su curso por la plata,
  Y la del mar rompiendo en blanca espuma,
Llevando cada prospera fragata
  El mar y el viento como leve pluma;
Dos navios encuentra y desbarata
  De aquella Inglesa referida suma,
Entre la Dominica y Matalino,
Islas del mar, y ventas del camino.

" Huye el uno, ganando el barlovento,
  Y abriendo los costados las espuelas
Al cavallo del mar, que yguala al viento,
  Lleno de paramentos de sus velas;
Echando el otro a fondo, y siempre atento
  A entender sus ardides y cautelas,
Diez y ocho Ingleses que tomó pregunta,
Y el cuero y nervios con los huessos junta.

" Al tormento confiessan los que tienen
  Tan gran odio, señor, al confessarse,
Que de Plemua con el Draque vienen," etc.
Dragontea, c. 4.

been accounted dangerous, but they found a good road, "in which 1000 sail might have lain in fourteen, twelve, and eight fathom, fair sand and good anchorage, with high islands on either side". They could find no fresh water, but plenty of fish to be taken either with hooks or net, and the men went ashore and fowled; after tarrying two days here, they lingered two more in a lesser sound, about a league distant, which Drake explored the preceding night in his barge. If it be true that a difference of opinion had arisen between the commanders, it may explain a delay for which there would otherwise be no apparent reason. That dispute is said to have caused or accelerated Hawkins's death: on the morning of the 12th the fleet passed through the strait; and at night, when it was off the easternmost end of Puerto Rico, he breathed his last. *

Sir Thomas Baskerville took the place of this brave old seaman in the *Garland*, and at two in the afternoon of the same day the fleet anchored in a sandy bay, two miles east of Puerto Rico city, and within reach of its forts. Drake paid dearly for this imprudence. One shot wounded his mizzen, another entered the steerage, where he was at supper, and struck the stool from under him: he, indeed, escaped unhurt; but several of the party were wounded, and two of them to death. Sir Nicholas Clifford was one, the other was Sir Francis's bosom friend, Master Brown, who had been christened by the unseemly name of Brute, taken, no doubt, from the fabled story of our Trojan descent. "Ah, dear Brute," said Drake, "I could grieve for thee! but now is no time for me to let down my spirits!" † No time was lost in removing to a safer distance; and on the following morning they came to anchor "before the point without the town,

---

* Hakluyt, 584. Lediard, 310, 311.

† Fuller relates this, "from the mouth of Henry Drake, Esq., there present," whom he speaks of as his "dear and worthy parishioner, ately deceased" (*Holy State*, 129).

a little to the westward : there they remained till nightfall, and then twenty-five pinnaces, boats, and shallops, well manned, and furnished with fireworks and small shot, entered the road ".

The galleon which was the great object of this enterprise had been completely repaired, and was even on the point of sailing for Spain, when the certain intelligence of this intended attack reached the island. The Spaniards prepared themselves with equal promptitude and determination for defence : they landed the treasure, sunk the galleon in the mouth of the channel, and made a floating barrier of masts, on both sides, almost to the forts and castle, so as to render the passage impassable. Within this barrier the five zabras were stationed : their lading had been taken out ; and, that nothing might be unnecessarily risked, all women, children, and unable persons had been sent into the interior, none remaining in the town but men who were able to defend it. A heavy fire was opened, both from the ships and forts, upon the English ; and it became more destructive when they had succeeded with their fireworks in setting the ships in flames, for by that broad light the forts were enabled to direct their shot. Yet the adventurers persisted in their desperate attempt, till they had lost some forty or fifty men, by their own account, killed, and as many more wounded ; consoling themselves with the thought that "there was also great death of the Spaniards aboard the frigates, with burning, drowning, and killing, besides some taken prisoners". Defeated, but not disheartened, they returned to the fleet, and remained at anchor the next day. One of the zabras had been consumed to the water's edge : the Spaniards employed the day in warping up the other four, all of which had been more or less injured ; and one, as they were removing her, was seen to sink. But no renewal of the attack was attempted ; Drake lingered another day as if unwilling to abandon the enterprise, though he now perceived it to be hopeless: two more he was detained by calms; then proceeded to the south-west point of the island, and there set up more pinnaces, washed his ships, and refreshed his men on shore.* And here a Spanish man and woman took refuge with him. The man's story was, "that he feared some great torment for not having repaired to the town, according to the governor's command, to assist in its defence,—and that the woman was his wife". Whatever may have been the motives for their flight, Drake was too humane a man to refuse them the means of escape.

Taking a final departure from Puerto Rico on the 25th of November, the fleet anchored under Cape de la Vela on the last day of the month; and on the morrow the troops were landed, and without resistance took possession of Rio de la Hacha, "one of the ancientest towns in all the main, although not very large". After a while the Spaniards " came in to talk of a ransom, but not to the general's liking"; finding this negotiation fruitless, Drake went with some 150 men by water to the Rancheria, six leagues distant, which was the station for the pearl fishery, and there a few soldiers were taken and many negroes, with some store of pearls and other pillage: after this an agreement was made that the Spaniards should pay 24,000 ducats for the ransom of the town, and one prisoner 4000 for his own. Four days elapsed: the ransom was then proffered in pearls; but these were rated so dear, that Drake refused to accept them, and sent them back, giving the Spaniards four hours to make a more satisfactory payment, or abide the consequence. His proceeding here was more honourable than theirs; for after a farther delay of two days, the governor having obtained a safe conduct, came into the town, and told Drake plainly that no ransom would be paid; that the pearls had been offered without his command or consent; and, in fact, that he had drawn out the time in negotiations for no other intent

* Hakluyt, 584. Lediard, 311.

than to send intelligence to those towns which were not strong enough to defend themselves, that so they might secure their property by carrying it into the woods. However incensed Drake may have been by this avowal (if it were actually made), he respected the word which he had given, and the Spaniard was allowed to depart in safety.*

The vengeance which the invaders took was to burn the town and the Rancheria "clean down to the ground," the churches only excepted, and the house of a lady, who wrote to Drake, requesting him to spare it. Proceeding now along the coast they came to Santa Martha, and found in the town nothing "but the houses swept clean"; but in the course of the night the lieutenant-general of the Spaniards was taken, and a little booty brought in from the woods. That town also they burnt on the 21st, and on the 27th entered the harbour of Nombre de Dios. The place was abandoned at their approach; but about 100 men kept the fort, played upon the invaders with a few small pieces of ordnance, waited till they could give also a volley of small shot, and then, as the English were running to the assault, took to flight, and struck into the woods. "The name of Nombre de Dios was greater than its strength," this fort being its only work of defence, "though they might have made it stronger if they would". So the invaders thought: they soon discovered that the Spaniards relied, with sufficient wisdom, upon the attachment of the natives, the strength of the country, and its climate—being "very unhealthy as any place in the Indies," and its abundant fruits—being "very dangerous to be eaten for breeding of diseases". The removal of property had been complete: nothing of any value had been left; and "there was a show in their shops of great store of merchandise that had been there". Nothing fell into the conquerors' hands except twenty tons of silver, two bars of gold, some money, and other pillage which they

* Hakluyt, 585.

found in a little watch-house, on the summit of a hill, in the woods.*

Drake remained here with the fleet while Baskerville with 750 men went for Panama, on the second day after their arrival. Two days longer Drake waited, apparently, to see whether the Spaniards would ransom the town : they had either been strictly forbidden to do this, or they were too high-minded, or, perhaps, did not think it worth ransoming ; for, though large, the houses were all built of timber, and the single church, "which was very fair and large, was of no better materials". On the last day of the year he burnt half the town, and the other half on the morrow, together with all the frigates, barques, and galliots, which were in the harbour, or drawn up on the beach, where houses were built over them to keep the pitch from melting. Baskerville, meantime, found the march on which he had entered "so sore as never Englishman marched before": the way was very narrow, cut through the woods and rocks, and at that season full of mire and water ; and the enemy, knowing the ground well, played upon them from every point of most advantage. When they had advanced some ten leagues, according to their computation, which seems to have measured the distance by the difficulty, they came suddenly upon a fort in a marvellous strait way, by which they needs must pass, and from which, before they were aware, a fire was opened upon them, whereby more than twenty men, including four officers, were killed. This check made Baskerville come to a stand ; and understanding then that if he succeeded in taking this fort † there were two other such on the way, and that

* Hakluyt, 586.

† Fuller says : " They had so much of this breakfast, they thought they should surfeit of a dinner and supper of the same. No hope of conquest, except with cloying the jaws of death, and thrusting men on the mouth of the cannon. Wherefore, fearing to find the proverb true, that gold may be bought too dear, they returned to their ships " (*Holy State*, 130).

Panama had been rendered very strong, "the Spaniards knowing of their coming long before," he thought it necessary to return; for which resolution, mortifying as it was, there was this farther urgent motive, that his men had no food left, nor any means of getting it. There had either been great improvidence on his part in not being better provided, or Drake had relied upon his old friends the Maroons, who on this occasion failed him. He returned, therefore, with a weary, hungry, and dispirited army to Nombre de Dios on the fourth day. *

Nor was this the last disaster that befell this unfortunate expedition. There was an Indian settlement some half a league inland, toward which a detachment of about 100 men advanced, while Drake and Baskerville were with a watering party in the river about a mile distant. The Indians broke down a bridge to impede their passage, and from an ambush killed an officer, and wounded several others; then taking to flight, fired their own houses, thereby manifesting the deep hatred against the English with which the Spaniards had now possessed them. On the 5th the fleet departed, having tarried there too long, and on the 10th anchored off an island called Escudo, some thirty leagues westward of Nombre de Dios, and nine or ten from the main. There was good anchorage there, on fair sand, in twelve fathoms, and the island was covered with wood, and abounded with excellent water. Here they washed their ships, and set up the rest of their pinnaces. But this also was "a sickly climate, and given to much rain: one of the captains died here, and Drake began to keep his cabin, being extremely sick of a flux". Death was now busy in the fleet. Two more captains and the chief surgeon died of the prevailing sickness. On the night of the 27th, Drake's disease stopped on him, but there was no symptom of amendment. His mind seems to have wandered at three in the morning: "he

* Hakluyt, 586, 587.

used some speeches a little before his death, rising and apparelling himself; but, being brought to his bed again, he died within an hour". Some have asserted that he was poisoned; * but of this there is neither proof nor probability: the climate was poison enough, and a wounded spirit †may, perhaps, have predisposed the body to imbibe it. ‡

* " Sir Francis Drake," says Monson, " who was wont to rule fortune, now finding his error, and the difference between the present strength of the Indies and what it was when he first knew it, grew melancholy upon this disappointment, and suddenly (and I hope naturally) died at Puerto Bello, not far from the place where he got his first reputation " (p. 167). And again (p. 368): " Fortune did much for him; but at his death she was angry with him: first, in that there was a doubt whether it was natural; secondly (and the best his friends can say), that it was caused by grief, for failing of his expectation in that voyage ".

Lope de Vega represents his own people as giving him poison, at the instigation of one of the furies. " Drake," he says, " was aware of this intention, and would taste no food till it had been tasted; upon which they administered the poison *en una medicina*, and by that means reached his heart.

"Mirad la desventura la ruina
De aquel hombre atrevido y indomable!
Mirad que triste genero de muerte
Del cuerpo el alma a los infiernos vierte."

Dragontea, p. 472.

† This was Fuller's opinion, who had heard the particulars from a kinsman of Drake's present in the expedition. His account is, that Sir Francis's discontent began " to feed upon him. He conceived that expectation—a merciless usurer—computing each day since his departure, exacted an interest and return of honour and profit proportionable to his great preparations, and transcending his former achievements. He saw that all the good which he had done in this voyage consisted in the evil he had done to the Spaniards afar off; whereof he could present but small visible proofs in England. These apprehensions, accompanying, if not causing, the disease of the flux, wrought his sudden death. And sickness did not so much untie his clothes, as sorrow did rend at once the robe of his mortality asunder " (p. 130).

‡ Hakluyt, 587, 588.

The fleet anchored the same day at Puerto Bello; and it was in sight of that place "from whence he had borrowed so large a reputation by his fortunate successes" that Drake received a sailor's funeral, * his body in a leaden coffin being committed to the deep, with the solemn service of the English Church, rendered more impressive by volleys of musketry, and firing of guns in all the ships of the fleet. He had made his will, appointing Thomas his brother and Captain Jonas Bodenham executors, and leaving all his lands to that brother's son, except one manor, which he bequeathed to Bodenham. †

The remaining history of the expedition may briefly be told. Baskerville succeeded to the command of the admiral, Bodenham to the *Defiance*. They found nothing to plunder at Puerto Bello and little to destroy. A council was held, and it was determined to "turn up again for Santa Martha," if by any means they could, otherwise to go directly for England; their whole number at this time, sick and sound, amounting only to 2000. Baskerville put all his prisoners

---

* Instead of an epitaph, these verses were written on him :—
  "Where Drake first found, there last he lost his name,
  And for a tomb left nothing but his fame.
  His body's buried under some great wave;
  The sea, that was his glory, is his grave:
  On whom an epitaph none can truly make,
  For who can say, '*Here* lies Sir Francis Drake'?"

"Nor shall I here pass over in silence," Prince adds, "what another in those days added on the same occasion :—
  "'The waves became his winding sheet, the waters were his tomb;
  But for his fame the ocean sea was not sufficient room'."

The notice of his death in the *Indice Chronologico Peruano* is curious for its double error, and as showing how important a personage he appeared to the Spaniards: "El año de 96 murió Francisco Draque el Cosario que dio tanto cuidado en ambos mares. Su muete fue de enfermedad en Portobelo. Su madre le abia parido en un navio en el mar, y fue harto muriesse en tierra."

† Hakluyt, 588.

ashore; an act of commendable humanity on his part, for two of them had been liberated on condition of returning with the ransom agreed on for some of the rest, and nothing had been heard of them. It was an act of consideration also for those of his own people who were in the Spaniards' hands. As he was setting sail, there came one with a flag of truce, to say that, if he would tarry eight or ten days, eighteen of his men, who had been taken prisoners and well used, should be brought to him from Panama. The Spaniards were probably sincere in this; but the English supposed their offer was meant only as "a delay to keep them there till the king's forces had come about by sea, as they daily expected"; and, perhaps, they were as desirous of hastening from that deadly region as of escaping a conflict with a far superior force. So they departed; and not being able to hold their course for Santa Martha, fell in off the Isle of Pinos with twenty sail, which having been refreshed at the Havannah, were then standing for Cape de los Corrientes. This was a third part of the Carthagena fleet, which was sent out with instructions to seek the English with its whole force wheresoever they might be heard of. "As soon as they descried us," says the writer, "they kept close upon a track, thinking to get the wind of us, but we weathered them. And when our admiral with all the rest of our fleet were right in the wind's eye of them, Sir Thomas Baskerville putting out the queen's arms, and all the rest of our fleet their bravery, bare room with them, and commanded the *Defiance* not to shoot, but to keep close by to succour him. The vice-admiral of the Spaniards being a greater ship than any of ours, and the best sailer in all their fleet, luffed by and gave the *Concord* the two first great shot, which she repaid presently again. Thus the fight began: the *Bonaventura* bare full with her, ringing her such a peal of ordnance and small shot withal, that he left her with torn sides. The admiral, also, made no spare of powder and shot. But the *Defiance*, in the midst of the Spanish fleet, thundering off her ordnance and small shot, continued the fight to the end; so that the vice-admiral and three or four of her consorts were forced to tack about to the eastward, leaving their admiral and the rest of the fleet, who came not so hotly into the fight as they did. The fight continued two hours and better. At sunset all the fleet tacked about to the eastward: we continued our course to the westward. That night, some half hour after, their fleet keeping upon their weather quarter, we saw a mighty smoke rise out of one of their great ships which stayed behind, which happened by means of powder, as we think; and presently after she was all on a light fire, and so was consumed, and all burnt, as we might well perceive." *

The English were evidently so weak that they did not seek a renewal of the action, and the Spaniards were glad to shun it. Baskerville touched at Flores on his way home, and there landed two Portuguese pilots whom they had taken with them from England. They reached Plymouth early in May; and as the expedition had utterly disappointed the expectation which had been encouraged of its success, Baskerville seems to have obtained little credit † for the concluding action in which he had deserved much. If Hawkins and Drake had returned, their characters, and the signal services which both had formerly performed, were such, that

---

* Hakluyt, 588, 589.

† Camden says: " Baskerville and Troughton, the latter in the vice-admiral, the other in the admiral, did so entertain the Spaniards, that with small loss received and greater given (if a man may believe them), our fleet escaped" (502). Monson's account is not more favourable: " Baskerville," he says, " met and fought with a fleet of Spain; though not long, by reason of the sickness and weakness of his men. This fleet was sent to take the advantage of ours on its return; thinking, as indeed it happened, that they should find them both weak and in want: but the swiftness of our ships, in which we had the advantage of the Spaniards, preserved us" (167). Monson here ascribes to the ships what was due to the courage of the sailors.

they would have retained their place in the queen's judgment, and soon have recovered it in the opinion of the people. There were no two commanders in that age whose names inspired their followers with more confidence, or struck so much fear into their enemies. Drake, indeed, has attained the highest degree of fame : no other military or naval name is so universally known among his countrymen ; and it is the only one of modern history which has acquired in local tradition a sort of mythological celebrity. This probably originated with the Spaniards, who may truly be said to have honoured his memory in the bitterness of their enmity towards him. Two days' holidays were kept at Panama for his death and damnation ; and the most popular of the Spanish poets composed an epic poem to revile him. It was likely, according to a Spaniard's belief, that being a heretic Drake should have dealings with the devil ; that notion prevented them from feeling any mortification at his successes, which they imputed to the devil's aid ; and it enhanced their exultation over the failure of his last expedition, which they considered as the triumph of their religion over heresy and magic. The imputation of magic, when it reached his own country, was readily received, not by the Hispaniolised Romanists alone, with whose persuasions political and religious it accorded, but by the common people also, who believed that there was a white as well as a black art magic ; and that Drake, like Shakespeare's Prospero, and Friars Bacon and Bungay, with whom they were better acquainted, employed the spirits under his command only in good works.

The fables which have been grafted upon this belief are fanciful enough for the legend of a British or Irish saint. According to the popular traditions of the western counties, it was not by his skill as an engineer, and the munificent expenditure of wealth the which he had so daringly obtained, that Drake supplied Plymouth with fresh water ; but by mounting his horse, riding about Dartmoor till he came to a spring sufficiently copious for his design, then wheeling round, pronouncing some magical words, and galloping back into the town, with the stream in full flow, and forming its own channel at the horse's heels. Nor was it with the queen's ships that he defied and baffled the Invincible Armada, but by taking a piece of wood and cutting it in pieces over the side of his own vessel, when every chip as it fell into the sea became a man of war. There is another version of this miracle,—that he was playing at *kalcs* (or skittles) on the Hoe at Plymouth, when tidings came that the Spanish fleet was sailing into the harbour, and that he heard the news without the slightest emotion, and played out his game. But when that was ended he called for a block of wood and an axe, bared his arms, chopped the block into smaller pieces, and threw them into the sea, when every piece became a fine ship, and presently formed a fleet by which the enemy were attacked and destroyed.

To sail round the world was in the popular belief an adventure of the most formidable kind, and not to be performed by plain sailing, but by reaching the end of this round flat earth, and there shooting the gulf, which is the only passage from one side of the world to the other: Drake shot the gulf, one day: when on the other side, he asked his men if any of them knew where they were, a boy made answer that he knew, and that they were then just under London Bridge: upon which, stung by jealousy, Drake exclaimed, "Hast thou too a devil? If I let thee live there will then be one greater man than myself"; and with that he threw him overboard. When Sir Francis left home to embark for this long voyage, upon taking leave of his wife, he told her that if he did not return within a certain number of years she might conclude him to be dead, and consider herself at liberty to take a second husband. One version fixes the term at seven years, another at ten. During those years, Madam Drake, though assailed by many suitors, remained true as Penelope to her absent lord; but after the term had expired, she accepted an offer. One of Drake's ministering spirits, whose charge it was to convey to him any intelligence in which he was nearly concerned, brought him the tidings. Immediately he loaded one of his great guns, and fired it right down through the globe on one side, and up on the other, with so true an aim, that it made its way into the church, between the two parties most concerned, just as the marriage service was beginning. " It comes from Drake!" cried the wife to the now unbrided bridegroom; "he is alive! and there must be neither troth nor ring between thee and me." This is the Devonshire tradition of the "old warrior," as they call him, and his lady. The story in Somersetshire is, that as they were on the way to church a huge round stone fell from the sky, close by the intended bride, and alighted upon the train of her gown. She said, " It came from my husband," and immediately turned back; and it was not long before he returned, and, imitating Guy, Earl of Warwick, asked alms of her at his own door in disguise: a smile betrayed that he was telling a feigned tale, and the faithful wife recognised him, and fell upon his neck. It is said that the stone still remains upon the estate where it fell; that it is there used as a weight upon the harrow; and is so well contented with this usage, unceremonious as for so extraordinary a relic it may be deemed, that if it be removed from the estate, it always returns thither, no person knows how.

This is the latest instance in which such fictions have been invented unconnected with Romish fraud or sectarian fanaticism; and it shows how strongly the romantic character of Drake's exploits, and the extraordinary celebrity which he obtained, impressed the imagination of his countrymen. He left a widow, Elizabeth, daughter and sole heiress of Sir George Sydenham, of Combe-Sydenham, in the county of Devon: she afterwards married William Courtenay, Esq., of

Powderham Castle. He had no children, and of his eleven brothers nine also died childless. The property which he left was much diminished by a prosecution which the crown instituted against his executor Thomas Drake, for what is said to have been "a pretended debt": it would have been becoming in the government to have relinquished even a just claim. Drake, however, though a bountiful man, possessed the virtue of economy; and the estate which remained placed his nephew in such a station that he was created a baronet by James I., and represented the county of Devon in the beginning of the ensuing reign. Sir Francis himself was twice returned to Parliament for Bossiney *alias* Tintagal in Cornwall, afterwards for Plymouth. He was of low stature, but well set; his chest broad, his hair a fine brown, his beard full and comely, his head remarkably round, his eyes large and clear, his complexion fair, and the expression of his fresh and cheerful countenance open and engaging. His temper was quick, and he is said to have been "hard to be reconciled"; but the same strength of feeling made him constant in friendship. The gift of eloquence he possessed in a remarkable degree, and was fond of displaying it. One who served under him says that he was ambitious to a fault; and the vanity which usually accompanies that sin laid him open to flattery: but he encouraged and preferred merit wherever he found it; and his affable manners gave him a sure hold upon the affections of his men, while they had the most perfect confidence in his unrivalled skill as a seaman, and his never-failing promptitude in all cases of emergency. At all times he was a willing hearer of every man's opinion; but for the most part—as a truly great man for the most part must be—a follower of his own.

Hawkins led the way to the West Indies, Drake to the South Sea; opening thereby a course for adventurers who at length rivalled the vikingar in atrocity. The effect upon the Spanish colonies was most injurious; for rising and flourishing settlements were some subverted, and others removed into the interior, to be beyond the reach of a descent: hereby much growing civilisation was destroyed, and the people were withdrawn from the influence of maritime commerce, which is of all things most conducive to its progress. The expeditions undertaken in Elizabeth's reign against the Spaniards are said to have produced no advantage to England in any degree commensurate with the cost of money and expense of life with which they were performed, though great evil was inflicted upon the enemy. If the advantage were to be calculated by the rule of profit and loss, and consisted only in tangible gain, this would be undeniable; but the effects produced upon the navy and upon the national character must be taken into the account. In these expeditions it was that those seamen were trained by whose skill, so far as human skill was rendered instrumental in our deliverance, the Spanish armada was averted from our shores; and a succession of such seamen has from that time been uninterruptedly maintained from generation to generation.

THOMAS CAVENDISH

THE most successful of all those adventurers who followed in Drake's track was Thomas Cavendish, who was born to a large possession and a fine mansion at Trimley St. Martin, in the county of Suffolk. Having in a few years almost consumed his whole estate in extravagance, and following the court, he "thought to recover himself by a voyage into the South Sea, at a time when the war having openly begun it was lawful to make any spoil upon the Spaniards". This resolution was taken while he had yet means enough remaining from the waste of his fortune to build from the stocks one ship of 120 and one of 60 tons, to purchase a barque of 40, fit them out, and victual them for two years; and with 123 persons of all sorts in this little squadron he sailed from Plymouth on the 21st of July, 1586. The names of his vessels were the *Desire*, the *Content* and the *Hugh Gallant*.

They made the Canaries on the 5th of August, and on the 26th anchored at Sierra Leone. The next day two negroes came aboard, but not without first requiring that a hostage should be sent ashore for their own security; for European villainy had taught them the necessity of such a precaution. They informed him by signs that there was a Portuguese ship farther up the river; and the *Hugh Gallant* was sent after her; but, after going three or four leagues up, returned for want of a pilot, "for the harbour runneth up three or four leagues more, and is of a marvellous breadth, and very dangerous". On the morrow some of the men went ashore, and played and danced all the forenoon with the negroes, with a view to learning some good news of the ship on which they had fixed their hopes. They spied a Portuguese among the bushes, whom they seized and carried aboard: the account of the navigation which they obtained from him convinced them that it was prudent to leave the ship unmolested; "Whereupon," says Master Francis Pretty, of Ely in Suffolk, a gentleman employed in the voyage, "we went not to seek her, because we knew he told us the truth; for we bound him, and made him fast, and so examined him". Whether this means that they tortured him is uncertain, and is of little consequence to the character of this commander. Cavendish landed the next day with some seventy men, and for no assigned provocation attacked the negro town, burnt some of the houses, and took what little spoil was worth taking. In consequence, when his people were watering and washing "very quietly afterwards, they were suddenly attacked, many of them hurt, and one mortally wounded". *

They now sailed for Brazil, went in between the Island of St. Sebastians and the shore, landed, and remained there from the 1st of November to the 23rd, building a pinnace, repairing their casks and completing their water. While they were thus employed, a canoe, bound from Rio de Janeiro to San Vicente, fell into their hands. One Portuguese was on board, with six naked Indian slaves. The Portuguese knew the master of the admiral, who had been at St. Vicente in the *Minion* of London five years before. There was an Englishman residing then at the port, probably the first of his nation who settled in Brazil: by his means Cavendish thought to obtain fresh provisions, little caring to what after account his countryman might be called for communicating with him; so pretending to the Portuguese

* Hakluyt, iii., 803, 804. Burney, iv., 84, 85.

that they were merchants, and would gladly traffic with him, he set him at liberty, on condition of his carrying a letter to Whital, and returning with an answer, or sending one in ten days. The distance was about twenty leagues. But the merchant seems to have been too wary to hold any intercourse with so suspicious a squadron: nothing more was heard of the messenger; and Cavendish, having despatched his business, sailed toward the south, and on the 17th of December anchored in a harbour, which he named Port Desire, the discovery of which is the only one of any importance that can be attributed to him.* This being a good place for laying the ships aground, they "graved and trimmed them" there, finding, meantime, "marvellous good meat" in the young seals, which, "being roasted or boiled, were hardly to be known from lamb or mutton"; and in the penguins, which burrowed in the ground like rabbits. †

The greatest inconvenience in this port was the want of fresh water. The best they could obtain was by digging, and that proved brackish; and some of their people, while engaged at this well, were attacked with bows and arrows by about fifty Indians. Two of them were severely wounded, and the savages were pursued in vain by Cavendish himself and some twenty men. These Indians had old wrongs to avenge, and nothing is more tenaciously remembered in that stage of society. On the 6th of January Cavendish arrived at the entrance of the straits, and in the evening anchored near what is called the first Angostura, or Strait of the Straits. During the night lights were observed on the north shore, apparently intended as signals to the ships, and lights accordingly were shown as answers. In the morning Cavendish went himself in a boat to that side of the strait, and three men were seen on the shore waving a white flag. Upon this the boat stood in: it was asked, in Spanish, what

---

* Burney, 93. † Hakluyt, 804, 805. Burney, 66.

ships they were? and answered in the same language that they were English, bound for Peru. Bitterly, no doubt, disappointed by this reply, the Spaniards were silent, till the English spokesman told them that if they chose to embark, the general would carry them to Peru. To this the reply was, that they would not trust themselves to the English for fear they should be thrown into the sea. The interpreter made answer they might very well trust themselves, for the English were better Christians than they. With this the boat put off, leaving them to abide by their own determination. But they presently considered that it were better at any risk to embark than remain where they must inevitably perish; and they called after the boat, which put back, took one of them aboard, Tomé Hernandez by name, and again pushed off, not receiving the other two. Hernandez entreated that they also might be taken, in reply to which Cavendish inquired how many Spaniards there were in those parts? The answer was, twelve more men and three women. Cavendish then bade him tell his companions to go to them, and bid them all come and embark, and he would wait for them. With this joyful message the poor men went their way. But when Cavendish got on board again, the wind was fair for advancing up the straits: he ordered the anchors to be taken up; and not thinking it proper to lose, even for two or three hours, a fair wind for the sake of humanity, sailed away.*

These men belonged to an expedition, which, in consequence of Drake's appearance in the South Sea, had been sent from Spain to fortify the strait, and form settlements there. The viceroy of Peru, D. Francisco de Toledo, apprehending, from the daring conduct of such an enemy, and that enemy an English heretic, that nothing less than the Spanish dominion in those seas, with the property, bodies,

* *Viage al Estreche*, etc., Declaracion de Tomé Hernandez, xvi.-xviii. Burney, ii., 67-70. Hakluyt, 806.

and souls of the inhabitants, was at stake,* had with great personal exertions and extraordinary speed despatched Captain Pedro Sarmiento de Gamboa, with two ships, to survey the strait, and take especial notice of all places therein which appeared convenient for a settlement, or to be fortified for guarding the passage. When this service was performed he was to send one ship back with advices to Lima, and proceed in the other to Spain to lay the business before the king and the supreme council of the Indies. Part of his instructions was, that he was to take and carry away some of the natives, in order to acquire by that means some knowledge of their language. Sarmiento, though abandoned by his consort, completed with great diligence and ability the service on which he was sent. He marked two points near the eastern entrance, in the narrowest part, as well adapted for defence; the breadth at the westernmost being a geographical league and a half, at the easternmost less than half a league; and he made it known to all men by a declaration, a copy of which was buried there in an earthen jar at the foot of a cross, which he erected pursuant to the usual form of taking possession, that "having, in conformity to the viceroy's instructions, taken our most serene Lady, the Virgin St. Mary, for the advocate and patroness of this voyage, for that reason, and because of the wonders which, through her intercession, had been wrought in its behalf, he had given to the strait formerly called after Magellan the name of Estrecho de la Madre de Dios,—the Strait of the Mother of God". †

When Sarmiento arrived in Spain he proposed that both shores of the eastern Angostura should be fortified, whereby, in his opinion, the passage would be completely defended; and he represented that there were places within the strait convenient for the settlement of colonies. The Duke of Alva opposed the project, though his own son had originated it: "if a ship," he said, "only carried out anchors and cables

* *Viage*, etc., 4. † *Ibid.*, 239. Burney, ii., 39.

enough for her security against the storms in that part of the world, she would go well laden". But it was believed by the Spanish government at that time that the English were making preparations for establishing themselves in the strait, and so taking possession of the passage; and under this belief an armament of twenty-three ships and 3500 men was equipped at Seville for South America. Diego Flores de Valdes was appointed commander; and with the whole fleet, which was formed into three divisions, each for a separate service, he was first to sail for the straits, and there assist Sarmiento in planting the projected colony, for the use of which one division was allotted. That done, another division was to proceed to Chili, and the third put back to Brazil. This expedition sailed at the autumnal equinox, against the pilots' remonstrance, but by peremptory orders from the government; and on the eighth day after leaving Seville, while yet near their own coast, five of the ships went down in a violent storm from the S.W., and 800 men perished. The remainder put back to Cadiz in distress, two of them being totally disabled for service.*

It was December before the fleet, now reduced in number to sixteen, was again ready for sea; and as the season was thought too far advanced for their proceeding directly to the strait, they were ordered to winter at Rio de Janeiro. Sarmiento and other officers objected against this port, because the ships, while lying there, would be liable to much injury from the worm. This objection, like that of the pilots at their first outset, was disregarded. The fleet sailed, stopped a month at the Cape de Verds, and took from thence a disease which carried off 150 men during the passage to Brazil, where they arrived toward the end of March: as many more died while they remained at the Rio, and many of the intended settlers (happily for themselves) deserted, and remained in a

* Burney, 45, 46.

good country. Here the frames of a brigantine and launch, intended for service in the strait, were set up, and those of two wooden houses were made for immediate use on their arrival there. But the evil which Sarmiento anticipated took place; the ships were attacked by the worm; several became leaky; one was abandoned as unserviceable; and when, at the end of November, the fleet proceeded on its destination, the brigantine and launch were lost in the first boisterous weather; and one of the largest ships, of 500 tons, with most of the stores for the new colony on board, and 350 persons, twenty of whom had embarked as female settlers, sprung so fatal a leak, that before any assistance could reach her she went down. Disheartened by this last calamity, Valdes put back toward Brazil, and, before he reached the island of St. Catalina, another of his ships was wrecked on the coast. After some dispute between the commanders it was at length agreed to make another attempt; but three of the largest ships were now in too shattered a state for such a service, and they were left here with 300 of the sick and least serviceable men, and with orders to return to the Rio.*

Once more this unfortunate fleet set forth for the strait, and as they were leaving the island another ship got on a bank, and was wrecked. Sarmiento's vessel became leaky and unfit for proceeding: it was again taken into consideration what should be done, and, against the opinion of Valdes, the determination was to persevere; but it was agreed that the part of the force which was intended for Chili, and which was now contained in three vessels, should make for the Plata, and from thence proceed to their destination by land. The remainder of the fleet, now reduced to five, arrived on the 7th of February in the mouth of the strait, and cast anchor in the first Angostura. During the night they were forced out by a gale of wind; and after beating about till the

* Burney, 47, 48.

end of March, without being able to regain an entrance, Valdes returned in despair to Rio de Janeiro. There they found four ships from Spain, laden with stores for their use, and bringing letters which exhorted the chiefs to perseverance. Valdes, however, quitted the command, and sailed for Europe, leaving Diego de la Ribera to act in his stead. On the 2nd of December the expedition again sailed, consisting now of five ships and 530 souls. They arrived safely in the strait on the 1st of February, passed the first Angostura, and anchored between it and the second; but the ebb tide forced them from their anchors, and carried them back into the open sea. They anchored again close to Cape de las Virgenes, and because Ribera would risk no farther loss of time, there they began to disembark. Three hundred persons had landed, when, on the 5th, a gale of wind compelled the ships to quit the anchorage; on regaining it one of them ran aground within the entrance, and was wrecked: the people, artillery, and provisions were saved, but the provisions damaged. Before all the stores could be landed, Ribera, with three ships, left the strait during the night, and returned to it no more. He has been reproached as if he had wilfully abandoned the settlers, and sailed for Spain; but it is more likely that he was forced from his anchors, and that his people, finding the opportunity favourable, insisted upon bending their course for Spain. *

Sarmiento was now left with one ship, 400 men, thirty women, and eight months' provisions. He laid the foundation of a town near the entrance, on the north side, and named it the City of the Name of Jesus, *la Ciudad del Nombre de Jesus*. Leaving Andres de Viedma in the command there with 150 men, he sent the ship to Point St. Anna, which is on the same shore, about twenty-five Spanish leagues within the first Angostura, while he, with 100 men, proceeded

* Burney, 50-52.

thither by land. During a difficult and inauspicious march skirmishes took place with the Indians, whom he should have sought by every possible means to conciliate: several of his own people were wounded, and one of their chiefs killed. Near the point he founded his second town, which he called San Felipe: the situation was well chosen. There was a port with good anchorage, from whence a boat could reach the first Angostura in one tide: there was a fresh-water river, the country was well wooded, the port abounded with fish, and the shore with birds; but the snow which, during the month of April, fell for fifteen days, without intermission, made the unfortunate Spaniards apprehend what sort of winter they might expect in this inhospitable region. This, however, was to be their abiding place: they surrounded it with a strong palisade, and at each of its three entrances, one towards the port, the other towards the interior, planted two pieces of artillery. Sarmiento, nevertheless, found it necessary for his own security to sleep every night on board, lest the dissatisfaction which was felt toward him as the promoter of so disastrous an undertaking should break into open mutiny, and end in his destruction. In fact, he was secretly informed that a soldier, by name Juan Rodriguez, and Alonso Sanchez, a secular priest, had formed a conspiracy for murdering him, seizing the ship, and escaping in it to Brazil. Of this information he made such good use, that he got Rodriguez, the priest, and three others of the ringleaders, on board, and charged them with their guilt. They confessed it: the four lay culprits were taken ashore, labelled as traitors on their shoulders; they were beheaded backwards for the greater infamy, and their heads exposed upon poles. The priest was kept prisoner on board. This execution is said to have made the settlers quiet and peaceable; and Sarmiento, with thirty men, left them for Nombre de Jesus on the 25th of May: his intention was to give directions for fortifying the Angosturas, to convey more settlers to San Felipe, and then sail for Chili in order to obtain supplies.*

He reached Nombre de Jesus, was driven from his anchorage, and, after contending twenty days against the weather, saw that his only course must be to steer for Brazil, and there obtain provisions, which it was now impossible for him to seek in Chili. It was midwinter in those regions when he arrived at Rio de Janeiro. There he procured a barque, loaded her with meal, and, leaving directions for her to sail at the proper season, proceeded along the coast in search of further supplies: his ship was driven ashore and wrecked, many of the crew perished, and he himself with difficulty escaped on a plank. He procured another barque, freighted her with necessaries for his colony, and sailed in her from the Rio: but when he had got as far as 39° S. a storm compelled him to throw everything overboard, and return to the port from whence he had departed more than seven weeks before; and where he found that the vessel which he had first despatched had put back without effecting her passage. Hitherto Sarmiento, when he reflected upon his multiplied disappointments, could call none but the elements unkind; but the Portuguese governors were now weary of his solicitations: they had learned from Spain that both he and his undertaking were out of favour there; Ribera having reported on his return that the strait was more than a league across in its narrowest part, and that if a ship had wind and current in her favour no ordnance on shore could stop her. Sarmiento, therefore, as a last resource, sailed for Spain, there to justify his own statements, and, it may be hoped, to urge upon the government the duty of taking some measures for the relief of the miserable settlers. After his departure, the governor of the Rio sent one ship with supplies for them; but this vessel also was driven back, and no farther effort was made for their relief, either by the

---

* Burney, 52-54. Tomé Hernandez, viii.-xiii.

colonial governors or Spain : those in America, upon whom any responsibility might be supposed to lie, transferred it in their own minds each from himself to another ; and all, no doubt, rested in the persuasion, that the Spanish government, having planted the colony, would take all necessary measures for preserving it. But in Spain ample provision having been made in fitting out the expedition, the possibility of so many losses, and of such repeated failures, had evidently never been considered as it ought. If Sarmiento's ill fortune had not still pursued him, his personal representations might, probably, have produced some effect in Spain. But he was captured by some English cruisers off the Azores, and carried to England ; and though Elizabeth, it is said, gave him his liberty, after an interview in which she conversed with him in Latin, provided him with a passport, and presented him with 1000 crowns, various misadventures retarded for some years his return to his own country. And from the time he left the straits no vessel reached them till Cavendish appeared there.*

There are few tales in colonial history more calamitous than the fate of this forlorn and forsaken colony. Sarmiento had left them at the end of May. In August (which corresponds to our February, and is, therefore, one of the severest months in that miserable climate), the settlers at Nombre de Jesus thought it necessary to remove to San Felipe. Thither, accordingly, they went by land ; but Viedma, who commanded there, having no provisions for such increased numbers, sent 200 men back under Juan Iniguez, to support themselves as they could by picking up shell fish, and in other ways, and to be on the look-out for a ship with succours. Spring and summer passed, and no relief : winter was approaching ; and lest those at San Felipe, who had thus long endured, should irremediably perish of

* Burney, 54,-56. Hernandez, xiv.-xviii.

hunger, as they must if they remained there, Viedma built two boats, embarked in them with all the survivors there, then reduced to fifty men, five women, a friar, Sarmiento's nephew, Juan Suarez, and Viedma himself. They had proceeded some six leagues toward Nombre de Jesus, when one of the boats got upon a reef and was lost. The people were saved; but in so hopeless a situation that it was deemed best for Viedma to return in the other boat with the friar and twenty men, and for the remainder to remain where they got to shore, hut themselves there, and find provisions as they could. The seals and penguins, of which our navigators made such use, were inaccessible to them; and they divided themselves into small parties of three or four, for the better chance of finding wherewith to prolong a wretched existence. When summer came, and Viedma collected the survivors, only fifteen men and three women were left; and with these Viedma was endeavouring to reach Nombre de Jesus when the English ships appeared. They had passed on their way many dead bodies of their countrymen. *

The utter want of compassion with which Cavendish left these poor wretches to their fate, after he had promised to take them on board, excited no animadversion in his own times. The single Spaniard, who was fortunate enough to escape with him, relates it without any expression of feeling: the weather was fair for sailing, he says, and he did not choose to wait. Whether there were any survivors at that time at Nombre de Jesus is not known: probably not; for it may well be supposed that they also would have made signals to the ships. An English vessel which entered the strait in the year following took one Spaniard on board near San Felipe: he had supported himself with his gun, having long lived in a house by himself, being the last survivor of these poor colonists; and, except Hernandez, the only one who

* Burney, 71-73.

escaped from the deplorable situation in which their government had first placed and then abandoned them. All that is known of the others, whom Cavendish might have saved, is that their intention was to travel towards the Plata, and that they must have perished on the way.

At San Felipe, which had been founded for the sole purpose of securing the passage of the strait against all foreigners, the English ships "watered and wooded well and quietly, and remained there five days thus employed". The journalist of Cavendish's voyage says, "they had contrived their city very well, and seated it in the best place of the straits for wood and water". By his account there were four forts, each having one cast piece: the pieces had been dismantled and buried, but the English dug for them, and "had them all". "They had built their churches apart," he says, "and they had laws very severe," of which the gibbet bore certain proof. But all attempts to raise provision having failed, their stores being consumed, and game rendered so scarce and wild that it was hopeless for men, in their weak state, to go in search of it, they had "died like dogs in their houses, and in their clothes". Thus the survivors, when they took their miserable departure, had left them; and thus they were found by Cavendish, who named the place, in memorial of their fate, Port Famine. That name it still retains in English charts; the Spaniards themselves have adopted it, and *Puerto de Hambre* marks in their maps the place where the Ciudad de San Felipe had been founded!

Cavendish buried one of his men on the northern shore. This was the only loss that he sustained in the passage; but he acted inconsiderately toward the natives, believing them to be treacherous cannibals, on the report of Hernandez, and seeing that they had fastened knives and pieces of swords to their spears.* Instead of endeavouring to make them under-

---

* Hakluyt, 807. Burney, 78.

stand that the English were not their enemies, like the Spaniards, he ordered his men to fire upon them after some friendly intercourse had previously taken place; and in this unprovoked attack many were killed. He entered the South Sea on the 24th of February, with a favourable wind; and in the middle of March a party landed on the Isle of Mocha, near the coast of Chili, "where the Indians attacked them with bows and arrows, but were marvellous wary of the calivers". The English supposed these to be Araucans, whose heroic efforts in defence of their country the Spaniards themselves had rendered famous; recording at the same time the magnanimity of their enemies and their own atrocious cruelty. Cavendish landed next on the Island of St. Maria with seventy men, where they were mistaken for Spaniards, submissively received, and "plentifully supplied with wheat and barley ready threshed, as fair, as clean, and every way as good as any in England; and with potato roots very good to eat," all stored in vessels, and lodged in storehouses, as tribute for the Spaniards, who had erected a church there. In addition to these welcome supplies, the Indians brought them hogs, fowls, maize, and dried dog fish; and Cavendish, in return, entertained some of the chief people on board, and made them merry with wine.*

Missing Valparaiso, where he meant to have stopped, Cavendish anchored about seven leagues N. of that port, in Puerto de Quintero. A herdsman who was sleeping on the brow of the hill at this time awoke; and seeing three ships, was observed to catch a horse that was grazing near, and to ride away as fast as he could. The general landed with thirty men: before he had been an hour on shore, three horsemen came galloping toward them sword in hand; but stopped short at respectful distance. He sent two of his people with Hernandez toward them: they made signs that

* Hakluyt, 808.

only one should approach, and without arms. Hernandez went; and after much talk returned, telling Cavendish that he had parleyed with them concerning provisions, and had been promised as much as might be wanted. He was sent back to complete the negotiation, and a man with him; but, as before, the Spaniards made signs that they would not hold parley with two persons; Hernandez was again trusted; and being at some distance from the English, after a few words he leaped up behind one of his countrymen, and rode off; "for all his deep and damnable oaths which he had made," says Pretty, "continually to our general and all his company, never to forsake him, but to die on his side before he would be false. Our general, seeing how he was dealt withal, filled water all that day with good watch, and carried it aboard; and night being come, he determined next day to send into the country to find their town, and take the spoil of it, and fire it if it could be found." In this he failed; the party which was ordered upon the service discovering nothing but great store of cattle which were "wonderful wild, and of horse which were unhandled," and of dogs as wild as the cattle, on which they fed. They returned after a whole day's march, without loss, though without success in their search for the town. But on the morrow, as they were carelessly watering about a quarter of a mile from the shore, a strong party of horsemen, who had been too cautious to attack them when they were on their guard the preceding day, surprised them, and twelve * of the English were cut off; of these

---

* Pretty states the loss at twelve, and gives the names of all and of the ships to which they belonged. He says the prisoners were rescued, and that some twenty-four Spaniards were killed in the skirmish, which continued an hour. Hernandez says no Spaniard was hurt, twelve English were killed, and nine taken; and he mentions the execution of six of these; the others, perhaps, called themselves Roman Catholics. Admiral Burney thinks this may have been an act of vengeance for the Spaniards in the strait, whom Cavendish, when he might so easily have

three appear to have been slain, and six of the prisoners were hanged at Santiago.

After this loss Cavendish remained in the road four days, and watered in despite of the Spaniards, with good watch and ward. On the 23rd he took a small barque coming out from Arica, which he kept, and named the *George*. The crew took to their boat, and were pursued by the admiral's pinnace into Arica road : they got ashore, and the pinnace laid aboard a great ship of 100 tons, in which, however, neither men nor goods were found. The admiral and the *Hugh Gallant* followed into the road, but the *Content* was out of sight, otherwise Cavendish " would resolutely have landed to take the town, whatsoever had come of it ". The *Content* had been more pleasantly employed than in attacking a town which was likely to be well defended :—she had found at a place where some Spaniards had landed a whole ship's lading of Spanish wine, and tarried to take on board as much as she could conveniently carry, then in the course of the same day joined the squadron. By that time Cavendish perceived that Arica was well prepared for defence, found reason for believing that the treasure had been carried away and secured upon the alarm of his approach, and saw that there was no landing without the loss of many men ; " wherefore he gave over that enterprise ". However, he fetched out another barque, in spite of their forts, and then sent a flag of truce to ask if they would redeem their ship. He did this in hope that he might recover some of his men who had been captured, otherwise he would have made no offer of parley ; but their answer was that they had received special orders neither to buy any ship nor ransom any man on pain of

saved them, had left to perish there. There could be no plea for putting them to death as pirates, because Spain and England were then at open war. But the law of nations was as little regarded by the one people as the other, when there happened to be both inclination and opportunity to violate it.

death : upon this he burnt the ship, sunk the barque, and so departed, having been three days in the road.*

On the 27th they took a small barque sent from a place near Quintero, where Cavendish had lost his men, with despatches concerning him to Lima. There were on board three Spaniards, an old Fleming, and one George a Greek, who was " a reasonable pilot for all the coast of Chili ". In obedience to their orders, and to an oath which had been administered to them by some friars before they set sail, these men, as soon as they saw themselves in danger, threw the despatches overboard ; but Cavendish " wrought so with them," that they confessed their errand : " But he was fain," says his journalist, "to cause them to be tormented with their thumbs in a winch, and to continue them at several times with extreme pain. Also he made the old Fleming believe that he would hang him ; and the rope being about his neck, he was pulled up a little from the hatches ; and yet he would not confess, choosing rather to die than be perjured. In the end it was confessed by one of the Spaniards ; whereupon we burnt the barque, and carried the men with us." This cruelty was a work of supererogation, for which there was no such pretext as in those days was thought to justify such actions. After plundering two little settlements, the ships were all separated for awhile, during which time the *Hugh Gallant*, with sixteen hands, captured, after half an hour's fight, a ship of 300 tons with a crew of twenty-four men. They took from her her foresails, and left her, " seven leagues from land, very leaky and ready to sink " :—it is to be hoped the men were taken out. On the 17th of May the fleet was again collected ; two other prizes meantime had been captured, of which one " would have been worth 20,000*l*. in England, or in any other place of Christendom, where it might have been sold ". They took out as much as

* Hakluyt, 809, 810. Burney, 82.

they could stow, and burnt the rest with the ship. The men and women, "who were not killed," were set on shore. *

The next enterprise was at Paita. Cavendish anchored in the road, landed with sixty or seventy men, and drove the inhabitants out of the town, " which was very well built, and marvellous clean kept in every street, with a town-house in the midst, and to the number of 200 houses at the least ". This flourishing place he burnt to the ground, he and his people deriving no other advantage from this exploit than twenty-five pounds' weight of silver among them, and the satisfaction of reflecting upon the mischief they had done. Thence they went to the Island of Puna, where most of the cables used in the South Sea were made : there they sunk a ship " with all her furniture," which was lying ready to be hauled ashore, being in " a special good place for that purpose ". It was learnt from an Indian, whom they took at sea, that the lord of the island, with most of the inhabitants, had fled to the mainland, seeing his fleet, when (luckily for them) it was becalmed ; and that they had taken with them treasure to the amount of 100,000 crowns. This lord was an Indian cacique, who, " by reason of his pleasant habitation, and of his great wealth, had got a beautiful Spanish woman for his wife ". His " sumptuous house," which stood by the water-side, was " marvellous well contrived, with very many singular good rooms and chambers ; and out of every chamber was framed a gallery, with a stately prospect to the sea on one side, and into the island on the other, with a marvellous great hall below, and a very great storehouse at one end, filled with jars of pitch, and bass for making cables. On one side was a fair garden, in which were fig trees, that bore continually, pompions, melons, cucumbers, radishes, rosemary, and thyme, with many other herbs and fruits. There was a well in this garden, and a cotton plantation round it. On

---

* Hakluyt, 810, 811. Burney, 83.

the other side was an orchard, stocked with oranges, sweet and sour, lemons, limes, and pomegranates. Hard by was a very large and great church, with five bells. There were at least 200 houses in the town, near the palace, and as many in one or two towns more upon the island, which is almost as big as the Isle of Wight." *

"This great cacique," says Pretty, "doth make all the Indians upon the island to work and to drudge for him." But if the description be not overcharged, he had brought his island to a degree of civilisation which had not then been exceeded in any part of Spanish America, if it has since. "The Spanish woman, his wife," he continues, "is honoured as a queen, and never goeth on the ground upon her feet; holding it too base a thing for her. But when her pleasure is to take the air, or to go abroad, she is always carried, in a conveyance, like unto a horse-litter, upon four men's shoulders, with a veil or canopy over her, for the sun or the wind; having her gentlewomen still attending about her, with a great troop of the best men of the island." Cavendish had been told by an Indian prisoner that he might easily take the cacique, and the treasure which he had carried off, for the place to which he had retreated consisted of only three or four houses, without any means of defence. Relying upon this, he crossed over to the mainland; and on reaching the place where he designed to land, found there four or five large balsas, which had newly arrived, laden with provisions. Marvelling "what they were and what they meant," Cavendish commanded the Indian to speak the truth, as he valued his life. The poor wretch was bound fast, for torture or for execution—he might well suppose,—or both: he answered, "being very much abashed," says Pretty, "as well as our company were, that he neither knew whence they came, nor who they might be; for there was never a man in any one

* Hakluyt, 811-813.

of the balsas; but he supposed they might have brought threescore soldiers, who he had heard were to go to Guayquil (six leagues from the island), and reinforce the garrison of 100 men, for the better protection of some king's ships then on the stocks there. Not discouraged at this, Cavendish animated his company to the exploit, and marched by night, "along a most desert path in the woods," till he reached the place of which the Indian had truly informed him. * But the cacique had kept a good look-out; the people and the treasure were gone. It would have been rash to pursue the one, and hopeless to search for the other in the woods and in the darkness; and the adventurers were fain to console themselves for their disappointment by regaling upon the food, which they found at the fire, prepared for the cacique's supper.

So little did Cavendish apprehend any activity on the part of the Spaniards, notwithstanding they had received this reinforcement, that he laid the admiral aground at Puna, to examine and clean her bottom; keeping, however, continual watch and ward on the cacique's great house night and day. In an adjacent island he discovered a great quantity of stores which had been removed thither for concealment, with all the cacique's "household stuff, and his chamber-hangings, which were of Cordovan leather, all gilded over, and painted very fair and rich". A Spanish wife had inspired him with a taste for the refinements and luxuries of Spanish civilisation; and he seems to have inspired the Spaniards with more promptitude and resolution than at this time they were wont to display. The English had got their ship into the water again; when, early one morning, every one of the watch being gone abroad marauding, "some one way, some another, some for hens, some for sheep, some for goats," about 100 Spaniards, who had landed during the night, with all the

* Hakluyt, 812.

Indians of the island, came upon them; and of twenty Englishmen who were ashore only eight escaped. In the course of the day, Cavendish landed, with seventy men, to revenge their loss, drove the enemy from the town, set fire to it, and burned it to the ground. He burned, also, four ships which were building on the stocks; burned the church, and brought away the bells, and "made havoc" of the fields, orchards, and gardens; then hauled the vice-admiral ashore "to grave at the same place in despite of the Spaniards," and repaired his pinnace, which they had set on fire, and in which one of his men had perished in the flames. There can be no excuse for the negligence which allowed his people to be a second time surprised, and little for the ferocious spirit of revenge in which he laid waste what, when in evil hour he landed there, was a happy and an improving island. A hundred years * afterwards it had not recovered from the devastation then committed.†

Having remained at Puna eleven days, Cavendish departed on the 5th of June, sunk the *Hugh Gallant* for want of men, proceeded to the coast of New Spain, and there captured a ship in which was one Michael Sancius, a Marseillois by birth, who was one of the best coasters in the South Sea, and who was, therefore, detained "to serve their turn in watering along the coast". He served it another way, by giving them news that a great ship, called the *Santa Anna,* was expected

---

* In Dampier's time there was only one Indian town in the island, consisting of about twenty houses, and a small church. The Indians were all seamen, and the only pilots in those seas. "The houses stand all on posts ten or twelve feet high, with ladders on the outside to go up into them. I did never see the like building anywhere but among the Malayans in the East Indies. They are thatched with palmetto leaves, and their chambers well boarded; in which last they excel the Malayans" (i., 151). What a contrast to the cacique's mansion, with its Cordovan hangings, and its gardens!

† Hakluyt, 813, 814. Burney, 84.

at Acapulco from the Philippines. There were six men more in the prize, whom they took out, together with the sails, ropes, and firewood, and then set the vessel on fire. She was going along the coast to give the alarm; and another vessel, upon the same service, came to the same fate, except that the men got to shore. Cavendish next landed at Guatulco, a town of about 100 houses, which he plundered and burned. In the custom house, "a very fair and large" building, they found 600 bags of indigo, valued at forty crowns each; and 400 bags of cacao, each worth ten crowns. "These cacaos go among them for meat and money: 150 of them are in value one *real* of plate in ready payment. They are very like an almond, but are nothing so pleasant in taste: they eat them, and make drink of them." The Spaniards found these nuts in use as currency among the Mexicans, and learned from that people the preparation of chocolate, which everywhere retains its Mexican name. *

Cavendish burned the church here as he had done at Puna. He might have known that by burning a church he excited, among the Spaniards, greater horror and hatred against England than was felt there when the Spaniards burned an Englishman; sacrilege being a crime less frequent in the one country than cruelty in the other, and a crime by which even criminals were shocked. Advantage was made of this feeling at Guatulco in another way. There was a wooden cross there, five fathoms in height, which, the Spaniards say, Cavendish's men pulled down, smeared it with pitch, piled dry reeds around it, and then endeavoured to consume it by fire. The reeds burned and the pitch,—not so the cross: more and more combustibles were thrown on; and when the invaders re-embarked after three days' tarriance, during all which time they had continued their vain endeavours, they left it under a heap of ashes and burning brands unconsumed.

* Hakluyt, 814.

And when the Spaniards returned to their ruined dwellings, they found it brightened and beautified by its fiery trial, and were consoled for their own injuries by seeing that Heaven had manifested itself in the protection of the holy rood. The cross, before it underwent this assay, had been in good odour: it was made of a fragrant wood which was not known to grow within forty leagues of that place : it had been presumed that one of the Apostles had planted it there, and that one was supposed to have been St. Andrew. Now, however, when it had merits enough of its own, the likelier opinion was preferred that it had been erected when Cortes built some ships there for a voyage of discovery. The report of its miraculous preservation spread far and wide ; and from all parts devotees who could came to visit it, and to carry away fragments, the smallest splinter of which, if cast into the sea, stilled a tempest ; if thrown into a fire, quenched the flames ; and if put in water, changed it into a sovereign medicine. This waste of its substance was not miraculously supplied ; and when about a fifth part only was left, the Bishop of Antiquera removed it to his city, built a chapel for it, and enshrined it there with all possible honours upon a holy day appointed for the occasion. There its history continued to be told to the reproach of the English name. *

Sailing from thence, Cavendish overshot the haven of Acapulco ; and on the 24th of August he landed with thirty men at Puerto de Navidad, where they surprised a man in his bed who had been sent with letters to give the alarm along the coast of Nueva Galicia : they took his despatches, killed his horse, set fire to the town, burnt two ships on the stocks, and re-embarked. In the river of Santiago his people dragged for pearls, and took " some quantity " ; and in the Indian town of Acatlan, from which the inhabitants fled at their approach, they " defaced " a church, the commander being of

---

* Torquemada, l. xvi., c. 28, pp. 205, 206.

the party. The Marseillois by this time had entered thoroughly into the interests of his captors; he guided a party of them from Chaccalla Road to a settlement some two leagues inland, "by a most villainous path through the woods and wilderness": there they surprised three householders, with their wives and children, some Indians, a Portuguese, and a Spanish carpenter; all whom they bound and carried to the seaside. The women were then ordered to fetch "plantains, lemons, oranges, pine-apples, and other fruits, whereof they had abundance"; and when this was done the rest were liberated, except the Portuguese and the carpenter. They tarried five days at the little woody Island of St. Andrew, where they dried and salted as many birds as they thought fit, and killed abundance of seals and yguans, which they describe as "a kind of serpents, with four feet and a long sharp tail; strange to them that have not seen them, but very good meat". In another week they reached the Bay of Mazatlan: "there is a very great river within, but it is barred at the mouth; upon the north side of the bar withal is good fresh water, but there is very evil filling of it, because at low water, it is shoal half a mile off the shore". Their intention of watering here was disappointed, and what little fruit they obtained was "not without danger". *

They trimmed their ships and new built their pinnace at an island about a league from this bay; "and there," says Pretty, "we found fresh water, by the assistance of God, in that our great need, and where no water nor sign of water was before to be perceived; otherwise we had gone back twenty or thirty leagues for it, which might have been occasion that we might have missed our prey we had so long waited for. But God raised one Flores, a Spaniard, which was also a prisoner with us, to make a motion to dig in the sands. Now our general, having had experience once before

* Hakluyt, 815.

of the like, commanded to put his motion in practice; and in digging three feet deep we found very good and fresh water: so we watered our ships, and might have filled 1000 tons more, if we had would." How much suffering might have been averted, and how many lives saved, had it been generally known that filtered water may always thus easily be obtained!

Cavendish now quitted the coast of New Spain, and sailed for the south Cape of California. Within that cape is the bay called Aguada Segura, into which " a fair fresh river falls ". They watered there, and lay off and on from the 14th of October to the 4th of November, looking out for their expected prey, " the winds hanging still westerly ". On that day, between seven and eight in the morning, the admiral's trumpeter going into the top, espied a sail standing in for the cape. The cheerful tidings were presently verified; and Cavendish, " who was no less glad than the cause required, ordered the whole company to put all things in readiness ". That done, he gave chase some three or four hours, standing with the best advantage, and working for the wind: in the afternoon he came up with her, gave a broadside with his great ordnance, and a volley of small shot, and presently laid the enemy aboard. The size of the ship, 700 tons, made it evident that it was the galleon for which they had been lying in wait, the *Santa Anna*, from the Philippines, with the king's treasure on board; and, in his eagerness for such a prize, Cavendish began the fight with more spirit than discretion. When his men, who were not more than sixty in his own vessel, were on their ship's side ready to board, they perceived that the Spaniards "had made fights fore and aft, and laid their sails close to the poop, the midship, and the forecastle," and stood close under their covering, so that not a man was to be seen, from whence they plied their pikes, and threw great stones upon the heads of the assailants so fast, that they beat them off, with the loss of two killed and some four or five wounded. For all this, the English "new trimmed their sails, and fitted every man his furniture, and gave them a fresh encounter with the great ordnance, and also with small shot, raking them through and through". The Spanish captain Don Tomas de Alzola, still, "like a valiant man, stood stoutly to his close fights,"* and this, "second encounter" was resisted as successfully as the first; but Cavendish appears to have fallen off in time to avoid further loss, and to have carried on the remainder of the action with guns, "encouraging his men afresh with the whole noise of trumpets". After an action of five or six hours, the Spaniards being "in danger of sinking by reason of the great shot, some of which were under water, set out a flag of truce, and parleyed for mercy, requesting the English commander to spare their lives and take their goods".

Then, in the characteristic words of one of the fortunate adventurers, "our general of his goodness promised them mercy, and willed them to strike their sails, and to hoyse out their boat, and to come aboard; which news they were full glad to hear of, and presently one of their chief merchants came aboard; and, falling down upon his knees, offered to have kissed our general's feet, and craved mercy. Our general most graciously pardoned both him and the rest, upon promise of their true dealing with him and his company concerning such riches as were in the ship; and he sent for the captain and the pilot, who, at their coming aboard, used the like duty and reverence that the former did. The general, of his great mercy and humanity, promised their lives and good usage. The said captain and pilot presently

---

* Yet Christoval Suraz de Figueroa represents the ship as unprepared for, and taken without, resistance: "Hallavase (por ser aquel mar pacifico) sin una espada, y bien segura de semejante novedad. Candi abordando, la entró y robó" (p. 211). He says also that Cavendish hung a priest who was on board.

certified the general what goods they had within board, to wit, 122,000 pesos of gold : the rest of the riches that the ship was laden with was in rich silks, satins, and damasks, with musk, and divers other merchandise, and great store of all manner of victuals, with choice of many conserves of all sorts for to eat, and of sundry sorts of very good wines."

On the second day after the action Cavendish brought his prize into the bay, then called Aguada Segura, but now Bahia de San Bernabé, on the east side of Cape San Lucas, and there he set "the whole company of the Spaniards, both of men and women, to the number of 190, on shore". It was not his intention to keep the *Santa Anna*, with which, indeed, it would have been unwise to encumber himself; nevertheless, he would not, "of his great mercy and humanity," after he had despoiled the ship, give it to these poor people.* His journalist, who seems to have had about as much humanity as himself, complacently relates that they had a fair river of fresh water, with great store of fresh fish, fowl, and wood, and that there were many hares and conies upon the mainland. How they were to reach the mainland, he neither knew nor cared; and he did not know that a colony which Cortes had sent to that part of California had abandoned it, because they could not find means of subsistence there. "Our general also gave them great store of victuals, of garvanzos, pease, and some wine. Also they had all the sails of their ship to make them tents on shore, with licence to take such store of planks as should be sufficient to make them a

---

* Fuller says: "Mr. Cavendish's mercy after, equalled his valour in the fight, landing the Spaniards on the shore, and leaving them plentiful provisions". Mercy, indeed! But this is not the only reprehensible passage in his brief and very inaccurate account of this commander. Speaking of the Spaniards' design to fortify the straits, he says: "But God, the promoter of the public good, destroyed their intended monopoly, sending such a mortality among their men, that scarce five of five hundred did survive".

bark. Then," says Pretty, "we fell to hauling in of our goods, sharing of the treasure, and allotting to every man his portion; in division whereof many of the company fell into a mutiny against our general, especially those in the *Content*, which, nevertheless, were after a sort pacified for the time." The discontents of the *Content* were soon, after another sort, put to rest for ever!

To stow their booty was a work of some time. It was on the 6th of November that they anchored in the bay. On the 17th, the day of Queen Elizabeth's "happy coronation," salutes were fired from both ships with all their guns and small shot; and at night they "had many fireworks and more ordnance discharged, to the great admiration of the Spaniards, for the most part of them had never seen the like before". This ended, he discharged the captain, and gave him, in Pretty's words, "a royal reward, with provision for his defence against the Indians, and his company, both of swords, targets, pieces, shot, and powder, to his contentment". But he took into his own ship three Philippine boys, and two Japanese youths, who could read and write their own language, and were both of very good capacity. He likewise detained one Nicolas Rodriguez, a Portuguese, who had "not only been in Canton and other parts of China, but also in the Islands of Japan, being a country most rich in silver mines, and also in the Philippines"; and a Spaniard, Tomas de Ersola by name, "which was a very good pilot from Acapulco and the coast of New Spain to the Ladrones, where the Spaniards, sailing between Acapulco and the Philippines, put in, and find fresh water, plantains, and potato roots". All having been done, on the 19th, about three in the afternoon, he set fire to the *Santa Anna*, which had still goods in her to the quantity of 500 tons, waited till he saw her burned, as he believed, to the water's edge, then fired a piece of ordnance; and, with this triumphant mark of barbarous animosity against the Spaniards, set sail "joyfully homewards toward England with a fair wind". Night was closing when they sailed out of the road, leaving the *Content* astern; when morning came that ship was not in sight, and she was never heard of afterwards. *

Cavendish had delayed his departure till evening, that he might see the *Santa Anna* destroyed; nevertheless, that malicious purpose was defeated. Down to the water's edge he saw her burned, but the fire then freed her from her anchor, and the hull drifted ashore, for the salvation of the Spaniards. † They lightened it by throwing out the ballast, fitted it with jury masts, and were thus enabled to reach Acapulco, instead of perishing, as in all likelihood they otherwise must, upon that dreary peninsula. ‡

The *Desire* (now the only remaining ship of Cavendish's fleet) pursued her course across the Pacific, with a fair wind for five and forty days, when they came in sight of Guahan, one of the Ladrones. Some sixty or seventy boats came off to them with fruits, potatoes, and fish, which they exchanged

---

* Hakluyt, 817.—It was supposed that the captain, Stephen Hare, "was gone for the north-west passage". The people in that ship were discontented with Cavendish, and probably had got their share of the booty on board.

Fuller says: "The ship called the *Content* did not answer her name, whose men took all occasions to be mutinous" (*Worthies*, ii., 339).

† Yet these Spaniards, though thus providentially delivered themselves, acted tyrannically and wickedly toward the natives, carrying away a man and woman by force, and in bonds. Fifteen years afterwards, when a Spanish squadron was sent from Acapulco to survey those parts, the loss of these two Indians was still lamented by their countrymen; and they would hold no communication with the ships. "This is related," says Torquemada, "that care may be taken to do no injury to such people, because it may prevent them from ever peaceably submitting to the Spaniards, or believing them when they preach the Gospel. The devil desires nothing more than that any handle should be given them for refusing to be converted."

‡ Torquemada, t. i., p. 699. Burney, 89.

for little pieces of old iron: but when the English were sufficiently supplied, and would have closed the market, these pertinacious traders were for forcing their commodities upon them; and swarmed so thick about the ship, that it stemmed and broke one or two of their canoes. Nor could Cavendish be rid of them till he ordered some half dozen harquebusses to be made ready, and struck one of them himself; the others then fired; but these islanders were "so *yare* and nimble, that it could not be seen whether they were killed or not, so ready were they at falling backward into the sea and diving". On the 14th they made the Philippines at Cape del Espiritu Santo, and passing on the morrow through the strait of San Bernardino anchored at the isle of Capul. A cacique, " whose skin was carved with sundry strokes and devices all over his body," came off to trade with them, taking them for Spaniards: under this notion a friendly intercourse was established; and the English refreshed themselves " marvellously well with hens, hogs, cocoas, and *camotes*".* This was an unfortunate tarriance for the Spaniard Tomas de Ersola: he prepared a letter to the governor of Manilla, intending to send it by one of these natives. Rodriguez the Portuguese betrayed him: the letter was found in his chest; and Cavendish " willed that he should be hanged, which was accordingly performed ".

Here Cavendish remained nine days, demanding and receiving tribute, as if he had been a Spanish commander, from that and the adjacent islands. It was paid in pigs, poultry, cocoa nuts, and camotes. The day before his departure he caused the chief of this island, "and of a hundred more," says Pretty, " to appear before him, and then made himself and his company

---

* The English took these for potatoes. But in the description of these islands, prefixed by F. Juan Francisco de S. Antonio to his *Chronicles of the barefoot Franciscans in the Philippines, China, and Japan* (a most rare work, printed in a convent at Manilla), the camote is mentioned with several other wild roots, *que equivalen á las batatas en el gusto*, (p. 28).

known that they were Englishmen, and enemies to the Spaniards; and thereupon spread his ensign, and sounded up the drums, which they much marvelled at. To conclude, they promised, both for themselves and all the islands thereabout, to aid him whensoever he should come again to overcome the Spaniards. Also our general gave them money back again for all the tribute which they had paid; which they took marvellous friendly, and rowed about our ships to show us pleasure, marvellous swiftly. At the last he caused a saker to be shot off, whereat they wondered, and with great contentment took their leave of us."

Leaving this place on the 24th, they chased on the 28th a vessel from Manilla, along the coast of Panamao, and came so near that she stood in to shore close by a wind until she was becalmed, and then struck her sail, and "banked up with her oars". Cavendish anchored, manned his boat with twelve men, and sent them to pursue this vessel up the river into which she had run. They were, luckily for themselves, not able to find the opening; but they took a Spaniard out of a balsa, though fired at by a body of Spaniards from the shore, and pursued by a frigate which was sent in chase of the only prisoner aboard. He proved to be neither soldier nor sailor, but "a very simple soul," and one who could answer to very little that he was asked concerning the state of the country. Cavendish dismissed him with a message to the Spanish commander, whom he desired to provide good gold against the next visit, which he and his company meant to make him in a few years: nothing, he said, but the want of a larger boat to have landed his men had prevented him from seeing him now.

After passing the Moluccas, several of the men sickened, " by reason of the extreme heat and untemperateness of the climate," and Captain Havers died, to Cavendish's no small grief. Three guns with a volley of small arms served for his passing bell: the corpse was shrouded in a sheet; and after a prayer said was heaved overboard with great lamentation of all. They passed through one of the straits formed by the islands east of Java, and anchored in a port on the south side of that great island, where, by means of a negro, * taken out of the *St. Anna*, they could communicate with the inhabitants. But when the rajah of that district knew of their arrival, he sent to visit them; and an interpreter came, who, being a mestizo, spoke Portuguese as his *father* tongue. Cavendish had now been taught by experience to guard against all surprise; and when the rajah's minister passed a night on board, he commanded every man in the ship to provide his harquebuss and his shot, and so with shooting off forty or fifty small shot and one saker, himself set the watch with them. "This was no small marvel unto these heathen people, which had not commonly seen any ship so furnished with men and ordnance." Here they were plentifully supplied by the rajah's orders; and two Portuguese came on board, "men of marvellous proper personage, each in a loose jerkin and hose, which came down from the waist to the ankle, because of the use of the country, and partly because it was Lent, and a time for doing of their penance (for they account it as a thing of great dislike among these heathen to wear either hose or shoes on their feet); they had on each of them a very fair and white lawn shirt with falling bands on the same, very decently, only their bare legs excepted. These Portugals," says Pretty, "were no small joy to our general, and all the rest of our company; for we had not seen any Christian that was our friend of a year and half before. Our general entreated them singularly well with banquets and music. They told us they were no less glad to see us than we to see them, and enquired of the state of their country, and what was become of Don Antonio their king, and whether he were living or no, for they had not for long time been in Portugal, and the Spaniards had always

---

* Pretty says he could speak the Morisco tongue. The Malay is probably meant.

brought them word that he was dead. Then our general satisfied them in every demand, assuring them that their king was alive and in England, and had honourable allowance from our queen; and that there was war between Spain and England, and that we were come under the King of Portugal into the South Sea, and had warred upon the Spaniards there, and had fired, spoiled, and sunk all the ships along the coast that we could meet withal, to the number of eighteen or twenty sail. With this report they were sufficiently satisfied. They told us that if their king Don Antonio would come unto them, they would warrant him to have all the Moluccas at command, besides China, Sangles (?), and the Isles of the Philippines, and that he might be sure to have all the Indians on his side. They took their leave with promise of all good entertainment at our return." *

Cavendish sailed from Java on the 16th of March, passed round the Cape of Good Hope on the 18th of May, and on the 9th of June anchored in the road of St. Helena. Landing there they found "a fair and pleasant valley, wherein divers handsome buildings and houses were set up, and a church tiled and whited on the outside, very fair, and with a porch". The inside was hung with stained cloths, "having many devices drawn on them. There were two houses adjoining the church, one on each side, serving for kitchens to dress meat in, with necessary rooms and houses of offices: the coverings of the said houses were flat, whereon was planted a very fair vine, and through both ran a good and wholesome stream of fresh water." Opposite was a fair stone causeway leading to a valley wherein a garden had been planted with great store of pompions and melons. And upon this causeway was erected a frame with two bells, wherewith they rang to mass; and hard by a well-made stone cross, bearing date 1571, in which year it had been erected. The Portuguese had stocked the

* Hakluyt, 821, 822.

island with all sorts of fruits and esculent herbs, partridges, pheasants, guinea-fowl, goats, and swine. They had thus colonised it for the use of their ships homeward bound from India; "and when they come they have all things plentiful for their relief, by reason that they suffer none to inhabit there who might consume the fruit of the island, except some very few sick persons which they stand in doubt will not live until they come home: these they leave to refresh themselves, and take away in the next year's fleet, if they live so long". Three negroes were the only persons there when Cavendish arrived. They told him that the fleet had left it twenty days before, consisting of five sail, the least of which was in burden 800 or 900 tons, "laden with spice and calicut cloth, with store of treasure, and very rich stores and pearls".

Having cleaned their ship, taken in wood and water, and refreshed themselves during eleven days, they now sailed for England, the wind and weather favouring them. On the 3rd of September they were informed by a Flemish hulk coming from Lisbon of the discomfiture of the armada, "to their singular rejoicing and comfort". And on the 9th, "after a terrible tempest which carried away most part of their sails, by the merciful favour of the Almighty they recovered their long wished for port of Plymouth, two years and fifty days after their departure from that place".* As the third circumnavigation of the globe, Cavendish's voyage deserved to be thus fully related: the circumstances are creditable to

* "He who went forth with a fleet," says Fuller, "came home with a ship. Thus having circumnavigated the whole earth, let his ship no longer be termed the *Desire*, but the *Performance*. He was the third man, and second Englishman, of such universal undertakings."

Suraz de Figueroa says, that he entered London with sails of green damask, and his sailors all dressed in silk (p. 211).

It is remarkable that Lope de Vega, in the explanation prefixed to his *Dragontea*, of "lo que se ha de advertir para la inteligencia deste libro," confounds Oxenham with Cavendish, and gives an account of him under the name of Thomas Candir.

his activity, and seamanship, and courage, but honourable in no other way. Immediately on landing he wrote to the lord chamberlain Hunsdon, to inform the queen of his success; "and as it hath pleased God," said he, "to give her the victory over part of her enemies, so I trust ere long to see her overcome them all : for the places of their wealth, whereby they have maintained and made their wars, are now perfectly discovered, and, if it please her majesty, with a very small power she may take the spoil of them all. It hath pleased the Almighty to suffer me to circompass the whole globe of the world, entering in at the Straits of Magellan, and returning by the Cape de Buena Esperanza. In which voyage I have either discovered or brought certain intelligence of all the rich places of the world that ever were known or discovered by any Christian. I navigated along the coast of Chili, Peru, and Nueva Espanna, where I made great spoils. I burnt and sunk nineteen sail of ships, small and great. All the villages and towns that ever I landed at, I burnt and spoiled; and had I not been discovered upon the coast, I had taken great quantity of treasure. The matter of most profit unto me was a great ship of the king's which I took at California; which ship came from the Philippinas, being one of the richest of merchandise that ever passed those seas, as the king's register and merchants' accounts did show, for it did amount in value to   in Mexico to be sold; which goods, for that my ships were not able to contain the least part of them, I was enforced to set on fire. From the Cape of California, being the uttermost part of all Nueva Espanna, I navigated to the Islands of the Philippinas, hard upon the coast of China; of which country I have brought such intelligence as hath not been heard of in these parts: the stateliness and riches of which country I fear to make report of, lest I should not be credited; for if I had not known sufficiently the incomparable wealth of that country, I should have been as incredulous thereof, as others will be that have not had the like experience. I sailed along the islands of the Malucos, where among some of the heathen people I was well entreated, where our countrymen may have trade as freely as the Portugals, if they will themselves. From thence I passed by the Cape of Buena Esperanza, and found out by the way homeward the Island of St. Helena, where the Portugals use to relieve themselves, and from that island God hath suffered me to return to England. All which services, with myself, I humbly prostrate at her majesty's feet, desiring the Almighty long to continue her reign among us, for at this day she is the most famous and victorious prince that liveth in the world." *

In what a different odour would the memory of Cavendish be held, if he could have said, in this brief summary of his proceedings, that having found in the Straits of Magellan the miserable remains of a Spanish colony, he had taken them on board to save them from perishing by famine, and on the first safe opportunity had landed them among their own countrymen!

The success of this voyage induced him to tempt his fortune in a second with three tall ships and two barks: one of the barks was the property of Mr. Adrian Gilbert, a great promoter of the attempts for discovering a north-west passage. The other four were fitted out by Cavendish: they were the *Leicester Galleon*, in which he sailed himself, his old ship the *Desire*, commanded by Master John Davis, one of the best seamen of those times; the *Roebuck*, under Master Cocke; and the *Black Pinnace*. The number of men is supposed to have been little short of 400: among them were the two Japanese youths whom he had taken out of the *St. Anna*. But the fleet was ill-fitted for such an expedition: his means would probably have been inadequate to the great expenditure that it required, had they been strictly applied to it; but he advanced 1500*l.*

* Hakluyt, 837.

to adventurers, who, instead of equipping themselves, absconded with the money.* Having reached the coast of Brazil, Cocke was sent forward with two ships to attack Santos, in order to obtain provisions. He surprised the inhabitants at mass; but instead of bargaining with them for a supply, made good cheer upon what he found, while they escaped and carried away whatever was portable. Here Cavendish waited five precious weeks, and departed worse furnished than he came: then having burned St. Vincente by the way, proceeded to the straits. The fleet was separated in a storm: Gilbert took the opportunity of returning to England, leaving his captain on board one of the other ships "without any provision more than the apparel he had on". Davis fell in with the *Roebuck*: both proceeded to Port Desire, and there the *Black Pinnace* and the admiral joined them.† Cavendish had lost his boats, and quarrelled with his company: in consequence of this he removed into the *Desire*.‡

By this time it was the middle of March: "such," says Cavendish, " was the adverseness of our fortunes, that in coming thither we spent the summer, and found the straits in the beginning of a most extreme winter". They entered it on the 14th of April with favourable weather; but on the 21st were stopped by a wind from the W.N.W., and put into a small

---

* "These varlets, whom the justice had before sought with great diligence, I saw, within a few days after his departure," says Sir Richard Hawkins, "walking the streets of Plymouth without punishment" (*Observations*, etc., 15).

† Mr. John Jane's remark, therefore, seems hardly to be warranted when he says, that his "captain (Davis) could never get any direction what course to take in any such extremities, though many times he had entreated for it, as often I have heard him with grief report" (Hakluyt, 842).

Jane's narrative is written evidently with a malevolent feeling towards Cavendish. And in this he is contradicted by Knyvet, who, though a liar, could have no motive for lying in this case.

‡ Hakluyt, 842, 843. Burney, 98, 100.

cove on the south shore opposite to Cape Froward. There they remained above three weeks, during which they endured great storms, with perpetual snow; and many of the men "died with cursed famine and miserable cold, not having wherewith to cover their bodies, nor to fill their bellies, but living by muscles, water, and weeds of the sea, with a small relief of the ship's store in meal sometimes".* Discouraged by these hardships, and doubting what the end would be, Cavendish asked Davis's opinion, "because he was a man that had good experience of the north-west parts in his three several discoveries that way, employed by the merchants of London". Davis, who felt as much at home among ice and snow as a white bear, or a walrus, told him the snow was a matter of no long continuance. However, he called together the whole company, and told them he would tarry no longer in the straits, but turn back, and make for the Cape of Good Hope. The general opinion was, that being within forty leagues of the South Sea, it was better to "stay God's favour for a wind," and endure any hardships rather than give over the voyage; nevertheless, what he determined on they would perform. Upon this he declared his resolution to go for the Cape of Good Hope. But when he returned on board the *Desire* Davis represented to him that this would be a desperate undertaking: "if the rest of your ships," said he, "be furnished answerable to this, it is impossible to perform it; for we have no more sails than masts, no victuals, no ground-tackling, no cordage more than is overhead, and among seventy and five persons there is but the master alone that can order the ship, and but fourteen sailors; the rest are gentlemen, serving-men, and artificers". Davis made the

* Jane says: "All the sick men in the *Galleon* were most uncharitably put ashore into the woods, in the snow, rain, and cold, when men of good health could scarcely endure it, where they ended their lives in the highest degree of misery; Master Cavendish all this while being in the *Desire*".

same representations to Cocke: the "chiefs of the whole company" drew up a petition in consequence; and Cavendish, yielding to the general voice so far as to give up his own rash intention, determined to leave the straits and return for Santos. But as if he had been displeased with Davis for having influenced others in this matter, he left the *Desire*, and went again on board the *Leicester Galleon*.*

On the 18th they were free of the straits: on the 20th the *Desire* and the *Black Pinnace* separated from the other two vessels; Cavendish thought wilfully: but, according to their protestation, by unaccountable accident. † They returned to Port Desire, thinking that he would put back there; waited there till that expectation could no longer be entertained; were driven to the Falkland Islands, "which had never before been discovered by any known relation"; entered and passed the straits; were driven back, and, after enduring such sufferings as none but sailors can be exposed to, and with a perseverance and patient fortitude which never has been exceeded, reached Ireland in the June of the follow-

---

* Hakluyt, 843, 844.

† Admiral Burney says: " The circumstances are certainly of a suspicious nature; and there is some reason for believing that Captain Davis considered the engagement mutual between Mr. Cavendish and himself to make a voyage into the South Sea; and that he was determined, if possible, not to be disappointed of an enterprise which he had been brought thus far to prosecute. Instances without number are to be met with of ships deserting their commander-in-chief, to escape the perils of a long or dangerous undertaking; but the case of Captain Davis is of a different character, and is one of the few in which the separation, if contrived, was for the purpose of persevering in a pursuit after it had been abandoned by the chief commander as hopeless and impracticable " (pp. 101, 102).

" This is the same distinguished seaman who discovered and has left his name to Davis's Strait. He afterwards made several voyages to the East Indies, and lost his life there in a quarrel with the crew of a Japanese vessel " (*ibid.*, 106).

ing year, having lost sixty men out of a crew of seventy-six. Jane was one of the survivors.

Cavendish, who had parted from the *Roebuck* also, arrived with only his own ship on the coast of Brazil, and landed twenty-five men about three leagues from Santos, to seize provisions for the relief of their sick and starving comrades. The principal persons in the ship were of this party, and not a man returned. The Indians, who carried two of their prisoners to Santos, entered that town in savage triumph with the heads of all the rest. After these mishaps, Cavendish was joined by the *Roebuck*: they coasted along, ravaging houses and plantations as they went, and attempted with their boats to cut out some ships which were at anchor in the river near the town of Espirito Santo. The attempt was rashly made, and ended in the loss of eighty men killed, wounded, or basely abandoned by their comrades; after which the master of the *Roebuck*, by whose orders they were thus abandoned, and whom Cavendish calls " a most cowardly villain that ever was born of a woman," thought proper to shift for himself with that ship, and desert his unfortunate commander. * Nothing remained for Cavendish then but to make for England; but his heart was broken. Assured by his own unerring feelings that death was at hand, he wrote a letter to Sir Tristram Gorges, giving a brief account of this unhappy voyage, and complaining of the conduct of his officers and men. Having vented his complaints, he proceeded thus :—

" And now to tell you of my greatest grief, which was the sickness of my dear kinsman John Locke, who by this time was grown in great weakness, by reason whereof he desired rather quietness and contentedness in our course, than such continual disquietness, which never ceased us. And now by this, what with grief for him, and the continual trouble I

---

* Purchas, b. vi., c. 6., p. 1195. *History of Brazil*, i., 359-364.

endured among such hell-hounds, my spirits were clean spent, wishing myself upon any desert place in the world, there to die, rather than thus basely to return home again; which course I had put in execution, had I found an island which the cards make to be eight degrees to the southward of the line. I swear to you, I sought for it with all diligence, meaning, if I had found it, to have there ended my unfortunate life. But God suffered not such happiness to light upon me, for I could by no means find it; so as I was forced to go towards England, and having gotten eight degrees by north the line, I lost my most dearest cousin.

"And now consider whether a heart made of flesh be able to endure so many misfortunes, all falling upon me without intermission! I thank my God that, in ending of me, He hath pleased to rid me of all further trouble and mishaps. And now to return to our private matters: I have made my will, wherein I have given special charge that all goods (whatsoever belong unto me) be delivered into your hands. For God's sake refuse not to do this last request for me. I owe little that I know of, and, therefore, it will be the less trouble; but if there be any debt that, of truth, is owing by me, for God's sake see it paid. To use compliments of love, now at my last breath, were frivolous: but know that I left none in England whom I loved half so well as yourself; which you in such sort deserved at my hands as I can by no means requite. I have left all (that little remaining) unto you, not to be accountable for anything. That which you will, if you find any overplus (yourself especially being satisfied to your own desire), give unto my sister Anne Candish. I have written to no man living but yourself, leaving all friends and kinsmen, only reputing you as dearest. Commend me to both your brethren, being glad that your brother Edward escaped so unfortunate a voyage. I pray give this copy of my unhappy proceedings to none but only to Sir George Cary, and tell him, that if I had thought the letter of a dead man acceptable, I would have written unto him. I have taken order with the master of my ship to see his pieces of ordnance delivered unto him, for he knoweth them. And if the *Roebuck* be not returned, then I have appointed him to deliver him two brass pieces out of this ship, which I pray you see performed. I have now no more to say ; and take this last farewell, that you have lost the lovingest friend that ever was lost by any. Commend me to your wife. No more ! But as you love God, do not refuse to undertake this last request of mine. I pray, forget not Master Carey of Coakington : gratify him with something, for he used me kindly at my departure. Bear with this scribbling ; for I protest I am scarce able to hold a pen in my hand." *

Cavendish's history cannot be concluded better than by these his dying words : they are most touching in themselves, and leave us with an opinion of him far more favourable than could be deduced from anything that is recorded of his life.

* Purchas, b. vi., c. 6., p. 1200.

NOTES.

LORD HOWARD.

Southey has not gone much into details in his account of Lord Howard, thinking, perhaps, that he was rather the nominal than the real commander of the different enterprises in which he took part. Lord Howard, however, it should have been recorded, had at least some share in founding the "chest" for disabled seamen at Chatham. He sat on the trial of Essex, and was one of the lords who had a share in all the various commissions appointed by the Government for administrative purposes. During his latter years as Lord High Admiral many abuses crept into the navy. His age, and perhaps his easy-going profuse habits, disqualified him for the work of vigilant minute administration. His retirement was hastened by the adverse report of a commission, and perhaps by the pressure of Buckingham, who desired his place, and offered him good pecuniary terms as an inducement to retire.

EARL OF CUMBERLAND.

Research has added nothing of moment to this account of the Earl of Cumberland.

HAWKINS AND DRAKE.

The fame of these two men has made all inquirers into the history of that time eager to discover all there was to learn about them in the long hidden records of public offices, or private libraries. As regards Hawkins some curious facts have been revealed which serve to intensify the opinion a shrewd impartial critic would from the first have formed of him from accessible evidence. We have learned, for instance, that on his first voyage he plundered Portuguese slavers whom he found upon the coast — a fact naturally left unmentioned in his own published accounts. It has been revealed also, that in 1570 he entered, with the knowledge, if not at the instigation of Cecil, into a plot to cheat King Philip out of money, and valuable information. He made an offer to the king's ambassador, Don Guerau (Gerald) de Spes, to betray a part of the queen's ships to the Spaniard for a sufficient reward. Philip was for a time incredulous, but finally fell into the trap. He released some of Hawkins' men who were in prison at Seville, sent him 40,000*l.* and a patent of Grandee. Some of the money at least must have remained in the pocket of Sir John, and Cecil gained evidence that the King of Spain's intentions were mischievous. Both were no doubt well pleased, and the story is characteristic of the diplomacy of the time. It is also quite in keeping with the methods of that heroic, but lying and intriguing, period, that Hawkins was contemporaneously engaged in a negotiation to supply ships to the King of Spain's enemy, Louis of Nassau. In 1573, he was stabbed in the Strand by a fanatic who mistook him for Sir Christopher Hatton. Before sailing in 1567, he had taken an active part in driving a packet belonging to King Philip which endeavoured to take refuge in Plymouth, into the hands of the Beggars of the Sea, who were cruising outside. Cecil, who did not like him, recorded his opinion that Hawkins had been guilty of malversation in office, but of this there is no direct evidence.

Investigation has rather disproved the truth of some of the stories told about Drake, than added anything of note to what was known. The story of the quarrel with Bernard Drake must be at least exaggerated. The family of Ash recognised Sir Francis' right to bear their arms though with the "difference" of a third brother. Perhaps he attempted to use them without a "difference". The statement that he was of "mean parentage" is a mere mistranslation of Camden's Latin, but his branch of the Drakes were sinking into the mass of working people when his energy saved them. His father cannot have been Vicar of Upnor, where there has never been a church, but he may have had the living at Upchurch. Nothing deserving to be called evidence has been published to clear up the supposed mystery of Doughty's execution, but there is a curious statement in the malignant narrative of one Cooke that Drake believed the man to be a wizard who raised unfavourable winds to spoil the voyage. As a sailor,

Devonshire man, and Elizabethan, it is probable that Drake did believe in witchcraft. During his voyage in 1587, he put his Vice-Admiral Borough under arrest for insubordination. During the Armada war he had a violent quarrel with Sir Martin Frobisher over their respective rights to the prize money of the galleon *Rosario*. Drake apparently had to be satisfied with the ransom of Don Pedro de Valdes, which amounted to 3000*l*.

CAVENDISH.

Contrary to his custom Southey has overlooked a voyage of Cavendish's. If was the first, and was undertaken, in a ship of his own, in 1585, in company with Sir R. Grenville. Raleigh was the promoter of the venture, and the design was to plant the first colony in Virginia. The adventurers spent some time among the West Indian Islands plundering the Spaniards, and some time in Virginia harrying the natives, and returned to England at the close of summer. Some of the party stayed, but Cavendish was not one of them.

www.ingramcontent.com/pod-product-compliance
Lightning Source LLC
Chambersburg PA
CBHW030554300426
44111CB00009B/980